THE BEST MADE PLANS:
ROBERT R. NATHAN

AND 20TH CENTURY LIBERALISM

KENNETH D. DURR

Montrose Press
Rockville, MD

Durr, Kenneth D.

The Best Made Plans: Robert R. Nathan and 20th Century Liberalism

Library of Congress Control Number 2013939695

ISBN 978-0-9827977-4-7

Published in the United States of America by Montrose Press,
Rockville, Maryland

CONTENTS

INTRODUCTION

Robert R. Nathan was a New Dealer. As a statistician with the Department of Commerce he helped develop what is today called the gross domestic product. As an administrator with the War Production Board he produced the "Victory Plan" that determined how much could be extracted from the American economy, and how soon, for the winning of World War II. Later, as an activist and consultant he was an advocate of the simplified Keynesianism that still pervades the popular consciousness.[1] During the 1950s, Nathan was a pioneer of international economic development and a leader of Americans for Democratic Action (ADA), the organization that did the most to keep New Deal liberalism alive during an inhospitable decade. In the 1960s Nathan undertook two ill-fated projects that demonstrated the demise of the New Deal coalition he had fought so hard to preserve: Lyndon Johnson's nation-building effort in Vietnam and Hubert Humphrey's presidential campaign. He was one of the few remaining at what historian Arthur Schlesinger, Jr., once called the "Vital Center" as the liberal coalition broke up.[2] For Nathan, the premise of the New Deal was Franklin Roosevelt's vow of "bold, persistent experimentation" in the interest of economic growth, and he dedicated his life to continuing that experimentation.[3] He was confident in his ability to study a situation, draw up the best-made plan to produce the desired outcome—and then to make another plan if necessary.

This tenacity was just one of the remarkable qualities of the man. He absorbed the progressive ideal dominant in his youth: that with knowledge and planning men could change the world. A technocrat who had faith in numbers, Nathan was also skeptical of complex formulas and esoteric information. A hormonal imbalance in young adulthood made Robert Nathan's physique as imposing as his aspirations. But just as his fingers were too large for a calculator, his ideas were too big to be confined by numbers.[4] For similar reasons he was an economist uncomfortable with a chief tenet of his profession—the idea of the efficient outcome. When he had a choice—and Nathan usually believed that he did—he chose justice over efficiency every time.[5] Finally, during most of his professional career, Nathan worked independently. Unusual among liberals who depended greatly on status imparted by a journal, think tank, or university, he made his own living as a consultant. He worked incessantly and wrote prolifically, but nearly always to advance his clients' interests rather than his own.

This helps explain why Nathan is largely unknown today. There are exceptions, but most history books give him little more than a footnote for the creation of the Victory Plan—a mention, perhaps, as a leader of the ADA.[6] There is simply no obvious place to situate him in the familiar categories of 20th century politics and economics—he straddled them all. Furthermore, Nathan left no real intellectual legacy: his convictions were profound but his ideas were pedestrian. Instead, he was a practical man, more intent on getting results than advancing an ideology.

Democratic liberalism from the New Deal to the 1960s was based on the conviction that the American system, despite its faults, was sound, and that only moderate adjustments were required as long as the essentials remained in place: standing up for a capitalist economy as the proper underpinning of society, tempering the excesses of the free market by democratic means, and fighting totalitarianism of the left or right—but especially communism—at all costs.

Nathan had little to add to this formulation but hard work and the dedication of nearly every hour of his life. Indeed, in common with many ambitious men of his era, Nathan's dedication to his causes and his work far surpassed his attention to home and family. He was willing to devote his energy and expertise to nearly any worthy cause, and even as a professional he nearly always sought to advance the greater good. Those who study the intellectual underpinnings of 20th century liberalism might see a "movement," but he did not use that term. For Nathan liberalism was the way life should be lived—friends, allies, and business associates working together to get something done that would, perhaps (and only perhaps, for Nathan was a realist), produce a more equitable world.

This is not the story of an intellectual fountainhead or a master strategist of American liberalism. Robert Nathan was more a first-rate field general who loved nothing better than being with his troops and plotting how to take the next hill. Unlike some theorists who love mankind but cannot abide company, Nathan reveled in fellowship. He made a remarkable number of friends, had a staggering number of acquaintances, and always maintained a disarming faith in the essential goodness of humanity. Given all the facts and pointed in the right direction, he believed, people would usually do the right thing. That may be why Nathan spent his life planning, because he believed that good people would follow good plans. Still, he was a practical man with no illusions about the brilliance of his designs—just as with the American system, there was always room for adjustment.

Nathan never stopped believing these things, even as the New Deal order fractured and flew apart. He never appears to have considered that the things that undermined liberalism—the rights revolution, identity politics, and stagflation—would not yield to incremental reform. The man who told a 1972 graduating class that "the risks of moving too fast are less serious than the dangers of moving too slowly or not at all," was not inclined to put aside his plans for fear of unintended consequences.[7]

My own plan for writing this book was one that Nathan would likely have approved. I take a straightforward narrative approach, sketching out historical background, documenting decisions made and actions taken in that context, and then draw modest conclusions. I usually avoid second-guessing Nathan's motivations or taking him to task for failing to see then what is evident today. Nathan was too occupied with what was coming up to worry much about what had gone before—he left a vast written record, but was not an introspective person, nor was he inclined to commit his mistakes and regrets to paper. I have, therefore, opted not to speculate far beyond what is actually in the record. A more psychoanalytically oriented biographer might have speculated about whether or not Nathan was greatly shaped by his Jewish identity, scarred by his acromegaly, or felt inadequate as an economist lacking a Ph.D. I have left such speculation to the reader, whose own conclusions are likely to be as valid as mine.

The political and economic context in which Nathan lived and worked is critical to this story and I have assumed a fair degree of historical knowledge on the part of the reader. To ensure context, I have nevertheless provided more historical background than one might find in an academic treatise. Perhaps those not requiring it will simply accept the opportunity to better understand the perspective of the author.

Another important thing to understand in that regard is that this is a commissioned biography, undertaken by History Associates Inc. on behalf of Nathan Associates Inc. It was the kind of contract that Robert Nathan would have appreciated: Nathan Associates insisted on an honest assessment of the man, and to win the project I had to demonstrate that I could produce an account that met the standards of the historical profession.

For providing this opportunity—and this freedom—I must thank Nathan Associates chairman John Beyer. For providing company resources (which he watches more systematically than the founder did) I thank President Lakhbir Singh. I am most indebted to director of communications Mary Miller, who managed the project for Nathan Associates and contributed resources, encouragement, and exceptional editing skills. Mary understood the potential of this story better than anyone else, and for her sake I regret that I could not put in the additional year or so of reflection and revision that would, perhaps, have made this a better book. But like Nathan, I am also a consultant and understand the importance of working to the terms of the contract signed rather than the one wished for.

Even so, for eighteen months this project has consumed most of my time and attention. That goes to show that more than a decade after his death, Robert R. Nathan can still command unusual dedication and sacrifice. Along the way, I found it helpful to remember that the subject of my book put in even longer workdays in living his life than I did in writing it. My reward was to be author of this book. To my wife Jean, whose time and attention were also taken up by the now-familiar economist, and who so often filled in for her distracted husband, the only compensation I can offer is my love and my gratitude.

History Associates colleagues Megan Anderson, Duncan Campbell, Robert Colby, Robin Filan, and Meaghan Ryan were better compensated for the time they put in helping me research this story. Andrew Simpson, Nancy Crenca, and Gail Mathews painstakingly proofed the text and notes. I am especially thankful that Kurt Hanson, who has provided me with the most and the best editing and historical advice by far over the years, finally agreed to make it official and review this manuscript as a consultant to History Associates. Thanks go finally to everyone who took time to talk with me about their lives with Robert Nathan. I am sorry that neither Maury Atkin nor Joe Gunn saw the finished book, but hope that their wisdom and enthusiasm lives on in the pages that they helped me write. I am deeply grateful to have spent a morning with Mary Nathan, whose preference for unvarnished facts and passion for justice gave me perhaps the best window on Nathan himself that I could have had. I have tried to heed the inclination that she shared with her husband to tell the story straight.

1

THE EDUCATION OF AN ECONOMIST

An ambitious and confident 21-year-old set off into working-class Philadelphia to start his first real job as an economist. Robert Nathan had come up from near poverty all on his own merit. He had worked hard, was determined to succeed, and nothing in his experience suggested that he would not. He had risen from blue-collar Dayton, Ohio, to one of America's top business schools, working constantly all along the way. Now he was helping to conduct one of the nation's first unemployment surveys.[1]

The time was April 1930, scarcely six months after the stock market had crashed. The reason it happened was a matter of interest to Nathan and his fellow business students, but not an urgent question—they remained intent on making their first million and saw few barriers to their success. The nation had yet to learn the magnitude of the "Great Depression" into which it was slipping. There was no reason to expect, therefore, much adversity in Philadelphia's neighborhoods.

Nathan began knocking on doors, talking to people, and checking up on the work of project enumerators—the workers who canvassed the neighborhoods.[2] It was not his first household visit, but it was not the last; somewhere along the way Nathan began to realize that if the American dream was working out for him, it was not working out for everyone—and it could not, in every case, have been their fault. "In my urge to 'make it' in the competitive world," Nathan said later, "I had adopted a kind of clinical neutrality toward most issues." But now Nathan recognized bewilderment, shame, and "a sense of loss that rippled through what the unemployed had to say when I questioned them." Robert Nathan had grown up believing in what the 1920s had celebrated as "rugged individualism." He would never give up his faith in the free market, but he had learned that personal welfare and human dignity were "nobody's individual responsibility, but everyone's collective responsibility," and that only an enlightened, activist government could ensure it.[3] It was among the most important lessons learned in the education of an economist.

DAYTON DAYS

The journey that put Robert Nathan face-to-face with unemployment in an American city began a generation earlier in rural Eastern Europe. In the far northwest reaches of the Austrian Empire was the Province of Galicia, and in the rolling hills west of the Carpathians, the shtetl of Burshtyn. Jews had settled there as early as the 1500s.[4] In the intervening centuries they formed deep and seemingly timeless attachments to the land; family and community had taken root. Then, in the late 19ᵗʰ century they began to break down.[5] In Galicia, the population doubled in just a few decades. Farms had been subdivided to the point where few could sustain their families—at the same time the encroachment of international commerce devastated centuries-old cottage crafts. Although more Jews worked in agriculture in Galicia than elsewhere in the Austrian Empire, about half worked in trade and small business—they were equally hard hit when heavy restrictions were placed on Jewish businesses in Galicia after 1893.[6] By the time of World War I, a million people had left Galicia forever, Robert Nathan's parents among them.[7]

Louis Nathan was born in Burshtyn in 1873; Hannah Schnee a year later.[8] How Louis Nathan made a living is unknown, but he was an educated man and had studied to be a rabbi.[9] He married Hannah at age 23, and together they had two children: Goldie, born around 1899, and Louis, Jr., born a year later. By then, the Nathans were intent on starting over somewhere else. In 1900 Louis ventured forth to the United States where Hannah already had family.[10]

The second great wave of eastern European migration that brought some 23 million immigrants to the United States had yet to crest in 1900. The economy was booming and employers were welcoming. At Ellis Island, Louis Nathan met the agent of a Dayton, Ohio, foundry. Asked if he knew anything about factory work, Louis, who spoke no English, somehow answered in the affirmative, and got a free train ticket to the Midwest. Work in the foundry appears to have paid for his family's passage to join him in 1902.[11] Louis then took up a more congenial line of work—by 1903 he was a peddler, supplying produce by wagon to his neighbors in Dayton's Jewish "East End."[12]

The Nathans were doing well enough to support a growing family—daughters Rose and Lily were born in 1903 and 1906 respectively, and in between the Nathans moved from one rented house on Rogge Street to another.[13] Curiously, the Nathans also moved from one name to another during these years—although they had clearly settled on the surname "Nathan" years before, late in the decade the family adopted the name "Nathanson" for a time.[14] Christmas likely meant little to the orthodox Jewish family—until December 25, 1908, when twins arrived. Lawrence was born first and Robert was the baby of the family by 15 minutes.[15] Although his birth certificate identified him as

Robert Roy Nathanson, and he is listed by that name in the 1910 federal census, the family returned to the shorter surname soon after. It is not certain, however, whether Robert Nathanson ever legally changed his name to Robert Nathan.[16]

As the children kept coming, Louis Nathan kept forging ahead. He moved his family from Rogge Street to a marginally better neighborhood a few blocks away. By 1910 the Nathans were settled in what in another context would be called a "shotgun" house at 1406 South Wayne Avenue where the inseparable Nathan twins grew up.[17] Throughout their Dayton years, the lives of Robert and Larry Nathan revolved around enterprise. At first it was the enterprise of their father. A fixture in Dayton's East End, Louis rose very early in the morning to pick up fruits and vegetables at the markets downtown.[18] By the time the twins were nine or ten, they often accompanied their father as he called on customers. "He'd ring their bells, and they would come down," Nathan recalled. Sometimes Robert or Larry would be dispatched to carry produce upstairs, but more often they held the horses in check while their father did business.[19] One of Robert's earliest memories was of a time that they failed—the wagon moved, and Louis Nathan fell to the ground and fractured his skull.[20]

Later in life Robert Nathan would realize that his father's existence "seemed to be consumed in a round of ceaseless work."[21] But it was to his credit that Louis inspired his sons to work so hard at so early an age. Neither Larry nor Robert spoke much about the influence of their mother. According to the 1910 census, Anna Nathan (she changed her first name upon arrival) could neither read nor write.[22] Louis Nathan on the other hand, could do both and knew his math as well. He liked to challenge the boys to bouts of "mental arithmetic" as they made their rounds.[23]

That provided Larry and Robert with an advantage when they went into business for themselves. In their first enterprise, the twins bought baskets of pretzels at a nearby bakery and sold them individually to the vendors and customers around the St. Clair Market and the City Market House.[24] On a few occasions they also loaded trucks at the commission houses on St. Clair Street. But mostly it was selling—Larry and Robert Nathan started early and spent their working days as salesmen. They sold flags at holiday parades, peanuts and popcorn on circus days, sandwiches to workers at National Cash Register, and even candy at the Lyric Burlesque Theater.[25] It was newspapers that they sold the most. Robert hawked the *Dayton Daily News* at the corner of 5th Street and Main. Larry staked out the intersection at 5th and Ludlow just a block away, eliciting frequent double takes from strangers encountering two nearly identical newsboys.[26]

Robert Nathan later insisted that his childhood was typical; that in their rough neighborhood the Nathans got in "lots of fights as kids," but the record suggests otherwise.[27] Even after they entered their first year of high school they remained so successful on their respective corners that the *Dayton Daily News* featured them on the front page of its December 22, 1923, "Newsboys Edition." The article quoted the twins as saying that their greatest aspiration was to form a law partnership and that they were saving their newspaper money for college. The boys had internalized both their father's work ethic and his faith in upward mobility.[28]

The Nathan twins (Larry above, Robert below) were featured in this special December 22, 1923, edition of the *Dayton Daily News*. (Courtesy of Special Collections and Archives, Wright State University)

Every Dayton freshman went to Parker High School at the time. Nearly all of the East End Jewish high schoolers, however, finished at Steele High. To the financially minded Nathans it may have been the extra carfare that convinced the twins not to go to Steele.[29] It may have been because Stivers Manual Training High School, built in 1908, was the best in town.[30] Larry and Robert were definitely in a minority at Stivers—as late as 1929, by one count, there were only five Jews out of a student body of about 1,200.[31]

While at Stivers the Nathans kept working: selling papers and clerking in downtown department stores, and serving as "high school correspondents" for the *Dayton Daily News*.[32] And they stayed together. For the first day of junior year they were assigned different home rooms, but some "earnest pleading in the office" convinced the administration to reconsider. Their curriculum was tough: Robert's included two years of Latin, three years of math, and chemistry and physics. Both boys earned "almost" straight A's.[33] They also found time for extracurricular activities—Robert as editor of the *Stivers News* and Larry as sports editor. During senior year Robert was secretary of the debating society the first semester and president the second.[34] They were the first children in their neighborhood to finish high school.[35]

The high school student in 1927.

PHILADELPHIA

In September 1927 Robert and Larry Nathan boarded a train for Philadelphia. Larry, who had once been to visit a sister in Poughkeepsie, made light of his brother's unworldliness; at age 18 the farthest Robert had ever been from home was nearby Springfield to attend a Stivers basketball game.[36] But Robert was hardly parochial in his aspirations. Although the boys had been accepted at Ohio State University they held out for spots at Pennsylvania University's prestigious Wharton Business School.[37] They expected the nation's oldest business school to be a gateway to, in Robert's words, "the expanding world of finance and commerce."[38]

There was another good reason to go to Wharton. Older brother Lew worked as a salesman for the Philadelphia Electric Company and lived with his wife, Fan, on 58th Street, about a dozen blocks west of campus.[39] That meant free room and board for Robert and Larry.[40] The two settled into a curriculum of applied business and economics courses and kept working to pay tuition. During his first year in college, industrious as ever, Robert sold "Real Silk" hosiery door-to-door after school. In his sophomore year he worked as evening manager of a "Nedicks" fast food stand in West Philadelphia.[41] He also worked at a downtown shoe store on Saturdays and at the Philadelphia Post Office during the Christmas season.[42]

Robert even found a way to make his studies pay off, starting a tutoring service with a classmate near the end of his sophomore year. The two ingeniously compiled and issued to new students handouts listing available room and board—along with descriptions of their own services. His classmate specialized in math and physics. Robert covered the rest, either personally or through hires—one of whom was Larry, who tutored insurance courses.[43] They obtained copies of exams given over a five-year period and concentrated on the questions that had been repeated. The system worked, making Robert's tutoring services very popular with athletic coaches.[44] As finals approached, Robert was able to clear $300 per week.[45]

Larry and Robert went home to Dayton during their first three college summers. There, Robert got his first and only taste of manufacturing employment, working for General Motors subsidiary Delco during the summer of 1929, hauling parts between departments and operating a drill press on the shock absorber line.[46] He began to understand that the realities of industrial employment and management were less clear cut than the black and white world of direct sales. Delco had a piecework incentive system—the more employees produced, the more they were paid. But when production went up, Robert noticed, management moved the baseline. He was surprised to find that, in this case at least, hard work was not justly compensated. Accordingly, he was amused to learn that his co-workers took production imperatives lightly, regularly disappearing for naps during the night shift.[47] Although he gained some valuable insights, the fifty cents an hour he earned at Delco was not enough to get him through his junior year, so Nathan took his predicament to *Dayton Daily News* editor Howard Egbert who obtained from eminent Daytonians $1,200 in contributions for a Robert Nathan college fund.[48] Some of them may have believed that they were making a good investment in the entrepreneurial youngster, but a few, perfectly consistent with the tenor of the times, appear to have wanted quick returns. During the first two summers, recalled Robert, "all they wanted to know was what stock should I buy?"[49]

Jubilant young people, perhaps during years at Wharton. Robert Nathan is kneeling, second from left, Larry is kneeling at the right.

Back at school, the continuing round of jobs and classes cut in to the time that Robert could devote to social and athletic pursuits, but his seemingly boundless energy made even these limited activities impressive. The former editor was selected historian for the class of 1931.[50] Somewhat uncharacteristically, the budding businessman joined Penn's literary group, the Zelosophic Society, acting as student manager for a performance of Shakespeare's *A Midsummer Night's Dream*.[51] Another surprise was that, although athletics seem to have mattered little during his high-school years, at Wharton, Nathan's physique developed impressively; his chest expanded and his face and hands grew large. He became something of an athlete and took up intramural boxing and wrestling.[52] Finally, Nathan served as chairman of Penn's Jewish Students' Association.[53]

Employment and extracurricular activities, however, were decidedly secondary; Nathan was determined above all to get everything out of his business education that he could. For the first few years his aspirations were conventional. Although Larry gave it up, Robert continued to look toward law school, convinced more on faith than on direct experience that it was a sure path to success. Still, there were more direct ways to wealth, and they did not escape his attention. At the end of the freshman year every Wharton student had to choose a thesis. Nathan settled on "Common Stock as a Long-Term

Investment," partly due to an influential professor and partly, he later admitted, "due to my get-rich-quick ambitions."[54]

During his first few years at Wharton, Robert Nathan was in many respects typical of the aspiring self-made man of the 1920s, determined to get ahead and making everything serve that goal. Wharton was accommodating. There were classes on insurance, banking, and the stock market, all approaching the subjects from a technical rather than historical or theoretical point of view. Nathan was encouraged to master the intricate machinery of the nation's financial system but discouraged from ever considering that the *status quo* might not be the best available. The experiences and studies during those years, Nathan said later, "made me a captive of narrow perceptions."[55]

By 1929, however, those perceptions had begun to widen. Nothing inclined Nathan toward intellectualism—he was more interested in results than the ideas that underpinned them. It is not surprising, therefore, that what finally began to move Nathan and a few of his business school classmates to question the sterile orthodoxies of the 1920s were the decidedly unintellectual economic expositions of a pair of writers known as Foster and Catchings.[56]

William Trufant Foster was a Harvard graduate, English professor, and college president. His counterpart was banker, businessman, and phrasemaker Waddill Catchings. During the 1920s, the two formed a foundation dedicated to protecting the interests of consumers and began writing the books that they hoped would enlighten people as to what was to their benefit—and especially against their interests—in America's market economy. Their most influential work, *Road to Plenty*, was published in 1928. This unassuming economic treatise was an account of a cross-country train ride by a cast of stock characters that included "The Gray Man," the "Thoughtful Professor," and "The Friendly Lawyer." It was a didactic novel that read like its 19th century predecessors, but its economic theory was decidedly modern.

The classical economics that underpinned the Wharton curriculum was premised on the understanding that it was production, represented by the individual actions of countless entrepreneurs, that drives markets. Established by French economist Jean Baptiste Say, the "law of the market" posited that all of those independent actions would automatically regulate production and sustain consumption. If either became unbalanced, the market would compensate—booms and busts therefore, were "self-correcting." Foster and Catchings, in contrast, identified a "paradox of thrift:" producers inevitably saved too much of their economic gain, drawing money out of the economy and making it impossible to keep consumption up. Foster and Catchings, in effect, turned classical economics on its head, arguing that consumers rather than producers were the mainsprings of a market economy.[57] It followed, as John Maynard Keynes would soon insist more academically, that government countercyclical spending might sometimes be required to keep an economy at full performance.[58] His professors may have been chagrined, but Nathan was soon in the thrall of Foster and Catchings, even though at first their ideas seemed more to intrigue and amuse than stimulate action.[59]

Nathan returned from Dayton and his stint on the line at Delco in September 1929 to enroll in a course on the business cycle taught by Professor Frank Parker. Neither Parker nor any of the other professors at Wharton anticipated the stock market crash that came the next month.[60] Parker was unimpressed by the event. An engaging lecturer, he stretched out a rubber band before the class and let it snap back, demonstrating that, as classical economics instructed, economic busts were "part of the inherent character of the capitalist free enterprise system."[61]

The students do not seem to have been terribly concerned about the crash either. Many of Nathan's classmates remained as determined as ever to wind up on Wall Street. But as the weeks stretched into months and the expected self-correctives did not engage, Nathan began to question what he had been taught. "Nothing I dredged up seemed to shed any light," he recalled.[62] In the spring of 1930, Nathan still considered the crash more an economic curiosity than a human disaster. Then, one of Nathan's professors, Frederic Dewhurst, asked him if he would like to do some part-time work on an "unemployment survey."[63]

Dewhurst, working through Wharton's Industrial Research Department, had already conducted one study on unemployment in Philadelphia in April 1929. Recent events had placed greater emphasis on the problem so Dewhurst planned a larger effort for April 1930. Nathan was eager to join. Statistical sampling was in its infancy—Dewhurst and Nathan simply divided Philadelphia into "representative" areas and prepared for a "complete canvass" of the selected neighborhoods. Their enumerators were 94 attendance officers from the Philadelphia Bureau of Compulsory Education who fanned out to interview 36,665 families.[64] One of Nathan's jobs was to check up on their work. He bought an old Moon sedan for $50 and got to know Philadelphia.[65]

The third largest city in the United States, Philadelphia had been, despite the national boom of the 1920s, in relative decline for years.[66] The 1929 study had shown unemployment already above 10 percent. After the crash, as much of the country waited blithely for things to "turn up," industrial Philadelphia went downhill fast.[67] Although it was the faces of the unemployed that most affected Nathan, it was the bleak industrial landscape that gave him his first understanding of not only the human toll, but also of the economic waste of the business cycle. "I'd look at a factory half idle when there were people out in the street who wanted to work."[68] "Here you would see Philco closed," he recalled, "and people wanted to buy radios. And certainly Philco wanted to produce radios. How could this be?"[69] "I could no longer distance myself from damaging problems and policies," Nathan concluded.[70]

So in the spring of 1930, out of his entrepreneurial upbringing, his Foster and Catchings curriculum, and his experience in Philadelphia's neighborhoods, Nathan developed the economic philosophy that he would hold for the rest of his life. During the next few years the Great Depression caused millions of Americans to change course. Some embraced fascism, some socialism. Nathan was too much a believer in the market to be drawn to either. He always upheld free enterprise "almost as part of a duty," but he was equally convinced that markets could be shaped, and their damaging effects moderated, by the intervention of an enlightened government.[71]

Having developed his message, Nathan soon found his medium. Dewhurst had been impressed with Nathan's work and employed him through the rest of his undergraduate years. Then Dewhurst suggested a special project. One of the new questions asked by the 1930 federal census was about unemployment. But as the figures came out through the spring and summer of 1930 they began to draw fire from statisticians certain that the census was underreporting unemployment. At Dewhurst's suggestion, Nathan meticulously cross-checked the 1930 census with the Philadelphia study and with others. He found the federal census to be woefully inadequate. Most importantly, he began to love statistical work, not as a mathematical exercise but as a means of gaining understanding. As he put it later, "columns of dry figures about unemployment translated into the despair of flesh and blood human beings."[72]

On June 17, 1931, Larry and Robert Nathan graduated from college.[73] They had averaged around 90 percent in their grades, worked hard to pay tuition, and lived together under brother Lew's roof on 58th Street.[74] Now, for the first time, they moved apart. Larry had hoped to become an accountant and stay in Philadelphia, but finding that "jobs were scarce" he accepted a position with Hecht's department store in Washington, D.C.[75] Robert still planned to become a lawyer one day, but statistics had captured his imagination—he decided to remain at Wharton and earn a Master's degree in economics.

KUZNETS

There were also financial considerations behind Nathan's decision to stay in school. The Wharton Industrial Research Department had agreed to convert his part-time job into a full-time research assistantship; tuition was covered and there was a "modest" salary attached.[76] Nathan seemed squarely on the academic track, and for a time did nothing to discourage the professors who pointed him toward a Ph.D.[77] If inspiration counted for anything, Nathan should have stayed on that track, for in the fall of 1931 he met the man who would guide his ascent into the New Deal.

Simon Smith Kuznets was born in Russia in 1901 and attended the University of Kharkov. His family fled Russia during the Revolution and Kuznets ended up at Columbia University where he studied with Wesley Clair Mitchell, a pioneer of empirical economics. Kuznets soon surpassed his mentor in analysis of economic data and in the late 1920s joined Mitchell at the National Bureau of Economic Research (NBER), a pioneering research institute in New York. During World War I, economic planners had been unable to put together a statistical picture of American economic capacity.[78] Afterwards, the NBER began developing the information. By the late 1920s, working at NBER, Kuznets had begun developing the most advanced statistical picture of the economy yet. He was also teaching at Wharton.[79]

He was only 30 years old and part-time, but Kuznets was already a star on the Wharton faculty—the one professor who taught only graduate students. He was a quiet man and a difficult lecturer—"he mumbled and he chewed his words," Nathan recalled— but there was something special in the words and in the thought behind them. Even in the 1930s, economics had not entirely shaken its origins as a branch of philosophy. Some of the best theorists eschewed empirical evidence and collectors of statistics often failed to use them to create a larger picture. "He had a rare capacity to find and analyze data that gave reality to economic theories and policies and practices," Nathan recalled. His immediate impression was simpler: "this is a genius."[80]

More traditional economics professors strove to impress their colleagues and attain standing in the academy. A few aspired to uplift the practice of business administration as well. Kuznets was committed to simply succeeding at the task that he had set for himself: "do the kind of research that would establish a clearer and essential picture of the nation's economy," as Nathan wrote.[81] Policy was a strong component of this work. Kuznets knew— and Nathan discovered—that gaining a clear picture of the economy was an important first step toward improving it.[82] Nathan spent two years in graduate school and attended two classes with Kuznets, always sitting front and center to catch every word.[83]

Nathan earned a record as one of Wharton's most distinguished graduate students. He wrote book reviews for scholarly journals.[84] In March of 1932, the U.S. Bureau of Labor Statistics published *Social and Economic Character of Unemployment in Philadelphia: April, 1930,* by J. Frederic Dewhurst and Robert R. Nathan. Anyone would have expected him to become a professor. Kuznets, who by his second year had begun to take a personal interest in his student, certainly did, but Nathan was growing restless.

By the time of graduate school, Nathan had completely abandoned his former "clinical neutrality" and was intent not on reaping rewards from the economy but on shaping it to create a more just polity. By the fall of 1932 he was convinced that the federal government had to take a more active role in turning the economy around. Someone persuaded him to join the local campaign for Franklin Roosevelt so he put his impressive baritone to work for the cause, speaking from the back of a sound truck, urging Philadelphians to vote for Roosevelt "in their own self-interest—because he would get America moving again."[85] Nathan was clearly inspired more by Roosevelt the man than by his as-yet traditional view of economics. The Foster and Catchings acolyte admitted later that he would have preferred to hear something about increasing purchasing power through federal spending. No matter. The next March, Nathan took the train to Washington and stayed with Larry to attend the inauguration of his candidate.[86]

It was a heady time for Nathan's chosen profession, the supposedly dismal science. Roosevelt proved to be a relentless experimenter and, not surprisingly, most of his experiments involved economics. The classical economists and budget balancers were still influential, but ideas about government intervention were becoming mainstream, particularly in the work of "braintrusters" Gardiner Means and Adolph Berle, who maintained that the rise of impersonal corporations meant that it fell to the state to shield individuals from the excesses of the market.[87]

Back in Philadelphia, Nathan read newspaper accounts of the developing New Deal and heard about the growing ranks of "New Dealers"—lawyers mostly, but some economists—who were putting the ship of state through unprecedented maneuvers. Simultaneously, because academics were obliged to specialize and to theorize, Nathan grew ever more detached from his studies. He had discovered that he would never be a good theoretician.[88] "My own temperament and interest pointed to the arena of conflict in Washington," he admitted.[89]

Kuznets was equally aware that Nathan would never be a top rank theoretical statistician, but he was nevertheless bitterly disappointed when he decided not to go for a doctorate.[90] "Why be a half-baked economist?" Kuznets asked.[91] Nathan countered that he hoped for "the chance of changing the economy."[92] Besides, Nathan continued, he still planned to go to law school: economist or attorney, he hoped to be a New Dealer one way or another.[93] In June 1933, Nathan received his Masters of Science in Economics. He kept at his job at the Wharton Industrial Research Department for a few months more and then headed to Washington.[94]

Nathan already had a job. By 1933, Frederic Dewhurst had moved to the Department of Commerce as Chief of the Division of Research and Statistics in the Bureau of Foreign and Domestic Commerce. It was a good place to be. During the 1920s, as a successful Secretary rather than as a failed president, Herbert Hoover had built Commerce into the biggest and best funded of all the agencies.[95] Dewhurst offered Nathan a job there at $2,600 a year.[96]

On a September morning in 1933, Nathan reported for work at Washington's largest office building. Three flights up, Nathan located the Division of Research, opened the door, and encountered Simon Kuznets. "What are you doing here?" a surprised Kuznets asked. "Well, what are you doing here?" Nathan countered. Kuznets explained briefly that he was "on loan," continuing his NBER studies on the national economy within the Department of Commerce.[97] They left it at that. In the afternoon Dewhurst called his newest hire into his office. He asked Nathan if he would be willing to work for Kuznets. "Willing?" Nathan boomed. "I would love to!"[98]

Nathan owed this newest occupation to a quiet yet earnest economist named Isador Lubin. A Lithuanian immigrant, Lubin ended up at the Brookings Institution where he counseled Wisconsin Senator Robert LaFollette, Jr., in his investigation into the causes of the depression. Lubin convinced LaFollette that the first step to fighting the depression was to understand its scope.[99] The result was a June 1932 Senate resolution that directed the Secretary of Commerce to make "estimates of the total national income" from 1929 to 1931. Commerce turned to Wesley Mitchell at NBER and Mitchell tapped Kuznets.[100]

The concept of measuring national income went back at least to 17th century England.[101] Adam Smith weighed in on the subject at the dawn of the economics profession. Alfred Marshall at Cambridge, who devised many of the most valuable tools of modern economics, developed the idea further in the late 19th century, as did Irving Fisher at Yale in the early 20th century. New York University professor Williford King took national income beyond an idea in the 1920s and his methods were further elaborated at NBER. Economists at the Federal Trade Commission had also made some early estimates.[102]

While still at NBER, Kuznets developed far better methods for determining national income than his predecessors.[103] Kuznets also obtained much better data and was more creative in using it. Earlier analysts had been most preoccupied with determining how the national wealth was apportioned. Kuznets was more interested in the causes of economic growth.[104] He factored in costs of production, excluded unpaid work, and ruled out illegal income.[105] In essence, Kuznets determined where, in the circular flow between producers and consumers, individuals actually received income, and then figured out how to measure it.[106]

The addition of Nathan brought the Kuznets team up to three; it also included Milton Gilbert, another Kuznets student, and Robert Martin, a more senior Commerce economist.[107] Kuznets had divided the economy into eleven main groups and allocated these among his team for study. Nathan was tasked with figuring out the employment and income of service and professional workers—doctors, lawyers, nurses, and engineers. Members of the team started with three basic data sets: the federal census of population, manufacturing, and agriculture. They had to generate the rest and received great latitude for creativity. "We found a survey here, a master's thesis there, or a Ph.D. dissertation somewhere else," Nathan recalled.[108]

The team members developed information, created tables, and did some writing, but the genius behind the work was Kuznets.[109] Somehow, Nathan wrote, he brought together widely differing sources, bridged hosts of informational gaps, and could still "produce a coherent nationwide picture of the American economy."[110] The study was completed in January 1934 and released that June by the General Printing Office as *National Income of the United States, 1929-1932*. It was immediately recognized as a landmark achievement, laying the foundation for the gross national product and gross domestic product measurements that have since become indispensable to politicians, planners, and business people.[111]

Commerce had already decided to make the national income study permanent, but for Kuznets, the challenge was over. He left in January and Robert Martin took over direction of the project. Within a few months of his mentor's departure Nathan's interest also flagged. The exhilaration of the achievement gave way to tedium once the project was past its innovative stage. More important, Kuznets was an impossible act to follow. "I liked Martin, but he wasn't a Simon Kuznets," Nathan admitted.[112] He had begun a habit of setting high standards for his bosses.

WELFARE

Nathan also expected a great deal of himself. Despite his successes in economics, Nathan remained determined, almost as a matter of principle, to fulfill his childhood aspiration of becoming a lawyer. In the fall of 1933 he enrolled in the evening program at the Georgetown University School of Law. He took classes five nights a week, five to seven p.m. Weekends he pored over cases. The schedule soon began to wear—Kuznets expected a great deal out of his assistants during the day. Many of Nathan's fellow students, in contrast, were political appointees with lighter daytime demands.[113]

More problematic was Nathan's realization, gained very early, that the law was not for him. Nathan's studies all seemed to indicate that when it came to lawyers, "the one who lied the best was the one who won." Georgetown was a Jesuit school so its liberal faculty were well able to counter such impressions, and Nathan spent a good bit of time in spirited argument with ethics professor and Regent, Father Francis E. Lucey. But he never changed his mind.[114] At the same time Nathan was ever more intent on influencing public affairs. He could see a direct link between economics and policy, but the law that he was learning seemed mostly irrelevant to the questions of the day.[115]

Nathan was receptive, therefore, when in the summer of 1934 he got a job offer from a former colleague at the Industrial Research Department. Emmett Welch was now affiliated with the Pennsylvania State Emergency Relief Board, the agency that dispersed funds from the New Deal's Federal Emergency Relief Administration.[116] Welch wanted Nathan to develop statewide unemployment data to help qualify Pennsylvania for funding—and he promised a raise.[117] Nathan would have preferred to remain in Washington, but he accepted the position in July 1934.[118] If his Harrisburg accommodations were any indication, it seems likely that Nathan expected to return to Washington before too long; he booked a room at the YMCA.[119]

Nathan had only been at work for a few months when he got a call from Edwin Witte, the Wisconsin economist administering Franklin Roosevelt's cabinet-level Committee on Economic Security, charged with preparing legislation to create government-sponsored unemployment insurance and old-age pensions.[120] A response to grassroots demands for government action in the face of the Great Depression, yet framed conservatively so that its success was ensured, the "Social Security Bill" promised to be a legislative landmark.

Nathan had just started a new job and was reluctant to let down his friend, but Welch and Witte worked out a deal. Nathan worked Monday through Thursday in Harrisburg, and Friday through Sunday in Washington. The State of Pennsylvania paid his salary and the federal government paid his travel and per diem expenses. That only left it to Nathan to put in seven-day weeks with a 250-mile round trip commute.

The task was to develop the statistical underpinnings for the legislation—the numbers that would determine how the program would work and how extensive its coverage could be.[121] Nathan began with the statistical base that he himself had created—the Philadelphia study and the unemployment figures that he had developed under Kuznets and had been keeping up ever since.[122] But most of his job with the President's Committee consisted of the kind of research that he had become used to doing at Commerce. He wrote countless letters to state statisticians, departments of public safety and labor, chambers of commerce, and life insurance companies, usually to request any figures that they might have and sometimes to clear up the inconsistencies that inevitably arose.[123]

It was perhaps fortunate for Nathan's health that the social security effort was on an accelerated schedule—Roosevelt wanted legislation in January 1935. By early December, Nathan had produced 48 tables of estimates and filled sizeable gaps in the unemployment data. Assuring Witte that "our work is in such condition that estimates can be prepared without delay or difficulty," Nathan resigned.[124] But the State of Pennsylvania was not to keep Nathan either. At Commerce, Robert Martin was not succeeding as administrator. Late in December, Willard Thorp, the Amherst economist running the Department's Bureau of Domestic and Foreign Commerce, asked Nathan to return as Chief of the National Income Section of the Division of Economic Research.[125]

Back in Washington in mid-January, Nathan and a staff of seven began reinvigorating the national income program.[126] They continued to seek new data, as Nathan put it, "off the beaten path of conventional research." They also worked hard to achieve closer ties with other federal agencies, easy to do because developing better numbers promised not only to help Commerce but to help the cooperating agency as well.[127] The Internal Revenue Service was particularly helpful, even conducting special runs of tax returns. The passage of time was also an ally. Every time a study was repeated the statisticians could sharpen the numbers in light of the new data.[128] In August, the Bureau of Commerce's *Survey of Current Business* carried an extended article by Nathan on the 1934 national income, which also revised the figures presented in the Kuznets study in light of new information. It was the first of many articles that regularly appeared in the *Survey of Current Business* under Nathan's byline.[129]

By then Nathan's personal situation had improved from bachelor's quarters at the Harrisburg YMCA. He was living with brother Larry in an apartment at 933 L Street in Washington's Mount Vernon Square district.[130] Larry and Robert had once been nearly identical twins, but no one seemed to think much of it as Larry remained slim and of medium height while Robert continued to grow through high school and college. He gained height on Larry—hitting 6 feet 1 inch, and developed a barrel chest and cavernous voice to match. Robert's face, hands, and feet also became much larger during those years, giving him the appearance less of a scholar than of a boxer.[131]

In early 1935, Nathan failed the medical exam required to renew his civil service status. His face and hands, the doctor explained, indicated that he was suffering from acromegaly, a condition caused by an overactive pituitary gland that could lead to gigantism and perhaps even mental problems. Larry took Robert for further consultation with a Johns Hopkins neurosurgeon who provided better news. For reasons unknown, the pituitary overactivity had ceased—the doctor wrote the civil service a letter.[132]

The L Street apartment was the scene of heartbreaking developments beginning later in the year. By 1935, the Nathans' older sisters Lillian and Rose were both working and living at home on Wayne Avenue in Dayton.[133] That fall, leaving his daughters to take care of his wife, Louis Nathan—who had taken no vacation since leaving Austria 35 years before—headed east to visit family.[134] He stopped in Washington for a time and then took a train to New York to visit Anna's relatives. After about two weeks, Louis returned to L Street with numbness in his arms. When it got worse, Robert took him to a neurologist who determined that Louis had suffered a series of light strokes. Anna and Rose came to Washington. The strokes continued for another three months until, in early 1936, Louis died.[135]

The brothers gave Louis Nathan, by setting the example of "ceaseless work" if nothing else, some credit for their achievements. Robert hoped that in the end his father understood the scope of what they had accomplished, although he admitted "I'm not sure he was fully aware of our progress."[136] Louis was taken to brother Lew's house in Philadelphia and services were held there.[137] In the meantime, Robert kept up his own round of ceaseless work, with less dire consequences for his own health.

When he left law school in mid-1934, Nathan had no plans to return. That changed when he opened his mailbox at the YMCA to find his grades and the news that he was first in his class.[138] In July 1935, settled in at Commerce once again, Nathan returned to the regimen: work all day, law school at night, and studying cases on the weekends.[139] Maintaining this rigorous schedule had been tough when he was working for Kuznets; it was even more difficult now that Nathan was a section chief, with administrative duties and staff to supervise. He pushed himself hard and in the fall of 1936 developed a persistent streptococcal infection. The doctor recommended time in a warmer climate. A friend who worked for the Works Progress Administration, the New Deal agency that supervised public works projects, suggested Key West.[140]

The last of the Florida Keys, 129 miles south of Miami, had been a tourist mecca in the early 20th century, thanks to the pioneering overseas railway completed in 1912. Then, on Labor Day 1935, a hurricane hit, killing hundreds on Key West and wiping out the railroad. Ever since, the WPA had been replacing the tracks with highway and trying to get the tourism industry restarted.[141] In late 1936, Nathan set out to clear up his strep throat and to explore Key West. From Miami he took a bus south—it took ten hours, including ferry service, to bridge the gaps in the highway.[142]

When the tired traveler finally stepped into the tropical night he heard the enquiry: "Robert Nathan?"[143] His guide was a WPA staffer who had been put on alert—the first of scores of friends that the itinerant economist made in the nation's southernmost city. That night Nathan moved into the first floor of a house on Caroline Street, rented for ten dollars a week. The next morning he awoke to an island still devastated and populated mostly by WPA staff, Navy personnel, and a smattering of intrepid tourists.[144]

For a few days Nathan was rootless, touring on a rented bicycle and taking in such sights as Sloppy Joe's bar and patron Ernest Hemingway, "with his air-conditioned sandals and old sweater and shorts."[145]   Although later in life he was usually up for a beer with friends and knew a good bottle of Scotch when he saw one, at the time Nathan was a light drinker, so he never pulled up a stool next to "Papa."[146]   He did, however, frequent WPA music and drama programs held every night.[147]

After about a week of wandering, Nathan found purpose after being introduced one day to Captain Manuel Lopez. Lopez, as Nathan described him, was a "dark skinned, oversized, cigar chewing Cuban." Having done his share of smuggling, he had since settled down as the captain of a deep-sea fishing boat. Nathan arrived on the pier the next morning with a sandwich and spent the day fishing. He claimed to have enjoyed angling before—Nathan had fished off Cape May with brother Lew during college—but going after tarpon, shark, and barracuda where the Atlantic met the Gulf of Mexico was different. Equally different was Manuel Lopez. He was, recalled Nathan, "the antithesis of everyone I had worked for or with in the 28 years of my life up to that time." The contrasts between Key West and Washington were endless, and to a man so much occupied with making the indeterminate finite through numbers, there was something refreshing in the endless expanse of sea and sky. Nathan spent one month fishing with Lopez. In early 1937 he returned to Washington with a clear throat and a lifelong passion.[148]

WIDENING HORIZON

By the time Nathan found Key West, his own horizon had widened. He began to find a place in the network of New Deal economists who were remaking Washington. Heading the national income page in the *Survey of Current Business* put Nathan's name squarely before domestic policymakers, and soon it came before an international audience as well. The Great Depression was an international crisis; unemployment was a concern across the western world. In late 1935, someone at the International Labour Organization in Geneva invited Nathan to write an article detailing his methodology for the organization's prestigious journal.[149] The article appeared in January 1936, with an introduction touting the author's contribution to the recently passed Social Security Act.[150]

Later that same year, Nathan published his second book-length study, *National Income in the United States, 1929-1935*, in which he provided extensive notes on methodology and carefully laid out the limitations of the study, setting a precedent that Commerce was to follow thereafter.[151] Nathan published another extensive survey in 1937.[152]

The National Income Division, Bureau of Foreign and Domestic Commerce, in 1936.
Nathan is in the back row, far right.

During the next few years Nathan's group at Commerce continued to expand its database through sample surveys and cooperation with other federal agencies. The National Income Section began issuing information quarterly and breaking it down by states. It was an exciting time to be doing the work: government agencies, research organizations, and trade associations were all learning to gather and use statistical data like never before. Still, "the national income" itself remained an arcane subject—Nathan spent much of his time explaining what it was.[153]

Some of the explaining was done to the press. Nathan became friends with influential Washington journalists including Al Friendly of the *Washington Post* and Drew Pearson and Robert Green, who had scandalized the city with their book *Washington Merry-Go Round* during the Hoover administration and parlayed it into a syndicated column of the same name. Pearson and Green even began mentioning Nathan's name in their columns—a heady experience for an economist in his twenties.[154]

Washington was full of young men equally dedicated to the national welfare in a time of seemingly limitless possibility. Far more than in any previous administration, many of them were Jews. Anti-semitism was still endemic in mainstream American culture, and although Roosevelt set an unofficial quota for high-level appointments, there were still widespread grumblings about the "Jew Deal."[155] Still, Nathan insisted that he encountered "almost no barriers" and "never felt any real prejudice."[156] Most of these young idealists were lawyers, but there were economists too. Isador Lubin, who had moved from Brookings to become commissioner of the Bureau of Labor Statistics, had been there longer than most. He recalled that in the New Deal "virtually every university in the country was combed by the various federal agencies for competent economists." By mid-decade Nathan had begun to meet most of them, even as Commerce and Georgetown Law still demanded most of his time.[157]

By then the big "brain trusters" of the early New Deal like Raymond Moley, Gardiner Means, and Adolph Berle had begun to step aside and the second generation of younger New Dealers—Nathan's generation—had come to the fore. Among the most influential were Isador Lubin at Labor, Lauchlin Currie at the Federal Reserve, and Leon Henderson, chief economic advisor to the WPA.[158] As Nathan recalled, "you could go around Washington, go to a meeting, go to dinner at someone's house—there would be a lot of technicians. It was just exciting."[159]

And because the young statistician from Commerce held the keys to the national income, more than a few in high places were eager to meet him, including Secretary of Labor Frances Perkins and Secretary of Agriculture Henry Wallace.[160] The latter was particularly impressed upon their first meeting. When Nathan reached out to shake, Wallace stared and remarked, "what a hand for shucking corn!"[161]

But among the top New Dealers, Nathan was closest to WPA administrator and Roosevelt confidante Harry Hopkins. There were two reasons for the affinity. First, the WPA was the fullest realization of countercyclical spending ideas to date. There had been other attempts to boost purchasing power through public works, but administrators had focused on project management more than pump priming, and expenditures had remained relatively low. Hopkins was determined to use the WPA as a vehicle for putting money in the hands of consumers first and foremost. When Hopkins wrote a book to explain his goals, Nathan was happy to provide statistics. Nathan was impressed. Hopkins did not just ask for numbers, Nathan recalled, he asked "how did you get these?" Although he was a sick man throughout the New Deal and the war that followed, Hopkins was remarkably effective, and Nathan deeply respected his "kind of inner determination."[162] After *Spending to Save* was published in 1936, Hopkins autographed a copy for Nathan and wrote "I hope your figures in this book will stand up. All inquiries will be referred to you."[163]

Nathan had no such relationship with his own boss, Secretary of Commerce Daniel Roper. When in a cabinet-level meeting Hopkins cited some of the figures on unemployment that he had used in his book, Roper claimed never to have heard of Robert Nathan and criticized his figures as "guesswork." When the president asked what agency Nathan worked for, someone deadpanned, "yours, Dan."[164]

Even as his name began to register in the upper echelons of Washington, Nathan kept a low profile. Through the mid-1930s, most of his networking had been done during professional lunches and the course of business; Nathan remained, in his own words, "virtually isolated" from social affairs.[165] There were two reasons for this. First, law school left little time for socializing. Although he passed the D.C. bar in late 1937, it was not until the next October that Nathan completed his degree, ranking 11th in his class with an 86.67 average.[166] Second, with his own life so highly scheduled, he had been content to stay in Larry's social orbit rather than establish one of his own.[167] The affinity between the Nathan twins, even into adulthood, may have kept other people out. "Larry gave me four eyes and two minds to work with," Robert claimed just a few years later.[168] By 1937 the Nathan family was unusually close. Robert and Larry had moved to a new apartment on Gallatin Street and sister Rose and mother Anna, who had remained after Louis Nathan died, were sharing it with them.[169] It was Larry who split things up. In 1937 he got married to Dora "Dee" Motter. Robert moved out.[170]

Nathan kept things in the family, however, sharing a one-room apartment on 16th Street with cousin Edward Jaegerman, an attorney with the Securities and Exchange Commission.[171] Jaegerman moved out in 1939 and Nathan was joined by Boston native Theodore "Ted" Seamon, a classmate at Georgetown Law School who was five years his junior.[172] After graduating, Seamon went into practice as an aviation lawyer.[173] About that time Nathan embarked on his one and only legal case—a divorce matter for one of the secretaries at the Commerce Department. He took the case but let Seamon handle it.[174]

Out of law school and away from family, Nathan made up for lost time, perhaps deliberately cultivating a reputation as one of Washington's most colorful bachelors. He piloted a bright red Pontiac convertible around town—fast, according to some accounts. He nursed a pipe thoughtfully and gathered acquaintances assiduously. On Christmas he drove around Washington delivering presents to the children of friends.[175] He was hardly handsome, but by one account Nathan was popular with women as the "great-big-love-able-bear type," and by 1940 he had a steady girlfriend, Frances E. Vaughan, who worked in the War Department. Early that year, when their conservative landlady protested Nathan's entertaining a woman overnight, he and Seamon indignantly moved out.[176] They set up in a larger apartment at 1308 18th Street Northwest near Dupont Circle and diligently split everything down the middle—excepting liquor: Nathan professed to be a near teetotaler.[177]

Despite the improvements in his social life, Nathan remained an outlier in Daniel Roper's business-friendly Commerce Department. One writer called Nathan's office "a lone outpost in hostile territory."[178] That changed after December 1938 when Harry

Hopkins succeeded Roper. "Hopkins drew me closer to the center of power," Nathan noted later.[179] Hopkins hired like-minded Richard V. Gilbert to establish an Industrial Economics Division and elevated Nathan's own group to division status.[180] In December 1939, Hopkins promoted Nathan to chief of the new National Income Division and charged him with conducting an unprecedented study of "sources and the distribution of national income."[181] Nathan's division was the largest in the Bureau of Foreign and Domestic Commerce.[182]

By then Nathan's name was associated with the Keynesian school of economics that had recently established a beachhead in Washington. The Great Depression had undermined classical economics, which could offer little more than the cold formula of Hoover Treasury Secretary Andrew Mellon: "liquidate labor, liquidate stocks, liquidate the farmers, liquidate real estate . . . purge the rottenness out of the system." Economists began searching for new solutions. Policymakers, including Hoover, understood that in the absence of anything else, federal spending might get the economy going again. By the time Roosevelt took office the concept and the term "pump priming" were both well established. Still, as yet there was no "legitimate" economic explanation for the Great Depression or justification for deficit spending. As a result, the New Deal never embraced deficit spending with any consistency. Franklin Roosevelt, who had campaigned against Hoover's reckless spending, still wanted to balance the budget.

"National Income Gain in 1936 Largest of Recovery Period," Nathan's article in the July 1937 *Survey of Current Business* breathlessly announced.[183] Even so, Nathan was privately emphasizing to his growing circle of friends that they were "not making enough progress."[184] As the article asserted, 1936 had brought what appeared to be a definitive end to the Great Depression—the most impressive and sustained period of growth since the crash. A few, Nathan included, believed the recovery to be mostly due to the liquidity injected into the economy by the WPA and other New Deal programs. But Roosevelt was not among them. He still worried about deficits and when Treasury Secretary Henry Morgenthau argued that it was time to trim Roosevelt listened.

That October, the stock market crashed again and the nation plunged into what was immediately dubbed the "Roosevelt Recession." From his post in Commerce, Nathan tracked the recession and argued that the president was being "held captive by members of his administration who insisted that the only way to regain the ground lost in the recovery program was by affirming again and again his dedication to a balanced budget."[185]

The Roosevelt Recession opened the way for a sea change in economic thought, and the captain of the Keynesian fleet was Nathan's friend Lauchlin Currie. The brilliant Canadian studied at the London School of Economics and was denied tenure at Harvard because of his unorthodox ideas about fiscal policy.[186] But Currie was welcomed at the Federal Reserve by Chairman Marriner Eccles, a Foster and Catchings reader. Currie was probably the first influential Washington economist to notice when Cambridge-based economist John Maynard Keynes published *The General Theory of Employment, Interest and Money* in 1936. In that work, Keynes explained in great detail that the government was not a passive bystander to economic activity but an active and indispensable participant. When business and consumer spending could not sustain current volumes of economic activity it was essential that government do so to prevent collapse. The alternative, Keynes argued, would be a sharp and sustained reduction in overall economic activity, like that which had occurred in the early 1930s.

By 1938, a few academic economists, most notably Harvard's Alvin Hansen, had begun to embrace Keynesian economics. A landmark in this transition was a series of seminars held at Harvard and Tufts in early 1938 and summarized in the book, *An Economic Program for American Democracy*. But it took the Roosevelt Recession to knock the budget balancers off guard and give the Keynesians ballast. From his post at the Federal Reserve, Currie began recommending Keynesians for government posts, among them Richard V. Gilbert and Walter Salant at Commerce and Gerhard Colm at the Bureau of the Budget.[187] When the young Keynesians talked, older liberal economists listened, among them Leon Henderson and Isador Lubin, who along with Currie, finally convinced Roosevelt to adopt Keynesianism in April 1938. Never again would a president try to balance the budget in recessionary times.[188]

Nathan never considered himself a Keynesian. It is no surprise, however, that many others did, for not only were his ideas the same in all essentials, his work was a concrete expression of Keynesianism.[189] Keynes taught economists and policymakers to think in macroeconomic terms, not to focus on fine-tuning the mechanisms of the economy but to look broadly at aggregate inputs and outputs. This is what Kuznets and Nathan had been doing since 1933. As John Kenneth Galbraith, another economist who had recently come to Washington put it, the national income studies, "almost as an act of nature, focused attention on the volume of savings that could be expected at full or near-full employment and the volume of public and private spending and investment that would be necessary as an offset." "Structural reform ceased to seem important," Galbraith concluded.[190]

As if to prove that economics in the 1930s was anything but consistent, within months Washington's policymakers took up the issue of structural reform. If the rise of Kenyesianism was one response to the Roosevelt Recession, the Temporary National Economic Committee (TNEC) was another. TNEC was created on the related premise that the rise of large corporations and "monopoly power" had contributed to the Great

Depression by keeping liquidity out of the system, depressing income and employment.[191] In a marathon of hearings, TNEC planned to determine how to break the monopoly and restore competition to the economy. In addition to the obligatory Congressmen, the committee contained a "who's who" of liberal economists. Isador Lubin of Labor and Willard Thorp of Commerce had seats. There were also a host of alternates, some notable like Gardiner Means and Adolph Berle, some less so like SEC economist Thomas Blaisdell. Of them all, Robert Nathan, age 29, was the youngest. Thorp's alternate, he was responsible for studying the flow of income at different stages of the business cycle.[192]

From the start, TNEC was all sound and fury. The highlight came early, when, in a move orchestrated by Currie, Alvin Hansen propounded the essentials of Keynesian thought.[193] The hearings continued for 18 months, and were steadily eclipsed by events in Europe. In the end, there was little to show from the effort beyond a 43-volume report that no one ever read. But TNEC turned out to have three unexpected benefits: Nathan learned more about the economy during the months with TNEC than he had during the years at Commerce and discovered how to excel in the company of equals—as Nathan later put it, "the cut and thrust of those associations braced my confidence in my ability to back my judgments with solid supporting evidence." Moreover, he became well acquainted with TNEC executive director Leon Henderson, a man who would become one of his closest allies in the "cut and thrust" that lay ahead.[194]

MILITARY REQUIREMENTS

In the United States, the Great Depression promoted political experimentation; elsewhere it spurred militarization. By the late 1930s, the militarists in Europe and Asia were on the move and no one was doing anything about it, certainly not in the United States. America in the 1920s and 1930s was staunchly isolationist. By the time that World War I rhetoric about making the world safe for democracy gave way to secret deals and a scramble for territory, many Americans were convinced that the country had been led into it by international bankers and munitions manufacturers. There was little sense among citizens of global economic ties, let alone a shared commitment to human freedom. These sentiments were represented in Congress, which had saddled the Roosevelt administration with neutrality acts designed to prevent the Great War from happening again. Then the Germans invaded Poland in September 1939, easily surmounting trenches that seemed so formidable 35 years earlier. This should have suggested that this time things were very different, but Americans were determined to stay out of another European war and only reluctantly began to prepare.

A lull following the onset of hostilities led even Roosevelt, who understood instinctively that America would eventually be drawn into the war, to reconsider. "Things here are amazingly quiet," he wrote in March 1940.[195] It was a good time to be out of commission and Nathan was, hospitalized for an illness and operation, most likely to remove the kidney stones that plagued him throughout his life.[196] In April, Germany invaded Denmark. The Low Countries soon fell. In May, the United States made its first real organizational response to the war in Europe. Roosevelt created a high level Office of Emergency Management, and below it, responsible for mobilizing the economy for defense, the National Defense Advisory Council (NDAC). On May 29, as the new NDAC met, beleaguered British forces were being driven off the continent at Dunkirk.[197]

The NDAC was a strange entity, fully reflecting America's ambivalence about war. Its authority was divided among seven members. A few, like union leader Sidney Hillman and economist Leon Henderson, were drawn from the ranks of the old New Dealers. But most, like Edward Stettinius of U.S. Steel, and William Knudsen of General Motors, represented big business. The trend was clear: as the nation moved toward defense and perhaps war, businessmen rather than brain trusters would call the shots.

New Dealer or not, Nathan had skills that the defense effort could use. One of the chief jobs of the NDAC would be to determine how much defense materiel could be produced and when. It needed a macroeconomic picture of the nation's productive capacity, and Nathan's national income experience uniquely qualified him to provide it. Former TNEC director Henderson also knew that the statistician had developed "a talent for one-sheet summaries."[198] Intelligent, opinionated, and aggressive, Henderson likely recognized a kindred spirit in Nathan, and offered him a job.[199]

Nathan talked things over with Henderson and also with Stacy May, the unassuming Dartmouth-educated Rockefeller Foundation economist who would be his direct supervisor at the Bureau of Research and Statistics. Commerce had provided Nathan with stability and the opportunity to study law, but he did not want to make a career out of national income and was ready for bigger things.[200] He took the job. Nathan turned the National Income Division over to Milton Gilbert, Richard V. Gilbert's cousin and also a student of Simon Kuznets. By 1942 Milton Gilbert had turned the national income effort into an even more powerful macroeconomic tool, the Gross National Product (GNP), which measured not only income but also fixed capital, government expenditures, and other assets. It was a tool that Nathan would soon have the opportunity to use.[201]

On June 21 Nathan took his place as Chief of the Military Requirements Branch of the NDAC Bureau of Research and Statistics.[202] Because he would have to deal directly with the armed services, his was the hottest seat in the Bureau of Research and Statistics.

But for a few weeks it looked like Nathan would never get the chance to fill it. Long before Joseph McCarthy, Martin Dies was making political hay out of finding communists in the government. In October 1939, the Dies Committee had discovered Nathan's name on a very long mailing list compiled by a communist-front group, the American League for Peace and Democracy.[203]

Nathan claimed to have no idea how his name got on the list and called its publication "pointless and ridiculous."[204] His colleagues at Commerce made light of the matter. In a mock ceremony they presented him with a garden sickle and a hammer mounted on cardboard. The inscription read: "to comrade Robert R. Nathan, from his fellow travelers in recognition of great statistical feats performed in the interest of the first international income."[205] A columnist wrote that "the nationally known economist is anything but pinko."[206] Six months later the FBI was not so sure. Nathan's security clearance was held up while the FBI investigated. Under oath Nathan swore that he had never been a member of the group and did not recall making contributions to it. He most likely made a donation. Frances Vaughan was sure that he had, and Nathan had already developed a penchant for giving to nearly every good liberal cause that came his way. But the FBI turned up nothing other than the grumblings of a few Commerce Department people who equated liberals with communists. After a few weeks Nathan was cleared and could go to work.[207]

His one and only brush with red-baiting behind him, Nathan became one of the chief advocates of the use of statistics in the developing defense effort with a staff of seventeen. His job was, in essence, to determine what the military would have to take out of the national economy on a month-to-month basis.[208] "We started asking a lot of detailed questions," Nathan recalled, "and became nuisances very quickly." The military, it turned out, did not have the answers.[209] There were three big problems. First, the structure and funding of the armed services made coherent information impossible to obtain; the Army, Navy, and Merchant Marine all had separate appropriations and established requirements differently.[210] Second, when Nathan queried Army-Navy Munitions Board officials they responded with questions: "are we preparing for a land war, a sea war, an air war, a European war, a defensive war on the U.S. Continent?"[211] The final problem was political. In 1940 America was still strongly isolationist. Franklin Roosevelt was seeking re-election, and any hint that the government was even thinking about war was off limits.

So in the second half of 1940, after exploring the blind alley of actual requirements, Nathan's group took another route entirely, calculating what the nation could theoretically produce at full employment and working backward from there to anticipate consequent raw materials shortages. Their approach focused almost solely on the three raw materials most basic to war production: aluminum for planes, copper for munitions, and steel for tanks, ships and guns.[212] It quickly became apparent that there would be shortages of all three, but to Nathan steel looked like the biggest problem.[213]

For Nathan, the military-requirements work, steeped as it was in statistics and theoretical production levels, was no academic exercise. He appears to have understood from the start that America would become involved in some way in the European conflict. He believed in the mission of the NDAC and had nothing but contempt for its opponents, which he characterized as "conservatives, America Firsters and advocates of 'peace at any price.'"[214]

In meetings, memos, and water cooler conversations, Nathan began making his case to anyone who would listen and to some who would not: unless capacity was immediately increased, steel would be in short supply before America got far into mobilization.[215] Common sense and experience seemed to suggest otherwise. The steel industry had not run anywhere close to capacity for years. During the Great Depression, mills had been producing at only 15 or 20 percent of their potential. Even in early 1940 they were only up to about 66 percent of capacity. No intelligent businessman would consider building, maintaining, and paying taxes on additional equipment before he could earn an income on what already existed.[216] Nathan understood this, but left the problem of how to spur mill construction—ultimately done through incentives and tax breaks—to others. His job was to identify military requirements problems and he did it vociferously. In the end, Roosevelt himself settled the debate by dictating that industry capacity be brought up to 10 million tons—below what Nathan suggested, but within range.[217]

By then, however, Nathan had earned a reputation alongside Henderson and others as an "all-outer," a pejorative term at the time.[218] Nathan's conduct in the steel issue put him in the middle not merely of a policy conflict but of a political one as well. After years in the New Deal wilderness, political conservatives and their business allies had begun to experience an end to exile. The Roosevelt administration showed every sign of inviting them both back to the table as the nation mobilized. The conservatives, however, wished to move slowly, deliberately, and to wring as much income from civilian production in the expanding economy as possible. To them, the "all-outers" looked suspiciously like liberal social planners in disguise. "We were accused of being the 'full-employment boys' or the 'long-hairs,'" Nathan admitted. There was some truth to the charge.[219]

As he dispensed with steel and moved on to aluminum and copper, Nathan found a supporter, a mentor, and an inspiration in a diminutive Frenchman who had been stranded among the Allies and was making the best of it. Jean Monnet was heir to a cognac distiller who in recent years had moved from international business to military diplomacy. When

France fell unexpectedly in June 1940, he had been in England as chairman of the Anglo-French coordinating committee. Winston Churchill appropriated the services of this particular French resource and detailed Monnet to Washington, D.C. His job was to find a way to get military purchasers and civilian manufacturers moving.[220]

By late 1940 Monnet had set up headquarters of the British Supply Council in a suite on the ninth floor of the Willard Hotel; Nathan had established himself not only as one of Washington's chief "all-outers," but also one of its most perceptive students of military production. Naturally Monnet was interested.[221]   One day Monnet appeared at his office door. "This little French devil comes in and asks what we're doing," Nathan recalled. He explained his raw material calculations, concluding that although he had solid numbers on steel, "what about aluminum?" Most would have been confused, Monnet was intrigued.[222]

Monnet understood as well as Nathan this macroeconomic approach to calculating requirements, what one scholar has called "the technique of the balance sheet."[223]   He understood even better than Nathan how important such calculations could be for preparedness. From a distance of years, it seems commonsensical that World War II would be won with American materiel, but in 1940 very few were thinking in such terms. Monnet was among the first in Washington to express what Nathan called "one simple idea which basically should have been obvious."[224]

Throughout late 1940 and the first half of 1941, Monnet and Nathan spent a great deal of time together. Early mornings brought walks in Rock Creek Park—Monnet liked to walk briskly without speaking, slow or stop to talk out an idea when it arose, and then pick up the pace again.[225] Nathan did even less talking during visits to Monnet's house on Foxhall Road, where the host would offer cognac from his family's cellars and gently plant messages that such notable guests as Felix Frankfurter then took directly to Roosevelt. Monnet always worked through others, keenly aware that a Frenchman seen talking about military production to the president of isolationist America would do far more harm than good.[226]

By the end of 1940, talk of all-out war still had what Nathan called "a political dynamite aspect," but the need for mobilization—for defense—was now open to discussion.[227] In late December, in a paper presented to the American Statistical Association, Nathan laid out the challenges of matching military items with raw material requirements. Hardly an inspiring topic in ordinary times, but these times were not ordinary.[228]

CELEBRITY MOBILIZER

In January 1941, a soft-focus, black-and-white photo portrait of Robert Nathan graced the cover of *Future*, the magazine of the United States Junior Chamber of

Commerce. While few Americans received *Future*, newspapers and magazine nationwide reprinted the list inside of the "ten young men of 1940." Even making the list was an honor; Howard Hughes and Orson Welles had been on the first list published two years earlier. Among those joining Nathan on the 1940 list were novelist William Saroyan and Polaroid founder Edwin Land.[229]

Just a few years earlier, Nathan had been a little-known daytime civil servant and nighttime law student. But thanks to his reputation as the all-outer who predicted the steel shortage before anyone else, he had become a minor celebrity. Nathan's formal associations helped. In the late 1930s he was president of the Washington Chapter of the American Statistical Association.[230] He was also deeply involved, along with other notable economists and social scientists, in the organization of the National Planning Association.[231] Perhaps more important, Nathan had learned to make the most of his contacts. By the early 1940s, Nathan's cumulative hundreds of handshakes, casual conversations, and lunchtime consultations had paid off. "Bob knows everybody in Washington and they all like him," said one acquaintance. "If the town had a mayor, Bob would be elected every year."[232]

Nathan owed some of his celebrity to his growing abilities as a public speaker. This had not always been the case. Nathan's early speeches could be heavily laden with bureaucratic phraseology, especially when he spoke from a script he had written himself.[233] But by the end of the 1930s he had learned to trust his instincts and let his remarks flow naturally, only lightly constrained by a set of notes. His speaking voice was impressive: tones rising from deep within his chest that seemed too big to control were expertly shaped at the last second by a strong glottis and a sharp intellect. By 1939 he was putting these facilities to regular use, addressing audiences that included the Justice Department staff in March, the Philadelphia Controllers Association in April, and a Foreign Service Officers group in November.[234] In the early 1940s Nathan's engagements ranged as far away as Chicago, New York, and Boston. Closer to home, the Chevy Chase Men's Temple Club of Keneseth Israel billed Nathan as "The Dynamo of Democracy."[235]

Nathan was industriously cultivating his reputation as a Washington character. Feature writers and columnists who started with his economics inevitably ended with his colorful personality. There was the jaw bone of 300-pound shark (caught off Key West of course) on his office wall, and the boxing gloves on the shelf, just in case Nathan could coax a caller into a sparring match.[236] There was the bright red Pontiac convertible with a swivel installed on the steering wheel so that Nathan could corner quickly as he careened about town, heckling slow-moving truck drivers. Perhaps less hyperbolic were accounts of long work days, beginning about 8 a.m. and ending at 2 or 3 o'clock in the morning.[237]

These colorful touches looked best on a backdrop of serious tones, and by 1941 no one was as serious about industrial mobilization as Nathan. He was encouraged when, on January 7, Roosevelt scrapped the NDAC and created the Office of Production Management.[238] Instead of seven heads the OPM had two: GM's Knudsen and labor's Hillman—"a hell of a strange wedding," as Nathan put it.[239]

But it soon became evident that in the OPM, as in NDAC before it, the "business as usual" crowd held sway. Mistrusting, or simply disliking, Nathan's estimates of steel capacity, the administrators asked for another opinion. In February 1941, American Iron and Steel Institute consultant Gano Dunn turned in a report predicting a surplus of steel capacity.[240] The all-outers—Henderson vociferously and Nathan in great detail—challenged the findings and Dunn went back to his balance sheets.[241] Meanwhile, automobile manufacturers, expected by the OPM to convert to aircraft production, continued to press claims that "we have inventories of axles. Please allow us to go ahead and use them up."[242]

Nathan always seemed to feel that one more study, a few more figures, and the stand-patters would see the light. In mid-February Knudsen formally asked the Army, Navy, and Maritime Commission for total requirements. The figures arrived in early March and Nathan and his staff worked overtime doing the reverse of the calculations they had made in 1940, working from products to raw materials rather than from raw materials to products. Using military "tables of allowances" that specified how much steel went into a tank, how much copper went into a shell, and how much aluminum went into an airplane, they translated materiel requirements into raw material estimates and put prices on everything. When on March 11, the United States embarked on the "Lend-Lease" program to supply armaments to Britain, those requirements were folded in, and by the end of March the estimates were completed. Stacy May announced that the U.S. economy would have to produce $48.7 billion of defense materiel by the end of 1942—just under half the entire national income of 1940. OPM all-outers were sure that "business as usual" was over.[243]

In February, Dayton's illustrious son returned home to deliver an idealistic speech to a Jewish group. In it Nathan blended the insights of Monnet with New Deal full-employment fervor. Germany had set the terms, "and democracies will have to meet that challenge," he said. But "if we had utilized this lost manpower this country could have accomplished anything it wanted," he continued. "The belief that there must always be millions of unemployed in this country is a defeatist attitude."[244]

By summer Nathan was more often angry than idealistic. From his office in the new Social Security Administration building at 4th Street and C—which was rudely requisitioned by military and civilian planners and never returned—Nathan posted a series of venomous memos. Richard V. Gilbert kept a file. "Ten months after the fall of France," Nathan wrote in one, "we are using to produce armaments only a fraction of the total resources which could be used for that purpose. For the past six months the OPM experts have spent their time spinning out reasons why we cannot do what has been done and is being done in Britain." The problem was worse than lack of organization or bad administration, Nathan concluded. "It is poverty of imagination and lack of drive that lie at the root of the inadequacies of our program."[245]

By the middle of the year some of the signs were looking better. Through 1940, the War Department had been exasperatingly uncooperative in providing requirements. When it did, the estimates were very low. In late 1940, Roosevelt appointed a new Under Secretary of War, Robert Patterson, who began to cut through the bureaucratic sclerosis. Other new top-level military appointees, many with legal or Wall Street backgrounds, did the same. In early June, the War and Navy Departments tripled their munitions programs.[246]

Despite these good signs there was still a big problem evident from Nathan's office. The $48.7 billion cited by Stacy May was just a compendium of different requirements. There was no grand strategy, no sense of how the parts would fit together, and no ideas about what had to be produced when. Through June and into July, the loudest demands from the all-outers were for scheduling. Word got to Roosevelt and on July 9 he instructed Secretary of War Henry Stimson to "establish a munitions objective indicating the industrial capacity which the nation will require." When two weeks later the Soviet Union entered the war on the side of the Allies and qualified for Lend-Lease, the task became even more urgent.[247] Special envoy Averell Harriman went to Britain, all-outer industrialist William Batt went to Moscow, and the military revisited its requirements yet again.[248] Nathan and his statisticians waited to put the pieces together.

But the OPM remained "more a political arrangement designed to fend off contending social interests," as historian Steven Fraser put it, than an effective administrative agency.[249] Nathan fulminated about large-scale planning and production deficiencies, but the OPM was even worse at allocating critical materials and stimulating smaller-scale production. New Deal utility man Harry Hopkins had taken over Lend-Lease. In August, two young lawyers working for him noticed that the Soviet Union had recently lost more heavy bombers than the United States even had on order. Phil Graham and Joe Rauh went to see Nathan, who confirmed that only one four-engine bomber had been delivered in August

1941. Graham and Rauh were not just run-of-the-mill lawyers; they had both clerked for Supreme Court Justice and Roosevelt confidante Felix Frankfurter. They fired off a memo to the president. Hopkins returned it, telling the young functionaries to get their facts straight. The frantic pair returned to Nathan who hauled out some of his abundant yellow data sheets, scrutinized them, made pencil marks, and reported: "I made a mistake. There wasn't one four-engine bomber delivered in August. There were no four-engine bombers delivered in August."[250]

The president was not privy to this particular bottleneck, but he was keenly aware that the OPM was incapable of getting materials to where they were most needed. When one approach failed, Roosevelt seldom started over; like the impasto artist, he simply added another layer. Accordingly, on August 28 he created a new agency on top of the OPM. The Supply Priorities and Allocations Board (SPAB) was intended to fix priorities and allocate raw materials.[251] Nathan and the growing cadre of all-outers were encouraged that Roosevelt had appointed Sears Roebuck executive Donald Nelson, who had a reputation as a "New Deal businessman," to head the SPAB.[252]

In September, Nelson formally requisitioned from the Army, Navy, Maritime Commission, and Lend-Lease Administrator all of the requirements that Roosevelt had requested. In November the numbers arrived. Nathan and his military requirements staff embarked on a round of 12- to 15-hour days and seven-day weeks running through the by now familiar calculations. Using manpower prospects, estimated national income, expected supplies of steel, copper, and aluminum, and their dog-eared tables of allowances, the statisticians assembled a picture of the production effort. Beyond the date of the initiation of the offensive against the Axis—September 30, 1943—the scheduling provided by the services was still rudimentary or non-existent, so Nathan and his staff made their own estimates. "We scheduled out the program by quarters as best we could," he recalled later.[253] Nathan drew up a document, and on December 1 submitted it to Stacy May. There was more work to be done, particularly better scheduling by the military, but his report formed the basis of what had already been dubbed "The Victory Program."[254]

By then, breathless headlines were reporting a military production program of tremendous scope. But Nathan kept one factor in mind that others let slip. All told, the services had asked for $27 billion in production for 1942 and $34 billion in 1943. These were reasonable if the national income of the United States remained flat. But, Nathan believed, "in terms of an all-out effort to maximize our national income, we should be able to accomplish more."[255] His projections indicated that even with allowances for civilian production, military expenditures could still hit $40 to $45 billion in 1942 and $60 to $65 billion in 1943.[256] Taking this into account, Nathan and May concluded, "three-fourths of the Victory Program can be achieved by September 1943. We believe the entire program can be accomplished by the spring of 1944."[257] On December 4, 1941, May forwarded the Victory Program to Donald Nelson. It was militarily viable, economically practical, but politically improbable—at least for another three days.

"Long Hairs" in the Limelight

By the time of Pearl Harbor, Nathan's personal life had undergone some small but significant changes. His mother and sister Rose had moved into an apartment together and Larry had moved to Boston, where he was a buyer for the R.H. White Department store.[258] Sometime after Larry left town, Nathan began assembling another family of sorts—one with the unlikely name "Goon Squad."[259]

It most likely began casually. Nathan invited some of his steadily widening circle of friends over and the talk inevitably focused on the subject uppermost in everyone's mind—the successes and failures of the defense mobilization program. Sometime in the latter half of 1941 the casual had become ritual: every Monday evening a group of like-minded junior officials from across the government agencies met for two or three hours at Nathan's apartment at 18th and Connecticut. Nathan provided beer, liquor, and snacks. His friends provided perspective on the progress of the mobilization and sympathy for the travails of the host.[260]

The numbers changed—there might have been a dozen or more on occasion, but more often there were about six to eight. The core group included Joe Rauh and Phil Graham, the lawyers from Lend-Lease; Ed Prichard, lieutenant to the OPM's Sidney Hillman; David Ginsburg, soon to be general counsel of the inflation-busting Office of Price Administration; and Nathan's Keynesian colleague from Commerce, Richard V. Gilbert. Higher-level officials were less frequent guests. They included Lubin, Henderson, Currie, and Wayne Coy, the director of the Office of Emergency Management who had access to the White House.[261] All were New Dealers. Except for former journalist Coy, they were lawyers and economists, men the conservative press dubbed "long hairs."

With the exception of Nathan and Henderson they were physically unimpressive. Nevertheless, they began to sow a certain amount of fear among the uninvited, earning the name applied to union-busting toughs in the labor wars of the 1930s. When the Goon Squad began, no one knew that America was going to war, just that mobilization was vital. Nathan described their goal in modest terms. "What we were trying to do," he said, "was to be sure that a group of us understood what the problems were and understood where we were going."[262] They clearly saw themselves, as Phil Graham's wife Katherine later put it, "waging a magnificent battle against bureaucracy and red tape."[263] They tried to promote the cause of people who were doing well, provide help to those who needed it, and "if we thought anybody was sort of playing games, or hurting the program, or even thought of a personal benefit," Nathan admitted later, "well we knew Drew Pearson well…"[264]

In the apartment at 1308 18ᵗʰ Street Northwest, Washington, D.C., the site of the legendary Goon Squad meetings.
(© Corbis)

It was natural for the Goons to become fully mobilized leakers. It was common practice for mid-level officials to individually enlist the leverage of journalists to turn the wheels of power. Nathan called it "an unauthorized government technique."[265] Of course Nathan had his ties with Al Friendly and Drew Pearson, but other reporters also claimed Nathan was "a good source of information" in wartime Washington.[266] When Nathan discovered that Army procurement officials had "ordered blankets in an absurd quantity," he tried to convince the Army to reduce the requisition, but to no avail, so "in general terms" he mentioned to some reporter friends that "the army is apparently stockpiling woolen goods." When that comment made print the order was cancelled.[267]

The most enthusiastic of the Goons by far was Ed Prichard. "Prich" was the most tactically brilliant of the group but the least disciplined, as his 250-plus-pound physique indicated. Before the fall of France, Prichard had been a pacifist; afterward he swung around to become the most fervent of all-outers.[268] He was not so much willing as driven to leak for a good cause. One evening the Goon Squad decided that Prichard's volubility with Drew Pearson had become counterproductive and instructed him to stop. Two weeks later, however, something came up that seemed too important to keep back. The Goons told Prich to leak it. "Are you sure?" asked Prichard. "Yes," they said. "Well, all right, then," Prichard replied, "I've already done it."[269]

By 1942, the mere existence of the Goon Squad was making the columns. Nathan always insisted that no one ever leaked classified information—that the Goons stuck to personalities and generalities. But their "needling" of the bureaucrats generated not merely bemusement but enmity and outrage. Out of the best motives, perhaps, they were playing a dirty game. The Goons were concerned about more than mobilization and their conservative critics readily recognized it. All were liberals, most were veteran New Dealers, and they resented Roosevelt's retreat from reform and cooperation with conservatives. As one presidential assistant put it, they are "no longer the king pins and they don't like it."[270]

In the weeks after Pearl Harbor, however, the Goons had reason to be optimistic— Roosevelt had become an all-outer. He was a president in dire need of reassurance, both for himself and for the nation, and Donald Nelson could provide exactly what Roosevelt required—Nathan's memo on the Victory Program. Late in 1941, Roosevelt requested a shopping list for 1942. Nathan was happy to oblige. The numbers were high, thought Nathan, but realistic: 50,000 aircraft, 40,000 tanks, 7 million tons of shipping.[271]

At the same time, Winston Churchill and British Minister of Supply Lord Beaverbrook were in Washington to attend what would come to be known as the first Washington Conference. Roosevelt shared the shopping list which he expected would be lengthy enough for the British. Instead, Beaverbrook, knowing how quickly war materiel could be consumed, encouraged Roosevelt to increase the figures, and he did.[272] Nelson and Nathan then tried to scale the numbers back a bit—a moot point when in his January 6, 1942, State of the Union Address, Roosevelt insisted that "we must raise our sights all along the production line." He promised 60,000 aircraft, 45,000 tanks, and 8 million tons of shipping.[273]

To get the job done, Roosevelt dispensed with the OPM and created a much more powerful agency, the War Production Board (WPB). This board included such high-ranking members as the Secretaries of War and Navy and the Administrator of Lend-Lease (who usually sent representatives). It included the administrators of all of the other war agencies as well, but Roosevelt appointed one boss and gave him potentially vast powers—Donald Nelson. The reason for this choice is open to conjecture. Nelson, ever the conciliator, had certainly been giving Roosevelt good news of late.[274] In the OPM and SPAB he had worked well with both businessmen and New Dealers—he "occupied the middle ground," as the official WPB history put it.[275] Nelson also had some effective advocates, Nathan chief among them. As wartime economist Eliot Janeway wrote, "these economists were exasperated with Knudsen because he lacked the imagination to believe that the objectives they visualized could be achieved. They believed in Nelson because he assured them these same objectives were practical."[276]

That the consensus builder was going to take strong stands seemed to be confirmed when on February 19 he created within the WPB an "alert, tough-minded and realistic" group that could spot problems in advance and have latitude to come up with solutions.[277] Nelson appointed Nathan as Chairman of the WPB Planning Committee, explaining that he was "the best thinker I can find."[278] Nathan's appointment, wrote the *Boston Globe*, "probably makes him the most important unknown in Washington."[279]

Photographs such as this one from the April 13, 1942 issue of *Life* helped cultivate Nathan's colorful wartime reputation. (© Corbis)

But *Barrons Weekly*, which claimed to have predicted the appointment, emphasized that Nelson was opting for toughness as much as brains. Nathan was "the man behind the hell-raising reports," *Barrons* announced, "predicting the shortages that have now arrived."[280] It may have been hoped that Nathan's reputation for toughness would rub off on his superior, who had none. The cover of the April 13, 1942, issue of *Life* carried the stern visage of General Brehon Somervell, the new head of the Army Services of Supply. But inside was a four-page profile of Nathan, the first page bearing the image of the hirsute, tee-shirt clad economist squaring off in boxing gloves over the subtitle "tough young brainstormer sticks pins in bureaucrats."[281] Profiles in countless other newspapers and magazines took the same tone. At age 33, Robert Nathan was tough, smart, and even more confident than ever, with the press to prove it. In college Nathan had no time for varsity boxing and may not have made the cut if he had. Now he was stepping into the heavyweight ring with Donald Nelson in his corner holding the towel.

The Feasibility Dispute

Nathan was chairman, but he had some formidable help on the WPB Planning Committee. The two other members were Frederick Searles, Jr., a 54-year-old former mining executive and engineer who had worked with the War Department, and Thomas Blaisdell, Jr., a 47-year-old former Columbia professor who had been with the SEC and TNEC.[282] There were some 25 professionals and about 75 staffers, most of whom reported to Nathan.[283] Executive director Edward Dickinson, a former research assistant at U.S. Steel, kept things running.[284] Simon Kuznets readily agreed to work for his former student as chief economist of the Planning Committee.[285]

Nathan was now more popular than ever, regularly receiving weekend invitations to the estates of industrialists-turned-mobilizers called "dollar-a-year men" after the nominal government salary that gave them employee status.[286] Nathan was careful in accepting. More than a few of the dollar-a-year men appeared to be using their influence to hold back mobilization rather than advance it.[287] On March 14, 1942, Robert Guthrie, head of the WPB Textile Division resigned, charging that his work had been stymied by his "business-as-usual" superiors, one of whom was the Chairman of the Board of General Electric. When the story broke, Department of Agriculture official Gardner Jackson sent Nathan information he could forward to "friends in administrative posts" and "likewise to other interested persons."[288] Nathan probably shared the information—this was a classic example of the kind of personality-driven dispute that the Goons liked. Pearl Harbor had also made Nathan more aggressive than ever. He told one reporter that "friendships don't count in fighting a war. What the hell! If we lose the war we lose everything."[289]

Senator Harry Truman also mistrusted the dollar-a-year men. His Senate Special Committee Investigating the National Defense Program took up the Guthrie case. Early on, a member introduced into evidence one of the first Planning Committee memos to

Donald Nelson in which Nathan declared that civilian production should be "ruthlessly ceased" and baldly asserted that manufacturers would not fully convert until left with no other choice.²⁹⁰ The memo made the April 15, 1942, headlines, but the next day, when Nathan testified personally, there were no sparks—he was duly respectful.

By then the Planning Committee had embarked on a dizzying number of initiatives: looking into objectives for construction, balancing military and civilian programs, and investigating manpower shortages. The committee also weighed in on relief for firms put out of business in the war economy, the concentration of civilian production, the adequacy of transportation, the supply and distribution of toluene and gasoline, and the mobilization of scientific research.²⁹¹

The War Production Board Planning Committee. From left, Thomas Blaisdell, Jr., Frederick Searles, Jr., and Chairman Robert Nathan. (© The Associated Press)

In one respect the Planning Committee was doing just what Nelson hoped, cutting across organizational lines to identify problems. Nathan seemed to enjoy this diverse agenda, but his colleagues grew concerned. Searles decided early that the committee tended "to consider too wide a range of subjects." He wrote Nathan in March that "we are shooting with a shotgun on a rifle range."[292] In mid-summer Kuznets also noted that the committee "has dealt with, or rather touched upon, an amazingly large number of problems." He worried that the group was not fulfilling its planning function.[293]

Despite the heavy agenda, Nathan maintained one overriding priority. The dispute between civilian planners and the military continued to revolve around the scale of requirements, but after Pearl Harbor the adversaries traded positions. In 1941, Nathan had been chagrined to get military orders amounting to $300 million or $500 million at most. By early 1942, the military, now with a real war to fight, was placing orders in the $5, $10 or $20 billions, and there was no coordination between the services requesting these great sums of materiel.[294] "The quartermaster corps evidenced no concern about ordnance," Nathan recalled, "nor did ordnance care about chemical warfare."[295]

Instead of worrying about raw materials shortages, Nathan was now deeply concerned with the "feasibility" of military "program objectives." If plants were built and orders placed regardless of supply, there was a good chance that resources would be haphazardly and inefficiently expended, resulting in aircraft with no instruments, tanks with no treads, and factories with no machinery.

The military was less concerned. Its leaders were enthusiastically commissioning the construction of new plants and turning the Army-Navy Munitions Board into what the WPB had been intended to be—a super purchasing agency for war materiel.[296] Donald Nelson was otherwise occupied. Ostensibly appointed because as a Sears executive he had been the nation's "number one buyer," Nelson had never succeeded in controlling military purchases. His solution, introduced by SPAB in late 1941, was the Production Requirements Plan, in which manufacturers applied for "priorities" allowing them to obtain critical materials. Unfortunately, these were little better than "hunting licenses" that enabled most major manufacturers to get some of what they wanted but not all.[297]

The problem of matching supply and demand was the biggest challenge facing the WPB in 1942. Blaisdell and Searles appear to have understood the task in immediate terms, as one of breaking individual "bottlenecks" to production.[298] But Nathan was inclined to see things in macroeconomic terms—as a problem of maladjustment of the national economy as a whole; by March 17, he had convinced his colleagues that the 1942 and 1943 Victory Program objectives were "considerably beyond attainment," and that they would have to work with the services to adjust them. They made a formal recommendation to Nelson.[299] This was a tricky situation: how could the civilians who had once criticized the military for keeping its expectations too low now insist that that the services were setting their sights too high? And besides, had not the president himself set the new, higher numbers?

Nelson agreed that he should try to negotiate with the military. Before doing so he took the problem directly to Roosevelt, who agreed to cut production expectations for 1942 back to a manageable $45 billion and to hold 1943 objectives to $75 billion. Searles still held that the WPB and services should negotiate, but Nathan was now convinced that they should hold the military to Roosevelt's figures instead.[300]

Nelson, however, was reluctant to pursue the matter much further. By spring of 1942 military production was finally beginning to take off. Both the president and the military made it clear that there would be no further reconsideration of goals until later in the year when ultimate capacity became known.[301] Nelson did not mind waiting—he liked to let the passage of time either resolve problems or to make them more manageable. With the military becoming more powerful and his Production Requirements Plan failing to take hold, the influence of the WPB was at an ebb. Manufacturers, in fact, had begun to consider the Army as "the source of orders" and the WPB as "a source of question-naires."[302] Nelson may have hoped he would have more leverage after his requirements plan began to work.

Nathan was not as patient. In mid-April he appealed to Nelson. "If this goes on and there isn't any real coordination in the military it's hopeless," he said. "Well what do you want to do?" Nelson asked. "I think we ought to do a feasibility study," Nathan responded, "rough and quick."[303] The work was not as quick as Nathan suggested, but by July, Kuznets had a new set of objectives, a bit higher than what Roosevelt had recently approved, but well below the $55 billion for 1942 and $87.4 billion for 1943 that the military had set.[304]

The military now understood that greatly expanded national income would allow for more production, but put less stock in the planners' other insights. Nathan believed that experiences in Britain and Germany suggested that civilian production could not be reduced below about 50 percent of the total without crippling the economy. This was the chief factor limiting the military's outsized requirements—not something that the military, always suspicious of coddling civilians, would want to hear. While Kuznets kept working on the study, Nathan attended luncheon after luncheon, trying to get backing from the rest of the civilian war agencies for the showdown with the military that he now believed was inevitable.[305]

On August 12, Kuznets forwarded a 140-page document to Nathan. It was really four different studies tackling the problem from the perspectives of dollar magnitude, raw materials, industrial equipment, and labor.[306] It determined that $47 billion for 1943 and $80 billion for 1944 "represented the limit of feasibility."[307] To his "feasibility study" Kuznets appended one additional recommendation, something that Nathan, Kuznets, and Nelson had discussed before, and what Kuznets had alluded to in March in his memo about the Planning Committee "not fulfilling its planning function."

Nathan put most of his faith in getting the big numbers to add up. Kuznets, however, was not convinced that scheduling could ever be so precise as to eliminate all problems.[308] What he recommended, therefore, was a "supreme war production council" composed of civilian and military members who could make fast and effective decisions to solve the smaller problems.[309] Nathan, having received his feasibility study, was now more willing to back Kuznets than before.[310] Nelson disliked the idea, well aware that what Kuznets described was precisely what had been expected of the WPB, which only underscored Nelson's own failings.

By late August, Roosevelt was, by one account, disturbed at "the rate at which tank treads were accumulating without armor plate, at which carburetors were accumulating without sets of instruments."[311] Feeling the heat, Nelson refocused on the failures of military planning, informing Under Secretary of War Robert Patterson and Under Secretary of the Navy James Forrestal, "I am convinced and have been convinced for some time that the total objectives for 1942 and 1943 are beyond attainment." He enclosed the Planning Committee's figures.[312]

Nathan was ready for the confrontation. He formally circulated the feasibility study to the top members of the WPB including the War Department, the Navy Department, and Harry Hopkins at Lend-Lease. Hopkins may have been intrigued, but did not respond; nor did the Navy Department. But the War Department did.[313]

The package sent by Nathan was received by General Brehon Somervell on September 12. Fifty years old, Somervell had served in the skirmish with Mexico during the Wilson Administration, was decorated in World War I, and had been an accomplished WPA administrator in the 1930s. He was a very effective administrator with a reputation for being tough—sometimes too tough. For that reason, when Robert Patterson was reorganizing the Army early in 1942 he asked for, and received, Nelson's recommendation before promoting Somervell.[314] Somervell took on a huge job. The Army Services of Supply was responsible for acquiring and dispersing all the materiel and supplies required, not only in the United States, but in every theater of war.[315]

Like his colleagues Somervell was suspicious of civilians; unlike them he was hot-tempered and undiplomatic. He knew Nathan—the fates had thrown them together in the April 13, 1942, issue of *Life*, Somervell glowering from the cover and Nathan pugnacious behind boxing gloves on page 47. Somervell cannot have liked what he read of the celebrated civilian "needler." Somervell definitely did not like Nathan's boss and was already engaged in a low-level war against Nelson through leaks to journalists and other off-the-record attacks.[316] The Goon Squad, of course, was up to the challenge. Nathan later admitted to employing his own leaks against Somervell.[317] Drew Pearson was delighted to document what he characterized as a tooth-and-nail fight between the military and civilians for control.[318]

Somervell found three documents in the envelope from Nathan. In addition to the feasibility study was an August 31 memo by Kuznets and a September 8 memo by Nathan. It was a lot to absorb and Somervell was not inclined to read closely. He was having his own problems just then with the military hierarchy. It was also a Saturday afternoon and he was still at the office.[319] Somervell dashed off a reply to Nathan and cc'd Nelson. Referring to Kuznets, the note began snidely—"I am in agreement that his data are unreliable"— and deteriorated quickly. Somervell complained about "ex cathedra remarks about cutting facilities" and questioned "Mr. Kuznets' military background." As for the discussion of production strategy and military strategy, the general wrote, "to me this is an inchoate mass of words."[320]

It is probably the recommendation of a "supreme war council" that incensed Somervell the most. He had been trying to get a more direct line of reporting to the Joint Chiefs and now an economist was promoting a committee to bypass him entirely.[321] Somervell ridiculed the idea of a "board of 'economists and statisticians' with military men without any responsibility or knowledge of production." Finally, concluded Somervell, in phrasing truly strange, "I am not impressed with either the character or basis of the judgments expressed in the reports and recommend that they be carefully hidden from the eyes of thoughtful men."[322]

Nathan read the response in disbelief. Somervell had overlooked the issues almost entirely. He had focused on minutiae and personally attacked an academic of nothing near his standing. Nathan hesitated to show Somervell's reply to Kuznets, but he did. After a while both men found some humor in the situation.[323] Nathan asked Nelson's permission to reply. Nelson agreed without hesitation. He and Kuznets crafted a response, sent under Nathan's name alone, that patiently distilled the findings of the report and impertinently prodded the general.[324]

"In view of the gravity of the problem discussed in these documents," it began, "I hesitate to take your memorandum seriously." After a point-by-point discussion of the findings, Nathan condescended that "the fact that we once urged that the sights be raised is no reason now for adopting an ostrich-like attitude when goals are established that are above probability of achievement." He reminded Somervell that the unreliability of data was due to "both the limited quality and quantity of the data derived from your department," and expressed regret that the memorandum of August 31 "was not phrased so as to be comprehensible to you." Nathan claimed to appreciate Somervell's frank comments on the report, but stated that "your conclusion from it, however, that these judgments should be carefully hidden from the eyes of thoughtful men is a non-sequitur." Nathan concluded that in the near future "thoughtful men" would no doubt sit down and discuss the issues, but dismissed as a "waste of time" any further "round-robin" with Somervell.[325] "For me to say that to a four-star general—that was a little hot," Nathan admitted years after the fact. "But he deserved it."[326]

Somervell soon realized that he had been mistaken to take on the two civilian economists, even though, in his mind, they had been stand-ins for Donald Nelson. The very next day he circulated a memo disavowing any conflict with the WPB and discouraging any public airing of an "alleged controversy." Similarly, Nathan might have been tough on paper, but soon realized that he had been punching above his weight. The two men sat in on several subsequent WPB meetings and the subject never came up—it was not yet time.[327]

During late September and early October Nathan continued to make his case. Isador Lubin was Hopkins' delegate to the WPB. Nathan sat with both of them on the back porch of the White House (Hopkins lived there at the time) to explain the feasibility study. He also met with Leon Henderson, now the nation's chief price controller and a WPB member.[328]

The time arrived on October 6, 1942. Attendance was up—14 regulars and 17 guests. Everyone knew that there would be a confrontation. Somervell brought along—and prominently displayed—a letter from Chief of Staff General George Marshall confirming that he was in charge of "interpretation of strategy" to the WPB. Nathan began by presenting the main findings on feasibility and making the plea for the supreme war production council. Wayne Coy asked whether the military would admit that the requirements for 1942 were too high. Somervell did not think that the difference was serious enough to worry about. To Nathan's point he added "what good would be a board composed of an economist, a politician and a soldier who does not know production?"[329] Nathan, conciliatory, assured Somervell that civilians would not question strategy, but had the military considered feasibility? Somervell, leaning over his letter from Marshall, deflected the question and insisted that the military could not fight on the $80 billion dollars Kuznets estimated would be available in 1943. He said that the military needed $92.9 billion.[330] More civilians weighed in, but the military held firm behind Somervell.[331]

Like Nathan, Leon Henderson appeared an unlikely "brain truster." He was short, weighed 200 pounds, and seemed always to have a cigar in his mouth. Henderson "looks like the operator of a second rate pool hall" one journalist wrote, and he could act like one too. He was not afraid to fight for a cause and he was good friends with Donald Nelson.[332] As the meeting stalled, Henderson began speaking, almost mumbling at first, in low tones. He was going back over all of the figures in detail, raising his voice as he raced toward the peak figure. "Maybe if we can't wage a war on $80 billion, we ought to get rid of our present Joint Chiefs, and find someone who can," Henderson snarled.[333]

There was dead silence around the table. Henderson filled it with a personal attack on Somervell's ignorance and arrogance. He accused the general of padding his figures. William Batt tried to settle things down, interjecting that Somervell did not make strategy. "Ain't he got a letter?" Henderson demanded. The meeting ended.[334]

The Planning Committee met a short time later. Stacy May sat in. They would have to drop the supreme war council idea, he insisted. Nathan agreed. The committee also decided that if the military did not wish to cut, it should be allowed to simply extend the 1943 timetable into 1944. The next meeting of the WPB was lightly attended and tightly controlled. Nelson, Lubin, and Henderson laid out the Planning Committee's compromise. Somervell, who had clearly had consultations of his own, accepted it.[335]

Nathan and his colleagues took this as a victory. It was actually a generous compromise. Somervell had already accepted the idea of an extension, and without the supreme war production council the package was palatable. By November, the Joint Chiefs had submitted a revised 1943 program totaling $80.1 billion, only slightly above what Kuznets and Nathan considered feasible. It also pushed back its own schedule.[336] In the end, the assault against the Axis took place in mid-1944—almost exactly when Kuznets and Nathan had first estimated that it should.

By then Roosevelt had had enough. In October he took South Carolina political veteran James Byrnes off the Supreme Court and put him in charge of a new mobilization agency, the Office of Economic Stabilization. He gave Byrnes the powers that Nelson had not used. The conservative Byrnes shored up his left by hiring Frankfurter protégé Ed Prichard, but cautioned him to "quit going to cocktail parties and gabbing to columnists."[337]

By the end of the year, the American production machine was going into high gear, but Donald Nelson's days were winding down. Ferdinand Eberstadt, a former investment banker who had run the Army-Navy Munitions Board, had joined the WPB and created the Controlled Materials Plan, an allocation system that worked where Nelson's did not. Eberstadt's system shifted the economic power strongly toward the military, which Nelson sought to correct by bringing in Charles E. Wilson of General Electric as director of production.[338] When Nathan took a position on the Combined Staffs of the Combined Production and Resources Board, intended to integrate American and British production, he also felt the effects of reorganization.[339] As the chairs shifted, Nathan feared for the Planning Committee. He implored Nelson to keep it reporting directly to the Chairman rather than let it be put under Wilson. For some reason Nelson failed to do so.[340]

By early 1943 Nelson had more on his mind than the fate of the Planning Committee. The military was arguing that the Controlled Materials Plan demonstrated that Eberstadt was best qualified for the job. Roosevelt was inclined to agree, but believed that it would be unseemly to slip him into the top spot. A good solution seemed to be to bring in Bernard Baruch, the legendary head of the World War I mobilization program, as a figurehead and put Eberstadt below him. James Byrnes made the offer to Baruch.[341] The switch was to be made February 17, 1943, but before he himself could be fired, Donald Nelson abruptly fired Eberstadt. Roosevelt backed out of the deal. What had happened?

No one is likely to know for sure precisely who provided Nelson with the information. Drew Pearson fingered Wayne Coy as the one who tipped off Nelson.[342] Eliot Janeway pointed to someone else and provided far more detail, which rings true. Late in the night of February 16 to 17, according to Janeway, Nathan called Nelson and arranged an early morning breakfast. There, Nathan told his boss about the announcement planned for 2 o'clock that afternoon. He knew because Ed Prichard, ensconced in Byrnes's office, had told him. Prichard also suggested that Nelson should fire Eberstadt beforehand.[343]

It was a discouraging time for Nathan. He respected Donald Nelson greatly. The two had become close friends and Nathan was intensely loyal to his boss. But the closer the nation got to realizing an economic miracle, it seemed to Nathan, the more recriminations there seemed to be at the top—most of them involving Nelson. "The military never forgave the civilians for getting as much power in the war as they did," Nathan believed.[344] If Nathan had helped save Nelson, he cannot have been proud of how he did it. Regardless, he had another boss now, GE President Charles Wilson, and he was not entirely pleased about it. "I wouldn't go with Charlie," Nathan insisted later. "I had no respect for him."[345]

There was another good reason for Nathan to plan a departure. The House Military Affairs Subcommittee, led by conservatives suspicious of the few New Dealers still in Washington, had begun probing the deferment lists. As Nelson had done for Nathan, Leon Henderson at the Office of Price Administration had gotten a deferment for his 31-year-old general counsel and the sometime Goon, David Ginsburg. The Congressmen fumed when Ginsburg resigned to take a commission as an Army captain. They began ransacking the agencies for other abuses of "essential man" deferments and threatened to name names.[346]

Nathan's deferment, obtained in October 1941, had been easy to get.[347] He was wearing a back brace at the time.[348] Sometime in the 1930s, Nathan had injured his sacroiliac playing handball.[349] Early in 1943 he aggravated it again.[350] On March 21, Nathan was named to yet another joint committee, this one coordinating U.S.-Canada production, but by then he had asked Nelson to have the deferment lifted.[351] Nelson resisted, but then granted the request. On April 3, Nathan submitted his resignation. He had no military post as yet, but believed that his resignation would leave Wilson "completely free to reorganize the planning function."[352]

Being sworn in as private at Fort Myer, Virginia, April 30, 1943. David Ginsburg is at left. (© Corbis)

On April 30, 1943, Nathan and Ginsburg were inducted together at nearby Fort Myer, Virginia. That night, back in Washington, Nathan made one of his first radio appearances, debating a Representative about the Congressional push to end deferments.[353] A few days later, Nathan fired off one last WPB memo. It went back over the ground of the last few months, lauding increases in production and the halt in extravagant construction. But it lamented that with the success of the program had come "a concomitant decline in interest concerning programming." Nathan also called one last time for an "authoritative programming body."[354] By then no one at the WPB was listening; instead they threw a farewell party. The next day, May 6, 1943, Nathan and Ginsburg reported for active duty.[355]

At age 34, Robert Nathan had already hit what, by most measures, would be considered the pinnacle of a career. Hard work and enterprise had taken him far beyond Dayton's East Side. Statistical talent and administrative expertise had carried him into the highest levels of the government where he had already done much for the nation. He had helped figure out how to measure its economy, develop its social safety net, and arm it for war. Nathan had also raised the stature of his profession. Late in life, economist John Kenneth Galbraith still recalled "the excitement generated by Nathan and the Victory Program."[356] Robert Nathan had adopted a set of ideas revolving around a simple insight: that people made the economy and that people—through their government—had the responsibility of seeing that it served the many instead of the few.

2

A LIBERAL'S HIGH NOON

A t the height of summer, 1949, a reporter came around a Washington, D.C., traffic circle on his way to visit the consulting firm at No. 3 Thomas Circle, a World War I-era brick row house between Massachusetts Avenue and 14th Street.[1] Horse-bound in the middle of the intersection was a man no one remembered: General Henry Thomas, an accomplished but unassuming Civil War general who had faded fast in the company of more self-promoting Union warriors. The man the reporter came to meet, in contrast, was unabashed in his efforts to make a name and advance a cause. Something of an intellectual, more of an ideologue, and very much the entrepreneur, Robert Nathan was eager to give one more of countless interviews about his favorite subject, liberal economics.

"Everybody calls me a son of a bitch" he told the reporter, leaning back in his office chair and pulling relentlessly on his ever-present pipe. "They say business isn't making any money." But he knew better and reveled in the knowledge. "Steel is fantastic," he crowed, "second quarter profits will be the highest in history. And I'd love to do a study on profits in the auto industry." Some of the profits should rightly remain with industry, Nathan admitted. He was no communist and no socialist, but Foster and Catchings, national income studies, the perspective from the heights of the wartime economy, and the intellectual penumbra of John Maynard Keynes all convinced him that to keep the nation's economic bloodstream flowing, a large part of those earnings had to get back to the consumer. "Our economy is too complex for us to have laissez-faire," Nathan explained. The reporter waited while he took one call and made another—the United Steelworkers Union needed him to help prepare for contract talks in Pittsburgh, so he postponed some upcoming Congressional testimony.[2]

The years from 1943 to 1950 were at once promising and perplexing for New Deal liberals. Although there had been no New Deal legislation since 1937 and Republicans and conservative Democrats rode high in Congress, most continued to believe that the electorate still backed liberal reform. Robert Nathan was among the few who expected even more. He expected former soldiers to become progressive crusaders. He expected government planning to get even wider rein than during wartime, business to willingly share its wealth, and labor to adopt a similarly civic-minded stance. He even expected the United States to convince the United Nations to become guarantor of a Jewish nation in a hostile Middle East. Because he was willing to help make these things happen Robert Nathan was a very busy man during this liberal's high noon.

SOLDIER AND AUTHOR

Riding a bus south from Washington in the spring of 1943, Nathan was no doubt relieved to be beyond reach of the Congressional assault on the "long-haired boys" left over from the New Deal. For Nathan—even more for David Ginsburg, who sat next to him—the experience had been painful. "You could sort of hear them hitting the steps as they went down," observed another Washington insider.[3] When the two arrived at Camp Lee, Virginia, it looked as if things might not improve. As they entered the first building, Ginsburg remembered glancing at a bulletin board to his right and a clipping from that morning's *Washington Post*, and "pictures of Bob and myself inanely grinning." Underneath someone had scrawled, "these two sons of bitches arrived today."[4]

Nathan's back was not much improved—he wore a brace of steel, canvas, and leather when he enlisted—but he did his soldier's duties and met with no resentment beyond the bulletin board.[5] Kitchen duty, cleaning latrines, and ditch digging were welcomed after Washington. "I was really enjoying the new life," he wrote his former Goon Squad friends. "You should have seen me swinging a pick and shoveling and raking dirt in the hot sun."[6]

But Nathan was hardly the average blue collar or farm boy recruit. He somehow got permission to spend four days rummaging through the files at the Camp Lee reception center correlating IQ results with age, education, and income. "Got some interesting results," he told his Washington friends. An inept marksman, Nathan allowed the recoil of his Springfield rifle to knock a piece out of his nose.[7] Fortunately, he was rejected for combat duty almost immediately.[8] The Quartermaster Corps and the Air Corps both wanted him—the former won, but then a request from the Office of Strategic Services, which Nathan hoped might send him overseas, trumped it. Only three weeks later his health betrayed him. While walking through camp, Nathan felt his sacroiliac slip and pain shot through his back. He spent five days in barracks and three weeks in the camp hospital.[9]

By July 1, the Army had nursed Nathan back to ambulatory status.[10] He returned to Washington to take a position with the European Industry and Trade Section of the OSS. It was undoubtedly as good as it could have been to be back in Washington under the circumstances. Days Nathan spent with Section Chief Moses Abramovitz, a

Columbia-trained economist who had worked with Simon Kuznets at NBER; nights he lived with Kuznets and his family at their house on California Street.[11]

What Nathan actually did at OSS is less clear. Newspapers stated that he was an "analyst of enemy economics."[12] Nathan recalled that he followed up on the old domestic data "to see where the bottlenecks were" and talked a lot to his old WPB colleagues.[13] Mary Tillotson, a pretty blonde from Minnesota who was working as a secretary to the European Industry and Trade Section, did not remember him doing much at all besides spending time flirting and following her on her rounds through the government agencies.[14] "I think the Army didn't know what to do with Bob while he waited for his discharge," she said later.[15]

In just a few weeks, though, Nathan relapsed and ended up in Walter Reed hospital.[16] On the advice of a physician friend he rejected back surgery—still experimental at the time. Instead he got into the habit of "eating aspirin like chewing gum" and waited for his back to heal.[17] The Army was not as patient, offering a medical discharge almost immediately, but Nathan rejected it—he hoped to go back to OSS and perhaps overseas.[18] So he spent the late summer in the company of his fellow soldiers, most clad in gray pajamas or red hospital lounging suits, most with wounds more serious than his. "The weather was hot and the pace of life was slow," he recalled, and after lights out the soldiers tended to talk in low tones, eventually getting around to their "almost universal concern over jobs and security and peace."[19]

What his comrades voiced as deeply personal concerns, Nathan inevitably understood in macroeconomic terms. In the presence of so many soldiers already facing demobilization, Nathan began to think harder about ideas that he had already begun to formulate about what should be done after the war. The economics were just a bit more complicated, but the idea was simple—the kind of economic planning that was helping win the war could help "win the peace." As he told a New York business group in April, "we can have real prosperity under free enterprise if we show the same kind of realism, imagination, and determination concerning the postwar period as we have been able to develop during the war."[20] Somewhere Nathan obtained an early magnetic recorder, and ensconced in Ward 48 at Walter Reed, he began dictating a book.[21]

The concerns that Nathan and his fellow convalescents shared were far more urgent than the average young adult's worries about making it in the world. Most Americans were quite sure that the nation would slip back into depression after the war. Younger people who had grown up during the 1930s knew nothing else but peacetime depression. Those with longer memories knew that World War I had been followed by an exceptionally sharp recession from which agriculture, for one, had never really recovered. Economists found far more compelling reasons for concern. They realized that mobilization had inflated the gross national product to a tremendous degree—government spending had gone from 6 percent of the economy to almost 45 percent.[22] As Nathan pondered, Harvard Ph.D. Paul Samuelson wrote that after the war "there would be ushered in the greatest period of unemployment and industrial dislocation which any economy has ever faced." European Keynesian Gunnar Myrdal agreed and predicted that free market mechanisms would crumble under the impact.[23]

That sense of urgency informed Nathan's book. The chief insight was that of Keynes, popularized in the United States by Alvin Hansen, that countercyclical federal spending could be used to keep a national economy at full employment. The biggest problem was saving—by individuals but especially businesses—that kept money out of circulation and exempt from the "multiplier effect" that Keynes had credited with creating economic growth. In practice, Nathan believed that postwar planners need merely do as the WPB Planning Committee had done: calculate the amount of gross income needed to maintain full employment and see that it went into the economy, either by higher wages obtained by forward-thinking employers or strong labor unions, progressive income taxes and social security insurance, or simply redistributionist government programs. The alternative, he posited, would be depression, the collapse of the free market, and even the rise of totalitarianism.

Nathan's project was no high-flown academic treatise, however. Instead he was determined to make the insights that economics had to offer available to the common man in words that they could understand—a kind of Foster and Catchings shorn of the parables and folksy characters for the postwar generation. Nathan filled chapters with titles like "Why We Have Had Depressions," "The Risk in Investment," "Government Spending Can Fill the Gap," and with breezy and overtly didactic text that sounded like a college professor put unexpectedly before a class of kindergartners. The text was punctuated by simple and iconic full-page illustrations. On page 213—fifteen pages before the close—Nathan drove his main message home. "While competition should be encouraged to constantly improve products and production techniques, there must be some other instrument to insure the maximum benefit of our economic operations to the people as a whole. Obviously, this instrument is the government, which in a democracy is the only agency representing the people."[24]

In November, Nathan wrote a preface acknowledging Keynes and penned a dedication to Kuznets.[25] Having given up on the prospect of going to Europe for the OSS, Nathan accepted a medical discharge—although he turned down a 10 percent disability payment.[26] Ready to leave government service after a truly remarkable decade, the convalescent sent his thanks to Franklin Roosevelt. "You have given me a fixed determination to work only in the interest of the people," he wrote. "It is my fervent hope that nothing will ever cause me to swerve from that objective."[27] He was discharged November 24, 1943.

In early December, *Newsweek* announced that citizen Nathan was going to Hot Springs, Arkansas, to further convalesce "with a magnum of aspirin, a sciatic back, and notes for a new book."[28] This one, on manpower readjustment, had been commissioned by the Council on Economic Development (CED), an organization of forward-looking businessmen created in 1942.[29] Its consonance with Nathan's aims was made clear in one of its earlier titles: *Toward Full Employment*, by John Kenneth Galbraith.[30]

Notes in tow, Nathan stopped in Dayton to visit Larry, who had joined a firm there, and to man his old street corner for a *Dayton Daily News* "old time newsboys" event.[31] By Christmas he had left Hot Springs for Los Angeles to stay with film industry friends made through Matthew "Matty" Fox, a colleague from the WPB.[32] He remained there until February, working on the CED project which shrank to report status somewhere along the way and then stalled.[33] While Nathan's second book evaporated on the West Coast, his first neared publication in the East. Nathan had tentatively entitled it "Let Freedom Bring." McGraw-Hill apparently considered that just a bit too clever, so it came out in March 1944 under the title *Mobilizing for Abundance* instead.[34] Nathan would have had high hopes for the book, as any author must. Donald Nelson had written an awkward but appreciative blurb for the dust jacket, and Nathan sent inscribed copies around Washington—Franklin Roosevelt hoped to read it but cautioned that "these are rather full days."[35]

The reviewers were not kind. The more generous faulted Nathan for removing too many complexities. One scholarly reviewer called it a "sprightly written little book," but noted that "intelligent laymen may be somewhat repelled by the simplicity."[36] Eminent Harvard economist Gottfried Haberler was tougher, calling it "a very popular exposition of a very simplified version of the familiar Keynes-Hansen theory of oversaving" with no discussion of alternate explanations for depressions or consideration of complicating factors. It can "impress only the unthinking but hardly convince the thoughtful," Haberler concluded.[37] Others faulted Nathan for blind adherence to the "mature economy thesis"—that henceforth population, not productivity, could be expected to expand the economy and that, therefore, putting money in payrolls would be far more productive than additional investments in enterprises or technologies.[38] Criticisms like these could only leave Nathan's intended readers scratching their heads. More damaging was the review that came out just days after publication.

For its effort, the *New York Times* enlisted its most prestigious and popular book reviewer, John Chamberlain, who got a full page for his assessment. Chamberlain rejected economic quibbling and went directly to the issue that would most inflame Nathan's critics throughout the postwar years, and one that he would never be able to adequately explain away: that the planner in him could not help but reduce producers, consumers, spenders, and savers into so many economic entities that were expected to act with great consistency and predictability—and largely as the planners decided. "The trouble with Mr. Nathan's prescription for running an economic system is that it requires constant doses of force," Chamberlain wrote. He may be a great technical economist, the reviewer concluded, "but like so many of his breed he is at least partially oblivious to the moral, the psychological and the political aspects of what he is saying."[39]

Nathan's response was to escalate the rhetoric. On an August 1944 radio program he warned that "if we have fifteen or twenty million people out of work, steadily, after this war, it may very well mean the end."[40] To some extent, Nathan seemed surprised that as the war wound down the national passion for planning seemed to evaporate. "It is time that this country stopped being afraid of the word 'planning,'" he said.[41] The problem was not planning, he maintained, but rather that "Conservative, do-nothing elements offer the most serious threat to political democracy in the United States and the World."[42]

Despite the reviews, *Mobilizing for Abundance* gained a readership—it was referred to in some circles as the "New Deal Bible" and it helped raise Nathan's profile. A British reviewer later compared it with a similar all-encompassing plan, the White Paper by English economist William Beveridge which became the blueprint for the full-employment Social Democracy created by the postwar British Labor government.[43] The difference, as Nathan was soon to understand, was that Americans were less inclined than the British, who had suffered far more wartime devastation, to trade economic freedom for social security.

Economist to Activist

It was, in fact, the need for the British Empire to narrow its horizons that posed a question that occupied most of Nathan's time in 1944 and much of his attention throughout the decade: what was the fate of Palestine? The Robert Nathan who came to Washington was not an observant Jew and no Zionist. Robert and Larry had been raised in an orthodox family and had gone through Bar Mitzvah. Robert had also led a Jewish social group at Wharton, but his interest was clearly more social than religious. Larry had committed the sin, unpardonable in the eyes of his mother and sister, of marrying a blonde-haired, blue-eyed gentile.[44] Robert claimed to have known nothing of Zionism before the war, ostensibly because there were no advocates of a Jewish homeland in

Dayton.[45] But Nathan could never turn down a worthy cause that offered a chance for some friendly conspiracy, and by 1942 Palestine was one of them.

Israel Sieff was a merchant, the wealthy director of the British Marks & Spencer retail chain, who had relocated to Washington for the war. He was also a firm believer in a homeland for European Jews and good friend of Chaim Weizmann, by then the undisputed leader of the Zionist movement. The Zionists had been hoping for a Jewish state in Palestine for nearly 50 years and Sieff decided that one way to further the cause was to enlist influential Washingtonians into a group that could make things happen behind the scenes. In October 1942 he began gathering them in meetings at his home. Some of the Goons were there, Ben Cohen and David Ginsburg along with Nathan. Another attendee was White House administrative assistant David Niles. During the war, this group helped Sieff in his goal of quietly "tending and watering the ground" around Washington.[46]

In late 1943 Sieff arranged a meeting between Nathan and Weizmann at the latter's request. The Zionist leader asked the newly discharged soldier what he intended to do next. "I said I didn't know," Nathan recalled. "I had to get my back straightened out, but where I was going I wasn't sure." Weizmann asked Nathan if he knew anything about Palestine. "Not much," he replied. Weizmann put the case for Zionism before Nathan. He believed that the British, in their 1917 Balfour Declaration, had promised the Jewish people a state of their own in Palestine.[47] In 1920, the British received a mandate from the League of Nations to administer Palestine, but Zionists suspected that Britain would relinquish it as part of postwar retrenchment. Weizmann told Nathan that he wanted to understand the potential of Palestine, asking "can it really be a Jewish homeland or are we plain *mashuga*?"[48] Could it provide not only shelter for a few true believers, he asked, but economic opportunity for millions? He asked Nathan to find out.[49]

Although Weizmann's hopes were clear, he knew that the study's integrity had to be unquestionable. Early in 1944 he pulled a network of private contributors together, Nathan's friend Isador Lubin among them.[50] Dubbed the American Palestine Institute, Incorporated, and administered by Sieff associate M.H. Blinken, it raised about $100,000 for the study and made much of the fact that a sizeable proportion—one tenth—was contributed by Lessing Rosenwald. Rosenwald was a Sears executive and president of the American Council for Judaism, which was against the creation of a secular state in Palestine.[51] Doing contract work was new to Nathan—he had no idea what to charge, but settled on $75,000.[52] Given his earlier involvement in the Sieff group, it is likely that Nathan was by now a committed Zionist, but he could truthfully say—and did—that "I wasn't hired as a Zionist or an anti-Zionist. I was hired as an economist." He got a free hand to conduct the study as he saw fit.[53]

The next thing Nathan did was find some help. He quickly engaged the brilliant but difficult, pugnacious and pudgy Oscar Gass, an economist from the Treasury Department and the WPB. Nathan was still in California when Gass began collecting all the books, reports, and articles on Palestine that he could find.[54] He then recruited Louis Bean, who had worked at the Department of Agriculture and the Bureau of the Budget.[55] Nathan rented an office and by mid-February had an outline for an "objective study of the economic potentialities of Palestine," circulated under letterhead of "Robert R. Nathan, Consulting Economist, 1731 K Street NW, Oscar Gass, Director of Research." Nathan's goal was to write a book of less than 250 pages.[56]

The American Palestine Institute had its own goal: "absolutely no publicity."[57] Weizmann and Sieff hoped that the study would become well-known, but not until the time was right. Word began to leak out, however, especially in mid-1944 when the British denied visas to the three economists on the grounds that their work was not war-related, but likely out of concern over "Arab disturbances."[58] The British did, however, provide documents and studies, and even prepared special reports.[59] Sometime after that, Bean dropped out and in his place Nathan recruited Daniel Creamer, an economist formerly with NBER.[60] By November Gass had written some of the book's early chapters.[61] In December, after intervention by Harry Hopkins, the team finally got its visas.[62]

While Gass and Creamer went ahead, Nathan stopped in London to visit the foreign office. For the worldly war mobilizer, this first trip abroad was a revelation. He was properly spooked when he heard his first V-2, knowing, as was legend, that you only heard the supersonic missile if you had survived. Nathan was far more affected than he expected to be by the devastation of the Blitz. "We at home haven't felt it at all," he wrote in his journal, the first that Nathan would keep while on nearly all of his travels abroad. He also visited Parliament and spoke with Clement Atlee, who would soon become the architect of the British welfare state.[63]

Nathan was in Paris during the Battle of the Bulge and in the Middle East by Christmas, where he consulted with the head of the British Colonial office in Egypt.[64] Two days before the New Year, he made the brief flight from Cairo, peering out the window at the Suez and then the forbidding Negev Desert. He was heartened to see irrigated land and orange groves.[65] But on the ground, he recalled, "as the road ascended from the airport to Jerusalem my spirits descended. Barren hills and fields of stone led to the question 'how could anyone pick such a place for settlement and development?'"[66]

The land may have seemed unpromising, but its inhabitants full of potential, and people were usually what mattered most to Nathan. As he established himself in Jerusalem and then began moving across the countryside—sometimes with Gass or Creamer, sometimes with Palestinian attendants—Nathan met scores of journalists, industrialists, scientists, and politicians. Chaim Weizmann ensured that Nathan met everyone who could help by throwing a big party for him. The next day Nathan had a more formal luncheon with British High Commissioner Lord Gort.[67]

Nathan did more socializing than Gass and Creamer and his share of the research was smaller: he focused mostly on water, power, and housing. But when it came to shaping the agenda and the analysis, Nathan's contribution was invaluable. As one colleague who worked closely with him in the mid-1940s put it, even if he knew nothing about a subject he "would start questioning and drilling. He always asked the right and the tough questions."[68] Gass, for one, was always ready with a bold response. The results, Nathan recalled, were invaluable weekends at Sieff's house in Tel Mond spent "arguing and talking, questioning and reading."[69]

As he soaked up information about Palestine, Nathan learned something else that made his work far more influential than it might have been. Almost no one in wartime Washington was aware of the extent of the Holocaust—Nathan claimed never to have discussed it with his friends.[70] He began to understand the horrific scope of the tragedy while in Palestine. It hit home when someone told him that some 100,000 Jews had been killed in Galicia, the land of his ancestors. "It's so damned barbaric it is hard to believe," he wrote, "but it is too well established for any doubt." By late January, 1945 he thought that perhaps 3 million had perished across Europe.[71]

By the time Nathan left Palestine the economist's free hand had been tempered by the activist's passion, which was never far from the surface. In mid-February he attended a planning committee meeting of The Jewish Agency for Palestine, an ostensibly non-political group led by David Ben-Gurion, which was a hair's breadth from outright Zionism and would soon be acting as the Jewish Palestinian government in exile. He spent countless hours talking economics with Eliezer Kaplan, the treasurer of the Jewish Agency. Nathan was back in Washington by March 20, 1945, arriving shortly after Creamer and Gass.[72]

"Robert Nathan, Consulting Economist" worked on the Palestine study through 1945. Nathan produced four of its 28 chapters—on water, power, and housing—working mostly evenings and weekends, while Creamer drafted seven. Oscar Gass wrote the rest.[73] As the book neared completion it became clear that its findings might have the power to change the face of the Middle East and global politics as well.

Behind Chaim Weizmann's pitch to Nathan was a contentious and highly political history. Whatever the intentions of the Balfour Declaration, after the British Mandate over Palestine was established, it became clear that creating a Jewish state in the Middle

East would generate violent and sustained backlash not only from Palestinian Arabs, but also among Arabs elsewhere living under British protectorate. Jews fleeing Hitler arrived in large numbers in the mid-1930s, spurring an Arab revolt not settled until 1939. At that time a British White Paper renounced the idea of a Jewish state, and expostulated at length about the low "economic absorptive capacity" of Palestine. The protectorate imposed sharp immigration restrictions. Weizmann's question to Nathan in late 1943 was, in effect, a request for a rebuttal to the White Paper.

By 1946, the British protectorate was being lifted in a delicate dance that involved the British, the Americans, and eventually the United Nations. The first steps were hearings by an Anglo-American Committee in Washington. When they opened in January 1946, Nathan, flanked by Gass and M. H. Blinken, was the first to testify on the Palestine economy.[74] Nathan made what one journalist described as a "blistering attack" on British immigration policy and testified that Palestine could absorb 100,000 people "almost immediately." His study, Nathan insisted, demonstrated that the presence of Jewish settlement actually raised the quality of life for nearby Arabs. One commissioner inquired whether Arabs might resist Jewish incursions—Gass replied that the more land Jews opened up, the better it would be for Arabs.[75]

Nathan well knew that Arab sentiment could pose a steep challenge to Jewish settlement. Although he met few Arabs in Palestine, he talked with enough of them to learn that settlement and statehood trumped every other issue. "They just didn't want any more Jews in Palestine," he confided to his diary.[76] Whatever the extent to which the impartial economists had become impassioned advocates, their study, published in April 1946 as *Palestine: Problem and Promise*, was widely praised for its scope and scholarly integrity.[77] Nathan's hoped-for 250 pages had expanded to 675. In two parts, one historical and analytical, one prescriptive, it covered the past and potential future of Palestine's water and power, agriculture and manufacturing, housing and construction, finance and commerce. It acknowledged that Arabs were "willing to forego economic benefits" to exclude Jews and attain an Arab state. But given a political settlement, it stated, Palestine should be able to absorb from 615,000 to 1,125,000 "immigrants" during the next decade.[78] Weizmann had a rebuttal to the White Paper; Nathan had a cause.

RECONVERSION

When he left the Army, Nathan wrote Roosevelt that he was "determined to work outside the government, not for financial reasons, but rather to carry your principles and philosophy ahead." It seemed easier to be a New Dealer outside, rather than inside, Roosevelt's increasingly conservative administration. Nevertheless, newspapers were soon speculating that Nathan was "slated to be offered a key job in government."[79] There was no shortage of options—in the few months that he was in Palestine, Nathan was offered positions with the Surplus Property Administration and with the State Department.[80]

Nathan turned everything down—he had had enough of government and wanted to write the book on Palestine. But then Ed Prichard got involved. His own military career had been similar to Nathan's, but even shorter; due to his weight he did not even make it through the first day of training camp. A month later Prichard returned to Washington and the Office of Economic Stabilization under Fred Vinson, a man with years of legislative and judicial experience who had emerged as one of the most courageous and effective administrators in wartime Washington.[81]

By April, both Prichard and Vinson were with another agency, the Office of War Mobilization and Reconversion. The OWMR grew out of the Office of War Mobilization, the super-agency that Roosevelt had created for James Byrnes to compensate for the faltering War Production Board. On April 4, 1945, as the end of the war approached, Roosevelt appointed Vinson to take over the agency that now had a longer name.[82] Vinson needed help, and Prichard recommended Nathan.[83]

Prichard prepped Vinson well for the meeting: he was familiar with Nathan's WPB work and said "we need the same kind of thinking on demobilization."[84] Nathan resisted, but the opportunity to once again do large-scale economic planning was hard to turn down. Vinson's reputation also made a difference. Isador Lubin had earlier confided to Nathan that Vinson was sharp and "evidently very loyal to the Boss."[85] Nathan accepted and expected to report on April 16.[86]

On Thursday, April 12, "the Boss," Franklin Roosevelt, died in Warm Springs, Georgia. Nathan asked to be let out of the agreement, but Vinson countered that given Harry Truman's inexperience "we're ten times more important now."[87] These were tumultuous days for the country. Even though it had been eight years since the last major New Deal reforms, and Roosevelt had been compelled to move steadily to the right ever since, as long as Roosevelt lived, what one historian has called the "myth and symbol" of the New Deal remained.[88] Most Americans felt a sense of loss. Liberals were devastated.

Nathan might have gone to the White House memorial service on the April 14, but for him it was an even more tumultuous time—that was the day that his mother died. When Nathan's father got sick in 1935, Anna Nathan and daughter Rose had moved to Washington. Nathan and his mother do not appear to have been close. Mary Tillotson, whom Nathan began courting at the OSS, may have been one thing that kept them apart at the end. Robert knew that his mother had been crushed when brother Larry married Dee—a gentile. Although he had been dating Mary for two years, he never did introduce her to his mother.[89] As the nation mourned Roosevelt, Robert and Lew arranged a funeral service for Anna Nathan in Philadelphia. She was buried on Sunday, April 15.[90]

The next day Nathan reported for work as Deputy Director for Reconversion at the OWMR.[91] Once again he was at the fulcrum of the American economy during a turbulent time. Once again there was a byzantine back story. By the summer of 1944 it was clear that it was only a matter of time before the war ended, and the big question was when to begin reconversion to a civilian economy. Nathan made his preference clear in newspapers and radio appearances. Things were perilous, he argued. If the nation waited too long to reconvert, former war workers and returning servicemen would be unemployed while manufacturers retooled. If the corporations took too long, unemployment dragged on, and savings ran out, there would be no purchasing power once conversion was accomplished. "We must make sure that this does not jump from transitional unemployment to the big, chronic unemployment of the depression years," he told a radio audience in August 1944.[92] Nathan therefore called for immediate reconversion to ensure that postwar unemployment was as low as possible.[93]

The military had another view—its leaders insisted that it would be gambling with victory and destructive to morale for the civilian economy to be restarted when soldiers were still fighting. Large businesses agreed for completely different reasons. During World War II the military found it far more efficient to deal with big producers than small ones. By 1944 the first linkages in what would someday be called the "military-industrial complex" were formed. Big business had done well, saved money, and reasoned that when reconversion came it would be better able to carve out big pieces of the civilian pie than small firms would.

As in 1942, big business and the military had formed an unbeatable pair against the lifting of production controls. The WPB was now led by Julius Krug, who bowed to the dominant pair rather than fight them as Nelson had done. The frightening reverse at the Battle of the Bulge silenced advocates of early reconversion for a time, but when Nathan started work at the OWMR everyone knew it was coming. Big business generally wanted controls to be either off or on. Public sentiment was for some reconversion.[94] The trick was determining what production controls to lift and when.

To do that, Nathan assembled a team of like-minded liberal planners, and Vinson gave them room to run. Moreover, Vinson applied pressure on Krug when necessary to ensure that his planners were heeded.[95] Nathan ostensibly had an equal, the Deputy Director for War Programs, but the push toward victory made that job obsolete and Nathan became Vinson's right-hand man, just as he had been Nelson's. It was a period, as the historian of the OWMR put it, "during which staff freedom resulted in extraordinary independent initiative," including the creation of interagency working committees.[96] Nathan relished the meetings when officials from agencies across the city—many close friends—came to his offices in the Lafayette Building overlooking the White House to compare and coordinate plans.[97]

The reach of the OWMR was wide, extending beyond production controls to wages and prices. Not surprisingly, Nathan believed that the government's wage-price policy should be geared to maximum output and maximum purchasing power. Like most observers he was worried that as war jobs evaporated and mandatory overtime was cut back—the standard work week during the war was 48 hours—incomes would shrink drastically and people would spend as little as possible and save the rest. "I believe that a general wage increase can be granted as overtime is eliminated, without a substantial increase in prices," Nathan advised Vinson. "The best insurance against deflation is not accumulated savings but the maintenance of the flow of current buying power."[98]

Organized labor was understandably happy with Vinson's OWMR.[99] Nathan was happy as well. Although the politics of 1945 would never allow Nathan to carry out his plans entirely, Vinson, whom Nathan described as "moderately liberal," let him develop them as far as possible. As Nathan remembered it, he and his boss would "argue and argue" before Vinson's keen sense of the politically possible helped him draw the line. Nathan undoubtedly liked the arguments more than the decisions.[100] He was likely equally pleased when at least a few in Washington started calling him "Mr. Reconversion."[101] Then things changed abruptly. On July 22, Vinson became Treasury Secretary, continuing the rapid rise in the government that eventually took him to the Chief Justice of the Supreme Court. Prichard went with him.

New Dealers were bound to be let down by Truman, but one of the things that disappointed them most was the quality of his appointments. Excepting James Byrnes and Fred Vinson, too many appointees were old Truman friends with little administrative talent or imagination. John Snyder, who took over the OWMR on July 23, seemed to exemplify this stereotype. He was one of Truman's old army buddies and his closest friend in the government. Even though Snyder brought along his own assistant from the wartime Defense Plant Corporation which he had directed, he asked Nathan to remain as Deputy Director of Reconversion. Nathan agreed.[102]

This was a gamble for both men. Snyder must have felt that he could keep the economist confined to his spreadsheets. Nathan must have felt that he could bulldoze a mediocre boss. Both proved more formidable than expected, and the personal relationship started off badly. Snyder had no interest in arguing, and when the arguments stopped real discussion did as well. Nathan attributed this to the fact that Snyder had no "depth of conception," and said that changing bosses "was like going from college to elementary school."[103] Snyder was an accomplished St. Louis banker, but like most American financers, nothing in his experience had compelled him to take Keynesianism macroeconomics seriously.

Nevertheless, Nathan kept pushing his own agenda. He created a transition planning committee led by economist Everett Hagen to promote "longer run objectives of full production and full employment."[104] His boldest move was to push through a report on reconversion aimed at the general public. *From War to Peace: A Challenge,* was a 19-page booklet penned by Nathan and published by the government on August 15. It was written in a popular, almost elementary, style much like *Mobilizing for Abundance.* The themes were familiar as well. "Our total victory over our enemies was the inevitable and just product of our total mobilization for war," it began. "The same energies, the same skills, the same cooperation that won the war must now be directed toward the winning of a total and stable prosperity in peace." In order to steel the citizenry for the task ahead, the report guaranteed "immediate and large dislocation to our economy." Statistics generated by Hagen's working group suggested—so *From War to Peace* predicted—that unemployment could reach "8 million before next spring."[105]

The only notable thing about *From War to Peace* was that last prediction, and it spurred either deep concern or rank derision. The OWMR immediately came under fire for what many considered its alarmist report. Snyder, whose name was on the document, was furious. He later claimed that he had not had time to review the report but signed off anyway—and that Vinson had refused to do so.[106] Snyder was not gaining much praise for his handling of reconversion anyway, and like Donald Nelson he resisted asserting authority over other agencies. *From War to Peace* only made things worse for Snyder, and he sidelined Nathan. There would be no more staff studies.[107]

From his perch in the Lafayette Building, Nathan kept his working committees busy and continued thinking about purchasing power. One issue was paramount in his thinking. The best way to put money in the pockets of people who would spend it was for employers to raise wages. But if they passed on those raises to consumers as price hikes, as corporations were apt to do, the benefit would be lost. During his OWMR time, therefore, Nathan became certain that the best way to maintain purchasing power and avert an economic collapse would be to convince or compel employers to raise wages without raising prices.

Although Nathan disavowed it later, a second factor cannot have helped but influence his thinking.[108] In 1945, S.380, the last hope of New Deal liberals, was passing perilously through Congress. The Full Employment Bill was authored by Leon Keyserling, an economics-minded lawyer and assistant to Senator Robert F. Wagner who had helped frame landmark New Deal legislation including the National Industrial Recovery Act, the Social Security Act, and the National Labor Relations Act. Liberals considered this newest piece of legislation the fulfillment of the first point in the Economic Bill of Rights laid down by Roosevelt in his 1944 State of the Union Address. It was overtly Keynesian— pledging the government to calculate the GNP necessary to create full employment and to make up any shortage with federal spending.[109] Indeed, a passage in one of Nathan's many memoranda on wages and prices explicitly concluded, "should adoption of S.380 at once, to create a permanent mechanism to investigate the question of insufficiency of demand, be urged even more vigorously?"[110]

It is likely that Nathan could not resist entering the full employment bill debate; it is certain that he was passionate about the wage-price debate. The result was even more damaging to the OWMR than *From War to Peace*. In late October, Nathan produced a 26-page report on a suggested wage-price policy. It was a "backgrounder" for internal use only but was highly influential and, as before, there was one point that people remembered. Truman's speechwriters relied heavily on this Nathan report in penning the president's October 30 radio address on wages and prices.[111] In it Truman ventured that "industry as a whole can afford substantial wage increases without raising prices."[112] That passage infuriated business leaders nationwide. Even liberals such as *New Republic* colum- nist Richard Strout were irritated, certain that it would embolden labor to make new wage demands in a time of economic turmoil. Strout wrote that the "practical result of it almost automatically will be a protracted period of argument, negotiation and striking."[113]

Truman immediately backtracked, but there was more damage to be done. The full report, which suggested that a 24-percent increase in wages without an accompanying increase in prices was possible, was leaked almost immediately and everyone, including Snyder, was pretty sure that Nathan had done it.[114] Nathan even received a letter from a labor leader, upset because his international union was one of the few with no copy.[115] By then Nathan and Snyder were feuding in the press, where Nathan was prevailing thanks to Drew Pearson. They were not even speaking at the office.[116] By November, journalists, citing the leaked wage-price report, were calling Snyder "one of the most harassed officials in Washington" and predicting Nathan's imminent departure.[117]

Nathan later argued that OWMR was by then ineffective. But he had played a big part in crippling it, and his resignation, submitted early in December and effective at the end of the year, was necessary.[118] Nevertheless, after Truman learned of the resignation he called Nathan to the White House and tried to change his mind.[119] Nathan seemed to consider his resignation license to once again go on the record. On December 17, he predicted to the *Wall Street Journal* that "if nothing is done to stabilize the economy at high levels and to get full employment in another two or three years, then we're going to have a depression that will shake the free enterprise system to its very foundation."[120] Two weeks later, Snyder was publicly gracious in his acceptance of the resignation, but he never forgave Nathan for what he believed to be rank insubordination. Somehow, Nathan and Truman remained on good terms.[121] Nevertheless, Nathan joined the long line of New Dealers who liked Truman but could never adjust to working for anyone besides Franklin Roosevelt.

CITIZEN FIRST

Even as he left government service for the second time, Nathan remained intent on fulfilling his promise to "work only in the interest of the people." Oddly enough, it was his undistinguished military career that gave Nathan his next opportunity. The American Veterans Committee (AVC) was no "beer and bingo" veterans group. It grew out of correspondence between two unusual veterans, Gilbert Harrison, who had edited the school paper at UCLA, and Charles Bolté, who had edited the paper at Dartmouth. Both had served overseas—Bolté had joined the British Army even before Pearl Harbor and had lost a leg in North Africa—and both knew how to reach people. Bolté got out of the service first and from his Greenwich Village apartment began assembling a liberal veterans group, one that could leverage the soldiers' sacrifice to build a better America.[122] The group's motto was "Citizens First, Soldiers Second."

Chapters began forming in 1944. By 1945, the AVC had come out publicly in favor of a variety of liberal measures including a housing bill for veterans, a Fair Employment Practices Commission, and the Full Employment Bill.[123] Nathan could hardly resist this new opportunity to win the peace. He joined in 1945 and in late March 1946 became chairman of the newly formed Washington, D.C. chapter.[124] Nathan had every intention of helping to make the AVC a "permanent progressive force" and as a first step he decided to involve his group in the ongoing battles over reconversion.[125]

By mid-1946 production controls had been lifted. But price controls, which affected every American far more directly, had not. Americans were flush from high wartime wages and impatient for consumer goods—so impatient in fact that without controls they would bid up the price of nearly everything. That could create a price bubble that would pop with dangerously recessionary results. Administered by the Office of Price Administration (OPA), price controls closely affected consumers, although they generally understood the need for slow relaxation over many months. Businesses, however, wanted controls removed immediately and were making headway with the increasingly conservative Congress.

Therefore, Nathan's first big initiative as chairman of the Washington AVC was to launch a "Save OPA" campaign.[126] If Congress does not extend OPA, he warned the month he took office, "it will be writing its own ticket to depression."[127] In May, the Washington AVC held a rally downtown at which Nathan spoke.[128] The campaign helped fuel phenomenal growth, with the Washington AVC going from 800 members in March to 2,000 in June. It can only have helped that the chapter chairman was fast becoming a liberal spokesman with a national profile. By mid-June, the Republicans in Congress, led by Senator Robert Taft, had prepared a bill ostensibly to extend the OPA, but actually intended to destroy it. Nathan was becoming expert at the radio forum format popular in the late 1940s, and got the better of Taft on the nationally broadcast "American Forum of the Air." Although his prepared prefatory remarks were wooden, he was unbeatable in debate, hurling in his heavy but remarkably agile baritone, facts, statistics, and well-honed rebuttals like so many missiles.[129] "Either we have no OPA or we have an effective OPA," he concluded.[130]

Truman was in a tough spot. If he signed the Republican bill he could be blamed when OPA failed. If he vetoed it he would have killed OPA himself. Nearly all of Truman's advisors told him to sign. Nathan wrote that "there is no point in beating a fast retreat under a hopeless law," and advised Truman to veto the bill and hold a "fireside chat" denouncing the Republicans. Truman agreed, vetoed the bill, and went on the radio to explain that it was the "only honest solution."[131] With controls off, food prices shot up. The Washington AVC responded by forming "price patrols." Most of the grocery store policing was done by AVC wives, but it was not beyond Nathan to get worked up by a 20-cent increase in the cost of strawberry preserves.[132]

In mid-June, the Washington delegation departed for the first convention of the AVC in Des Moines, Iowa. The presence of such notables as Nathan and Franklin Roosevelt, Jr., helped draw photographers to the tarmac, but the organization's phenomenal growth and idealistic charter convinced at least one reporter that the AVC "is worthy of attention far out of proportion to the organization's relatively small membership."[133]

Reporters elsewhere agreed and the AVC Convention drew a great deal of press interest. Observers were surprised, and local tavern-keepers dismayed, when the 2,000 delegates stayed sober and stuck to business.[134] Nathan, who now chaired the AVC's largest chapter, figured heavily in the proceedings as a decisive and sharp parliamentarian who knew how to keep meetings on track. Many of these meetings involved the consideration and adoption of the national platform Nathan and his companions wrote in Washington before the convention.[135] Nathan even ran for the AVC's number two post, although he withdrew at the last minute.[136]

Bleary-eyed but resolute at the AVC Convention in Des Moines, Iowa, June 1946.
(Mark Kauffman/Life Magazine/Getty Images)

Nathan was elected, however, to the governing body that mattered most: the AVC National Planning Council (NPC). "The NPC was an impressive group," remembered author Merle Miller. "At least we impressed each other, and we were forever being interviewed and photographed." Joining Nathan, Miller, Bolté, and Harrison were other equally distinguished members, including Michael Straight, a J.P. Morgan heir who ran the *New Republic*, Chat Paterson, who had served in the State Department, and Cord Meyer, an aide to the founding conference of the UN.[137] The group might have been even more august but John F. Kennedy turned them down and Ronald Reagan was rejected as being too radical. Even with its existing members, the NPC inevitably had long and hard meetings, which Miller said, "always lasted into the early morning."[138] By late 1946 the NPC had a great deal to argue about, particularly what should be done about the communists taking over the AVC.

In the 1940s communist infiltration was a serious, sometimes fatal, problem for liberal organizations. As the war began almost every liberal group in America had its share of far left idealists, convinced during the Great Depression that Soviet communism was better than democratic capitalism. Most of them had always been underground, and as the wartime "Popular Front" dissolved they began working in surreptitious earnest to convert liberal groups to communist outposts. A number of international labor unions and many more locals had come under communist domination by the end of the war. Then the Party began thinking about veterans. The communists had first considered taking on the American Legion, but by early 1946 they had switched to the more fertile field of the AVC, making sizeable gains in New York City. The AVC's founders were delighted with the growth—until they realized why it was happening.[139]

Communists were already well represented at Des Moines, which made approval of a constitutional provision that pledged AVC members to uphold "full production and full employment in our country under a system of private enterprise" difficult.[140] Good liberals were not at first eager to get too exercised about communism in general, considering its influence minimal and its support welcome. Besides, they reasoned, squabbling on the left only empowered the right. But communist chapters grew and even managed to get members on the NPC, so by late 1946, recalled Miller, "every meeting was a battleground."[141]

It usually took personal experience with communists to convert a New Deal liberal into an anti-communist liberal: the AVC was Nathan's experience. Party members had already attempted to take over the Washington, D.C., chapter, but assisted by Gus Tyler, an International Ladies Garment Workers Union staffer with experience fighting communists in the labor movement, Nathan kept them out.[142] By late 1946, the national leadership seemed ready to fight also. The NPC considered an explicitly anti-communist position with party members in the room at a November meeting. Nathan was unable to attend but sent a statement read into the record maintaining that "the tendency of reactionary and fascist forces to destroy and defeat constructive American liberalism by sweeping with a wide brush and smearing all liberals with the label of 'communism' represents a great danger to be fought relentlessly."[143]

By June, things had gotten much worse. Some staunch anti-communists had already abandoned the organization, leaving only 1,500 delegates at the Milwaukee convention. Those remaining had their choice of three slates: left, right, and center. Behind the day-to-day of the convention was a shadow convention as communists fought anti-communists for control of the AVC. Bolté and Harrison both stepped down. Chat Paterson, a Washington member and good friend of Nathan's, ran for the top spot on the right wing slate. The communists fielded their own slate, and Michael Straight assembled a compromise slate. Both the right and center slates included the most popular candidates, like Nathan and Franklin Roosevelt, Jr. In the end, the anti-communists won handily, with only Michael Straight, who was on all three slates, receiving more votes than Nathan.[144]

Some pronounced it a victory, but the AVC was rapidly becoming a remnant. "After the triumph in Milwaukee," recalled Miller, "almost everybody's interest in AVC seemed to dwindle, as if meetings weren't as much fun once the communists had been defeated."[145] There was an equally powerful force at work—the idealistic young veterans with lots of free time on their hands were starting families. Even Robert Nathan.

In late 1945 Nathan had moved into number 415 at the Carlyn apartments at 2500 Q Street.[146] Apparently Ted Seamon also stayed there briefly, but by the summer of 1946 he had moved out and Nathan and Mary Tillotson were spending more and more time together.[147] When the OSS became the CIA, Mary transferred to the State Department. Her first trip abroad for State in 1947 convinced Nathan that they ought to get married.[148] Nathan's schedule was not the kind to allow a big weekend event. Instead the couple was married on a Wednesday, July 16, 1947.[149] Although the groom was not an observing Jew, the Nathans were married by a rabbi at an Alexandria temple.[150] Nathan might marry, but he could never settle—or even slow—down. There was a reception dinner at the Washington Statler that evening. The next morning the couple boarded a plane for Chicago to attend a meeting of the AVC Planning Committee.[151]

The AVC was ahead of things. It was 1948 when communism did its greatest damage to New Deal liberalism with the complicity of Henry Wallace, the top-tier liberal who had once marveled at Nathan's potential for shucking corn. The nation's rocky postwar reconversion—especially the administration's tough stand on labor unrest—had done much to thin out Harry Truman's New Deal support. The 1947 promulgation of the Truman Doctrine, which averred an American "obligation" to support those fighting Soviet expansion, and marked a clear beginning to the Cold War, alienated smaller sources of support from far-left apologists for the Soviet Union. One of these was Henry Wallace, the former secretary of agriculture, vice president, and secretary of commerce under Truman. Dismissed by the president for publicly differing with U.S. foreign policy, but still considered golden by most New Dealers, Wallace was in fine position to run as the presidential candidate of the left. His campaign began in early 1948 under the banner of the Independent Progressive Party, whose most energetic and enterprising advocates were members of the Communist Party.

Mary Tillotson and Robert Nathan, wedding day, July 16, 1947.

Nathan was no happier with the situation than other New Dealers. In March 1948 he allowed that Wallace was definitely the best liberal candidate on domestic issues, but the next month he wrote a tough critique of Truman's record for the *New Republic*, which concluded that liberals would have to support him nonetheless.[152] He was certain that the communists within the Progressive Party would "double cross" Wallace eventually.[153]

In this politically turgid climate, the AVC had expressly forbidden its members from endorsing candidates on its behalf. But in April, one New York City member was charged with speaking for a local party allied with the Progressives. The AVC's deliberative body, the National Administrative Committee (NAC), was designed to deal with just such situations and Nathan was on it.[154] The group investigated and returned what amounted to a guilty verdict. In July, two newspapermen informed the NAC of a problem hiding in plain sight; John Gates, editor of the Soviet Communist organ *The Daily Worker*, was an AVC member from New York. He had already been indicted as a party member by the Department of Justice under the Smith Act.[155]

On a hot and sticky day in August, the NAC met in New York to look into the matter. Outside the narrow and shabby Hotel Whitehall at Broadway and 100th, a crowd of about 150 had gathered, most of them communist sympathizers. Inside with Nathan was Joe Clorety, a Department of Labor economist. Publisher Michael Straight and history professor Bernard Bellush also sat on the committee. It did not take an advanced degree to determine the outcome—the group recommended that the NPC expel Gates.[156] There was "no reasonable doubt," Nathan said later.[157]

In September the NPC met. Nathan declared that the group had "a clear obligation, in light of legislative history, to proceed to oust communists if AVC is to grow and strengthen along liberal lines." Nathan also noted that it was abundantly clear that, counter to what liberals had believed a few years earlier, there was no working with communists; they would destroy what they took over. That left the NPC "no choice but to oust Mr. Gates here and now," he concluded. Everyone agreed except Morris Pottish, a sympathizer if not a party member, and Bellush, who believed it was a matter for the convention.[158]

The once-promising AVC was in decline. When the New York members ignored the edict, Pottish himself was expelled and 40 AVC chapters were suspended. Early in November the Progressive Party demonstrated its irrelevance by garnering 2.4 percent of the vote. Late in the month the AVC met in Cleveland and expelled 13 more chapters. The NPC chose not to publicize the delegate count, which was dismal.[159] Nathan had a tough time giving up the idea that the AVC could be a "permanent progressive force." In late 1948 he was behind the creation of a Women's Auxiliary—Mary was among the charter members.[160] In January 1949, a son was born, John Louis Nathan. Three months later the proud father put a photograph of "Johnny" in the AVC Bulletin, claiming that his "purchase" of a ten dollar share made him the youngest investor in the AVC.[161] Through the early 1950s, Nathan remained on the planning committee and continued to line up speakers for Washington chapter luncheons from a long list of friends.[162]

INCORPORATION

The AVC might remain an inspiring, if time-consuming, avocation, but as 1946 began, Nathan needed a job. Naturally he turned to his friends. He had more of them than ever, including political friends—the kind that mattered in Washington. In 1944 Nathan and Leon Henderson formed the "Independent Committee for Franklin Roosevelt."[163] Having raised a respectable amount of cash for that fall's presidential race and established partisan credentials, Nathan seemed a good candidate when Truman political fixer Bob Hannegan put together an "informal brain trust" for the Democratic National Committee. Because its members included Nathan, Henderson, and Prichard, among others, one journalist dubbed it the "legislative goon squad."[164] At about the same time, word in Washington was that Nathan and Prichard would take formal positions on the DNC.[165] Nothing came of either—Truman was certainly not looking for a "brain trust."[166] More surprisingly, even though the Employment Act of 1946—which conservatives had shorn of any commitment to "full" employment—had created a group of high-level economic planners, Nathan, who was the liberal's pick, appears to have turned down the opportunity to be on the DNC.[167] After a second very difficult exit, Nathan was determined to get into private business and out of government for a long time.

It was not an entirely original idea. Leon Henderson had left the OPA in early 1943 to head the Research Institute of America, a business information service, and a year earlier had done contract work for the Foreign Economic Administration.[168] Isador Lubin signed on as president and chairman of Confidential Reports, Inc., a theater auditing group owned by the major movie studios, in January 1946.[169] By then, however, Nathan and Lauchlin Currie had already decided to go into business together.[170] It is significant that both Henderson and Lubin joined existing firms. In most cases, something about an economist does not an entrepreneur make.

Nathan's good friend, Universal Pictures executive Matthew "Matty" Fox, however, was very much the entrepreneur. Fox worked his way up in the industry from theater manager to vice president at the studio. Having saved Universal from bankruptcy in the late 1930s, he had a reputation as a business wizard.[171] Fox had been a curiosity on the WPB, but Nathan respected his commitment to the cause, and used him to great effect as a "dynamic pusher for an all-out effort."[172] A Planning Committee staffer called him "one of the best hatchet men I've ever known in operations."[173]

As an outsider and entrepreneur, Fox could appreciate better than the economists what might be possible in the free market. "He was fascinated by the capacity of the guys he met," remembered Nathan, "and wanted to put them together."[174] His idea was that a network of highly credentialed and connected former government men might be in a position to reap sizeable postwar profits advising investors and exporters, both in the United States and abroad, and perhaps even undertake overseas economic development projects. He promoted his plans during the war but held them for the duration. In November 1945, with the war over, Fox incorporated World Wide Development, and established offices in lower Manhattan. Somehow, Fox had lined up as president a man with the kind of reputation needed to sweet-talk foreign governments, former Eisenhower Chief of Staff Major General Royal B. Lord.

Fox's idea was still more complicated, however. World Wide might be in the headlines, but much of the day-to-day work would be done by subsidiary operations run by eminent economists Lauchlin Currie and Robert Nathan. Currie established his firm in early 1946. Robert R. Nathan Associates was incorporated in Delaware two days later, on January 14, 1946.[175] Both founders assigned all of their stock to World Wide, and in return they got equity and the funds required to get their own enterprises up and running. The first meeting of the board of directors of Nathan Associates was held January 15, 1946, at Lauchlin Currie's offices, 19 Rector Street, in New York City. Nathan was elected president, Currie, vice president. The secretary-treasurer was World Wide executive Herman Starr.[176]

That done, Nathan headed to Key West. He returned with a pencil-thin moustache and letters of acceptance from new recruits, including his former administrative assistant from the WPB, Edward Dickinson, who took over the treasurer's position.[177] The office was originally intended to be at a Vermont Avenue location, but soon Nathan was moving into the row house at No. 3 Thomas Circle.[178] Nathan's new quarters reflected his new determination to be behind the scenes—although the building faced the circle, all activity, including the parking lot and Nathan's office, was in the back.[179]

Nathan Associates officially hung out its shingle in late March, declaring its office open to conduct "tailor made" economic studies of all kinds for manufacturing and commercial establishments, investment and banking houses, importers and exporters, and trade associations. Last on the list were foreign governments seeking economic planning.[180] The author of *Mobilizing for Abundance* and *From War to Peace* could not help being a bit condescending. A self-penned press release touted the firm's "service to the business community which will help in its understanding of the basic economic forces at play in our complex economy." "Economic thinking and action," Nathan cautioned potential clients, "must be based on facts and knowledge rather than hunches and bias."[181]

Businesses were not as quick to see the value of Nathan's services. The first customers came from personal connections.[182] The Dayton-based company NCR was having trouble getting steel and aluminum in the shortage-plagued and price-controlled postwar market. Nathan used his connections to see that it did.[183] Connections made through brother Larry gave the firm a toehold in retail, producing a pamphlet for a local "group buying" firm that catered to churches, labor unions, and social organizations.[184]

Nathan tried to expand his turf in another retail-related venture done in cooperation with Bert Sarazan. Although he had been a colleague of Larry Nathan's at Hecht's, Sarazan also had government experience, having done publicity for War Loan drives. In late 1946, while fishing off the coast of Florida, Nathan and Sarazan decided to form a public relations firm—and that whoever took the first fish would become president. Sarazan ascended to the presidency with the assistance of a very small mackerel.[185] In December 1946, they formed the Bert M. Sarazan, Inc., advertising and public relations firm.[186] The idea was to provide off-the-shelf institutional advertising campaigns. Sarazan completed an 11-pound "brochure" by mid-1947, but the service found few takers.[187] Within two years Sarazan was back at Hecht's.[188]

Nathan did get a few chances to educate business leaders about economic issues. In July 1946, Nathan Associates entered into an arrangement with the Lester Harrison advertising agency in New York.[189] Harrison arranged luncheons in which Nathan offered up-to-date assessments of business prospects. In return the businessmen could "fire questions" at the economist. Nathan's message remained consistent—he warned retailers to avoid speculation and to reject high-priced goods such as $3 men's shirts and $29.95 cotton dresses.[190]

It was a modest start for a company with big ambitions, but Nathan was not daunted. Indeed, during 1946 he appeared to identify himself more fully with World Wide Development than with his namesake. This is not surprising given that World Wide had attracted headlines and secured financial backing for offices in Paris, London, Rome, Cairo, and Rio de Janiero to complement Nathan and Currie's "semi-autonomous branches."[191] Despite the headlines, Nathan did not like what he saw when, in the late summer of 1946, he spent time at World Wide's Paris office. "If I were not occupied on government matters I'd like to dig in and get things going for the outfit," he confided to his journal.[192] But at the time Nathan was working neither for his own company nor for World Wide; he was fulfilling a personal commitment made nearly three years earlier to Jean Monnet.

In November 1943, Nathan had agreed to assist the French Committee for National Liberation with economic planning.[193] Given the many challenges France faced, however, the effort did not seem urgent until the winter of 1945 when industrial production in the recovering nation began to level off. In early 1946, the French government established the *Commissariat du Plan* to draw up a five-year economic plan under the direction of Monnet.[194] Nathan made two trips to France during 1946 as a consultant to the plan.[195] His role was in an advisory rather than fact-finding capacity—most of the time he found himself pressing the French simply to work harder. As the plan neared completion, however, Nathan spent a month in Paris consulting with Monnet and his staff and generating one memorandum after another to sharpen the presentation and policy recommendations. On the night of August 25, Nathan "went to bed to write" but was interrupted by the ringing of bells and fireworks exploding beyond the Eiffel Tower outside his window—it was the anniversary of the liberation of Paris. He was back in Washington on September 1. By then, his firm's largest project to date was getting underway, although regrettably from a marketing standpoint, one that was kept entirely secret. [196]

Although *Palestine: Problem and Promise* had effectively countered the British White Paper and established that the area could support large numbers of immigrants, it also emphasized that substantial economic development of Palestine could not be accomplished internally; in academic terms, the economy "would have to be maintained for a prolonged period on a non-self-sustaining basis."[197] In laymen's terms it meant that American donations would be required to support the Jewish population in Palestine. Indeed, by late 1946 Nathan had become an inveterate fundraiser for Palestine, traveling and speaking for the United Jewish Appeal (UJA), an international philanthropic organization, and the American Palestine Trading Corporation (AMPAL), set up by the labor movement in Palestine to fund cooperatives. His message was always the same: "invest, invest, invest in Palestine."[198]

But how much investment could reasonably be expected? Columbia economist Eli Ginzberg had looked into it in 1941, but things had changed considerably since then, so in June 1946, Nathan Associates received a $50,000 contract from the United Jewish Appeal to "help provide an intelligent basis for setting quotas."[199] This was a big boost for the fledgling company. Nathan hired a number of employees who spread out to poll the population in 75 cities across the United States.[200]

In the Washington office, Gass and Creamer, both of whom also worked part time for the UJA, appear to have kept the effort on track. Other fixtures around Nathan Associates in its earliest days included Lorraine Hobday, who had been Nathan's secretary at OWMR and had typed *Mobilizing for Abundance*, and Ruth Aull, who also had a long record as a secretary in government agencies, and eventually took over the duties of office manager.[201] Staff came and went with the projects during these early years, but Aull and Gass—who gave about two-thirds of his time—became the core employees. Their first effort for the UJA paved the way for several even more extensive efforts in subsequent years and linked the firm tightly—if invisibly—with Jewish philanthropy in the United States. But that was only one of the studies with profound consequences for the future of the firm. The other was far less remunerative, bringing in only about $12,000, but it made the reputation of the firm—for good or ill.

Stumping for the United Jewish Appeal in 1946.

"A Liberal Firm"

Sometime in the fall of 1946, another friend paid a visit to No. 3 Thomas Circle. Philip "Phil" Murray had emigrated from Scotland as a child, risen to lead the United Steelworkers of America and then to the top of the entire industrial labor movement as president of the Congress of Industrial Organizations (CIO). For decades before the Great Depression, the labor movement had been synonymous with the American Federation of Labor (AFL), an association of unions mostly organized on the basis of craft: machinists, painters, and lithographers, for example. The AFL proved reluctant to organize the workers who began furiously organizing by industry—steel, auto, electrical—after the passage of one of the chief pieces of New Deal legislation, the 1935 National Labor Relations Act. During the war, a deal had been struck: the government guaranteed relatively generous wages and protected the right to organize; the industrial unions agreed not to strike and to work closely with mobilization efforts. It was during those efforts that the generous and gentlemanly Scotsman got to know Robert Nathan. Now he asked Nathan to develop economic information for upcoming wage negotiations. "Could you undertake a study and advise and suggest a policy?" Murray enquired.[202] It was a question as innocuous as Chaim Weizmann's—and with consequences equally explosive.

The AFL unions, rooted in construction and transportation, were still able to exert power by withholding skilled labor so they tended to stick to "bread and butter" unionism—bargaining about wages and working conditions, leaving the rest to their employers. Murray and the leaders of the CIO unions understood that they owed their existence to friendly legislation and sympathetic agencies, so that success, if not existence, depended on keeping their cause in the mainstream of liberal reform. One very good way of doing this was to argue that wage increases were good not only for their members, but also for the country. How that could be may have been tough to explain, unless Robert Nathan and a few others had not already been doing so for years.

Nathan started the chorus with the OWMR wage-price memorandum that leaked into the headlines in October 1945.[203] Henry Wallace—who claimed to have read a chapter or two of *Mobilizing for Abundance*—pitched in the next month when the Commerce Department issued a report stating that industry could afford wage increases with no price increases.[204] At the end of 1945, United Autoworkers President Walter Reuther put the idea into policy—he demanded a 30-cent raise for GM workers with no increase in prices.[205] Impossible, the automaker said. Reuther made a bald challenge to the sovereignty of management: he told GM to "open the books" and prove it. The automakers were just the first—by January other CIO unions had made their demands and gone on strike. The Truman administration countered with fact-finding panels and one-by-one settlements. Murray's steelworkers accepted an 18.5 cent raise. The UAW finally settled in March for a penny more—and no one opened the books.[206] This "first round" set a pattern of industry-wide strikes and government-brokered settlements that persisted through the 1940s.

Nathan sat out the first round. On a January evening in Key West, he told a Rotary Club audience that wages could certainly be raised "just a little" with perhaps even a small price hike. He also assured the audience that labor troubles would soon be over.[207] But the troubles only got worse and 1946 became by far the most strike-torn year in American history as nearly 5,000 strikes involved some 14.5 percent of the nation's labor force.[208] President Truman seized the coal mines twice that year and threatened to draft striking railroad workers—who settled at the last minute. Under the circumstances, all but the most sympathetic liberals ignored Reuther and Murray's efforts at labor statesmanship, and infuriated by the industrial upheaval, Americans responded to the campaign question "Had Enough?" by voting Republicans into control of Congress that fall.[209]

Nathan, therefore, faced an uphill battle when he agreed to help make the case for labor in the second round. With help from Gass, two research assistants, and a graphic designer, Nathan produced what Murray wanted. In early December the report went to the printer and Murray scheduled its high-profile debut.[210]

An impressive crowd gathered at the Washington Statler on December 11, 1946. Among the 130 in attendance were reporters, publicists, labor leaders, and government officials including the Chairman of Truman's Wage Stabilization Board, the Chairman of the Council of Economic Advisors, and the Secretary of the Interior.[211] Flanked by large-scale charts and graphs, Murray introduced Nathan, who made his ambitious case, not just for some pay hikes, but as the report's title indicated, for *A National Wage Policy for 1947.*

The nation, Nathan began, was "flirting with collapse." Prices had risen too quickly and purchasing power lagged too far behind.[212] Then he provided specifics. From the beginning of 1945 to October 1946, the average factory worker's pay envelope could purchase 21 percent fewer goods. Corporate profits, in contrast, were 50 percent of their wartime peak. That meant that industry could offer raises averaging from 21 to 25 percent—with no price hike—and still keep their profits where they were during the late 1930s.[213] Those scanning their reports found the same propositions, phrased in slightly less alarming terms: first, that "recent economic tendencies" meant the "prospect of a sharp decline in employment sometime in 1947," and second, that "never in recent years has the national interest so clearly required a major general increase in real wage rates."[214]

At 2 p.m., as Washington insiders listened, a press release hit the wire services. Robert Nathan had "warned that a sharp drop in the purchasing power of the weekly pay envelope is seriously endangering our entire economic fabric."[215] Nathan's message was more nuanced than the headlines suggested. Like a good "labor statesman," Nathan cited a litany of legislative and administrative steps—including curbs on monopoly and expansion of social security—that should be taken to guarantee the success of his national wage policy.[216] But it is likely that few remembered these details, either too pleased or too irritated to notice. Then question-and-answer time came and someone asked the obvious question: why, absent compulsion, should business charge less than the market will bear? *The New Republic* described the response. "Nathan stuck out his jaw and softly expressed the hope that when business sees the full case against such a policy it may experience a change of heart."[217]

Nathan explains his "National Wage Policy for 1947" on December 11, 1946. At left is Nathan's client, labor leader Philip Murray.

On the morning of December 12, reporters asked Harry Truman about "The Nathan Report"—no comment. Other cabinet officials responded likewise. At the Department of Commerce, Henry Wallace's successor Averell Harriman drafted a highly critical formal response and then filed it away—he was infuriated, but he was a friend of Nathan's.[218] On Capitol Hill, a Colorado Democratic senator demanded that Treasury investigate Nathan's findings. "Either they are true or false," he demanded of Treasury Secretary John Snyder, who no doubt had hoped he would never hear of his former deputy again.[219]

During the next few days, scholars, journalists and especially backers of business began picking apart the report while Nathan scrambled to hire clerical staff to meet the demand for copies.[220] Al Friendly of the *Washington Post* noted that Nathan was at least consistent—the report looked "strikingly similar" to OWMR report of a year ago, he wrote.[221] *Business Week* also mentioned the earlier "extremely mischievous report," which it claimed had "wrecked the price control machinery completely."[222] Other ad hominem criticisms invoked OWMR, pointing out that Nathan had erred by 4 million when he predicted 8 million unemployed in early 1946.[223]

Most however, were content to criticize the report itself. George Romney of the Automobile Manufacturers Association called Nathan the perpetrator of an "economic fallacy" by treating wages, prices, and profits as a whole—even in good times, he noted, some industries lose money.[224] Others had problems with the idea of generalizing wage hikes. "Its counterpart in the clothing industry would be to make all men's suits size 40 because that happened to be a rough average of all customers," wrote *Business Week*.[225]

While good New Deal liberals and friends of labor tended to stand behind the Nathan Report, statisticians easily detected flaws. Nathan and Gass had used one baseline for wages—January 1945; and another for profits—1936-1939. They had also assumed on little evidence that 1947 would be as profitable for industry as the last quarter of 1946 had been. Economists noted that Nathan and Gass, in the best tradition of the "mature economy thesis," downplayed the importance of capital formation and the potential of investment. They also pointed out that even if all CIO members gained raises without price hikes, that would little help the largest group of workers of all—the unorganized.[226]

There were also the ideologues, of course: the *Cleveland News* complained that it was "economists such as Nathan who pull strings for the hidden hand of socialism."[227] Disillusioned New Dealer Raymond Moley wrote that the Nathan Report epitomized New Deal liberalism's drift toward collectivism and "its political alliance with the CIO."[228] A more thoughtful Dorothy Thompson questioned the extent of government intervention in the economy required by Nathan's scheme.[229]

In search of a more even-tempered response, Averell Harriman asked the Director of Economic Research of the Commerce Department to take a look. The assessment took a week. "The tables are special pleading tables—they are not a dispassionate presentation," was the verdict. The assessment criticized the use of different baselines and the assumption of full employment and high profits for 1947. "The report is a lawyer's brief. It is not meant to be a judge's decision," it concluded. After a week of controversy, Harriman was not the only one still interested—the assessment appears to have gone to Truman's full cabinet.[230] Even out of the government, Nathan was still sticking pins in bureaucratic backsides.

Nathan was well-known before, but now, as he took to public appearances, print, and the airwaves to defend his report, he was truly a celebrity. He repeatedly took on economists in the opposing camp, including George Terborgh of the Machinery and Allied Products Institute and Ralph Robey of the National Association of Manufacturers. They were both fine debaters, with a few points in their favor, but Nathan never gave much ground. He got the better of Minnesota Republican Governor Harold Stassen on "Town Meeting of the Air" on January 22. Stassen had only run for the presidency once—he was not yet a "perennial candidate" joke. But Nathan ridiculed Stassen's position with a parable about the Republicans who had killed OPA: "their pleading reminds me of the story of the boy who murdered his mother and father. Then he went into court and asked for mercy because he was an orphan." Threadbare or not, Nathan's joke got a big laugh, sustained applause, and undercut Stassen effectively.[231]

Debating wages and prices with Dr. Ralph Robey, chief economist for the National Association of Manufacturers (right) on the "People's Platform" radio program, January 5, 1947. Moderator Dwight Cooke is at center.
(© Corbis)

The Nathan Report may have been a lawyer's brief, but it was a good one, and all of the CIO unions pressed it into action. Holding a copy of the report, Walter Reuther called for 22.5 percent wage hike—right in the report's range—although he settled for half that.[232] Employing a "Little Nathan Report," unveiled in April, Murray's own steelworkers settled as well, ensuring that the second round would be nowhere near as bloody as the first and helping the Truman administration and the CIO repair its relationship in time for the 1948 election.[233] Prices, however, still went up, if not as quickly as before.

By then, the annual highly publicized trip to the bargaining table, with labor attempting to compensate for inflation and business insistent on holding the line, were commonly called "rounds." Nathan was out of the ring for the third round of wage nego-tiations in 1948, although he testified before Congress for the AVC that there would be no need for one if business would simply roll back prices.[234] Instead, in a booming economy business and labor settled for a 13-cent wage increase.[235] When Phil Murray next turned to Nathan in 1949, things were not so good.

A mild recession had set in late in 1948. In addition, the CIO had been chastened by the Taft-Hartley Act, passed by the Republican Congress over Truman's veto, which halted the expansion of industrial unionism. The luncheon that July in which Nathan, as one paper put it, "laid the foundation for the foundation for 'fourth round,'" was not as well attended as the one two years earlier, although there were still a few cabinet members and congressmen. The *National Wage Policy for 1949* acknowledged that some businesses could not afford pay increases, so that there could be no pattern across industries. Still it insisted no less on a "return to high levels of production and employ-ment."[236] To his earlier list of required administrative actions Nathan added two more: a public works program to combat the recession and the repeal of Taft-Hartley.[237] The report itself was a bit more circumspect. "Economics is by no means an exact science," it read, "but enough is known to permit not only intelligent diagnosis but also general corrective prescriptions." Nathan concluded that he "hoped that the report will be read and discussed objectively."[238]

Again, Nathan prepared a report just for the steel industry that turned out to be even more useful. By mid-July steel talks had broken off and a strike loomed.[239] The day after speaking in Washington, Nathan went to Pittsburgh where he told another audience that industry profits were up five times over 1939 while purchasing power was only up 14 percent. Nathan's report justified a 30-cent wage increase, but the industry was not buying. Things looked grim as the Truman administration prepared to send in a fact-finding commission. Murray also looked grim, but when a reporter ventured that perhaps Robert Nathan might be on the fact-finding board, he smiled.[240]

Nathan helped the United Steelworkers make its case, testifying for six hours before the presidential board.[241] In the end, though, Truman's fact finders instructed Murray to scale back his demands, on the grounds that its bid was inflationary.[242] The economist who chaired the group noted that Nathan had erred in suggesting that wages had any relation to the demand for steel.[243] He did not understand that for Nathan, who had been thinking in macroeconomic terms for nearly two decades, everything was related. In any case, there could be no missing the relationship between the 1940s wage-price wars and the future of Nathan's firm. "From then on we were never going to be a middle-of-the-road firm," recalled Nathan years later, "we were going to be a liberal firm."[244]

"The Discrete Insider"

Although *Palestine: Problem and Promise* acknowledged that Arab resistance to Jewish settlement would likely be stiff, in public Nathan seemed surprisingly sanguine about the political implications of substantial Jewish settlement in Palestine. He acknowledged in his journal that, "the losers will raise holy hell, be they Arabs or the Jews, and there will be plenty of justification for it."[245] But in public, Nathan was more apt to provide assurance that economic growth would eventually reconcile the two peoples—somehow.

In April 1946, the Anglo-American Committee that was wrestling with the Palestinian knot issued its recommendations. It rejected the idea of creating either an Arab or a Jewish state. Instead it called for a UN trusteeship to keep the peace until the passage of time and rising living standards made a stable, multi-ethnic Palestine possible. Nathan agreed of course, telling a reporter that a UN-imposed settlement and economic development "is the key to peace."[246] The alternative was "partition," splitting Palestine into Arab and Jewish states. The Committee rejected that step, as did Nathan.[247]

But the Anglo-American Committee also agreed that 100,000 Jews should be allowed to enter Palestine immediately, thus ensuring a powerful backlash. Through 1946 and into 1947 violence between Arabs and Jews steadily escalated. While Nathan fought for the CIO back home, his friends in the Middle East were fighting for a homeland in Palestine.

In February 1947 the British turned the problem over to the United Nations and the question was reopened. This time it was harder to be optimistic about the potential of a trusteeship. Nathan agreed. To make development succeed, he was beginning to understand that "you have to have a sympathetic government:" only partition could create that.[248] In Palestine and the United States, advocates of partition and Jewish statehood were gaining strength. Still, it would not be Jewish activists, but rather the U.S. government, through its influence at the United Nations, which would have the power to recognize or deny a Jewish state. By the summer of 1947 it was time for Israel Sieff's Washington circle to stop "tending the ground" and start pulling some strings.

Five years after Sieff's first meetings, David Niles had become an aide to the Truman White House. Niles was well-placed to act as a Zionist advocate in the administration and, because he kept an exceptionally low profile, he was able to do so without creating enemies. That was important because while Truman was leaning toward partition, the State Department was resolutely against it, certain that establishing a Jewish state could only lead to endless war in the Middle East.[249]

In July 1947, its permanent headquarters still under construction, the United Nations convened at a former defense plant at Lake Success, Long Island, to debate the future of Palestine. Recognizing that his UN contingent was against partition and determined to keep his options open, Truman sent General John Hildring to Lake Success to make the case for the administration. The job was too much for one man, and Hildring found it impossible to deal on his own with the Jewish pressure groups that had converged on New York. Niles suggested that Nathan would be an effective liaison between Hildring and the Jews.[250]

So in mid-July, the newlywed Nathans moved into a suite at the Sherry-Netherland Hotel overlooking Central Park. The hotel was jammed with UN delegates and hangers-on. Nathan began working night and day, consulting routinely with notables such as head of the Jewish Agency David Ben Gurion, Abba Eban, and Golda Meir. He routinely reported to Hildring and Niles and consulted with other members of the UN delegation.[251] As time went on and the deadline for the vote on partition approached, Nathan moved well beyond his role as liaison.[252]

The situation at Lake Success, and at the Sherry-Netherland where many of the negotiations took place, grew byzantine. The U.S. delegation was now committed to partition, but State Department officials on the scene, led by Director of the Office of Near Eastern Affairs Loy Henderson, were hoping that the vote would fall short. Stepping into the resulting vacuum was a small group of influential Jews—including Nathan, financier Bernard Baruch, and judge Joseph Proskauer—who lined up votes for partition from among the UN's undecided members. Some State Department men marveled at their approach, as Fraser Wilkins recalled, "they always had a beautiful case to present."[253] At least one official never forgave what he saw as the trespassing of private citizens into the affairs of state. Henderson's assistant, Edwin Wright, ran into Nathan frequently at Lake Success and described him as willing to do anything for the cause including threaten the Costa Rica delegation with loss of construction funds unless it fell into line. Wright even accused Nathan of impersonating Truman during a phone call to Haiti.[254]

That the baritone Nathan could have done Truman's alto convincingly is unlikely, but it is more certain that Nathan put critical pressure on Liberia. When Niles informed him that the Africans were wavering, Nathan got on the phone to tell the Liberian delegation that if they did not back partition, he would have his friend, former Secretary of State Stettinius call *his* friend, Harvey Firestone, Jr., whose rubber company dominated the Liberian economy. Liberia voted for partition.[255]

Nor did Nathan restrict his politicking to foreign nationals. Under Secretary of State Robert Lovett reported to Defense Secretary James Forrestal that "never in his life had he been subject to as much pressure" as during the days before the partition vote. He named Nathan among the most dogged of those who "importuned him."[256] The vote was postponed once, but on November 29, the United Nations voted 33 to 13 in favor of partition, achieving the necessary two-thirds majority. Isador Lubin was among the many who thanked Nathan, congratulating him on the "heroic job that you did at Lake Success."[257]

Zionists had little reason to exult, however. While Jews accepted the UN partition and began building a state, Arabs rejected it entirely and prepared for war. Palestine was soon ensnared in a civil war. The State Department slapped an embargo on arms shipments to either side.[258] Nathan countered that the United States "should let arms go to defenders but not aggressors."[259] Jewish Agency colleagues did more than talk—they began funneling weapons through back channels to Palestine. That gave Nathan yet another opportunity to take the Jewish side in the undercover battle between Zionist idealists and State Department realists for the soul of American foreign policy.

Trouble arose one night along the border between New York State and Canada. A young Jewish Palestinian was apprehended with a shipment of supposed textile machinery that turned out to be mortar-making equipment bound for the port of New York. The FBI was notified. The Palestinian called the highest contact in his notebook, a Washington-based official of the Jewish Agency. There was more at stake here than one arms shipment and one courier, the official realized. If word got out, an invaluable supply line could be cut. It was 4 a.m. The official called Robert Nathan anyway.

Men like David Niles, Robert Nathan, and David Ginsburg "knew as much about the arms traffic to Israel as they chose to," wrote historian Peter Grose, "and if any trouble arose they knew where to turn." Nathan waited until dawn and turned to J. Edgar Hoover.[260] The incident on the border was far from routine, Nathan told Hoover bluntly. If the FBI went forward "some prominent people and some important organizations could be hurt." Hoover asked if the arms would be used in the United States. "No," Nathan replied. He asked whether they would be used against U.S. citizens. "Absolutely not."[261] Playing it straight with J. Edgar Hoover worked: the messenger was merely fined and the "textile machinery" made it overseas.[262]

While the Jews in Palestine fought for their existence, sympathizers in Washington began the fight for statehood. On February 3, 1948, Nathan, Gass, Benjamin Cohen, Richard V. Gilbert, and Eliahu Epstein of the Jewish Agency, which was essentially the Jewish government of Palestine, met at David Ginsburg's house. For three hours they considered how best to persuade Washington's influentials to back U.S. recognition of a Jewish state. Again, the State Department was on the other side of the issue, but the group was convinced that a sizeable portion of public sentiment was on their side. Behind the scenes at the White House, Clark Clifford and Truman's influential army buddy and former business partner, Eddie Jacobson, were also backing statehood. On March 6, Nathan's group advised Ben Gurion to make a bold move—ignore the diplomats and declare a Jewish state.[263]

Instead the State Department made the bold move. The diplomats believed that the president had approved a predetermined policy: if that proved to be unworkable, then the United States would reject partition and push for trusteeship. The fighting in Palestine certainly seemed to discredit partition. On March 19, shortly after Truman assured Chaim Weizmann that the United States was behind partition, UN Ambassador Warren Austin declared a reversal of policy.[264]

That night, Nathan lamented on radio station WINX that the day "will go down as one of the blackest days in the annals of United States foreign policy."[265] "The State Department pulled the rug out from under me," Truman admitted privately the next day. He assured Weizmann that if Israel declared statehood and the United Nations stalled that the United States would recognize it.[266] But for a while the State Department policy held. On March 24, Nathan posted a long letter to Robert Lovett. "Our new policy strikes me as a tragic mistake," he wrote, but by now Nathan had discarded any pretense that economic development under any political arrangement would solve the Palestinian problem. "We should not kid ourselves that a solution by agreement is possible."[267]

Nathan's letter did not convince Lovett, but a meeting in May with Truman top aide Clark Clifford did. Lovett realized that the Truman administration was going to back a Jewish Palestinian state no matter what the diplomats did and advised Secretary of State George Marshall to accept the situation. More because the U.S. reversal imperiled the very existence of the UN than anything else, Marshall did. Now all that was needed was a formal request. On May 14, 1948, Eliahu Epstein made it. At 6:11 p.m. the United States formally recognized the state of Israel. At Lake Success, Warren Austin got in his car and drove home—he could not face his colleagues.[268] In front of the Jewish Agency headquarters on Massachusetts Avenue in Washington, D.C., a crowd gathered. At 6:12 a photographer snapped a picture. Front and center beneath the Star of David flag was Robert Nathan.[269]

On May 17, Nathan was in Pittsburgh, regaling the B'nai B'rith with a history of the new state of Israel. It was a speech he would give many times during the next few years, usually with a request for donations at the end. "The man is tremendous," effused the columnist for a Jewish newspaper, after one such occasion. "He completely captivated his small audience with his history of the economy of the new Jewish state." For most it was familiar, she wrote, "yet everyone listened as if the tale which was unfolded was a revelation."[270]

Outside the Jewish Agency on the day of Israel's recognition, May 14, 1948. Nathan is in the middle of the crowd just below the upper tip of the flag.

Nathan devoted much of the rest of the decade and beyond to helping to keep afloat the country that he had played a small part in creating. In March 1949, the Jewish Agency created an Economic Department, with its chief mission attracting investments in Israel. Nathan agreed to head up the department, even though it was based in New York City, and for several years fielded queries from interested businessman and promoted opportunities in Israel in the press.[271] A reporter seemed surprised to find that Nathan "now frequently speaks not as an objective advisor on the basis of his professional experience, but as a man who has taken upon himself the job of encouraging American Jewry to invest in Israel."[272]

But the "objective advisor" had one more job to do. Israel had a strong contingent of socialists who preferred cooperatives and contributions to the free market. Nathan saw that as a big mistake and told one Israeli labor group that the state would have no choice but to welcome private capital.[273] Philanthropy was fine for helping immigrants adjust, but the building up of Israel, he insisted, should be an investment rather than a charity.[274] The U.S. government was the biggest investor. When a $1 million Export-Import Bank loan came through, Nathan thanked Truman for his support, writing that "economic development in Israel will serve to spearhead the development of the whole Middle East."[275]

The United Jewish Appeal was also considering the various attributes of philan-thropy and investment. In January 1948 the UJA offered Nathan Associates one more "top secret" contract. Some believed that issuance of Israeli bonds might choke off the philanthropy that was the UJA's mission. Its leaders wanted to know if that was true.[276] For this sophisticated polling Nathan brought in experts. He solicited proposals from the leaders in the field, including Roper and Harris.[277] In mid-February the University of Michigan's Institute for Social Research agreed to do the job for less than $10,000.[278] By October, the survey established that Americans would buy bonds without giving up charitable donations. Nathan urged Ben Gurion to launch a drive, but the latter remained concerned about losing donors.[279]

In 1948 charitable donations to Israel topped out at $150 million and began declining. By 1950 the total was heading toward $90 million, and Ben Gurion was ready to take Nathan's advice.[280] On September 5, he convened a conference in Jerusalem that included fifty influential Americans and Israeli government officials. Nathan made his case again. "You have undertaken a bold adventure," he pronounced, turning to Ben Gurion. "You must have a daring financial policy to go with a daring immigration policy."[281] The convention approved a $1.5 billion bond issue. Three days later Nathan Associates released another report based on the 1948 survey that established a blueprint for the bond issue. It estimated how much was available from various types of investors and suggested what mix of bonds would attract the most investment. The report recommended that the bonds not be tied to specific projects. People would rather invest in Israel, Nathan believed, than bridges and dams.[282]

Nathan Associates prepared the report, but Robert Nathan personally helped execute it. Nathan took a seat on the board of governors of the American Financial Development Corporation for Israel, a group with a New Deal connection—its chairman was Henry Morgenthau, Franklin Roosevelt's Treasury Secretary.[283] From the beginning of 1951 into the spring, Nathan traveled across the country, from the Deep South to Detroit and from New England to Texas, promoting Israeli bonds.[284] In his appeals Nathan invoked history and economics. He also reverted to some of his earlier idealism: "a prosperous Israel will help raise the standard of living in the whole area," he told a Kansas City group.[285] Through the first half of the 1950s Nathan Associates kept doing top secret surveys and Nathan kept speaking. "From an outsider, unaffiliated with Zionism and Israel," wrote historian S. Ilan Troen, "Nathan had become the discrete insider."[286]

SEARCH FOR DIRECTION

For its May 4, 1947, edition, the *New York Times* gave Nathan about 1,200 words on the topic, "If I Headed a Business." There was a lot he would do, Nathan wrote, including writing congressmen, studying labor laws, raising wages, cutting prices, and by all means avoiding "short sighted practices."[287] But nowhere did Nathan mention that he actually *did* head a business. Perhaps there was a reason. Nathan's business ventures were far from booming at the time—not at all unusual for a beginning businessman but perhaps not the right sort of thing for the *Times*.

By then World Wide Development had led Nathan into an uncomfortable corner and a hasty exit. Matty Fox was not the type to agonize over nuances, so when the prospect of a big overseas opportunity appeared he was for it. So were General Lord and another World Wide catch, Rear Admiral Howard Flanagan. In October 1946, they negotiated a deal with Juan Peron in Argentina with the potential of some $1 billion in industrial and technical aid contracts.[288] By early 1947, all of the World Wide subsidiaries had people there. Currie himself was in Argentina and Nathan had dispatched G. Griffith Johnson, an economist who had moved quickly through Treasury, Commerce, and the OPA.[289]

Johnson's career with Nathan turned out to be equally fleeting. Although Argentina was in the middle of a major state-controlled industrialization push and appeared to be in earnest, it was also harboring quite a few Nazi war criminals. The State Department had, in fact, put an embargo on Argentina for that reason. But now, worried more about communists than Nazis, the State Department lifted the restrictions exclusively for World Wide. When the news broke in January, reporters made sure to name New Dealers Nathan and Currie. Nathan told one reporter that he was "unfamiliar with the details." Liberals were furious. The Jewish Agency told Nathan in no uncertain terms that the deal "stinks."[290] Nathan resigned from World Wide Development, and the venture stalled.[291]

World Wide had promised a safe harbor for Nathan's fledgling consulting firm, an entity to take care of the details and keep the coffers full while Nathan pursued his dazzling array of private and public interests. It had been too good to be true. Nathan had been impressed by Jean Monnet's "almost unparalleled capacity of figuring how to move and sell and get backing and put things over." Now, to keep his business going, Nathan would have to do this himself.[292]

The first task was restructuring the business. Nathan did not own his company, only stock in World Wide Development, which with the collapse of the Argentina venture, was of dubious value. He may have gotten financial help from his partner in the advertising initiative or he may have simply opted to use that company as a new shell for his own. In any case, it was an "amicable arrangement." By 1949, Bert M. Sarazan, Inc., Robert Nathan president, was the sole owner of the Robert R. Nathan Associates.[293]

Through the late 1940s, Nathan, Gass and a handful of other employees built up the business. Two early contracts also involved Latin America. In the postwar years Puerto Ricans had begun to migrate to New York City in large numbers. By early 1947 the Puerto Rican population of the city was at least 350,000. O. Roy Chalk, the owner of Trans-Caribbean Airlines, was interested in opening a San Juan-New York route. Nathan Associates found that not only were hundreds of thousands leaving Puerto Rico, there were tens of thousands returning regularly. The potential for traffic was beyond expectations, Nathan reported.[294]   Chalk started what became Trans-Caribbean's staple route.[295] Another venture that year was an apparently unsuccessful one, producing color Sunday supplements for 41 Latin American newspapers.[296] A similar enterprise involved helping a University of California team produce a study on anti-Semitism.[297]

Besides the surveys of Jewish communities (which were secret) and the wage-price studies (which most definitely were not) the most notable of the 1940s projects was work done for another labor union, the Actor's Equity Association. Broadway was not doing well during the postwar years. Plays were expensive, motion pictures were cheap, and actors and stage managers were unemployed. Isador Lubin suggested that his friend might be able to help. In late 1947 Nathan Associates completed a small pilot study. In early 1948 Nathan himself conducted nine work sessions with Actors Equity and interviewed some 50 people in the industry. The firm pored over the history of every theatrical project available. By April, Nathan Associates had prepared a 120-page prospectus with preliminary recommendations and a quote for a larger study. Actors Equity paid $3,000. That summer the union approved the much larger study, although there is no evidence that it was ever completed.[298]

A number of international initiatives fizzled during the company's first years. In the spring of 1946 Nathan got overtures from the governments of Poland and Czechoslovakia about economic development projects of some kind.[299]   Only the former opportunity materialized and that on an exploratory basis, but it earned Nathan Associates a badly needed $13,750 and provided Nathan and Gass with firsthand experience in a communist country.[300] In mid-1947 the two made the rounds of the top economic offices and were taken on tours of the countryside. Nathan was struck by the fact that during his entire visit he saw only one steam shovel cleaning up the wreckage that lay all around two years after the end of the war, but he felt that he had received full access. "As for the iron curtain," he wrote, "it sure didn't exist for us."[301] But Nathan Associates did not get the contract either—Poland was just beginning to enter the deep freeze of the Cold War.

In June 1948, Nathan set out on another first, island-hopping the Pacific with an "overwhelming desire and need to achieve success on the rubber and pepper deal."[302] The cloak and dagger enterprise had the hallmarks of a Matty Fox production. In 1947 Fox had quit the movie business to work on a new venture owned 51 percent by American investors and 49 percent by Indonesians, called the America Indonesia Company. The company was to get a monopoly on the sale of Indonesian exports and the purchase of imports—and 7.5 percent of the value of every ton. There was a small complication—Fox very much needed the help of Meyer and Brown, a seasoned import-export firm. There was a very large complication as well—Fox's contract was with the budding Indonesian Republican government of Sukarno—still technically in revolt against the Dutch colonial government of Indonesia. The U.S. Government was not happy. Two months earlier Fox and Nathan had been called to the State Department and told that the deal flouted Dutch sovereignty and might imperil negotiations between the Dutch and Sukarno. Neither man appeared to have been daunted.[303]

Nathan should have been. It was his task to conduct the negotiations with the Dutch government in Jakarta required to pull off the deal—and neither the Dutch nor Meyer and Brown had any use for Matty Fox. Nathan spent a lot of time waiting in hotel rooms for meetings to materialize, and in the end returned to the United States empty-handed.[304] He did, however, reach an insight that may have been even more valuable. "Whites who go to the far corners of the earth," he wrote in his journal, "seem to…get some sort of satisfaction out of their self-assigned superiority." Nathan confessed to being intimidated by the fact that the whites were outnumbered and concluded, "perhaps that is why they act so superior."[305]

While Nathan was in Jakarta for Matty Fox, Nathan Associates was withering in Washington. By then the UJA study was winding down and Nathan had been cutting staff routinely. The only full-time professional employee was Sidney Lerner, an economist from the University of Wisconsin and WPB veteran who had been with the company since 1946, and he was looking for work.[306] Nathan planned to "convert it into an individual operation, assuming Sid leaves and business isn't better soon."[307] But Lerner hung on and so did Nathan Associates.

The fourth-round labor talks seem to have convinced Nathan that if his was going to be a "liberal firm" it should go more forthrightly after labor. In some respects Nathan became a champion of organized labor by default, because his ideas about maintenance of aggregate demand spending dovetailed nicely with CIO wage aspirations. He also had some credentials of his own—during his time at the Commerce Department, Nathan had been a member of the United Federal Workers of America, CIO.[308] In the fall of 1949, he embraced that identity as never before, officially opening a "Labor Division"[309] At the end of the year the CIO gave Nathan an assignment as an on-air personality in its weekly radio series on ABC. Every Tuesday night at 10:45, Nathan expounded from "only the briefest notes" on the economic topics of the day, bookended by Joe Glazer's union songs and James Crowley's news reports.[310] Nathan continued doing radio spots for the CIO at least until early 1953, and well before the run was over, reporters were referring to him as a "noted labor economist."[311]

Late in 1950, the Labor Division embarked on the only speculative work that Nathan Associates ever undertook. Working with Louis Walinsky, yet another WPB veteran, Nathan put together a few sample issues of "Bob Nathan's Washington Labor Letter."[312] It was not an entirely original idea. A publicist named Chester Wright had been producing his own brief labor publication since the 1930s. That had recently been taken over by a journalist who changed the name to *John Herling's Labor Letter* and kept it going for years. Nathan must have believed that a market opportunity remained, however. He promoted his four-page newsletter as "terse, crisp in manner and highly factual in content." Nathan expected laborites from international offices down to shop stewards to read it for economic news, collective bargaining facts, and "inside stuff," and persuaded Phil Murray to allow him to make his case to CIO officials in person and by mail.[313] By March 1951 the venture was over. Nathan needed 5,000 subscriptions to make his labor letter viable, but received only 620.[314]

The years from 1943 to 1950 were remarkably crowded ones for Robert Nathan and a topical account can hardly do them justice. Nathan was continually shifting from intense periods of study to endless stretches of travel to long days of meetings. The subject could be veterans' affairs in the morning, wage-price fights in the afternoon, and the future of Palestine in the evening. Nathan learned a great deal during these years. He read diligently when he traveled—not detective novels, but works of literature.[315] But most of what Nathan learned he seems to have acquired in the course of tackling whatever challenge he had most recently set for himself.

Throughout, he spoke and acted first and foremost as a liberal—one of the last of the formerly bright-eyed but now tired New Dealers headed for the wings. Nathan was above all an economic liberal. He believed in, and supported, all of the social causes that his friends did, but in activism usually stuck to economics. The first stirrings of the Civil Rights movement came during these years, but Nathan did not seem to notice. When he spoke at an AVC dinner in Miami in March 1947, it was the venue's first integrated event since the onset of Jim Crow. Others mentioned it. Nathan does not appear to have done so, but he did warn there would soon be a depression unless there was a big wage increase.[316]

Second only to the question of how Nathan was able to accomplish everything he did during these years, must be how he was able to hold onto his convictions about wages, prices, and depressions through this period of impressive postwar growth. The GNP bottomed out at $231 billion in 1947, rose to $258 billion in 1948, paused at $256 billion in 1949, and took off again, hitting $285 billion in 1950.[317] Still, in a 1950 essay published in *Twentieth Century Unlimited*, a compilation of articles by left-wing intellectuals and activists, Nathan warned "that the distortions which developed in the postwar period will sooner or later bring on a serious decline in business activity."[318]

Although he got some of the best headlines, Nathan was hardly alone in underestimating the power of pent up savings, deferred demand, and the capacity of private enterprise to accommodate them both quickly after the war.[319] In an early 1947 article, Everett Hagen noted that he, along with other alarmists in the OWMR, should have at least considered that the economy might reconvert after the war as quickly as it had been mobilized. Hagen admitted forthrightly that he had been far too preoccupied with deflation at the time.[320] Nathan never made any such admission. Why was he among the last to realize that even without a full dose of Keynesian medicine the crash was just not coming? One answer was later provided by Herbert Stein, a more conservative economist. "Macroeconomists can feel confident in wartime," said Stein, "because in wartime they deal with large numbers—large enough to override the noise in the data."[321] It took time for Nathan to leave the war behind and there was a great deal of noise in postwar America. And perhaps, consciously or not, Nathan enjoyed the crusade too much to question its premises too closely. "The young energetic liberals are forever dissatisfied and disgruntled and impatient," he wrote in his journal after one late-night bull session. "That's OK, and I hope we remain that way."[322]

3

New Dealer in Exile

Robert Nathan liked to hold meetings in the Congressional Hotel's "Veto Room." He could have chosen the Filibuster Room, with art by *Evening Star* cartoonist Clifford Berryman on the walls, or the Caucus Room, or even the Committee Room.[1] But he invariably asked for the Veto Room for executive sessions of Americans for Democratic Action (ADA), the non-partisan political group that occupied much of his time during the 1950s.[2] When he had taken the national account in depression and mobilized the economy in war, Nathan was an insider. Then, as an administrator in the executive branch, Nathan really had a veto. That was no longer the case.

Nathan was a New Dealer in exile during the 1950s. The exile was self-imposed, at first. Like many of his economist, lawyer, and social scientist contemporaries from the Roosevelt era, Nathan had opted not to serve Truman—and then criticized the administration that "provided a rather dry, arid climate for intellectuals."[3] Nathan might have had another chance in 1951 when he was considered for a post in one of the foreign aid agencies, but that July he assured the *Dayton Daily News* that he would not join the administration: "the men in charge are not liberals."[4]

His assumption might have been that things would get better. They did not. In 1952, the wildly popular and apparently unintellectual General Eisenhower won the presidency. "If you had a high IQ," grumbled Nathan later, "the Eisenhower team thought something was wrong with you."[5] For the rest of the decade, Nathan was shut out of the administration. He worked hard to influence policy, but always from the outside. Nathan's consulting firm also went into exile during the 1950s. It grew and prospered, but more from an economic development contract with far off Burma than from the variety of domestic "odd and end" contracts that barely paid the bills.

There were some victories. Nathan kept the ADA alive through its own years in the wilderness and helped defeat Joe McCarthy before he sapped the integrity of the American political system altogether. These were in some sense negative achievements, the New Dealer's symbolic veto of a political culture that had set aside the lessons of depression and war. For most committed liberals it was a dispiriting decade. Robert Nathan had his moments, but they were few. He loved to fight too much, whether from within or without.

A New Start in Asia

Today, the concept of "development economics" is assumed to be of postwar origin and revolve around the growth of Third World economies. But since the Great Depression had laid low even the most advanced economies, Nathan had been thinking about development economics most of his life. Before the mid-20th century, economists had generally focused on how nations create their own wealth, trying to understand why major industrial powers succeeded. By World War II, they began wondering instead why some nations seemed stuck in an underdeveloped state. Some theorists focused on the structural argument: states had to be arranged both politically and economically so as to foster the creation of an internal industrial base. The imperative under this model became "import substitution:" generating "foreign exchange" from exports that could be used to build up protected domestic enterprises.

A collateral theory was that it took a "big push"—a single large influx of capital—to move underdeveloped economies out of stasis, an infusion that could only come from external investment. Although the circumstances were not exactly applicable, optimistic economists took the Marshall Plan, launched in the spring of 1948, as proof that the theory worked. Its $13 billion infusion of U.S. capital had an immediate effect and lifted Western Europe above prewar standards in just four years. Nathan was already involved in another "big push" on a smaller scale, obtaining and helping plan the expenditure of funds from the United States to build up Israel.

Economic development was in the air when the Truman administration began drafting its January 20, 1949, inaugural address. There were three obvious planks in the foreign policy platform: support the United Nations, continue the Marshall Plan, and assist free nations in military defense. But Truman's speechwriters hoped for a big finish. They fixed on an idea developed by Benjamin Hardy, a staffer for Nelson Rockefeller, Coordinator of Inter-American Affairs during the war.[6] Hardy was thinking of Latin America, but the idea put forth by Truman as "Point IV" in his inaugural address had universal application as a "bold new program for making the benefits of our scientific advances and industrial progress available for the improvement and growth of underdeveloped areas."[7] The Marshall Plan had been mostly about resources—Western Europe had all the technical expertise required to rebuild. Point IV, however, introduced a new phrase into development lexicon: technical assistance. The developed world would still have to provide resources, but it would also have to provide the expertise required to build an economy.

Nathan, like other liberals, was inspired by Point IV. It seemed to extend the New Deal's promise of economic security overseas. It "really put into words the realization that we had to live in a world where people had better opportunities," Nathan said later.[8] Nelson Rockefeller thought so too. In early 1947, Rockefeller created the International Basic Economy Corporation to promote development in Latin America. In 1950, Truman asked Rockefeller to chair an International Development Advisory Board and Study Group. It was a homecoming of sorts—Stacy May, Simon Kuznets, and Robert Nathan all served on the 20-man Advisory Board.[9] Their report, submitted in March 1951, put American assistance firmly in a Cold War context. "Ours must be a positive strategy of strengthening the ties of cooperative progress which band the free peoples together," it stated.[10]

The administration had already transferred many of the activities of the Economic Cooperation Administration (ECA), the funding offshoot of the Marshall Plan, from Europe to Southeast Asia, the other frontier between communist regimes and the Free World.[11] It had also established a second "Point IV" agency, the Technical Cooperation Administration, administered by Nathan's friend Averell Harriman.[12] A 1952 national conference on international economic and social development indicated that a new discipline had arrived. Rockefeller gave the keynote address and Nathan participated in a panel on Southeast Asia.[13] By then he was rapidly becoming an expert on that particular corner of the world.

Burma was an ancient kingdom the size of Texas, situated directly below China near the center of South Asia.[14] When they conquered it in 1886, the British were not inclined to distinguish between vanquished Asian peoples, so Burma became a province of India. For the next 50 years, with British in the top posts and Indians dominating the labor force, the Burmese were third-class citizens in their own country. The British and Indians did create the world's top exporter of rice, but to the Burmese the market economy would always be emblematic of exploitation. By the 1930s, an indigenous socialist movement was seeking restoration of the monarchy and the overthrow of capitalism. Among its leaders were philosopher-politician U Nu and General Ne Win.[15]

It was a third man, Aung San, who led the freedom movement that prepared to take power from the British, who were eager to shed their Empire after World War II. Before the cession, however, Aung San and most of his cabinet were assassinated. U Nu became Burma's first Prime Minister.[16] U Nu began promoting economic development in terms evocative of Buddhist mythology—he wished to create for the people a contemporary version of the legendary "Padaytha Tree," a fount of plenty and fulfillment that had been destroyed by man's greed.[17]

U Nu also required economic development for less mystical reasons. In 1949 he had nearly been overthrown—only Ne Win and the army could save him.[18] A Ministry of National Planning had been established in 1946. Already there had been five years of study by both Burmese and Oxford economists.[19] But U Nu wanted something far more ambitious—an eight-year plan that would bring Burma to the threshold of the developed world. The Ministry of Planning would be closely involved in framing and implementing the plan, but needed outside expertise in devising it, for which it turned to the United States.

Burma had experienced almost no infiltration by Soviet or Chinese Communists. Although socialist, it promised to serve as a western bulwark in hotly contested Southeast Asia. "Would you be interested in advising Burma?" an ECA official asked Nathan in early summer 1951.[20] The offer came with a guarantee of autonomy—Nathan's team would be paid by the ECA but work only for Burma. Nathan accepted and in late August 1951 headed across the Pacific. Having had no experience in Asia, Nathan read up on the flight.[21] In Tokyo he picked up a friend who did know something about Asia. University of Wisconsin-trained economist Michael Sapir had participated in the reconstruction of Japan and agreed to join the team.[22]

Nathan's first important meeting was with the Secretary General of the Ministry of Planning. Hla Maung began with an air of stern authority to underscore the fact that Nathan's team would be working for Burma rather than the United States. "They are independent and like it and show it," Nathan wrote afterwards. But the Secretary General was also an economist and warmed to the discussion and to his colleague—who he was soon calling "Bob." The next step was to meet U Nu. U Nu was so committed to economic development that he had kept the title Minister of Planning for himself. One of the first things that Nathan noticed when ushered into the presence of U Nu was a picture of Mahatma Gandhi on his wall. The next thing he noticed was the "intent and penetrating character of his eyes."[23] As the talk unfolded it became clear to Nathan that U Nu's intentions were good and that he was a "highly motivated idealist, but also a mystic." He reminded Nathan of the visionary New Dealer Henry Wallace.[24] U Nu was reflective and serene. Nothing, Nathan wrote later, like an "operation-minded F.D.R."[25]

If there had been a test involved Nathan had passed it—Burma signed a two-year contract with the ECA for the services of Robert R. Nathan Associates.[26] Back in the United States the news made the papers with conservative columnists castigating the waste of U.S. funds on a "Burmadoggle" to benefit an old New Dealer.[27] The battering by conservatives helped to burnish Nathan's image with the socialist Burmese. Referring to a piece in the right-wing *Chicago Tribune*, the U.S. Ambassador to Burma said, "the editorial was the best recommendation."[28]

The Burmese had hired more help than just Nathan Associates. Nathan was not even in charge—that fell to Homer Pettit, project manager for the lead partner in the group, the industrial engineering firm, Knapp, Tibbetts and McCarthy. The mining engineering firm, Frank Pearce and Company, rounded out the team.[29] The engineers would plan projects and implement them, but the fundamental job of determining how best to help the Burmese economy reach its full potential capacity fell to the economists. This was something that Nathan, with his national accounts and wartime agency experience, seemed qualified to do. Hla Maung thought so—he specifically wrote into the agreement that all economic planning would be directly supervised by Nathan.

Nathan never had any intention of moving to Burma for two years. To lead the in-country effort, he hired Everett Hagen, the Wisconsin-trained economist who had worked for him at the OWMR. Hagen had gone on to the Bureau of the Budget, consulted for the ECA, and then returned to academia at the University of Illinois. After losing a dispute between the Keynesian and classical economists at Illinois, Hagen was ready for work elsewhere—Nathan hired him as Director of Field Staff.[30] Working for Hagen was an agricultural economist, a trade economist, and economists who could handle large-scale financial and fiscal planning.[31] "Backstopping" the overseas team was Ajay J. Creshkoff, a University of Pennsylvania-trained economist who would help with logistics, reporting, and analysis from Washington.[32]

The overseas consulting work provided incentives that had allowed Nathan to make some good hires: housing was provided free of charge by the Burmese government and living costs were very low. Nathan noted in one of his journals that Scotch was $2 a bottle.[33] The Burmese had agreed to sizeable paychecks that would be largely tax exempt. Given the hard work and health hazards his team would face, Nathan decided, "they deserve it."[34]

If the salaries were generous, the timetable was not—it gave the American team only 20 weeks to complete a preliminary survey, the foundation for a comprehensive study and plan. The Burmese had also identified programs that they wanted to begin immediately—regardless of what the engineers and economists concluded. Nathan had hoped to have a clear picture of the situation in Burma before he returned to the United States. Instead he confessed to being "quite confused about the underlying forces at work here."[35]

When Nathan returned to Burma in early January 1952 to help pull together his team's part of the preliminary survey, Louis Walinsky was already there. Mike Sapir, who had his own consulting firm in Tokyo, had too freely discussed the contract with his clients, so Nathan had to let him go.[36] That, and the fact that a few team members had only recently arrived made the survey a hasty effort. But by the end of the month Nathan was convinced that even if the chapters were less than perfect, "they are damn good."[37]

On January 30, Nathan, Walinsky, and the engineers presented the recommendations laid out in the *Preliminary Report on Economic and Engineering Survey of Burma* to U Nu in person. As requested, it was an eight-year plan running from January 1952 to September 1959 that provided a path for steady economic development. "The whole conception of Point IV is damn good and seeing it work is encouraging," Nathan wrote.[38] Nathan was equally encouraged that the work in Burma would provide a springboard for his consulting firm.[39]

In August, the preliminary survey was formally approved by the government at its "Pyidawtha" Conference.[40] U Nu was optimistic—overly so. He predicted that every Burmese family would soon have its own automobile.[41] The mystical U Nu was not alone in having great expectations. One senior administrator told a Nathan team member, "we need experts to help us do the impossible."[42]

The next step was preparing a far more comprehensive study that provided the technical data necessary to implement the projects sketched out in the preliminary survey. Completed in 1953, the *Comprehensive Report: Economic and Engineering Development of Burma* established specific programs by sector. Because the socialist Burmese were committed to industrial development, the report emphasized transportation, power, and construction more than agriculture, irrigation, forestry, and mining. The overall plan included 13 distinct projects. Some, such as a steel plant, were included at the insistence of the government. It "seemed to have symbolic and prestige value," recalled Walinsky.[43] The overall goals were relatively modest—to increase industrial production by 63 percent and agricultural production by 77 percent by 1960.[44] This would essentially restore Burma to its postwar standard of living and make possible the kinds of social development—boosting education, strengthening institutions—necessary for Burma to one day join the ranks of developed nations. "I think Burma will be satisfied with our work," Nathan wrote. "I can only hope there will be some implementation."[45]

The effort to develop Burma was taking place in the shadow of a more fundamental struggle over the path of economic development in Southeast Asia. In the summer of 1950, after Chinese Communist-backed North Korean troops attempted to take back South Korea, the United States—as the preponderance of a United Nations force— once again went to war. At the outset of the Korean conflict, Nathan took his old "all-outer" clothes out of the closet. He announced on his CIO-sponsored radio show and in regular letters to major newspapers that "mobilization efforts hardly attest to any significant degree of a continued sense of urgency."[46]   But the Truman administration intended neither to fully mobilize the national economy nor to call upon Nathan to reprise his old role. Instead, it was the United Nations that recruited Nathan.

In Karachi, Pakistan, June 1953. From left: Cushman Reynolds of the United States International Information and Educational Exchange; Burr Smith and John Tallman of the Technical Cooperation Administration; Nathan; and John K. Emmerson, Deputy Chief of Mission in Karachi.

There were some personal connections at work. Donald Kingsley, the executive director of the United Nations Korean Reconstruction Agency (UNKRA), was an old friend, and former Goon Isador Lubin was working in the U.S. mission to the United Nations.[47] By May 1952, Nathan had been asked to consider helping plan for peace. He prepared a dense four-page memorandum on "an economic survey and program for Korea."[48] On October 1, 1952, Nathan left for Korea with a one-year, $125,000 contract, to plan the country's reconstruction.[49]

Nathan assembled a stellar team. It included Gerhard Colm who had worked for the Bureau of the Budget and the Council of Economic Advisors, and John Lewis, an Indiana University economist. Much of the work in Korea was done by specialists who came into the country for brief periods. Besides Nathan and Walinsky these included Richard Musgrave, a public finance economist formerly with the Federal Reserve, and employment specialist Bertram Gross.[50]

Upon arrival, Nathan surmised that "the job is a very tough one and there will be plenty of obstacles and pitfalls."[51] Much of Korea's historical information had been kept by Japan, its former colonizer, and lost during the war. The team was stationed in Pusan, only 200 miles from the fighting, at a dust-ridden "wired in" military base called "Hialeah."[52] Nathan often emphasized the importance of working directly for the host country. But there was no chance of that in Korea. Most of the Nathan team's contacts were army and State Department officials who monitored—and closely regulated—their travel.[53]

By far the biggest pitfalls were political. South Korean President Syngman Rhee was an ardent anti-communist. He knew of Nathan's work for the CIO, considered him to be little better than a communist, and refused to cooperate.[54] Nathan concluded on more than one occasion that the effort was futile, but Kingsley reminded him that he worked for UNKRA, not South Korea.[55] Kingsley had his own political problems. By late October 1952, right-wing newspapers were reprising the attacks they had made about Nathan and Burma with even more vehemence. The story began circulating that UNKRA had turned down an offer by the Rockefeller Foundation to produce a study for free so that it could funnel funds to Nathan.[56] By November, Kingsley himself was under attack and on his way out of UNKRA, hauled before Congress to testify about the Nathan contract. "What a day," Nathan wrote in his journal on November 5, 1952. "Eisenhower won the election. President Syngman Rhee wants UNKRA to send the Nathan team home."[57]

Under these depressing circumstances the "wired in" Nathan team pounded out its preliminary report. Nathan admitted to "driving the staff very hard, but no more than myself."[58] The survey was done by December 15, 1952, but held back due to objections by "certain governments," most likely South Korea itself. When in February the report was finally leaked to the press, the grounds for resistance became clear.[59] The Nathan survey was tough on Rhee and noted that black marketeering and illegal profiteering were rampant. The report was not much easier on the army and the United Nations, criticizing the expenditure of $400 million with no integrated plan.[60] South Korea could become self-supporting by the end of the decade, the Nathan team reported, but only with outside assistance totaling some $1.75 billion.[61]

When Nathan returned to Korea in 1953 he found that the dust had settled—at Hialeah anyway. But if the base was a bit less depressing, the political situation remained as disheartening as ever. Nathan called Korea "a place of inconsistencies and conflicts on all matters."[62] Not surprisingly, Nathan opted to have his team produce the final report back in Washington, its 460 pages comprising what one scholar has called, "a fine representative of a genre of twentieth-century development planning documents."[63] The document supplied more detail to support the preliminary economic objectives. It stated that a $1.9

billion overall economic investment would be necessary—$1.25 billion of it from outside South Korea. Much "social investment" was also necessary to raise health, education, and housing standards.[64] The report encouraged the South Koreans to change their diet, making more rice available for export and thus creating more foreign exchange.[65] It also stated that South Korea had no choice but to normalize relations with Japan, given that its former enemy was now its logical trading partner.[66] The report was diplomatic toward Rhee, noting that South Korea required the "highest quality of intelligent and dedicated democratic leadership."[67] It was also philosophically eloquent. "To the free world," the report stated, "Korean reconstruction affords an opportunity to constructively participate in a great endeavor—an endeavor to build a progressive and dynamic economy in a part of the world where millions are unable to eke out a bare subsistence, where competing systems of government and economics threaten freedom and peace."[68]

Nathan had an invaluable ability to believe the best about an endeavor that he was heavily involved in, whatever the complications or ultimate prospects. That was true during the days and weeks surrounding the completion of the report in December 1953. But this report, like the preliminary survey, was also suppressed for a time. "I would love to blast the whole thing in the papers," Nathan confessed to Walinsky.[69] Nathan appears to have restrained himself, in this case at least, but the release of the report in June 1954 was hardly grounds for celebration at Thomas Circle. The published version had been shorn of the acknowledgements page and UNKRA delivered only five copies, informing Nathan that if he wanted more he would have to purchase them.[70] It was even more depressing for Nathan to see South Korea struggle through the remainder of the 1950s. Rhee ignored the Nathan study, refused to trade with Japan, and used U.S. aid funds mostly to patch together a corrupt regime.[71] In 1958 Nathan admitted feeling "that we had wasted our time and that UNKRA had wasted its money."[72] Incredible as it seems in hindsight, as late as 1961, the economy of South Korea lagged well behind that of the North.[73]

A Liberal Fight

As disconcerted as he was about economic backwardness abroad, Nathan was even more concerned about political backwardness at home. It is therefore surprising that he was late to wade into the organization that, more than any other, made it a mission to pull America out of its conservative slump. It is not at all surprising that by the 1950s he was in it up to his neck.

The Americans for Democratic Action was shaped by two profound postwar pressures. One was the perceived waning of the New Deal—"perceived" because even though the last flurry of New Deal reform ended in 1937, it took the death of Roosevelt and the presidency of Truman to convince liberals that something really had changed in the American polity. The other was the attempt to consolidate the political left under Henry Wallace's Progressive Citizens of America (PCA). The PCA and Wallace himself had become emblematic of one of liberalism's biggest New Deal faults—a tendency to overlook Soviet Communist totalitarianism on the left while fighting fascism on the right. Like the AVC before it, the PCA was rapidly infiltrated by Party members. Unlike the AVC, the PCA did not choose to fight, which left Party members controlling America's largest supposedly liberal organization.

In the winter of 1946 some began thinking about creating an organization and a program for liberals that would help extinguish domestic communism and keep the New Deal coals glowing until they could be rekindled. James Loeb, a former New York socialist and high school teacher, offered up the organization that he had run since 1941, the Union for Democratic Action, as the vehicle.[74] He called a meeting in Washington for early January 1947. David Ginsburg invited his old Army buddy informally. Loeb gushed in a letter to Nathan, "We have an opportunity of a lifetime. We are counting on your participation."[75]

Nathan was among the few hundred liberals who gathered at the Willard Hotel on January 3, 1947, but he opted not to join. Perhaps he was preoccupied with his celebrity as author of the "Nathan Report." Perhaps he wished to focus his extracurricular attention on the AVC. For whatever reason, this was an unusual case of Nathan limiting his involvements.[76] Among those who did sign on were former Goons David Ginsburg and Joe Rauh, economists Leon Henderson and John Kenneth Galbraith, Harvard historian Arthur Schlesinger, Jr., and the crusading mayor of Minneapolis, Hubert Humphrey. As Nathan later recalled, Eleanor Roosevelt admonished the group to move beyond her husband's old administration and "face new problems of new times."[77] Nevertheless, the ADA's first press release insisted that "the New Deal program must be expanded to ensure decent levels of health, nutrition, shelter, and education."[78] Everyone assumed, as former Office of War Information Administrator Elmer Davis put it when he opened the meeting, that the ADA was the "New Deal government in exile."[79]

Nathan's next brush with the organization came later that year when he and fellow New Deal economists served on the ADA Committee on Economic Security. Their report was predictably depression-minded, recommending immediate wage increases and price reductions.[80] The ADA needed some of its own medicine during the late 1940s, even then leading a precarious financial existence despite hefty contributions from labor.[81] The ADA's programmatic path was also precarious. Its biggest blunder and its greatest accomplishment both came during the 1948 presidential election: the former when it tried to dump Truman and make Dwight Eisenhower the Democratic candidate, and the latter when it obtained a strong civil rights plank that first began to loosen the Democratic Party from southern segregationist moorings.[82]

Nathan joined the ADA shortly afterwards, but was not active until 1952.[83] That summer, after the newly elected executive committee chairman resigned, Nathan took the post.[84] He was formally second in command, serving under former Roosevelt Attorney General Francis Biddle. In practice, however, Nathan was the operational leader of the group. He presided over a policymaking executive committee that consisted of veteran ADA leaders and the representatives of prominent legislators and labor leaders too busy to attend. He supervised a National Director and a modest staff.[85]

More than a few believed that Nathan's influence might spur a new period of activism. Upon his taking over the executive committee *The Jewish Criterion* wrote that, "if it's adrenalin the ADA needs—and we suspect that it does—Mr. Nathan has it in abundance to give."[86] Certainly Nathan's energy as an organizer and advocate was put to good use. He began convening informal, off-the-record meetings with old and new colleagues on foreign policy and national affairs.[87] In some cases, his personal interests informed his policy positions—he wrote from Korea that the 1953 ADA platform should support "substantial relief and rehabilitation aid, given as fully as possible through UN agencies."[88]

But it was probably widely understood that the most valuable thing that Nathan brought to the ADA was his book of contacts. Within a week of taking over, Nathan lamented the "failure of the National Office to do a decent job of fund raising." He decided to establish a finance committee with a strong chairman. When no one volunteered for the job he took it himself.[89] In some respects it was a good fit. Nathan was an ace fundraiser, having gained years of experience selling Israeli bonds. He did so out of loyalty to the nation that he had done so much to help create certainly, but also because the compensation for his efforts added to the Nathan family finances. Soon the bond campaign was also helping underwrite ADA appearances.[90] On Nathan's seemingly ceaseless cross-country trips during 1953 and 1954, he sandwiched his official duties for the Israeli bond drive between ADA chapter luncheons and evening fundraisers at private homes. Fundraising and organizing were twin priorities and the best way to do both, Nathan knew, was to castigate the reactionaries.[91] A skeptical columnist commented on Nathan's late 1953 "tour for the ADA-ers whipping up political spirit." "He mixes politics with economics," wrote J. A. Livingston. "When he's right, he's very, very right, and when he's wrong, he's sensational."[92]

About communism the ADA was unambiguous. "We reject any association with Communists or sympathizers with communism in the United States as completely as we reject any association with Fascists or their sympathizers," read its statement of principles.[93] Because it refused to assume that communists were just "liberals in a hurry," the ADA came under fire from the left in the 1940s and 1950s, and from radical scholars in later decades. Average Americans on the center or right were just confused—it was difficult to understand in the seemingly black and white 1950s how a group could be against communism but for the civil liberties that communists seemed intent on hiding behind.

Joe Rauh had no such problem. By the 1950s the former Goon was building a career as the top crusading lawyer for the left. He had helped Hubert Humphrey put across the 1948 civil rights plank and represented the unfortunates hauled before the House of Representatives Un-American Activities Committee. Some, like playwright Lillian Hellman, who claimed not to "cut my conscience to fit this year's fashions," were celebrities. Others, like William Walter Remington, were not. It did not matter to Rauh. Nathan had had his encounter with anti-communist investigators years before when he was being considered for the NDAC, and although he considered the charges ridiculous he cooperated completely with investigators. Similarly, when the hapless Remington, who had married into a radical family and was purported to have given state secrets to a Communist Party member, was investigated by the FBI, Nathan cooperated fully, providing all the information that he could about the junior economist who had worked at both the WPB and the OWMR.[94]

Regardless, as the 1950s went on and the anti-communist crusade passed from HUAC to Joseph McCarthy, Nathan could only have been chagrined at the toll it took. Remington was convicted of perjury in 1953 and murdered in jail the next year. And the anti-communist crusade hit even closer to home. In 1948, friend, fellow economist, and first vice president of Nathan Associates Lauchlin Currie was charged by a friendly witness with being part of a Washington spy ring. Under suspicion, Currie moved to Latin America to do economic survey work. In 1953 his U.S. passport was not renewed and he retired to a ranch in Colombia. Nathan could not know that his friend had by then turned up as an informant in the decrypted Soviet Venona cables. He only knew that Currie was no communist and did not deserve what he got.[95]

In drawing his bright lines between "us and them," Joseph McCarthy made no such distinctions. To him, an ADA member might as well have been a member of the Politburo. For a while after launching his career with a February 1950 speech in Wheeling, West Virginia, McCarthy was a boon to the newspapers and blight only on the Senate. Nathan was always proud that the ADA had been among the first to consider him a national problem. The making of political hay out of anti-communism already seemed old and tired when McCarthy first appeared. When a committee under Maryland

Senator Millard Tydings sought to discredit him it seemed a sure thing—then McCarthy helped unseat Tydings in a dirty campaign. The Wisconsin senator's enemies were good allies, providing him with publicity and coining the term that forever linked his name with anti-communism. But his best friends were a group of Senate Republicans who supported his double-fisted anti-communist stances and appreciated the buoyancy his ever more destructive campaign gave their party. Elsewhere in Washington were a handful of opponents and a great deal of silence, particularly from President Eisenhower who refused to sully himself with the Senator. After the 1952 elections, McCarthy became far more dangerous when he was appointed Chairman of the Permanent Subcommittee on Investigations, a post that allowed him to act as inquisitor toward the Voice of America, the State Department, and even the Government Printing Office.[96]

By 1953, Nathan, who well understood the destruction that communists could sow, believed McCarthyism to be far worse: "the psychopathic hysteria which has taken hold of the American people," he called it.[97] In the summer of 1951, William Benton, a Democratic senator, ADA supporter and Nathan friend, introduced a resolution to consider expulsion proceedings against McCarthy for misuse of funds. McCarthy refused to cooperate and nothing was done. Benton was defeated in 1952, but that same year a subcommittee investigated the matter and produced a damning account. Some 1,500 copies were printed by the GPO and promptly disappeared—and no more could be printed unless McCarthy's backers approved.[98] The next April, ADA chairman Biddle and executive committee chairman Nathan sent a letter to Attorney General Herbert Brownell stating that the Department of Justice had the authority and duty to investigate the charges.[99] McCarthy lashed back that normally he would sue for libel but the "crowd of Communist defenders may even be doing me a favor." [100] The ADA dared him to sue.[101]

The names of Nathan and Biddle were all over the newspapers, and few of the mentions were favorable. A week later the ADA's second most prestigious founder after Eleanor Roosevelt, theologian Reinhold Niebuhr, praised the fight "so courageously led by Francis Biddle and Bob Nathan," and announced that the ADA would republish the Senate subcommittee report.[102] It was an expensive venture—most of the report consisted of documents, so the entire thing was reproduced photographically. But Nathan, who would ultimately have to raise the funds to pay for it, did not hesitate.[103] Nathan always remembered the ADA as playing a major role in the McCarthy fight, but outraged press releases and the reprinting of the report did not a campaign make. Working through another organization, Nathan and fellow liberals accomplished much more.

Maurice Rosenblatt, whose father was an economist, was himself a tireless and committed liberal. He was also a lobbyist who could get things done on Capitol Hill. He and Nathan would certainly have met in any case, but they also had a friend in common, the inimitable Matty Fox.[104]   In 1948, Rosenblatt cultivated yet another of the many "letterhead" groups that sprang from postwar liberal soil. The National Committee for an Effective Congress was much more modest than the ADA—its only goal was to assist the deserving with campaign funds. It helped out six legislators in 1948, five in 1950, and ten in 1952.[105] By then the group had grown tenfold, and Rosenblatt wished to do something more sustained, like take on McCarthy.[106] Rosenblatt routinely confided in Nathan. "If we can mobilize three thousand key people around the country to be informed and interested in Congress then this can be a profound and creative influence," he wrote in June 1952. He saw the challenge as helping people "understand the underlying struggle for domination."[107]

By November 1952, NCEC was preparing for its campaign. Not surprisingly, much of the fundraising fell to Nathan.[108] Before he left for Korea, he sent out a number of requests typed on his personal stationery by Ruth Aull at Thomas Circle.[109] In early 1953, Nathan, Rosenblatt, William Benton, and Kenneth Birkhead, a staffer for the Democratic Senate Campaign Committee, shaped the as-yet inchoate plans into a program.[110] Rosenblatt laid out the constitution of what came to be called "The Clearing House" in a 1,500-word memorandum to Nathan. The reason McCarthy was succeeding, he began, was due not to lack of opposition but to a lack of informed opposition in Congress—"there are vacuums which nobody is filling and McCarthy is exploiting," he wrote. McCarthy received abundant professional advice and assistance from the right wing press, he wrote, but liberals had no comparable advantage. "It is clear that we must start operating on the Hill," he concluded.[111] By May, the group included AVC member and *New Republic* editor Michael Straight and William Benton's attorney, Gerhard Van Arkel, among others.[112] They promulgated a statement of principles pledged to "contain and oppose McCarthyism at the source of its power—the Congress," and to "show that it is essentially not anti-communist but a radical movement aimed at destroying the foundations, liberal and conservative, of our democratic society."[113]

The group began meeting regularly, sometimes at headquarters established at Washington's Carroll Arms Hotel, sometimes at Van Arkel's residence, and often at Nathan's house.[114] They may have preferred Nathan's house since they hoped to keep the Clearing House as low-profile as possible. By June 1953, the Clearing House had hired assistant Lucille Lang Olshine and began stockpiling its principal weaponry—information. Jack Anderson contributed the files that he had collected to write a book on McCarthy, and Olshine compiled more. They began feeding facts to liberal senators and reporters.[115]

After McCarthy appointed Joseph Brown Matthews to head his committee staff, Olshine compiled a dossier detailing Matthews's strange career as a disillusioned radical who had raced to the right and now fingered the protestant clergy as communist supporters. At the same time, an article stating these unconventional—even for an anti-communist—views appeared in a major publication. Clergymen nationwide protested, Matthews resigned, and McCarthy suffered his first notable setback. The Clearing House also obtained material that kept Robert E. Lee, a close friend of McCarthy's and compiler of the enemies list that had launched his career, out of the FCC.[116]

Everything came together when at last McCarthy took on one target too many. For the hearings that pitted McCarthy against the U.S. Army, the Wisconsin Senator was forced to cede the chairmanship to Senator Carl Mundt. The hapless Mundt chose as Subcommittee Counsel Samuel Sears, a slavish supporter of McCarthy. Within hours, Nathan, likely tipped off by Olshine, protested on behalf of the ADA that Sears's record "disqualifies him on grounds of both ethics and objectivity."[117] Committee Democrats were furious at the deception and demanded an immediate resignation.[118]

In the spring of 1954, McCarthy's slide began. Edward R. Murrow aired an indictment in March. In early April, Nathan watched as McCarthy rebutted Murrow on television. "Some were frightened, others were confused and still others felt a growing sense of urgency to fight back," he wrote. "My own reactions were in the latter category."[119] One way the ADA fought back was to purchase and redistribute 35,000 copies of the magazine *The Progressive* detailing McCarthy's record.[120] McCarthy finally self-destructed on television on June 9, when the mild-mannered Army counsel Joseph Welch begged, "Have you no sense of decency, sir, at long last, have you left no sense of decency?"[121]

That has gone down in history as the moment of McCarthy's downfall, but at the time things were not so clear. Nathan did not believe that the Army-McCarthy hearings had accomplished much.[122] It was crucial, therefore, that the Clearing House support Senator Ralph Flanders who pressed for action against McCarthy directly afterwards. Having hired former Hill staffer Larry Henderson, the Clearing House launched what was originally dubbed "Operation Nut-Cutting." Perhaps thinking of posterity, someone renamed it "Operation Anti-McCommunism."[123]

While Olshine continued research and Henderson worked the Hill in support of the Flanders effort, Nathan went in search of funds, putting himself at risk for the cause. Insisting that "it would be criminal to allow the present situation to cool off," Nathan secured big donations on the West Coast from an insurance executive and on the East

Coast from organized labor.[124] By then the Clearing House had lost its anonymity. In July, McCarthy chief investigator Don Surine visited L. B. Nichols, the Assistant Director of the FBI, to inform him that the McCarthy forces intended to fight the Flanders initiative by attacking the ADA and the NCEC. Pointing out that "Robert Nathan is one of the active individuals," Surine raised a few bogus charges by which Nathan's reputation might be smeared. None were compelling and neither Nichols nor his superiors took the bait.[125] The next month, the *Chicago Tribune* publicly lashed out at Nathan.[126]

When it came to liberal fundraising, organized labor had the dollars. The McCarthy fight was tough because few of the rank and file cared much about the issue, although their leaders could be mobilized.[127] On July 7, Nathan chaired a luncheon at the Willard Hotel for 20 labor and liberal Washington insiders. Henderson explained what Flanders was trying to do. Rosenblatt gave a pep talk, and Nathan sent them to the Hill to exert what pressure they could. In early August, 67 senators supported the resolution to censure McCarthy. Congress approved the measure in December.[128] Nathan remained in NCEC for a few years longer, but ultimately it was fundraising that forced him to choose one organization or the other because contributors were confused as to whether they were giving to NCEC or the ADA. He resigned in 1962, proud of his efforts to the end.[129] "That was when we all worked together," he recalled late in life.[130]

FAMILY MAN OF THE FIFTIES

By the mid-1950s, the youthful "all-outer" who had been celebrated in World War II-era publications had noticeably matured. There was no bright red Pontiac zipping around Washington. Instead, Nathan carpooled most days when he was in town.[131] Since the spring of 1949, the Nathans had lived five miles north of Thomas Circle in a brand new cookie-cutter postwar residential neighborhood. The three bedroom house at 1419 Whittier Place was near Rock Creek Park and only a block from Walter Reed Hospital, a place Nathan knew well. The old back trouble had left a mark—he liked to say that marriage cured it, but the pain reappeared at times. Between the sore back and the challenge of carrying his big frame around, by mid-decade Nathan had a slight but perceptible stoop.[132] He also carried another burden from earlier days. Nathan wore conservative suits and ties—few would have recognized the tiny ADA button he wore on his lapel—but he was still recognized by businessmen who inevitably said, "oh, so you're the S.O.B. who wrote that report."[133]

As the 1950s unfolded, the Nathan family grew up in suburban Washington. A second son, Richard, was born in May 1950. Nathan was proud of his children and loved his family—judging from his travel journals, "missing the family at 1419" was the worst thing about working overseas.[134] He marveled like every young parent does. Missing Johnny on the third birthday of his eldest Nathan wrote, "he has become a real character in a hurry. It doesn't take long for them to blossom into distinctive personalities. Dick is right there too."[135] And when Nathan returned home, there was Mac the Scottish terrier to meet him in the driveway.[136]

Then, in March 1952, the Nathans shouldered the heaviest burden of all. At three years and two months, Johnny became ill. A surgeon at a modern hospital would likely have determined that he was suffering from an extremely rare congenital intestinal obstruction and removed it. But the family was vacationing in Key West, far away from expert medical care. By the time they headed back north, John Louis Nathan had died. He was buried in a private ceremony at a Falls Church, Virginia, memorial park. For months afterward Nathan relived that "tragic early morning departure" in his mind.[137] He remembered it as a "great sorrow whose pall did not lift for a number of years."[138] "I don't think he ever quite got over it" said one of his closest friends.[139]

The Nathans kept going and better news came. A daughter, Ann, was born in October 1953. Son David arrived in September three years later. The Nathans were also fortunate to have a more extended family for support. Whether intentionally or not, both Robert and Larry made adult careers in Washington, so they could continue the partnership established long ago. Mary was also close to Larry's wife Dee—both were gentiles in Jewish families, after all. When Nathan mentioned the family in his journals it was common for only a comma to intervene before Larry and Dee were mentioned as well. Nathan still found solace at sea. The family traded Key West for Kitty Hawk for a few years after the tragedy, but the fishing was never as good and the water never as clear. They finally returned in 1957.[140]

In Washington, Mary raised the children mostly by herself. By the time Nathan came home from work, the family housekeeper had fed them and put them to bed. Husband and wife usually had a late dinner together and then Nathan gathered his papers and, as Mary recalled, "he'd stay up late, working, working, working."[141] "I know it isn't fair to my family to be away so much, and for that reason every effort is made to spend Saturday and Sunday at home," he wrote a friend in 1955.[142] Although Nathan was a political outlier, culturally he was a mainstream American professional man. Weekend fatherhood was not merely sufficient, but appropriate.

Nathan did take a deep interest in his children's religious upbringing. Although he fondly remembered the family attachment to the Wyoming Street Synagogue back in Dayton, he had never in early adulthood been an observant Jew—he had no qualms about Mary's unapologetic atheism.[143] But he insisted that she take the children to temple, so the Nathans joined the Rauhs at Washington's Temple Sinai Reform Jewish Synagogue.[144] As Nathan grew older he did begin to more closely embrace Judaism. There was always a political angle of course—not only was Nathan a leading backer of the Israeli state, he and Larry were also members of the Maryland-District of Columbia Chapter of B'nai B'rith Anti-Defamation league. Nathan had a seat on the group's executive committee by the end of the decade.[145]

Nathan clearly was concerned with the economic and political aspirations of the Jewish people, but when Mary asked him why he believed in God he dismissed the question with a flip reply: "Because Arthur Goldberg does."[146] Goldberg, a Temple Sinai member and liberal labor lawyer who eventually sat on the Supreme Court, was an exemplary man, but what really lay in Robert Nathan's spiritual depths, no one ever knew.

If there was a key to Nathan's personal success, whether in government, business, or liberal advocacy, it was an enthusiastic embrace of company. He collected people so he could talk to them—he enjoyed nothing more than "after dinner sessions of six to ten persons who can have a pleasant evening of good and interesting talk."[147] Some, like Joe Rauh and Arthur Goldberg, helped advance his causes or career and made headlines from time to time just as he did. Like Nathan, they were comfortable surrounded by gold leaf, burnished walnut, and grave deliberations at Washington's prestigious Cosmos Club.[148] His closest friends, though, were less celebrated Washingtonians like Howard Grieves and Maxwell Conklin, old friends from the Census Bureau with whom the Nathans owned a cabin on the Chesapeake Bay.[149]

With weekends at the shore, a mother raising a house full of young children, and a father dutifully serving on the Home and School Association (the local version of the PTA), the Nathans might have appeared to the neighbors an unexceptional postwar professional family.[150] They could hardly have known about the late night strategy sessions on their block aimed at unseating Joe McCarthy. But there could be no mistaking something exceptional going on when, early one July morning in 1955, the Secret Service cordoned off Whittier Place and a fleet of seventeen dignitaries arrived in the company of the Prime Minister of Burma, stopping by for breakfast. Sleepy two-year-old Ann rubbed her eyes, but five-year-old Dick was more impressed by the Secret Service agents than the dignitaries they were protecting. Mary demonstrated the washer and dryer in the basement to Mrs. U Nu.[151]

Robert Nathan had unusual, even extraordinary, associations, but as a family man of the 1950s he was entirely conventional. He was moderate in his habits and more comfortable in his skin than he had been at a younger age. The Nathan that comes through in the 1950s correspondence and journal entries is not the personality depicted in the World

War II-era articles. He was no longer inclined to speed about Washington in a convertible. The classical records he collected in the 1940s went missing a decade later—he was among the least musical of men.[152] It was claimed that he was a teetotaler during the war—he most definitely was not afterward. He favored Scotch on the rocks but seldom drank to excess—when he did he was far from home.[153] His real vice was profanity. Four letter words were remarkably prevalent in private conversation, although Nathan managed to employ them in public only for effect. He also tried from time to time to keep his smoking under control—mostly cigarettes now, sometimes cigars.[154] The fact that Nathan no longer affected a pipe suggests that having attained a comfortable persona with time and maturity, he no longer felt the need to cultivate an exaggerated one.

Deep sea fishing was the stuff of legend, but Nathan's second favorite pastime was decidedly pedestrian: he was a numismatist. It is a hobby that comes naturally to paperboys who handle a lot of change, and in later years Nathan's overseas travels turned his interest from domestic to foreign coins.[155] Nathan also read good books—Hemingway, Tolstoy, Eliot, Kafka, and Orwell (he read *Burmese Days* on his way to Rangoon) among them.[156] Mary Nathan did not know that her husband was a reader of literature, perhaps because Nathan read not compulsively or reflectively, but dutifully in quest of self-improvement, and mostly when time dragged in airplanes and far-off hotels—at home in Washington it never did.

There were other things Mary never knew about her husband's endeavors. It was not, at the time, expected that husbands would share professional concerns with their spouses. In a way, he did not even share them with himself for he was a master at compartmentalization, able to fully immerse at will in whatever demanded his attention at the moment. As he wrote in his journal in characteristic Nathanese, "usually I'm able to finish up a job or any major division thereof and go on to something else without carrying over too many persistent thoughts of the former."[157]

LEARNING FROM ODDS AND ENDS

Nathan's ability to compartmentalize became essential as he built up a diversity of domestic contracts. He realized that his company was overly dependent on the Burma project. A few more like it might have helped, but the Burmese project was unusual—it was more common for American development professionals to report to the U.S. government than to the host country. Any chance that Nathan would win similar contracts ended abruptly in January 1953 with the changing of the guard in Washington. In the Eisenhower administration the Technical Cooperation Administration was transformed into the International Cooperation Administration under the direction of Minnesota

Republican partisan Harold Stassen.[158] The illegal, and thus unofficial, policy of Stassen's ICA was no contracts for liberals.

The Nathan firm was among those summarily "Stassinated."[159] In checking Nathan's file in 1955, the FBI tried to determine why he was "persona non grata with Governor Stassen." He had passed a 1951 security check easily—what was different this time?[160] Stassen's assistant cited the bitter criticisms of former OWMR Director John Snyder, to date the only negative testimony in an expanding FBI dossier.[161] During the years of Democratic exile, therefore, the firm scrambled for domestic clients and what Nathan later called "odd and end" contracts, learning much along the way about putting economic consulting to work for paying clientele.

If Nathan Associates was going to specialize, the obvious alternative to international development was labor economics. It had, of course, been Nathan's first choice, and although he remained personally involved—lecturing at union institutes, debating at labor conferences, and manning the radio microphone for the CIO through 1953—work for his consulting firm was hard to get.[162] This was proved again in 1954 when Nathan pitched a "financial advisory program" to unions that did not get even as far as his "labor letter" project.[163]

A more promising prospect was the loose affiliation of unions called the "Railroad Brotherhoods." Edward Hickey had been a fellow student at Georgetown Law and general counsel to the Brotherhoods. As wage negotiations approached in late 1953 he asked Nathan to help prepare testimony for the negotiations and government fact-finding boards expected to follow.[164] "It gets us back into the labor fold," Nathan wrote to Walinsky.[165] But by the 1950s the railroads were in a noticeable decline brought about by the rise of trucking, the collapse of the passenger business, and a perverse regulatory regime. The Brotherhoods settled quickly, which kept the firm's earnings down. Lacking the "good inside track" he had hoped for, Nathan was not above working for the opposition. In 1955 he provided a study and testimony for New York State trucking companies hard hit by a railroad-sponsored ton-mile tax.[166]

The United Steelworkers Union was Nathan's most reliable labor client—until Phil Murray died in 1952. Murray's successor, David McDonald, was a vainglorious man and barely a liberal by Nathan's standards. Nathan nevertheless was always willing to come to Pittsburgh, where he worked mostly with USW general counsel Arthur Goldberg.[167] Nathan prepared yet another industry study for the mid-1956 labor negotiations, although he had only two weeks to do so and there were recriminations about compensation afterwards.[168]

Nathan's last chance to help make labor history came when the firm assisted in a landmark 119-day steel strike. The Taft-Hartley Act empowered the Eisenhower

Administration to force the workers back into the mills through injunction. Nathan's economic brief demonstrated that there was no national security justification for the move, but it was Goldberg's argument that the Taft-Hartley Act was unconstitutional that took the case to the Supreme Court.[169] The injunction held, but the four-month strike marked the moment at which the U.S. steel industry began losing out to foreign competition. Nathan and Goldberg matched briefs again in 1958 when the New York City Transit Workers Union attempted to prevent a Consolidated Edison takeover of transit generating plants. This time, however, neither Nathan's economic brief nor Goldberg's legal brief gained traction.[170]

Some efforts to land new business got Nathan into trouble with old friends in labor. David Dubinsky of the International Ladies Garment Workers Union was particularly unhappy about work that Nathan Associates did for the Commonwealth of Puerto Rico.[171] In 1948 the Commonwealth, with U.S. funding, launched a comprehensive economic development effort. "Operation Bootstrap" was intended to convert a backward agricultural economy into a modern industrial one. The problem was that wages in Puerto Rico averaged about a fifth of what they did on the mainland; employers could not afford to pay their industrial workers on parity with U.S. firms.

The Puerto Rican government got an exemption to the Fair Labor Standards Act and the unions cried foul. That left Congress with the task of brokering industrial growth in Puerto Rico without creating unfair wage competition for mainland employers. The Senate and House returned to this issue regularly during the 1950s. Nathan Associates helped the Puerto Rican government prepare exhibits, provided testimony supporting continued exemptions for a wide variety of industries, and published a 428-page report, *Evaluation of Minimum Wage Policy in Puerto Rico*, in 1955. That publication led to further assignments including a survey of the trucking industry and a study of manufacturing industries in Puerto Rico.[172]

As a result of his work for long-time client O. Roy Chalk, Nathan found himself not just at odds with labor but on the opposite side of the table. At mid-decade Chalk diversified beyond airlines with the purchase of Washington's transit system. Nathan Associates undertook a number of projects for D.C. Transit, making the economic case for a new limousine service from Washington to New York, supporting an application to launch a tourist line in downtown Washington, and even planning management conferences at West Virginia's posh Greenbrier Resort.[173] When, in 1956, Chalk pulled Nathan into labor negotiations on the side of D.C. Transit, Nathan insisted that he had acted only as a mediator.[174] But the fact was that Nathan was learning how to run a business—providing services that his clients required, regardless of ideological complications.

One of Nathan's other long-term clients was the Commercial Metals Company, a recycling and steel brokerage firm in Texas. The company relied on Nathan Associates mostly for regulatory advice and assistance in handling its import and export business. Sid Lerner had done the work before joining Commercial Metals himself in 1951.[175] After that Maurice Atkin took over.[176] Atkin worked for the Department of Agriculture during the 1940s on agricultural marketing programs. He knew Nathan through membership in the AVC and work for Palestine—Atkin was deeply involved in the underground movement to funnel arms to Palestinian Jews and even worked for a time at the Israeli Embassy. When Atkin's application for a State Department job got snarled in red tape, Nathan offered him a job instead.[177]

In addition to taking over the Commercial Metals work, Atkin provided advice and assistance on the Hill to Israel. By the end of the decade much of Atkin's time was spent helping clients qualify for the Food for Peace Program, also known as PL (Public Law) 480. The program was intended to make surplus U.S. agricultural products available to developing countries on very good terms, helping provide foreign exchange and drawing the recipients more tightly to the United States. Atkin spent a great deal of time working to get Israel qualified under the program, finally succeeding in the 1960s.[178] The work for Israel kept Atkin and an occasional other consultant employed. But they were neither economic studies nor a "meaningful part of the total revenues," so Nathan never took much interest in the trade-related tasks.[179]

Perhaps because so much of Nathan's business came from personal contacts, and because so many of these were made through his work on behalf of Palestine, there was a pronounced Jewish component in the firm's client base of the 1950s. Commercial Metals, for example, was run by Jacob Feldman, a big contributor to the Israeli Public Affairs Committee.[180] After Henry Montor, former chairman of the United Jewish Appeal and driving force behind the Israeli Bond campaign, established himself as a stockbroker, he hired Nathan to do a study of the growth—and thus investment potential—of the cement industry. This led to the unusual presence of tombstone ads featuring Robert Nathan's name in the financial pages of papers like the *Wall Street Journal*.[181]

The labor and PL 480 work gave Nathan Associates the opportunity to work on the fringes of administrative law, the body of rules that govern the regulation of the economy by federal agencies. Nathan got directly involved in the transportation realm. By the end of World War II, trucking, shipping, and aviation were all tightly regulated. In order to stop cutthroat competition the right to establish new routes was circumscribed. The best way for a newcomer to get into the transportation business was to purchase an existing route. To establish a new one, companies had to obtain a "certificate of public convenience and necessity" from the appropriate regulator.[182]

The Civil Aeronautics Board (CAB), like the other regulatory agencies, favored established operators. It was not receptive when a group of veteran aviators who had "flown the Hump" into China during World War II started a company called North American Airlines and applied to offer low cost non-scheduled service between U.S. cities.[183] The CAB's director was former Democratic Senator Joseph O'Mahoney, who had run the TNEC investigation, during which Nathan first experienced the "cut and thrust" of political wrangling. By 1953, Nathan Associates had been pulled into the case on behalf of North American. The firm began with an industry survey demonstrating that even if the big scheduled airlines tripled their service volume, there would still be room for new entrants. The survey was submitted to the CAB in June 1953.[184]

This was a big contract for Nathan Associates. With the general survey done, the firm agreed to provide support for all of North American's individual route applications. The firm—and often Nathan himself—testified in direct and cross examination as to the public convenience and necessity of each application. The economic analysis was tough and the testimony likely tougher, so Nathan brought in Franz Wolf, an economist with a doctorate from the University of Freiburg.[185] Although he had been in the United States with the Korean War-era Office of Price Stabilization, his German accent was strong. What Atkin described as a "permanent blue smoke screen" created by his ever-present pipe was even stronger.[186]

There were similar projects for shipping companies. Wolf remained to conduct a study for Zim Shipping, a commercial line that grew out of the Jewish postwar exodus from Europe.[187] Nathan himself testified before the Federal Maritime Board on behalf of Lykes Brothers and American Export Lines.[188] In 1959, Nathan Associates compiled an 81-page report and testified for American Banner Line, which hoped to establish a new tourist route to Europe. Nathan stated that there was sufficient capacity for the service and predicted that the airlines would not cut into sea travel—although he himself always flew.[189] By then, the firm had made the jump from administrative law into the judicial system, working in some cases directly for law firms as expert witnesses. "Frankly," Nathan confided to a lawyer friend, "I like the economic work better than law and that accounts for the fact that only occasionally do I work on a law case."[190]

The firm developed a surprising expertise in sports-related studies during the late 1950s. In 1958, Nathan Associates conducted a feasibility study for the New Latonia Race Track in Northern Kentucky. The next year the firm looked at the economic performance and potential of the venerable Churchill Downs in Louisville.[191] There was also an extended effort for the City of Philadelphia. What appears to have begun as an examination of financing options for a new sports stadium ended up as a full-scale study weighing the benefits of a new stadium in South Philadelphia versus a move to Camden, New Jersey.[192] Done in conjunction with an architect-engineering firm, the 1959 report found both options viable but underscored the resentments that would result from the Phillies moving to New Jersey.[193] A big weakness of the Philadelphia proposal that had to be overcome, the study pointed out, was the prohibition of beer sales at city sporting events. Philadelphia "seemed to be very satisfied with the project," Nathan remarked, but no decision was made for years.[194] When Veterans Stadium finally opened in South Philadelphia in 1971, beer was available.

Nathan was good at catching details for his clients, but tended to let them slip for his own business. It was tough figuring out what to charge. Atkin recalled that through the end of the decade the company's pricing was determined by the answer to the question "what might the client afford?"[195] Louis Walinsky had hoped that the North American Airlines contract might be a lucrative one or at least that "for a change we might make some money on one of these damn jobs."[196] It was not to be, most likely because Nathan— whose billing rate was very high—did a great deal of the work on the long and complex project himself. He confided to Walinsky in late 1953 that the North American contract was "going to turn out to be the biggest loss job which we have ever had."[197]

Personnel policies were similarly informal. Atkin signed on in 1951 with nothing but a handshake.[198] Walinsky spent several years in Burma with no firm agreement about what his final compensation would be.[199] That Walinsky would allow that to happen is as much a testament to Nathan's generosity as to his managerial indifference. Indeed, Nathan was apt to be liberal with bonuses during the good years, which included most of the 1950s, thanks to Burma.[200] Nathan was especially benevolent at his annual Christmas "open house" events, which were attended by scores of legislators, jurists, journalists, and liberal activists—and some employees as well.[201]

Nathan could be as generous as he wished and put his office at the disposal of the ADA and other good causes because throughout the decade the firm belonged to him alone. During the 1950s, shareholder meetings were held in the Wilmington offices of the Corporation Guarantee & Trust Company, where a lawyer voted Nathan's 50 shares by proxy.[202] The Board of Directors met regularly at Thomas Circle but its initiatives were purely pro forma. In 1950, Maury Atkin replaced Sid Lerner as Secretary-Treasurer, and through the decade the board consisted of Atkin, Robert Nathan, and Larry Nathan.

If Nathan did not worry unduly about corporate democracy in those days, he did stress accountability and review. On Monday mornings when he was in town, the entire company convened and project leaders took turns reviewing their work and waiting for the boss to weigh in. He had "an innate sense and feel about these individual projects," recalled Atkin, and "he always asked the right and the tough questions." Nathan was usually wise enough to let minor worries go, but if an issue came up in a project that he cared about, he was sure to have much to say, expletives included.[203]

Although Nathan's tough front could be hard to take, most people understood that his strong words stemmed from strong convictions. For there was nothing casual about working at Nathan Associates, where even the water cooler talk revolved around politics and economics. Atkin made hundreds of commutes with Nathan over the years. "I don't think we ever talked about a football game or a baseball game," he recalled.[204]

"RESTLESS LIBERALS"

In 1955, Nathan intended to serve only one more year as chairman of the ADA executive committee. "Indefinite tenure is not conducive to the greatest vigor either for the officer or the organization," he wrote.[205] By then, both Nathan and Joe Rauh—dubbed "Mr. ADA" by the *New York Post*—were dedicating much of their free time to the group. "Bob and I are partners in this ADA venture," Rauh wrote Walter Reuther.[206] As Rauh's 1956 term as chairman expired, he and Nathan tried to convince a young Congressman named Eugene McCarthy to accept the job. He refused.[207]

After that it was not hard to convince Nathan to take it—he seldom turned down a post in a good cause.[208] In his acceptance speech at the March 1957 ADA Convention Nathan backed a program that would "utilize more fully and effectively America's great material and spiritual resources," and vowed to "unilaterally oppose the coalition of isolationists, reactionaries and penny-wise pound foolish economizers who would destroy our foreign aid program."[209] One could say it was a professional move, but there could be no mistaking a genuine sense of mission. In a piece contributed to the 1956 ADA voter's guide Nathan lauded the nation's rising standard of living but lamented that it had not been "shared by all"—the old, the sick, those from broken homes and depressed areas. "The tragic point is that it lies well within the country's means to help them."[210]

In June 1957, Senator Hubert Humphrey hosted a party to let Washington liberals know that henceforth Nathan would be "Mr. ADA."[211] Nathan Associates also became part of the ADA apparatus: reports to Nathan in the field usually detailed not only what was going on at Nathan Associates, but also what was up in the ADA.[212] Nathan also put in time at the ADA office just south of Dupont Circle on Connecticut Avenue. He had a good staff there, including Edward Hollander, who was one of Washington's most committed liberal activists. During the war he was president of the local Union for Democratic Action chapter and afterwards became a charter member of the ADA.[213] In 1953, Nathan convinced him to give up his post in the Department of Labor to become ADA National Director.[214]

Nathan and Joe Rauh at Ninth Convention of ADA, May 11, 1956.
(© The Associated Press)

Hollander became invaluable to the organization. He was among the few to write speeches and press releases for Nathan, and on rare occasions critiqued Nathan's own writing.[215] He was also unusually forthright with Nathan about ADA prospects. In 1954, the ADA had to cut its expensive organizing staff. Nathan and Rauh tried to make it up by frequenting the chapters and shoring them up, but it was not enough. "It's inescapable that we have lost our organizational dynamic," Hollander informed Nathan in 1955.[216]

The ADA's biggest problem, however, was a complex identity crisis. For one thing, the organization was in practice Democratic—for every congressional Republican it backed 20 Democrats—but the group put a great deal of effort into appearing to be officially non-partisan.[217] In the summer of 1957, Honorary Chairman Eleanor Roosevelt urged Nathan and Rauh to reconsider. "Unless we are in the party we cannot do the work that needs to be done to aid the parties," she wrote.[218] Then there were those who argued that the ADA should drop short-term politics for long-term education like the Fabian Society, which had laid the groundwork for Britain's social democracy, rather than engage in day-to-day partisanship.[219]

Then there was ADA economics. In an August 1957 *New York Times* piece, former ADA co-chairman Arthur Schlesinger criticized liberal preoccupation with anti-depression measures that now seemed dated. He suggested replacing "quantitative liberalism" with "qualitative liberalism dedicated to bettering the quality of people's lives and opportunities." Schlesinger was astute as usual, identifying themes that would gain resonance in the 1960s, but he was also swiping at Nathan and Leon Keyserling, guardians of the old-time economic religion, and Hollander was furious.[220] John Kenneth Galbraith piled on with his 1958 bestseller, *The Affluent Society*, which questioned the wisdom of obsessing over abundance and neglecting "social balance."[221]

ADA National Director Ed Hollander in April 1954.
(Wisconsin Historical Society, WHS- 99110)

Nathan was not an intellectual on par with Schlesinger and Galbraith. He was a manipulator of signs and symbols that usually stood for concrete things rather than abstractions. He stuck to practical matters and let others debate the ADA's identity crisis.

And the most practical issue of all was pressing—money. The McCarthy years brought steady increases in the ADA rolls, but the fight was expensive, and left the organization $30,000 in debt by the time the Army-McCarthy hearings closed.[222] The big problem was labor. As New Deal scarcity gave way to Eisenhower abundance, a new generation of leaders took office. They rejected new crusades, seeking better wages and working conditions within the federal administrative apparatus that the old battles had made possible.[223] The United Steelworkers Union under Phil Murray gave the ADA $12,000 every year. That stopped under David McDonald.[224] Walter Reuther's UAW remained steadfast, but smaller unions also scaled back their contributions, cutting total receipts from labor by half. The ADA never managed to offset the loss of those big donations with small contributions, although Nathan tried.[225]

There is something about the cash nexus, especially fundraising, that makes liberals squeamish. After bungling one meeting, Rauh admitted to Nathan that "I probably shouldn't go talk to large contributors without you around."[226] Nathan was an effective fundraiser for several reasons: he had a big book of contacts left from the Palestine campaigns; he had the entrepreneurial ability that most liberals lacked; and he was not ashamed to talk bluntly about money.[227] When he returned from overseas in August 1954, Nathan found the ADA in debt for $34,000. He declared a crisis and activated the national finance committee. No one would agree to direct it so he did.[228] Next he asked everyone on the executive committee to raise $500. "I have no talents as a fund raiser," Arthur Schlesinger wrote in refusal.[229] By the end of the year Nathan was doing little but fundraising. "I fear my effectiveness as chairman of the executive committee is being seriously impaired," he confided to Rauh.[230]

But Nathan could never raise enough. By the summer of 1956, the organization was four issues late paying for the printing of its newsletter, *ADA World*.[231] In November 1957 there was not enough cash to cover payroll. Nathan went hat-in-hand to his top contributors.[232] It was perhaps ironic that a handful of wealthy New Yorkers had to save the organization that scores of earnest liberals would not support. The former included Marshall Field, Mary Lasker, and Mrs. David Levy—all Nathan confidantes.[233] In December 1957, another New Yorker, executive committee chairman Marvin Rosenberg, informed Nathan that he was going to have to serve another term as ADA Chairman. "At the present time you are the only one who can do the job adequately," he said, with finances likely uppermost in his mind.[234]

Regardless, the ADA remained in perilous financial condition. By 1959 Hollander was desperate. He had tried to drum up enthusiasm with attacks on the heir apparent to the Republican presidency but to no avail. "ADA has been steadily declining for the past five years" Hollander wrote Nathan. Liberals had hated McCarthy as an organization, he observed, but they tended to hate Nixon on their own.[235] This suggests that beyond its identity crisis and financial shortfalls, the ADA's biggest problem was that it had no positive agenda.

During the Eisenhower years, the organization sounded less like a voice in the wilderness and more like a tiresome scold. It started in the McCarthy years. Afterward, Democrats hoping to tap into the decade's conservative consensus would have preferred the ADA to whisper rather than to shout.[236] Presidential hopeful Averell Harriman refused to speak to ADA audiences and the Democratic National Committee chairman ventured that "we can get along without it all right."[237]

Neither Rauh nor Nathan were inclined to moderation. Nathan promised as chairman "to give voice and effect to the country's restless liberals."[238] His voice was heard on Capitol Hill. From March 1950 to March 1960 Nathan testified before Congress 26 times, usually on behalf of the ADA. These sessions were not always pleasant, Nathan admitted, as legislators were often "provoked by the nature of ADA and the uncompromising position we often take."[239]

The ADA also worked behind the scenes on Capitol Hill. Legislative director John Gunther did most of that work before resigning in 1958. The biggest accomplishment under Nathan's watch came during the passage of the 1957 Civil Rights Act, one of the first, and not entirely successful, skirmishes in the battle between southern conservatives and northern liberals for the heart and soul of the Democratic Party.[240] In retrospect, it appears that Senate Majority leader Lyndon Johnson did a masterful job getting any bill at all through Congress, but that is not how Nathan saw it at the time. He claimed that the ADA should get credit for "what was left of the bill" when Johnson was done with it.[241] After Eisenhower enforced the law by sending soldiers into Little Rock, Nathan sent a telegram to the president supporting his stand.[242]

The ADA's active participation in the Civil Rights Act was exceptional, however. Most often the organization's engagement with the public came through the press. Hollander worked hard to make ADA press releases newsworthy by highlighting the "verbal pyrotechnics" in Nathan's speeches. Hollander worried that it made the ADA sound shrill—it did—but he believed that he had little alternative, and Nathan could always be counted upon for rhetorical fireworks.[243]

Early on, Nathan took issue with Eisenhower's overall conservatism. He warned that the General had been co-opted by business and congressional conservatives and criticized appointees like Charles E. Wilson of General Motors, who famously told Congress, "I thought what was good for our country was good for General Motors, and vice versa."[244]

In 1953, as economic complacency seemed to set in, Nathan urged citizens to remember that "whatever the prospects, the government does have the power in the tax, spending and credit fields to prevent extreme movements up or down."[245]

Testifying before a Senate committee on campaign contributions, October 8, 1956, Nathan shows off recent ADA publications. On his lapel is a Stevenson/Kefauver campaign button. (© The Associated Press)

The ADA promoted nuclear disarmament and normalization of relations with Red China late in the decade, but was otherwise in agreement with the Eisenhower administration on foreign policy.[246] Not surprisingly, however, Nathan differed on foreign aid. In 1955 the ADA put out a pamphlet and program called *Partnership for Freedom,* which promoted foreign aid as a means to combat communism. Written largely by Haldore Hanson, a former "China hand" who had been tarred by baseless McCarthy charges and then "Stassinated," the program echoed Nathan's warnings that the United States must not let the Soviets co-opt foreign aid.[247] "We don't sell our ideas as revolutionary and we don't have the zeal and fanatic and evangelistic spirit to lead the tide," he lamented in 1952.[248] Three years later, in defending *Partnership for Freedom,* Nathan assured Congress that "when it comes to the know-how and capital for economic growth, the U.S. holds the trumps. Gentlemen, this is our dish."[249]

It is difficult to tell whether the ADA was distressed or delighted as the economic picture darkened in late 1957. Keynesians were ready to charge in with a tax cut, but economists surrounding Eisenhower worried more about inflation, so no cut was forthcoming.[250]   In early 1958, Nathan insisted on behalf of the ADA that "what we need immediately is an unbalanced budget."[251]   Then David McDonald, likely briefed by Nathan, met with the president and presented a stimulus program. "I guess I'm just too stubborn to act fast until all the facts are in," Eisenhower replied.[252] Nathan scorned what he characterized as the idea that "the only way to fight inflation is through unemployment and recessions and depressions."[253] The ADA countered with a Full Employment Commission, staffed by Nathan, Leon Keyserling, and Harvard economist Arnold Soloway. The result was a ten-point program, with top priorities of lower and middle class tax cuts, liberalization of unemployment benefits, and acceleration of public works.[254]

Nathan's chief contribution to the 1958 congressional election cycle was a strong stock speech offering Little Rock, Sputnik, and recession as evidence of Republican failures.[255] When the off-year election yielded a new crop of liberals, the ADA was ready with a program of legislative priorities entitled, "A New New Deal for the 1960s."[256] In his last report as National Chairman, delivered at the May 1959 convention, Nathan claimed that the ADA was "organizationally good and politically fruitful." "Even if progress at times seems slow, the outlook is encouraging," said Nathan. "The next year will be decisive."[257]

Nathan was abroad in the weeks before the convention. In his absence the organization's leaders decided to thank Nathan for "all he has done to sustain and inspire ADA over the years." "We came up with the notion that the thing dearest to Bob is his association with people," Rauh recalled, so they solicited letters from influential friends ranging from Abba Eban to U Nu, varnished them onto a Japanese shoji screen, and presented it to him at a May 9 banquet.[258] The group also raised funds for the "Robert R. Nathan Educational Fund of ADA"—although without him doing the fundraising they do not appear to have been very successful.[259]

Nathan's colleagues acknowledged the heavy price that he had paid to keep the organization going. "I suspect that most of us could live comfortably on what ADA has cost you in terms of dollars and cents," wrote James Loeb, who had helped start it all back in 1947.[260] They also understood that it had been an accomplishment just to keep the liberal group going during the wilderness years. "When I was first a member I used to be surprised from year to year to find that we still existed," wrote Harvard political scientist Samuel Beer. "I am convinced now that we are indestructible."[261] But typically, Nathan allowed himself to be importuned one last time. Beer agreed take over as chairman—but only after the November elections. Rauh broke the news that Nathan would have to serve a few extra months while he was overseas. "If Mary doesn't shoot you, we could at least have a telephone conversation," he wrote.[262]

LAST YEARS IN BURMA

In mid-July 1954, the Nathans were on a well-deserved vacation in Vermont when the Burmese government called the office. The office found Nathan. It was a message from U Nu. Nathan was wanted in Burma immediately for "high policy decisions."[263] Nathan was not happy, but U Nu was, after all, the client. He changed his plans.

U Nu really was the client. Under the original contract, the development team reported to Burma but was paid by the U.S. Economic Cooperation Administration. In 1953, after Nationalist Chinese forces made incursions into northern Burma that U Nu thought the Americans should have stopped, he terminated the ECA agreement and contracted with Nathan and the engineering firms separately.[264]

That was perhaps the Burmese government's most decisive action when it came to development. The team led by Everett Hagen had run into a number of obstacles during the first two years of the original contract. One was common in developing countries: the Americans were assumed to be able to effect change with little help from the host country. As Hagen put it, "no political official soiled his hands and none who headed any operating agency felt responsibility for its performance."[265] Nathan believed that since these officials were essentially functionaries, "there was little incentive to exercise initiative."[266] "The lack of managerial and entrepreneurial talent and enterprise is serious," he wrote in 1952.[267]

Another problem was Burma's commitment to socialism. That meant that private enterprise, the most constructive tool in a development economist's toolkit, was suspect. Without government support, Burmese businessmen were reluctant to risk anything.[268] The team convinced the government that it had nothing to fear from small business, reasoning, as Nathan recalled, that "everybody loves children, and children can't do you much harm."[269] Nathan later credited these small business initiatives with doubling Burma's industrial output from 1953 to 1957.[270] It was more difficult to get much performance out of the big state-run enterprises upon which Burma had staked its future. Even if the responsible officials had been interested in running them, few were competent to do so.[271]

All of this left Hagen disillusioned. He was also too much the academic to be a good team leader. Hagen was, remarked Nathan, "a bit deep for the others."[272] After two years Hagen returned to academia to take up a new subject—the cultural factors that discourage development. The timing was good because the task ahead was less big thinking—that had all gone into the comprehensive report—than "keeping a sense of perspective," as Nathan put it, and maintaining control of the details: monitoring the economic indicators diligently, adjusting the program accordingly, and most important, keeping foreign exchange reserves up so that everything could be paid for.[273]

In 1953, as Hagen prepared to leave, Louis Walinsky arrived. He faced an exceptional task but Walinsky was an exceptional man. The son of a labor leader and an artist, he had studied economics at Cornell and done graduate work in Berlin. Walinsky had served on both the WPB and its successor agency. He had probably inherited a penchant for public service from his father. In the late 1940s he worked in European refugee camps, rehabilitating and training displaced persons. He joined Nathan Associates in 1950.[274] Besides his professional experience, there were other things to recommend Walinsky. He was active in the ADA, serving on the executive committee before Nathan did, and even testifying before Congress on its behalf.[275]

Under Walinsky, the Burma project made an effective new start. Three new economists joined the team in the fall of 1953.[276] Three even more distinguished professionals came in 1954. Philip Locklin specialized in transportation, Richard Musgrave in public finance, and Irving Swerdlow in public administration.[277] Also a former WPB economist, Swerdlow became Walinsky's second in command as the project progressed. If there was a hot seat on the staff, it was filled by agricultural economist Shig Takehashi. Because rice exports would generate the needed foreign exchange, they were key to the Burmese development program.[278] "The whole thing swings on rice sales," Walinsky wrote.[279]

When Nathan visited in February 1954, he claimed to see "very considerable progress." Inflation was low, rice prices were high, and the team was engaged in a host of studies covering financial controls, tariffs, national income, and foreign exchange.[280] True, the big industrial projects had been grounds for at least one "long and bitter session" between Nathan and Burmese government officials, but in general the Burmese had been moderate in their goals.[281]

But in the summer of 1954, it was a new ambitious agenda that took Nathan away from his vacation. Nathan had actually been discouraged by the modesty of the Burmese goals—they seemed more targeted at inflation or depression than calibrated to economic expansion. Now it had all turned around. With economic signs good, the ministries were suddenly ambitious—overly so Nathan believed. It reminded him of the shift on the part of the armed services that had touched off the feasibility dispute more than a decade earlier. Nathan settled into the Rangoon office and began reviewing the records in search of "ambitious but feasible goals."[282] The staff universally thought the Burmese goals too high. Nathan was less worried about the goals than the data behind them—it seemed shaky.[283]

Nathan's visits abroad were tiring—"enervating," as Nathan often put it—in part because of an endless round of obligatory dinner parties, many in black tie.[284] His summer 1954 trip brought more of the same but also something new. U Nu asked Nathan to purchase traditional Burmese garb and promised to reimburse him as a gift. Nathan did so. Near the conclusion of the trip he breakfasted at the Prime Minister's house in his longyi and gaung baung, and U Nu took to calling him "U Nathan."[285] Nathan generally tried to keep a low profile, but a short time later, also at U Nu's request, Nathan gave a press conference announcing the new goals. It was easy to be optimistic at such moments. As he prepared to leave Rangoon Nathan remarked that "we really made an impact at the very top," although he also reminded himself that "it is their country." "We can only help and support. We can't lead or guide."[286]

In 1954, U Nu gave Nathan a Burmese outfit as a gift. He wore it at a working breakfast with the Prime Minister on August 20. From left: Walinsky, labor economist Saul Nelson of the Nathan staff, Nathan, U Nu, KTA official Edward K. Bryant, and Hla Maung.

Burma badly needed guidance. Only weeks later, inflation began to rise as government spending pumped funds into an economy offering too few goods. Within six months there were also big problems in the rice market. Prices had begun declining as early as 1953, but Takehashi was confident that they would recover.[287] By 1955, however, both the United States and Burma were running big surpluses—the competition drove prices down and raised resentments.[288] "It is natural for the Burmese to feel that the U.S. is inclined to sacrifice the well-being or even independence of Burma for its own selfish interests," wrote the *Burmese Review and Monday New Times.*[289]

By the time Nathan returned to Burma in 1955, foreign exchange was only half of what it had been two years earlier.[290]   The combination of the expanding program and contracting rice receipts had left the government, in Nathan's words, "panicky." Nathan urged more efficient operations and "modest curtailments," but the Burmese were talking retrenchment.[291]   One casualty of the crisis was Hla Maung, who was eased out of the Ministry of Planning and sent to be Ambassador to Yugoslavia. Hla Maung had been behind the government's hiring of the firm and Nathan was a friend. If he had been "more of a politician he would be a world beater," Nathan wrote.[292]   Nathan was equally concerned about Walinsky, who had taken the stepped-up program upon himself to the detriment of his health. "We just cannot do the economic work for each and all government agencies in Burma," cautioned Nathan.[293]

The 1955 crisis led to the creation, late in the year, of a three-year plan that called for the piecemeal implementation of the government's pet projects (like the steel mill and a pharmaceutical factory) and those likely to generate foreign exchange.[294]   The plan had two disheartening effects. First, it completely undercut any systematic basis behind the Burmese economic program. Second, it obliged the consulting team to endlessly oppose what Nathan called "wild projects," like a car and truck assembly plant.[295]   This was not easy to do. Walinsky called it "a major cause for soul-searching" whether to tell the client how to do what it wanted or that it should do something else instead. As most consultants would, the Nathan team probably erred on the side of the former. To convince the Burmese they were serious, Walinsky wrote, they would have had to renounce the contract. "And even this would probably not have sufficed."[296]

There were some bright spots during the next few years. After Hubert Humphrey mentioned to Nathan that the Soviets accepted rice in payment for technical advisors, Nathan (in Washington) and Walinsky (in Rangoon) began putting together a similar deal. They ultimately obtained four new technicians to augment the staff.[297]   In late 1956, Walinsky was also featured in an episode on Burma of Edward R. Murrow's "See it Now" program.

By mid-1957 Walinsky was ready to quit, tired of making recommendations not acted on and seeing only "endless evidence of inefficiency."[298]   Nathan came to Burma and exhorted officials there, including U Nu, to take more effective action, but to no avail.[299]   The team even picked up two new hires late in the project: Haldore Hanson, who worked on U.S. loans, and David Chewning, who advised the Civil Supplies Management Board, the government-owned consumer goods company. Chewning was surprised to find that the chief of the board worked only three hours a day.[300]

The dismal outlook took a toll on the team. Walinsky could be tough on people in the best of times, and his leadership alienated as much as it inspired in the worst. Nathan had already concluded that "personality and a good sense of human relations is about as important in overseas assignments as is ability."[301]   Ultimately Walinsky appears to have suffered from lack of inspiration. Upon being hired in 1958, Chewning received no guidance from Walinsky as to what they were trying to accomplish. "I don't think he knew."[302]

Despite the rice crisis, Burma renewed its two-year contract with Nathan Associates in 1955 and again in 1957, but the Burmese opposition was always looking for an opening.[303]   After Nathan's 1954 press conference, the Burmese opposition paper, *The Nation,* charged that the consultants were running the government.[304] The Burma Workers and Peasant Party (BWPP) presented a "People's Budget" in opposition to the one influenced by Nathan Associates and the other foreign contractors.[305]

In the end, U Nu's failure to bring about dramatic economic change led to his downfall. In 1958 his party, the Anti-Fascist People's Freedom League, split in two. That October, with the BWPP threatening to gain undue influence, U Nu transferred power to a caretaker government under Ne Win that was to restore order so that new elections could be held.[306] Ne Win set out to wipe away the traces of U Nu's program. He replaced almost all of U Nu's cabinet—the consultants could not be far behind.[307]

There were plenty of reasons to reconsider the Nathan contract. After the rice crisis the Burmese had gone to the United States for a $25 million loan.[308]   Only after the Soviets offered to help was the loan approved, and it was not even allocated until June 1958.[309] Ne Win was convinced that Burma's employment of a Democratic firm during a Republican administration had held up the process.[310] Nor did the Nathan team do much to help itself. It was well known that the American consultants were expensive. The Burmese ambassador called them "white elephants."[311] People may not have known that the top advisors made ten times the salary of Burmese cabinet members, but they likely noticed that the Americans had nice houses and well-tended gardens.[312] When Walinsky took over he discovered that everyone had two gardeners. One of his first unpopular acts was to insist that they cut it down to one.[313]

On Monday, December 1, 1958, Walinsky was at a luncheon when the U.S. Ambassador mentioned that he had seen in the papers that the consultants had been fired. Walinsky disputed it, and returned to his office to find a 90-day termination notice.[314] Nathan was not entirely surprised when Walinsky's cable arrived on December 2.[315] His biggest concern was what official Washington would read into the dismissal.[316]

Although the Burmese government cut off all official contact, the team remained occupied, pulling together the last of its work.[317] In Washington, Ajay Creshkoff, who had backstopped the project for seven years, began compiling a "Summary of Policy Recommendations, 1953-1959."[318] Ne Win insisted that Nathan come over. When he did in early 1959, Nathan found a "completely strange place from the one I visited just a year ago." Nathan tried to emphasize the "continuing usefulness of our accumulated work," and left Ne Win with a set of 17 studies.[319] It is unlikely that Ne Win read them. In the end, he jailed U Nu and drove Burma into depression and repression from which it has yet to fully recover.

Nathan's years in Burma marked an important interval in the history of economic development, the period in which the structuralist import substitution idea was tried and found wanting. As Walinsky pointed out in the book he wrote on the experience, the "big push" theory was wrong—it took more than capital to create sustained development. What Burma did, he pointed out, was "teeter on the development tightrope from imbalance to imbalance." Nathan Associates may not have been able to stop the act entirely, but Nathan and Walinsky probably always wondered if they could have done more to stabilize the process.[320] The sequence of events is important in another way. As a somewhat cynical development economist pointed out later, the Burmese experience roughly overlapped with the years when the liberal firm was on the outs with Washington. This may have been fortunate, but it could hardly have been intentional.[321]

In From the Cold

"Cats fought, a baby cried, roosters crowed, ducks quacked," and there was something that sounded distinctly like a fog horn. It was 4 a.m. February 9, 1957, and a sleepy Robert Nathan got out from under the mosquito netting to get ready for a day of marketing in South Vietnam.[322] Later that day he met with Ngo Din Diem, whose death six years later helped propel the United States more deeply into war. Nathan met with Diem three times in the late 1950s and picked up a retainer with the South Vietnamese Embassy in Washington, but never got work in-country.[323] It was a pity, Nathan thought after his last visit in 1959, "because neither the U.S. nor President Diem sense the full impact of what this stagnation could mean in another two or three years. Scapegoats will fall all over the place and lots of them will be Uncle Sam's people."[324] It was also a pity because Nathan Associates needed the business.

Just ten years earlier Nathan had been prepared to shut the firm down entirely, but by the late 1950s, he was committed—at least in principle—to making this unconventional business a success. In 1960 Nathan produced a marketing brochure that explained what was so different about it. *Three Steps from the Ivory Tower* compared the trajectory of economic consulting with Nathan's own career. The first step was into the government, the second was industrial mobilization for war, and the third step came when economists went to work on a consulting basis.[325]

This consulting firm's greatest strength was also its greatest handicap—Robert Nathan himself. He would do anything for it except give up his other activities. Sometimes Nathan believed that if not for professional obligations he would have been able to erase the ADA's deficit.[326] After Burma fell apart, Walinsky suspected that there might have been more work to come home to, were it not for the ADA. In late 1958 Walinsky wrote from Rangoon that he hoped the domestic business was "paying its own way." If not, he advised Nathan "either to curtail your outside activities and to concentrate harder on additional business or else to scale down your operating costs."[327]

In Saigon meeting with South Vietnamese President Ngo Dinh Diem, March 8, 1958.

Operating costs were up. By 1957, the firm had outgrown Thomas Circle, and that summer Nathan closed the deal on a "far more beautiful and more suitably located" building at 1218 16th Street.[328] He bought it himself and leased it back to the firm which occupied it in mid-November 1957.[329] At Thomas Circle Nathan had been in back; at 16th Street his office was right up front.[330]

By the next fall, Nathan knew that he had to put the company first as well. He was sure "we have depended too heavily on Burma and we need to diversify."[331] There might have been plenty of "odd and end" projects, but Walinsky was right—there was no way to cover the overhead.[332] When it came to international work some bridges had been burned beneath Nathan. He was still "Stassinated" but continued to bid on ICA projects anyway.[333] Some of the bridges he had burned himself. When he tried to land an Indonesian project, the U.S. Ambassador remembered Nathan's exploits for Matty Fox and objected.[334]

Walinsky, at least, let Nathan off the hook—he went on part-time status, spending much of the next two years writing a book about his experience in Burma.[335] In November 1959, Walinsky accompanied Nathan on an exploratory trip to Iran, invited by the Deputy Prime Minister and funded by the government. Nathan was "hopeful of landing an assignment" but had no idea what it might be.[336] Nathan went straight to the top, but instructed to defer to the Shah, he put on a poor performance. "This cramped my style a bit because it is my tendency to jump right in and pour it on," he admitted.[337] There had been numerous pitches in Japan. Nearly every time Nathan went to Burma he also went to Tokyo to visit Mike Sapir, who marched him from office to office to meet potential clients, but nothing ever materialized.[338]

Nathan did get a break after a marketing visit to Latin America in October 1958.[339] There was a specific opportunity—a survey of the economic potential of Colombia's Magdalena River Valley. Again Nathan went to the top, meeting with the president of Colombia. He also lunched with old friend Lauchlin Currie, who expressed no interest in giving up his new life as a gentleman farmer.[340] In the end, Nathan landed the project and convinced Currie to help out. The survey was a challenge since the Magdalena River Valley was home to the primitive Motolones Indians who preyed on the oil industry employees living there.[341] Five economists worked on the project during 1959, looking in particular at transportation problems and the impact of coffee prices.[342] The final report, *Program of Economic Development of the Magdalena Valley and North of Colombia*, co-authored by Robert R. Nathan Associates and Lauchlin Bernard Currie, ran to 1,712 pages and was published in 1960. It was nothing on the scale of Burma or Korea, but signaled a new start in economic development work for the firm.

While he worked to gain new ground for the firm, Nathan was working to gain new ground for liberalism as well. In 1956, he got deeply involved in electoral politics, personally contributing to more than a dozen legislative candidates and soliciting funds for several of them.[343] He also ran for delegate to the 1956 Democratic Convention, but since it was against ADA policy to endorse candidates before they were nominated, Nathan had to run as an independent, ensuring that he would not win.[344]

In Bogota, Colombia, October 1958. In the center is Nathan friend and first vice president of Robert R. Nathan Associates, Lauchlin Currie.

In presidential politics, the decade was a strange interlude for liberals like Nathan. Perhaps because they thirsted so much for intellectual sparkle during the bland Eisenhower years, they made a champion of Adlai Stevenson. He was from an old family—his grandfather had been Grover Cleveland's vice president—and much more an establishment Democrat than a liberal.[345] But he dealt in issues rather than emotion and expertly delivered speeches carefully crafted by the likes of John Kenneth Galbraith, although his extemporaneous remarks seemed to bear out Eisenhower's description of an intellectual as "a man who takes more words than are necessary to tell more than he knows."[346]

Nathan testified before the Democratic Platform Committee in Washington and then, even though he was not a delegate, went to the convention on behalf of the ADA.[347] Things looked good for Stevenson at a meeting of key backers in his suite the night of August 10. They looked doubtful for the strong civil rights plank that the ADA was determined to drive through the convention. The liberals hoped for a reprise of their 1948 achievement. They ignored the fact, as Stevenson and the establishment Democrats did not, that the 1948 move had also driven the southern wing of the party out of the hall. The committee held the plank up until it was too late for Nathan, Rauh, Reuther, and NAACP leader Roy Wilkins to launch an effective floor fight. Nathan was particularly disappointed when Hubert Humphrey, eyeing the vice presidency, temporized. "I don't think Hubert Humphrey can succeed as a moderate," he wrote.[348] One might have taken the defeat as a sign of impotence; Nathan considered it evidence that the ADA was all the more necessary.[349]

While Nathan was out of the political mainstream he was also in exile from the economics profession. By the mid-1950s Nathan's tag as a "labor economist" had dropped off. The WPB mystique had also faded. The last time an audience wished to hear about it was on May 25, 1950, when Nathan spoke to the Industrial College of the Armed Forces exactly one month before the start of the Korean War.[350] The next year, *Forbes* carried an article entitled "Who Are the Economists." The piece (which Nathan clipped) ranked Kuznets number five in the top ten and mentioned dozens of other names, none of them Nathan's.[351] He admitted to Walinsky that work for the ADA and Israel had probably led to "some dilution of my status as an economist."[352] At the end of the decade, however, Nathan was invited back to the table.

The Aldrich Commission was legendary in U.S. financial history. Created by Congress after the 1907 panic, it scrutinized the American financial system and led to the creation of the Federal Reserve. By 1950 there were calls to take another look, but Congress ignored them. So the Council of Economic Development, the left-of-center organization for which Nathan had once begun a study of demobilization, took up the challenge. In 1957 it established the Commission on Money and Credit, funded by $1.5 million in foundation grants. The 27 members chosen from government and industry included luminaries like David Rockefeller and New Dealers like Willard Thorp, Isador Lubin, and Robert Nathan.[353]

The challenge set for the Commission was to determine what changes were required in the financial system to promote an adequate rate of growth, sustained high levels of production and employment, and reasonable price stability. The members convened in six task forces; Nathan sat on four of them. They reviewed more than 100 research papers prepared by outside scholars and trade associations.[354] Nathan held the expected ground; one scholar identified Nathan and AFL-CIO economist Stanley Ruttenberg as the group's "radical wing."[355]

But the radicals were not far from the mainstream: Ruttenberg and Nathan believed that the economy could be expected to grow 5 percent per year. The group settled on 3.5 to 4.5 percent per year.[356] The Commission's assertion that the president should more closely coordinate with the Federal Reserve to help achieve full employment raised a few eyebrows, but in general, the Commission on Money and Credit report, issued in 1961, broke no new ground.[357] Nathan, it turned out, was not far from the mainstream of the emerging Keynesian consensus.[358] "Flattered and pleased" to be asked to participate on the Commission, Nathan began burnishing his reputation by writing book reviews for the first time in years.[359]

By 1959, when the Commission did most of its work, Nathan thought that he had found the presidential candidate to usher the liberals back into power. Hubert Horatio

Humphrey, having renounced his mid-decade dalliance with the center, was now the darling of the ADA. In late 1959 Nathan became treasurer of "Humphrey for President" and held one of the first fundraisers for the 1960 campaign at the Nathan Associates office—he raised $15,000.[360]

Rauh became Humphrey's unofficial campaign manager for a time and David Williams, editor of *ADA World*, wrote speeches.[361] In early March 1960, Humphrey thanked both the Nathans for their efforts on his behalf. "Bob is a tower of strength" he wrote Mary.[362] Later in the month there was another testimonial and fundraiser at 16th Street.[363] This time the ADA did not keep its members from the convention. Both Nathan and Rauh won seats on the Humphrey slate.[364] Things looked great until political realities intruded. First, Humphrey hired a professional campaign manager, James Rowe, who counseled him to keep his distance from old friends. ADA people, Rowe said, "have become inbred and doctrinaire; while they fight magnificently they always lose."[365] Then, in the West Virginia primaries, John F. Kennedy brought all of his family resources to bear and ended Humphrey's candidacy. Nathan's best efforts paled in comparison to patriarch Joe Kennedy's fortune. "You can't beat a million dollars," Humphrey admitted.[366]

Nathan had met Kennedy, who was on the Senate Labor Committee, during the Puerto Rico wage study. He was struck by the senator's impressive personality, but also by his "extreme youth." As Kennedy's profile rose, Nathan was glad to have him speak at ADA Roosevelt Day Dinners, but assumed that he lacked the experience or breadth of knowledge required of a serious candidate. Liberals also held Kennedy's failure to come out against Joe McCarthy and his father's old isolationism against him.[367] Most important, they just did not like him. Humphrey visibly burned with political passion, but Kennedy seemed too coldly, clinically, capable. Kennedy returned the sentiment. Asked why he never joined the ADA he said, "I'm not comfortable with those people."[368]

Schlesinger and Galbraith were exceptions—they came out for Kennedy early. Rauh made the jump after West Virginia, but Nathan clung to his mid-fifties favorite. If ADA people were chilly about Kennedy, they were icy about Lyndon Johnson. Nathan could never understand Johnson's attempts—successful as it turned out—to keep the party from breaking on the rock of civil rights. If Democrats opt for "complete party unity," Nathan scolded on one occasion, "there will be no Democratic program."[369] Some party-minded liberals warned Nathan to let up on Johnson, but neither Nathan nor Rauh could bring themselves to do so.[370]

At the Los Angeles Convention in July, Nathan undertook the Sisyphean task of trying to float Stevenson against the Kennedy tide. Every day, Nathan boomed and buttonholed for Stevenson. Every night Stevenson made another noncommittal speech.

Nathan kept at it despite "strong fights with some of my associates in ADA," but Kennedy won the nomination and it started to look, to some anyway, that Johnson might get the vice president spot. Nathan later claimed that he had no idea that the Texas senator might be nominated.[371] Rauh's biographer, however, noted that as the Stevenson drive collapsed, Nathan warned that Kennedy would pick Johnson. Rauh definitely asked Kennedy for assurance that this was not so and he apparently got it.[372]

An enthusiastic Stevenson delegate at the 1960 convention.
(© The Estate of Garry Winogrand, courtesy Fraenkel Gallery, San Francisco)

Once again, an establishment politician succeeded where the ADA would likely have failed. Kennedy picked Johnson, nailed down Texas, and strengthened his hand in the South.[373] Rauh stood on the floor, waved his hands and shouted "Jack, if you can hear my voice, please don't do it." Nathan caucused the D.C. delegates, who decided to back Minnesota Governor Orville Freeman, an old friend of Nathan's from AVC days. Nathan gave the news to a CBS reporter as Johnson watched in dismay from his hotel suite.[374]

The ADA executive committee meeting the next month was as tumultuous as the convention floor in Los Angeles had been. But in the end, with nowhere else to go, the organization endorsed the Kennedy-Johnson ticket.[375] That fall, Nathan put in his time making the rounds of the chapters, placating the grumblers and promoting the party ticket.[376] Not surprisingly, for this last-ditch Stevenson man there was no invitation to join the Kennedy camp.[377] Nathan's path out of the political wilderness had been tortuous and not calculated to ingratiate him with either the top or bottom of the ticket, but he seemed to have gotten what he had wanted. Now, he told the *Dayton Daily News*, "professors again will be welcomed in Washington."[378]

4

TAKE-OFF POINT

"Times have changed for us" Robert Nathan wrote in May 1961.[1] His firm's overseas credentials had been established by two projects: a development plan ignored by the Koreans it was intended to help, and a consulting engagement for Burma that sputtered into political and economic chaos. In the latter case, the country itself would soon sink from view under military dictatorship. This inauspicious history notwithstanding, less than two years later Robert R. Nathan Associates was suddenly very busy. More importantly, at the outset of the Kennedy Administration the foreign economic development component of the liberal project seemed to be blossoming from Cold War adjunct to idealistic crusade. Soon, the energetic young president was calling for "A Decade of Development," and the enterprising older economist was in the thick of it, building his company from a still shaky venture into strong self-sustaining concern. In the language recently popular among development economists and opportunistic politicians—Nathan Associates had reached the "take-off point."

For the term, credit must go to Walt Whitman Rostow, an economic historian whose work entered the mainstream in a 1960 book entitled *Stages of Economic Growth: a Non-Communist Manifesto*. As the title suggests, Rostow's idea was to give First World promoters and Third World participants something to believe in, something as inexorable in its logic as Marxian dialectical materialism. Although the book arrived just in time for the New Frontier, the ideas were not new, having been worked out by Rostow and others through the 1950s. But the overall scheme was engaging: rigid "traditional" societies are jarred by external forces into the "preconditions for take-off," becoming more productive and investing in a few dynamic sectors until they reach the take-off point. In the "drive to maturity," economies diversify and develop until an "age of mass consumption" brings plenty to the multitudes.[2]

Careers have been made by criticizing it, but for all the simplicity—or perhaps because of it—the Rostovian model remains compelling not merely for nations but for institutions. In 1961 Nathan's firm really was at the take-off point: gross revenues doubled from fiscal 1964 (the year ending January 1964) to fiscal 1967. Over the same period, Nathan's staff tripled to 60 working in the United States and 20 working overseas.[3] The company diversified its areas of expertise, and even began to flourish without the direct intervention of the founder.

Two other things appeared to have reached the take-off point in 1961. Since reconversion, Nathan had routinely renounced minor positions in the government, but retained a desire to serve. The chance for a spot in the highest levels of a Democratic administration for a time seemed close to realization as Nathan helped Hubert Humphrey pursue the presidency. The campaign took off but the candidate did not prevail. Worse, the entire postwar liberal project, embodied in the Americans for Democratic Action, and to which Nathan had given so much, never took off at all—it remained on the runway through two Democratic administrations. There have been times in American history when a generation's worth of change seems packed into a few short years. During the New Deal, Nathan had been near the epicenter of one such period. During the years from 1961 to 1968 he was near the center again—with as much to remember and more to regret.

LESSONS FROM THE FIELD

Things were different in the early 1960s, not only because there was a Democratic administration, but also because economic aid had a new look. Cold War foreign assistance had too often been considered a process—the helping of friends and the indirect punishing of enemies. Now there was a clear goal—to get to the take-off point where economic aid could stop. Kennedy billed this as "aid to end aid."[4] The new approach also acknowledged that economic growth could be traumatic unless a society was prepared socially as well as economically to adjust to it. Social as well as economic change, therefore, had to be promoted in a package known as "country programming." Finally, leaders understood that long-term development goals should trump temporary political differences between nations.[5] "Kennedy's great contribution was his idea of foreign aid without ties," recalled Nathan.[6]

To accomplish these ends, the administration created the Foreign Economic Assistance Task Force to restructure aid agencies into a super organization providing social and economic expertise, technical aid, and development funding as a coherent whole. Nathan served on the task force, which reported to international lawyer Fowler Hamilton, the first director of the United States Agency for International Development (USAID).[7] No one downplayed the need for capital infusions—these were to be provided by the USAID Development Loan Fund—but development specialists were determined that the capital rain on fruitful rather than barren ground, and it would take economists to tell the difference.[8] Nathan Associates was thus the beneficiary of the lessons learned during that first decade of overseas aid. Robert Nathan was determined to share the lessons of his own work widely. He began using a portable dictation machine in 1962, and his customary travel journals became ever more elaborate and explicitly aimed at providing those who would come after with all the details they might need—and then some.[9]

The lessons of the largest Nathan Associates project of the decade, providing economic advisory services to the Royal Government of Afghanistan, should have been evident early. On May 25, 1961, Nathan was conducting a three-week preliminary survey of Afghanistan when his host, Deputy Minister of Planning Abdul Hai Azziz Khan, led him to a site near the mountainous Pakistani border and pointed to a large cemetery. "You know who are buried there?" Khan asked. "No," replied Nathan. "The British."[10] The government of the landlocked nation the size of Texas might have wanted roads, dams, and better living standards, but the people were stoutly resistant to change. Afghanistan had never been colonized or remotely westernized—the British were the most notable among those who had tried and failed. Only later did Nathan understand the poignancy of that example, at the time he was actually optimistic.[11] Khan, he discovered, "really had a good idea of what he wanted and he had a good idea of what Afghanistan needed."[12] Khan also believed that Nathan could help him get it—the government signed a two-year contract in August 1961 and the team went to work the next month.

By then, staffing had already emerged as a recurrent headache. The opportunity to do applied work in an exotic location while earning a substantial tax-free income should have been widely appealing, but it was not. For the Afghanistan project Nathan quickly lined up fiscal, industrial, and agricultural specialists, but by September he was still lacking a senior economist and team leader—what USAID would call a "chief of mission."[13] The ever-accommodating Louis Walinsky agreed to fill in until, a few months later, Richard Huber, an old friend of Nathan's, arrived in-country.[14]

As the team settled in to work on a series of five-year plans, signs were indeed good. The government gave the team open access to the highest levels of the Afghan Ministries of Planning, Mines, and Industries and Agriculture, and officials welcomed open discussion of sticky issues and equally frank advice. Nathan also believed it critical that his team report solely to the Royal Government of Afghanistan, although the work was financed by U.S. foreign assistance grants.[15] But there were challenges as well. For one thing, the Americans were, to some extent, in competition. Since the mid-1950s the Soviet Union had been providing direct assistance to the country at its southeastern border. Soviets were also building dams, highways, and other projects—more glamorous work than economic consulting. Perhaps the biggest immediate problem was that the Soviets had also done some planning. They had written Afghanistan's second five-year plan before the Nathan team members had even arrived and their first job was to review it. The team found the plan unrealistic, and Nathan worried about how to persuade the Afghans to adopt a more feasible approach without looking less ambitious or dynamic than the Soviets.[16] That was the major problem that Nathan worked on during his second trip to Afghanistan.

As he began to field teams across the world, Nathan's professional life became largely a matter of remote monitoring punctuated by quick trips with big intentions. In Afghanistan, as in most of the firm's projects during the 1960s, Nathan was contractually required to visit at least once a year. But that was hardly enough. Lacking dynamic high-level leadership, the teams tended to bog down. Walinsky did "field inspections" in Afghanistan in late 1961 and late 1962, and Nathan himself did eighteen from the inception of the contract to its conclusion eleven years later.[17] Each trip had a specific mission: sometimes to lay the groundwork for contract renewal, sometimes to put a new team in place, sometimes to put his stamp on a particularly important plan or report.[18]

Whatever the mission, the trips took on a pattern. The team met Nathan at the airport (when they did not they heard about it) and dropped him off at a familiar hotel. At the outset Nathan laid in supplies for the customary two-week stay: western amenities like soap and tissues, breakfast or snack fare like jam and crackers, and a bottle of Scotch for after hours.[19] Nathan had less recourse to the Scotch than he might have liked, however, because social rounds were as imperative as professional consultation. The host government always staged formal gatherings and every team member felt obliged to have Nathan over for an informal dinner with the family at least once.

The workday tempo increased with the social whirl. When Nathan came out, recalled one team member during the 1960s, "everything speeded up."[20] Visits to Afghanistan in 1964 and 1966, for example, were largely dedicated to drafting or revising the second and third five-year plans.[21] Nathan not only spurred on employees; he also took his concerns directly to the ministries. In mid-1966 he went to Afghanistan because he perceived that there was "paralysis" at the highest levels and wanted to encourage the prime minister to take "bold steps."[22] There was never any question about seeing the prime minister either. In every country, one of the most important benefits of Nathan's presence was his ability to open doors closed to other members of his team. Nearly every trip abroad ended with a personal audience with a king, president, or prime minster, followed by an all-hands staff meeting. As economist Joe Gunn, who was in Afghanistan for the Asia Foundation in the early 1960s and worked closely with the team put it, Nathan would "talk with everyone he could and stir up lots of dust, and then turn it over to his team to take care of these things, then go off and do something else."[23]

By early 1968, the Afghanistan contract had been renewed three times and the team had produced a third five-year plan. But despite Nathan's efforts and Afghan officials' willingness to talk, it had become clear that progress was going to be slow. Abdul Hai Assiz Khan was dead. The economy was in trouble, with mounting inflation and declining reserves of foreign exchange, and the prime minster had recently resigned. Vietnam was also starting to affect budgets, and U.S. loans had been scaled back accordingly. Out of necessity the plan emphasized "quick producing and high yielding projects," and it was going to demand sacrifice and change from the populace.[24]

Everyone had much higher hopes for Latin America, the Kennedy Administration most of all, which had singled out the region for special attention with its 1962 "Alliance for Progress." The program pledged a decade's worth of support for economic development in Latin America. In financial terms that meant $20 billion in direct aid from the U.S. and $80 billion to be raised by the Latin American nations. In organizational terms it meant employing experts to see that the money was invested effectively.[25]

Nathan Associates' involvement in El Salvador began even before the "Allianza" was in place, with a 1961 International Cooperation Administration contract to examine conditions pertaining to investment and industrial development there.[26] Within a year El Salvador was considering a much larger role for the company: Nathan and Walinsky both paid visits during 1962 to discuss it.[27] By the time a two-year economic advisory contract was in place, El Salvador was receiving more Alliance funding than any other nation—$63 million all told from 1962 to 1965.[28] Nathan meanwhile continued to sharpen his approach to providing foreign economic advisory services—in broad outline, he saw his role as assisting and challenging the host country's ministers. Nathan's own challenge was to hire and deploy an effective and harmonious team. That proved to be impossible in El Salvador.

Doing economic work in a developing country "takes dedicated people or odd balls or sort of automatons," Nathan noted in 1961. "Unfortunately, there are not many in the first category."[29] It was tough to find economists in any category to go to work in El Salvador; the contract was a year old before a full staff was in place.[30] The toughest thing to find was a mission chief, which Nathan believed should be an "outstanding man." "Usually those who are available are not up to the caliber of what we want," he wrote.[31] The customary procedure for finding staff was for Nathan to put soundings out to his many friends and acquaintances and for them to do the same. By the time Nathan hired Glen Parker to lead the El Salvador project, the rest of the team had spent a year working unsupervised. They rebelled.[32]

It was bad enough when staffers fought among themselves, but too often they ended up in uneasy relationships with peers outside the company. In sharp contrast to Burma in the 1950s, Nathan teams in the 1960s were almost always surrounded by a large number of Americans working directly for USAID. The government employees found ample reason to resent contractors who were considered too free-wheeling and too highly paid—the salaries of government employees were not tax exempt.[33] In El Salvador as elsewhere, Nathan employees paid too little attention to mending fences with USAID staff, so Nathan came down to sort out the trouble. "It is strange how adult people can get themselves so fouled up," he wrote.[34]

Parker was ultimately unable to solve the personnel problem, so Nathan finally dispatched Sid Lerner as chief of mission.[35] One of Nathan's earliest employees, Lerner had rejoined the firm in the early 1960s after a decade in industry. Lerner was tough to the point of being peremptory. He kept the project moving but could never make it work well, especially when a junior staffer, having ingratiated himself with one deputy official, took every opportunity to undermine his leadership. Not until the project was nearly over did Nathan realize that the rest of the team, himself included, had ignored the seemingly incompetent—but no less influential—deputy official. It was a valuable lesson.[36]

These personnel problems hurt performance. When Nathan took stock of the work that his team was doing for the El Salvadoran planning agencies he had to admit that it was "not our best exhibit." Still, he was convinced that "our performance, with all its inefficiencies, is far superior to that of our competitors."[37] One of Nathan's chief objectives, in El Salvador as elsewhere, was to press for more taxes. El Salvador, however, was ruled by an oligarchy of influential families that held the line. Nathan knew it was a political, rather than an economic, problem, but still he personally pressed hard on the issue of taxes.[38] In the end, El Salvador implemented new tax laws and modest land reforms, enough for the country's growth rate to hit 12 percent by the end of the Nathan contract in 1965. The Johnson Administration called it "a model for other Alliance countries."[39]

It was Costa Rica, the most democratic and pro-American of Central American nations, that should have been the model for the Alliance for Progress.[40] In the summer of 1963, Costa Rican officials came to El Salvador to evaluate Nathan Associates' work, and in 1964, Nathan himself went to Costa Rica.[41] At first officials told him that they wanted only short-term technicians. "I emphasized that we were economists," Nathan reported, and prepared to leave. "The tone changed quite quickly," he noted, and a contract was signed that summer.[42] Nathan made plans to obtain a mission chief, but was informed that the host country did not want one. Instead, three economists worked away in relative isolation—largely elbowed out of the consultative and decision making process. Later it became clear that the Costa Ricans had never really wanted economic help. Rather, they believed that they had been imposed upon by USAID, and made to accept the Nathan team as a condition of receiving development loans. It was not the last time that would happen.[43]

As these large projects continued, Nathan Associates also undertook short-term work across the globe. In 1960 the company conducted a four-month study of administrative, managerial, and technical manpower in Ghana.[44] Three years later, Sid Lerner led a similar project in Nigeria, but he ran the effort imperiously and quickly alienated his staff. One of them, David Chewning, described it as "wholly atypical of the work of Robert R. Nathan Associates."[45] There was a visit to Nigeria in 1964 to discuss further work, but it turned mostly into a sightseeing trip.[46] In 1968, however, Nathan Associates landed a contract to produce an economic feasibility study for a road from Port Harcourt to Aba. But Nigeria was again unlucky. As John Beyer, a young economist on the team recalled, the engineering firm assigned to the project did not wait for the Nathan study—it designed the road to its own liking, infuriating USAID officials.[47]

Other international projects Nathan left up to others, such as the feasibility study Franz Wolf conducted for a rail link between Turkey and Iran for USAID in mid-1963.[48] Israeli economist Kurt Mendelsohn attempted throughout the early 1960s to get a Jerusalem office of Nathan Associates up and running from the headquarters of an old client, the Zim Shipping Company. "It really isn't much of an operation and throws off only a modest profit," Nathan admitted before closing it around 1967.[49]

By the early 1960s, Nathan had developed a mature philosophy of economic development. He well understood that neither visiting economists nor big infusions of cash could do much to promote self-sufficient growth. To the contrary, as development funds flowed ever more freely in those years, he worried that the infusion of liquidity might actually be counterproductive. "The process of muscle-building for a nation requires that a tremendous internal effort be made and that not everything should come from abroad," he wrote in one of his journals.[50]

COALITION COMING APART

Early on Friday, February 10, 1961, the stalwarts of Americans for Democratic Action filed into the "Fish Room" across the hall from the White House Oval Office. Joe Rauh sat back on a lustrous leather couch beneath a mounted sailfish caught by John F. Kennedy. Nathan stretched his lanky frame out on the brass-tacked, matching chair and propped his forearm—cigarette in hand—on the armrest. Less at ease were ADA executive committee chairman Marvin Rosenberg and ADA chairman Samuel Beer.[51] All stood as acquaintances dropped by—Beer's former student Kenneth O'Donnell, Nathan's friend Ralph Dungan, and the cigar-puffing, irrepressible Pierre Salinger.[52]

In the White House Fish Room, February 10, 1961, the ADA delegation prepares to meet with President Kennedy. From left: Pierre Salinger, Nathan, Joe Rauh, Samuel Beer, Marvin Rosenberg.
(George Tames/The New York Times/Redux)

In the early 1960s, as one scholar put it, the ADA represented, "for all practical purposes, the active 'left' of American liberalism."[53] Its leaders now gathered to pay their respects and offer help to the new president.[54] All were in an expansive, optimistic mood for the 9:30 a.m. meeting. As they crossed the hall, someone, probably Nathan, remarked that he had not "been inside the White House in eight years."[55] In the Oval Office, Nathan and Rauh got very different receptions—that difference underscores the fault lines along which the coalition that both men had worked so hard to build would soon come apart.

Beer began with platitudes about how much the ADA supported the president, and then noted that they wished to discuss two topics: he deferred to Nathan to introduce the first. The nation was just emerging from the second wave of a double-dip recession and the unemployment rate was at about seven percent. Nathan said that this called for decisive action. "The president was very cordial with Bob," recalled Rauh. Kennedy agreed that the unemployment rate was too high, but reminded Nathan that any remedy would have to be welcomed by the 93 percent of Americans who were still working. "Sell it and then I can pick it up," Kennedy told Nathan, "but I can't do that in the present political climate."[56]

Economic growth would, of course, wipe out unemployment, the discussion continued, but how, the president asked, could that be achieved?[57] Nathan told Kennedy not to be afraid of the mounting deficit, which was actually shrinking as a percentage of GNP. He figured that running a $5 billion deficit every year for ten years would make unemployment a thing of the past. "I think this was a little bit of a shock to him," Nathan admitted later.[58] Kennedy was actually quite surprised to have gotten any answer at all. Unlike most economists, Nathan had been frank, Kennedy confided to Walter Heller a few days later, and he appreciated it. But he also admitted that he could not afford to be tagged as a "big spender" so early in his administration.[59]

History credits Heller, chairman of the Council of Economic Advisors (CEA), with putting over the "Kennedy Tax Cut" that economic historians still call the capstone of "the golden age of economists' influence on American policy."[60] But Heller gave much of the credit to Nathan, whose frank advice prompted the president to talk at length early in his administration about "the fact that a $5 billion dollar deficit every year, year in and year out, wouldn't really hurt the economy." Kennedy put it directly to Heller at a cabinet meeting. "Do you agree with Bob Nathan that we could have a five billion dollar deficit without much trouble?" Heller explained how that could be possible. "Gradually," Heller recalled, "his full understanding of modern fiscal policy and economics won out."[61] In early 1963, Kennedy proposed an $11.4 billion tax cut—a massive stimulation of the economy that when finally implemented, furthered, if it did not entirely fuel, America's longest economic expansion up to that time.[62]

Next it was Rauh's turn. When he raised the subject of civil rights, Rauh recalled, "Jack Kennedy tightened up like a drum."[63] He had told Nathan that the ADA should push him on economics, but warned Rauh against pushing him on civil rights—it was too explosive a subject and he would have to go slowly. The delegation left after 40 minutes, most of those minutes occupied by Nathan. "We are greatly excited to know that we have a president so completely on top of his job," the group announced for ADA consumption.[64] But Rauh was not happy. Kennedy might be preferable to Eisenhower or Nixon, he told a journalist, "but compared to the high hopes we had, he's a bitter disappointment."[65] Nathan, oblivious to his own influence, was also disappointed. Kennedy's economic policies, he wrote two months later, were insufficient to "fulfill the objectives of the Employment Act of 1946."[66]

Nathan and Rauh were learning that it is harder to keep a movement together when it is in power and has to compromise than when it is on the outs and acting on only abstract principles. In Kennedy's "New Frontier," and to an even greater degree in his successor's "Great Society," liberals began fighting among themselves over the appropriate goals of the movement and the rightful recipients of social gains.

In his *Mobilizing for Abundance* days, Nathan had assumed that economic growth would solve all problems. By the 1960s he had moderated that position, perhaps under the influence of John Kenneth Galbraith's landmark 1958 book *The Affluent Society*, which called for more social and less private investment. As Nathan asked an audience in early 1963, "do we want urban redevelopment, more schools, better teachers, more and better hospitals, safer streets and roads, more assured worker supply and the like; or do we want more cars, more television sets, more private swimming pools and bigger houses?"[67] At heart, however, Nathan, like fellow New Dealer Leon Keyserling, would always be an old-fashioned "full employment liberal." He believed, as he told a religious group in late 1962, that full employment would bring about "true equality of opportunity for all American citizens."[68]

Joe Rauh did not agree. A lifelong concern about "civil liberties" turned, by the 1960s, into firm commitment to "civil rights," the issue that was quickly becoming the revolution that the postwar liberal project had never been. ADA liberals were more comfortable joining letterhead committees, convening seminars, and reasoning together, than they were marching in the streets and manning barricades. As African-Americans in Montgomery, Alabama, Little Rock, Arkansas, and Greensboro, North Carolina, began risking their lives for their principles, the old liberal orthodoxy paled.

On July 30, 1960, Rauh, Nathan, and Harriet Cipriani, all delegates to the recent Democratic National Convention, joined the cordon of protesters who had been picketing the whites-only Glen Echo amusement park in suburban Maryland for a month. Typically, they had party politics more on their minds than direct action—they carried signs that said "Democrats, support your party platform" and "Republicans, support your party platform."[69]

As black militancy increased, and white resistance mounted, Kennedy temporized and disappointment gave way to opposition. In May 1963, a different, less cordial ADA contingent met with the pesident. The group was headed by one of the old leaders, James Wechsler, but it demonstrated a new intransigence, taking the president to task for his lack of support for the civil rights movement. A new, more aggressive brand of liberalism was emerging—more moralistic, more activist, and far more interested in "rights" than in economics. Among the rights these liberals claimed was more democratic leadership in the movement itself. Even from within the ADA, members in the chapters and the national office began to criticize the group's long record of leadership by the same seemingly self-appointed clique of Washington insiders.[70]   Although the old New Deal liberals were still tolerated under the tent, power on "the left" was increasingly demanded for women, minorities, and the young. The ethnic working class and old-line labor unions were conspicuously absent from this emerging coalition.

Near the end of the old liberal order: Nathan and Eleanor Roosevelt at an early 1960s ADA function.

By the mid-1960s, Americans of all kinds, from college students to old-world ethnics, were taking a page from the black freedom movement and asserting group identities. Nathan was no exception, joining for the first time a Jewish group that was based on identity rather than politics. In November 1964, he became the first president of the John F. Kennedy Lodge of the B'nai B'rith. The lodge was dedicated by Nathan's friend and Supreme Court Justice Arthur Goldberg.[71]

As sixties liberalism emerged, the acolytes of the old order tried one last time to draw together. By 1963 the ADA was again deeply in debt and on the verge of collapse. At a luncheon in May, New Deal liberals Nathan, Humphrey, and Rauh met with labor liberals to begin putting together a deal.[72]   Throughout the summer, people on both sides tried to do something to keep the ADA and labor from "drifting apart." When the president of the Machinists Union agreed on the need for "an effective liberal center," Rauh insisted that he and Nathan were willing to work for it.[73] Meanwhile, Nathan begged funds from Walter Reuther and other labor leaders and promised to hire a "new vigorous executive director," and get an organizing drive going.[74]

But the effort collapsed, in part because labor had long ago slipped from the vanguard of progressivism. On one hand, blue collar workers who had done so well during the postwar years were now more inclined to bargain than to fight—particularly when it was someone else's fight. On the other hand, working whites felt increasingly threatened by the changing tone of liberalism. Southerners—and plenty of northerners—harbored the endemic racism that the New Deal had never really challenged. Moreover, working-class whites across the industrial heartland were increasingly uneasy as black settlement in white neighborhoods seemed to bring economic decline, and liberal employment programs threatened to increase job competition. True, in matters like civil rights, labor leaders had never entirely followed their members. But now, organized labor had its own political action efforts and its own problems—union membership had been declining since the mid-1950s.[75]

Then the fault lines splitting liberalism apart began to undermine the once-great electoral hope, Hubert Humphrey. From the time of his stand for civil rights at the 1948 Democratic convention, Humphrey had been the standard bearer for postwar liberalism. In 1960, he earned, not for the first time, a 100 percent on the legislative scorecard that the ADA used to rank vote-worthy candidates. *Progressive* magazine stated that he "accepts without apparent dissent the basic outlines of the modern welfare state proposed by liberal Democrats."[76] Nathan and Humphrey had become increasingly close through the 1950s. In 1961, on the occasion of Humphrey's fiftieth birthday, Nathan sent him a congratulatory cable from Afghanistan.[77]

In 1964, some liberals had implored Humphrey not to accept the vice-presidency under their old irritant, the deal-making Texan, Lyndon Johnson.[78] Nathan did not agree, believing that Humphrey could be of more use to the movement from within the administration than from without. He was sorry to miss the 1964 Democratic convention because he was overseas. He was equally disappointed when he awoke one morning, asked local USAID staffers who had won the vice presidential nomination, only to find that no one cared. When he learned it was Humphrey he sent another congratulatory cable.[79] Barry Goldwater's running mate unwittingly helped patch things up for a time when he called the ADA an agent of "foreign socialistic totalitarianism," and brought a spike in membership applications.[80] Arthur Schlesinger called Johnson and Humphrey's landslide victory the "greatest opportunity for constructive liberalism in a generation."[81] He was wrong.

The year 1964 had brought the Civil Rights Act. This was the greatest liberal landmark of the late 20th century, championed more aggressively by Humphrey than anyone else in Congress, but with it the South began to tip inexorably to the Republicans. The year 1965 brought Medicare and seemed to herald the full flowering of the Great Society, but the liberal hour was short. By the end of the year, to a growing number of idealists, these greatest political accomplishments of a generation meant nothing so long as there was war in Vietnam. And that, too, was ever more associated with Hubert Humphrey.

By the time of the ADA Convention in April 1966 the destruction of the "Happy Warrior" had begun, although as yet, things remained civil. The vice president asked to speak, so the leadership moved the scheduled debate on Vietnam up so that it would not be considered an attack on Humphrey. At the end of the debate the ADA discarded the uncompromising opposition to communism upon which it had been founded—a move strongly opposed by Nathan. "I value your advice and counsel on any matter," Humphrey had written Nathan in 1962. Now, as other friends dropped away, Humphrey valued it all the more.[82] Nathan helped Humphrey write a speech intended to affirm the administration's Vietnam stance yet mollify ADA progressives. It did neither.[83]

That October, Nathan tried one last time to make the old tricks serve. He chaired an ADA conference intended "to reappraise the central goals of liberalism for the next decade." That might have been possible in the era of Eisenhower, but as the Great Society shattered it was not. Battered by Vietnam, the old ADA liberalism was going down fast and conferences could not save it.[84] By 1967 it seemed as if everything was about the war. The March 31, 1967, edition of the *Washington Post* covered a reception for Afghanistan's new ambassador. Reporters had noticed a tête-à-tête between Robert Nathan, Russian Ambassador Anatoly Dobrynin, and Secretary of State Dean Rusk. They caught Nathan telling a mildly racy story about a beautiful Russian interpreter in Afghanistan. As Rusk put his arms around them, Nathan chuckled, Dobrynin managed to smile, flash bulbs popped, reporters scribbled, and the Secretary quipped, "Just watch. They'll call these peace talks."[85]

Ed's Shop

Nathan was not the only Washington economist to build his company to the take-off point in the 1960s. By then there were some 50 firms doing economic consulting work in Washington and the business was worth, by one estimate, about $12 million. The largest, C-E-I-R, was founded as the Council for Economic Research in 1954. That firm specialized in large-scale statistical projects involving computers, although it took on some smaller projects as well.[86] A few branch offices of the older firms, mostly based in New York City, specialized in market and investment research. One of the oldest was Lionel

D. Edie and Company. It was notable because for a time in the 1960s one of its leading economists, Pierre Rinfret, reprised the role Nathan had played in the 1940s—making bold, headline-garnering predictions to the press.[87]

Other economic consulting firms worked in the international sphere. Vincent Checchi started his development firm in 1951 after a stint as chief of mission for the Economic Cooperation Administration in the Philippines.[88] Edward N. Bernstein, the first research director of the International Monetary Fund, had a small firm specializing in studies for the IMF. And a handful of lone economists worked for foreign and domestic clients, among them Nathan's old friend Louis Bean and his first employee, Oscar Gass.[89]

Two Washington shops carved out highly profitable niches. W. B. Saunders set up his firm in 1947 after serving in the Army Transport Service. By the mid-1960s he employed 47 people doing transport analytics.[90] Hanina Zinder parlayed experience in the Rural Electrification Administration and the Federal Power Commission into a business providing expert witnesses for natural gas pipeline companies and oil producers. Zinder and Associates claimed 100 employees in 1962.[91] Robert R. Nathan Associates was not quite as large, with 88 full-time employees in 1966, but no other Washington firm provided as wide a range of economic consulting services.[92]

That was possible in part because by the mid-1960s Ed Hollander had taken much of the responsibility for domestic work over from the globe-trotting Nathan. In a 1967 letter to Isador Lubin, Nathan called that side of the house "Ed's shop."[93] Nathan trusted Ed Hollander as he did no one else in the firm. Their relationship was tempered not in the tepid bath of the workaday world, but in the cold, quenching water of political activism. After spending a decade serving with Nathan in the ADA, Hollander made the jump to Nathan Associates, becoming a vice president of the firm in early 1962. A measure of his importance is that Hollander replaced Larry Nathan, who was by then busy building up the Washington-area Bruce Hunt men's clothing chain.[94]

Nathan also held Hollander in the highest esteem. He was an economist—having done graduate work at American University in Washington—but he was not an academic. He had worked for the NRA in the 1930s, the War Manpower Commission during World War II, and the Department of Labor in the 1940s before joining the ADA staff. Although he left the ADA payroll in the early 1960s, Hollander remained committed to it. In 1963, precisely ten years after Nathan did, Hollander became chairman of the ADA executive committee.[95]

Hollander was, if it was possible, even more of a labor liberal than Nathan. During the mid-1960s, new recruit John Beyer joined Hollander for a luncheon date with a prospective client. When they arrived at the hotel where the restaurant was located, they found it being picketed by the Hotel and Restaurant Workers Union. Hollander had never crossed a picket line and would not let Beyer do so either. The prospect dined alone.[96] For Hollander some things—lots of things—were more important than business. When Harriet Kriesberg, a colleague at Labor Department, joined "Ed's shop" part-time in 1967, she asked for a $10,000 salary—Hollander informed her that she would have to have more.[97]

Nathan was a bit more willing to compromise—the business was his responsibility, after all. But there were limits. As mid-decade approached, Nathan was still working hard to build up the domestic side of the business.[98] Then the opportunity to do a big study appeared. It was from the tobacco company, Lorillard. In the wake of the 1964 Surgeon General's report, Lorillard wanted an assessment of the economic benefits of the industry, and was willing to pay $300,000. "We desperately needed it," Maury Atkin recalled. Nathan sought higher counsel—he called Hubert Humphrey. The two agreed that if the study were truly objective there could be no harm in it. Nathan and Atkin visited Lorillard's lawyers to talk. At one point, someone produced a sheet of paper detailing some "hoped-for" findings. "Gentlemen," said Nathan, "we can't do it."[99] The study was ultimately undertaken by C-E-I-R, which insisted on its objectivity.[100]

Nathan Associates was not without its own objectivity problems. In 1967 the firm did a study for Nathan's old colleague Edward Hickey, counsel to the Railroad Brotherhoods. It found that a "spectacular increase in net railway income" justified a 7 percent wage hike.[101] Had the word "net" been omitted, however, the study would have had to conclude—as most Americans did at the time—that the nation's railroads were deep in crisis, crumbling and going broke. Another labor project, for the International Chemical Workers Union, was on firmer ground when it established that earnings for workers in the chemical industry were well below those in other major sectors like steel and auto.[102] One of the most notable projects conducted by Ed's shop focused on employers rather than employees. The $98,000 study was commissioned by the Small Business Administration primarily for internal use but was published in 1967 as *The Future of Small Business*.[103] Precipitated by worries about the big business dominance of the economy summarized in John Kenneth Galbraith's 1967 book, *The New Industrial State*, Hollander's study found to the contrary that small business would remain strong during years of economic growth.[104]

At least one domestic project bore a striking resemblance to overseas work, and not surprisingly, Nathan took a keen interest in it. During the 19th century more mineral wealth in copper came out of Michigan's Upper Peninsula than had come out of the entire California gold rush, but by the early 20th century the mines were tapped out. The industry and the economy of the Upper Peninsula had collapsed entirely by the

1950s. When the Mackinac Bridge opened late in the decade, however, it seemed possible that the remote, depressed region might be revived. The 1961 Area Redevelopment Act was intended to make revival possible. In 1962, the Department of Commerce Area Redevelopment Administration and the Upper Peninsula Committee on Area Problems (UPCAP), consisting of representatives from the State of Michigan and 14 counties, hired Nathan Associates to devise a redevelopment plan.[105]

At a seminar for labor leaders held by the Brookings Institution, March 16, 1963, in Williamsburg, Virginia. From left: C.C. Killingsworth, Michigan State; Joseph Keene, Electrical Workers Union; Max Greenberg, Retail, Wholesale and Department Store Workers Union, and Adolph Berle, Columbia University.

Nathan dispatched a program specialist and a field representative to the Upper Peninsula.[106] He flew up himself in the middle of a snowstorm in January 1963 to launch an 18-month, $125,000 technical assistance effort.[107] Evidently Nathan made an impression on the populace—a month later, in exhorting the citizenry to back a school levy, the *Escanaba Daily Press* quoted Nathan in saying that development most often fails, "because people are not willing to pay the price."[108] That summer Nathan returned for a day to attend three meetings, one luncheon, and appear on television to rally support for his firm's economic redevelopment program. A Marquette newspaper reporter who did not know Nathan well speculated that his day in the Upper Peninsula must have been "one of the busiest of his life."[109] The UPCAP project ended in 1965 with a six-month task in which the Nathan staffers trained locals to take their place.[110]

The UPCAP project formed the basis of a more durable practice in the firm, the Department of Urban and Regional Development, directed by Malcolm Rivkin, formerly of MIT.[111] Projects undertaken included a study of the impact of the creation of the Delaware Water Gap National Recreation Area on surrounding communities and an assessment of the redevelopment potential of tourism and recreation for the Appalachian Regional Commission.[112] Hollander helped direct three 1968 studies on recreation, marine industries, and the bicentennial for the New England Regional Commission.[113]

Another landmark in the domestic line came in 1962 when the firm landed an $86,000 contract from the Department of Interior Office of Coal Research for a study of the export opportunities for the U.S. coal industry.[114] To conduct the study Nathan hired economist Ralph Trisko who had helped implement the Marshall Plan and served in the Mutual Security Agency during the 1950s. Trisko was assisted by three full-time staff members and two consultants.[115] Nathan also took a personal interest in the project, editing the first volume of the study during off-hours in an El Salvador hotel room.[116] The study found that American coal could be competitive in the world market despite transportation costs, and recommended ways to boost the export industry.[117] In 1968, Nathan testified before Congress about the study's findings.[118] By then Trisko had completed another assessment, this time of the market for coal and lignite from western U.S. mines.[119] Both studies were landmarks for the industry as well as for Robert R. Nathan Associates: U.S. coal exports climbed steadily through the 1960s and by the end of the century western bituminous accounted for more than half of all U.S. coal production.[120]

BACK TO ASIA

In the 1940s and early 1950s Nathan had undertaken international air travel with youthful enthusiasm, recording the time required for each leg of the journey and documenting every stop. Air travel was more of an adventure then, and also more of a luxury; the passengers were sometimes outnumbered by flight crews that plied them with ample drinks, gourmet meals, and tucked them into berths at night. By the 1960s jets had arrived and the age of adventure had departed. "It seems more and more like work," Nathan wrote of traveling in early 1961.[121] Nathan made six international trips that year, and six more in 1962.[122] The age of luxury was over too. USAID regulations required contractors to fly coach, leaving Nathan to scramble for an aisle seat and hoping to be able to move the arm rest out of the way to accommodate his ample frame.[123]

Nathan was now well into his fifties, and the travel required to monitor the overseas assignments wore him down. More important, it led him to worry that the workload "may be about as much as we can handle."[124] When it came to overseas work, Nathan was used to reading "every bit of correspondence and every memo that arrived." By 1965 that was no longer possible. Nathan had leaned hard on Louis Walinsky and rewarded him with the title vice president of economic development, but Walinsky resigned in May 1963.[125] Hollander and Trisko had little interest in overseas operations, and although Nathan gave Sid Lerner some important overseas leadership assignments, the two never really got along.[126]

Something had to be done. Nathan was out of the country seven of the first twelve weeks of 1965 and too often he was arriving in-country with little foreknowledge of the chief goals and challenges.[127] Then Nathan found someone whom he thought could fill in for him. Jerome "Jerry" Jacobson had been Deputy Assistant Secretary of State for Economic Affairs during the Kennedy Administration. He joined the firm in July 1965 as vice president responsible for international work and undertook a travel schedule only slightly less punishing than Nathan's.[128] That left the founder free to devote considerable attention to one of the opportunities he most worried about grabbing—a second shot at Korea.

Syngman Rhee, the strong man who had buried the 1954 UN plan, finally lost his hold on South Korea in 1960. A democratic administration came in after that, but it quickly lost support, mostly due to its inability to right South Korea's foundering economy. Another coup followed in May 1961, this one led by Park Chung Hee. Park was a general, but he was determined to succeed more through economic efficiency than through armed intimidation. To that end, Park and his American-trained economists came to Washington shortly after the coup to meet with Walt Rostow, now Kennedy's Deputy National Security Advisor, along with other American development experts.[129] The Americans advised the Koreans to proceed slowly, but Park was determined to move as rapidly as possible, producing a five-year plan that focused on heavy industrial development.[130] USAID was concerned. The mission director in Korea, who did not even know of Nathan's earlier work for the UN, asked him to come out and discuss an economic planning assignment, which Nathan did in December 1962.[131] There was a long wait, during which Park was "elected" president of South Korea, but the contract was approved in August 1964. There were more problems in staffing up, particularly since USAID had final approval authority—"it is damn hard to get good people, let alone to satisfy all the whims and idiosyncrasies of every official who wants to second guess a contract team," Nathan wrote.[132]

Some of this can be attributed to the fact that USAID was unusually involved in Korea. The United States was watching South Korea closely, concerned, particularly after the two coups of the early 1960s, that it might slide into anarchy as South Vietnam was doing.[133] As a result, the USAID mission was putting the pressure not only on contractors but on the government itself. As early as 1962, Nathan noted, "here there has been too much spoon feeding."[134] After getting a closer look he concluded that USAID "worked hand in hand with the Korean government in running the economy in a kind of joint venture."[135] While Nathan later lauded the close relationship between the United States and South Korea, at the time he was appalled, believing that USAID had stepped across an important line and was actually guiding policymaking rather than facilitating it. By 1965, Nathan expected trouble, writing that "someday there is going to be a terrible political or personal explosion because the Koreans resent this sort of partnership in which they are in many ways the junior partner even though it is their own country."[136]

The Nathan team tried to stay focused on its own responsibility, helping Park's ministries produce a new and more realistic five-year plan. The team began going over a proposed plan in 1965. When Nathan arrived in June 1966 he was not happy with the results—it was still too ambitious—and he spent much of that trip rewriting it.[137] The Koreans approved the plan a short time later. "For the first time in Korean experience," as one scholarly study put it, "a plan combined an adequate technical base, realistic political dimensions in terms of national objectives, and the involvement of key interest groups in the preparation and review of the plan."[138]

In general however, Nathan was deeply disappointed with his firm's second stint in Korea.[139] With USAID staff so heavily concentrated in the ministries, "there really is not a place for us," he wrote.[140] On his visits he urged his staff to work to get a higher profile in South Korea's economic planning board and operating ministries, but they were unable to do so.[141] As a result, the Nathan team ended up in a reactive role, responding to work orders rather than exerting much policy influence. Ultimately Nathan placed the blame on personnel who were too weak to challenge USAID staff or too academic to communicate effectively with the South Koreans.[142] One standout did emerge, but too late for the team. Robert Johnson, a University of Iowa economics professor, had worked in Vietnam for the Ford Foundation before joining the team in Korea.[143] Johnson, Nathan wrote, knew "how to get involved in subjects in such a manner as to evoke a sense of confidence and of practicality."[144] Johnson kept working in-country for a few years after the rest of the team left in the fall of 1966.

In May 1965 the South Korean newspaper *Choson Ilbo* ran an article on the economy that cited both Walt Rostow and Robert Nathan. Rostow was reported as having pronounced the country "now in the take-off state." Nathan said not yet. Another article noted that Nathan believed that take-off might be possible, given more taxation and lower consumption, by 1971.[145] Nathan's estimate was closer. Around 1970 the South Korean GDP, which had only been inching up through the 1960s, began to soar, but by then Korea had been working largely on its own for years.[146]

No one had any expectation that Micronesia was near the take-off point. There were 90,000 people living on the group of islands scattered over an area as large as the United States. These northernmost South Pacific archipelagos, including the Marianas, Carolines, Marshalls, and Gilberts, had switched hands several times. The Spanish and Germans had extracted coconuts and phosphates. Then the Japanese fortified them and fought their bloodiest battles of World War II there. In the postwar settlement, the United Nations had made the islands "Trust Territories" of the United States, and with the notable exception of nuclear testing in the Marshalls, not much happened after that.[147]

In early 1965, a friend of Nathan's called the office. The United Nations was unhappy with the United States for failing to fulfill the obligations of its trust. The president had made it Secretary of State Orville Freeman's problem—Freeman handed it to Nathan.[148] On the first of April, the Trust Territories entered into a contract with Nathan Associates for a preliminary survey and a two-year study. In late April, Nathan stopped at Saipan in the Marianas where he spent about a week meeting with top U.S. and Micronesian officials before heading on to Korea.[149]

The firm had its usual troubles getting a strong team in place. "We are advisors and helpers," Nathan reminded his staff at every opportunity, "ours is not the direct and operational responsibility."[150] But the first chief of mission nevertheless became too emotionally invested—when progress was slow his frustrations mounted and Nathan had to send him home. As in Korea, however, one valuable team member and future full-time staffer did emerge from the mix: James "Jim" Leonard, a development economist from Ohio State University. Nathan was struck by Leonard's assessment of the toll the "glass-enclosed and exposed kind of environment" took. "Most people are either neurotic when they come here or get neurotic before they leave," Leonard told him.[151]

And leaving was not easy. Not surprisingly for a far-flung island entity, air and sea transportation were big subjects covered in the two-year study. It was a coup when Nathan personally convinced one of the major airlines to schedule a stop there.[152] The Nathan team also assessed the potential for sport and commercial fishing, tourism, and agriculture. There was also the usual attention to economic planning. One of the Trust Territories' biggest economic problems Nathan recognized at the outset, was, in fact, too much U.S. money. With so many U.S. citizens spending money in Micronesia, the minimum wage had risen far beyond actual productivity.[153] When it was finished in April 1967, the Trust Territories study occupied 735 pages in three volumes. Micronesia had a path forward and Orville Freeman had some breathing room.[154]

TESTIFY

In late 1965, Nathan jetted into Puerto Rico for the first day of the "Status Commission" hearings intended to consider whether the island should remain a commonwealth, seek independence, or opt for statehood. Nathan had been working with Puerto Rican leaders since the mid-1950s. He knew everyone and everyone knew he had just circumnavigated the globe to get there.[155] When Nathan took the stand to testify on behalf of the commonwealth position he was perhaps too comfortable or just too tired. When an advocate of independence asked him whether or not Puerto Rico had resolved its status problems, Nathan replied that as far as he was concerned it had. His opponent threw up his hands and asked, "why then are we all here?" The audience laughed; Nathan did not.[156]

This mistake was unusual. Nathan had been testifying for nearly three decades—much of it before mostly unsympathetic congressional committees. Before Congress he put his reputation as an economist and an activist on the line, and by the 1960s he was often putting his company on the line as well. Expert witness testimony had become one of the integral offerings of Nathan Associates.

Transportation-related regulatory work like that done by Nathan in the 1950s continued. Trans-Caribbean Airlines remained on the client list, entailing route studies and appearances before the CAB successor agency, the Federal Aviation Administration. Nathan Associates did similar work for Continental when it wished to start a trans-Pacific airline route.[157] Then, in the early 1960s, the FAA became a client, commissioning a comparative study of U.S. international air transport policies conducted by Franz Wolf.[158] In 1964, Nathan testified for bulk-cargo barge lines backing construction of a Lake Erie–Ohio River Canal. Nathan's testimony detailed economic decline in the Ohio River basin and projected new economic activity that would result from a canal.[159] That project drew fierce opposition from trucking companies and railroads threatened by the potential new service.

More Nathan testimony, on behalf of the City of New York and the State of New Jersey, drew railroad fire as well. In the early 1960s the New York Central and the Pennsylvania Railroads, both staggering under the load of increased costs, deteriorating equipment, and federally mandated, yet money-losing passenger routes, were trying desperately to combine. That merger would be fine, Nathan informed the Interstate

Commerce Commission, but the combined company should pick up the decrepit Erie Lackawanna as well.[160] Nathan's arguments came early in a long process; when the merger was complete in 1968 the Penn Central was minus the Erie Lackawanna, but it went bankrupt anyway.

Nathan could hardly have been expected to become an authority on air service, barge lines, and railroads on his own—but he had Nathan Associates, which had become an effective expert witness shop. In the railroad case, for example, Ed Hollander did all of the research and prepared the testimony.[161] When it came time for cross-examination, Nathan was on his own, however, so he had great incentive to concentrate—albeit in furious bouts of study in between other professional and political projects. In those cases Nathan could rely, to some extent, on sheer tenacity and mastery of the process, which he gained to some degree through legal training but mostly through practice. He was not afraid of sparring with opponents, but most importantly, as one associate who helped prepare him for some of his appearances recalled, "he knew what to say and what not to say."[162]

From legislative and regulatory testimony it was a short step to the courtroom. Nathan's first antitrust work, undertaken during the 1950s, was for a department store that had sued a supplier for refusing to sell to it because it offered discounts.[163] The first big landmark, however, came in the 1960s with the "Automatic Radio" case. Automakers customarily included a generic "knockout plate" in their dashboards enabling customers to buy, and dealers to install, any radio they liked, and Automatic Radio was among the manufacturers of kits that dealers could install. In 1961, however, Ford had acquired Philco, its own radio maker. In its 1964 models Ford changed the knockout panel, making it difficult for dealers to install any radio but a Philco. Automatic Radio sued and hired Nathan as an expert witness. This case established a model that Nathan followed for the rest of his career. The staff would assemble materials, prepare reports, and brief Nathan. He would then, as Joe Gunn said, "think his way through a scenario, which he would present in court."[164] Nathan stood ready to testify that Ford's move was in restraint of trade, but after five years of motions, affidavits, and briefs the company settled in 1968. The court never heard from Nathan, and consumers never again heard of Automatic Radio.[165]

In the meantime, Nathan did appear in court for another underdog—the City of Milwaukee, which had lost its major-league baseball team. There were two problems. Milwaukee was a small market and, since 1961, the Minnesota Twins had been drawing attendance away from its hinterlands. At the same time the formerly winning Braves consistently finished fifth or sixth in the National League.[166] When the League announced that the Braves were moving to Atlanta for the 1966 season, the state of Wisconsin filed an antitrust suit and hired Nathan Associates.[167] Within a month the firm had prepared a 108-page report estimating the economic damage that Milwaukee would suffer from the Braves' pending departure.[168]

In early March, Nathan took the witness stand in state circuit court with much fanfare. He testified that the city stood to lose $18 million in income and 2,600 jobs. Cross-examined by Bowie Kuhn, then National League counsel, Nathan informed the court that his firm had determined statistically that Milwaukee was "a good baseball city." Nathan spent two days in court with Milwaukee residents rooting him on. A sympathetic local journalist wrote that no one "was as indisputably qualified as the big, craggy faced man who was on the witness stand."[169] It was not a particularly remunerative project—the firm netted about $25,000—but it garnered Nathan national attention. He was the sixth witness, but the *Sporting News* called him "the most impressive figure yet to appear."[170] Although Nathan helped carry the circuit court, the Wisconsin Supreme Court overruled its decision.[171]

Regulatory work also garnered headlines for Nathan, but in sharp contrast to the Automatic Radio and Milwaukee Braves matters, it was not entirely clear that Nathan was working for the underdog. It all began with some rate cases for Chesapeake Bell.

Regulated utilities could not raise prices, they had to convince the regulator—in this case the Federal Communications Commission (FCC)—that the rate increase was necessary and in the public interest. This had not been a problem through the 1950s and early 1960s, but as inflation began to rise at mid-decade, more and more utilities needed help with the regulators and Nathan was happy to provide it.[172] The work for Chesapeake Bell eventually led Nathan to a traditional sweet spot with a look at the Bell System's obsolete, arbitrary, and unfair geographically based wage differentials for the Communications Workers Union.[173] Nathan claimed later to have received permission from AT&T to do the wage scale work, but John Beyer, the young economist who helped prepare him for his testimony was impressed nonetheless with Nathan's ability to work both sides of the street. "At the same time Bob's testifying on behalf of AT&T, we're doing work for the CWA."[174]

And it was not just one of the regional Bells for which Nathan was testifying; it was for the second largest corporation in the United States. AT&T had few regulatory problems up until the 1960s, but then a newly activist FCC began looking at its 10 percent rate of return on toll calls and its seemingly predatory pricing in services that competed with Western Union. AT&T began building its defense case and it called Nathan up from Chesapeake Bell to the big leagues.[175]

On June 7, 1966, came the unlikely scenario of Robert Nathan arguing that a major corporation needed a raise. Moreover, he made his argument in the language of Wall

Street, insisting that AT&T could not compete with other blue chips for capital unless it could offer sufficient rewards.[176] Nathan also pointed out that AT&T needed sufficient returns in order to continue investing in research and development.[177] As he put it in his written testimony, "the Bell System has risked $27 billion in the past 15 years and will be expected to risk even more in the years ahead."[178]

A trace of the old Bob Nathan reappeared when he insisted that the equity of both consumers and investors could be reconciled in a full employment economy, but business journalists with long memories could not help but notice Nathan's change in tone.[179] It was a tough summer in that respect. Just a few days after his testimony for AT&T Nathan appeared in another regulatory matter, defending Roy Chalk's D.C. Transit against activists who wished to see government subsidies go to a public transit agency rather than a private company. Nathan cautioned that the advantages of public ownership should not be overemphasized. None of the other witnesses agreed.[180]

Nathan went on to do more work and give more testimony for both D.C. Transit and AT&T, but aside from an acknowledgement in later years that his liberal friends and those "who are activists in the consumer area were occasionally critical," Nathan never expressed regrets.[181] In retrospect, the question may not be why Nathan backed a rate increase for AT&T, but why he did not consider arguments about the need for competitive investment returns or research and development outlays when he was so intent on squeezing the profits of companies like U.S. Steel during the 1940s. His opponents then had made the same arguments that Nathan was making in the 1960s.

"We select assignments carefully and like to feel we are working in the public interest," Nathan insisted to a reporter in 1966. It is evident that that was usually the case, but on at least one occasion Nathan also wondered why it was widely acknowledged that every defendant had the right to legal counsel but the same did not go for economists.[182] Nathan may not have been sorry to "run interference," as one journalist put it, for AT&T.[183] His understanding of what constituted the public interest may have become more sophisticated over time. No one will ever know for sure.[184]

A View from the Fifties

"Bob and Mary Nathan, their three youngsters, and a collection of art occupy a new, ultramodern contemporary home perched on a wooded slope in Maryland." So went an installment of "Capital Coffee Break," a column written during the 1960s by the wife of an Ohio congressman for the *Dayton Journal Herald*, documenting the best sort of "small Washington dinner party."[185] By then things had changed for Nathan's family as well. Nathan was now in his fifties, a bit older than the typical postwar father of young children, but with a booming consulting business he had more than typical earning power and with it he built a new and beautiful home for his family in one of Maryland's best suburbs.

At the new house, early 1960s. From left: Robert, Ann, Richard, David and Mary Nathan.

How and why they got there was, by the mid-1960s, a familiar and—for liberals like Nathan—a somewhat uncomfortable story. Whittier Place was in what was often called at the time, a "changing neighborhood." During the 1950s, and with greater speed late in the decade, the mostly white neighborhood began to transition into a mostly African-American neighborhood. At first, the Nathans appeared to have had no intention of moving to the suburbs and Nathan confidently helped lead the liberal crusade against "white flight." He and Rauh were among the handful of celebrity sponsors of a "Good Neighbor Pledge" campaign advertised in the Washington newspapers, and on one occasion Nathan even called his neighbors together and urged them not to yield to prejudice.[186]

Nathan "held himself to be the great humanitarian," one of those neighbors recalled, which made it all the more galling when, "he soon sold his house for a handsome profit and moved."[187] But as in so many cases, humanitarianism takes a back seat to one's children. The Nathans had no problem when the schools integrated, but "they were getting rough," Mary recalled, and someone brought a gun to school.[188] The Nathans bought a lot in the upscale Bannockburn neighborhood in Bethesda, Montgomery County, Maryland, and began building in May 1961.[189]

The house at 7101 Crail Drive was designed by Hugh Jacobson. It was strikingly modern in the now-dated Bauhaus style—all rectangles and white stucco. It was not entirely practical (the flat roof always leaked), but the house, especially the pool, made an impression. The house and the architect were Mary's ideas, but the result was commensurate with the reputation of one of Washington's greatest progressives.[190]

Nathan put it to good use. There was a fundraiser for the Student Non-Violent Coordinating Committee in the summer of 1965. While Harry Belafonte chatted with Mary inside, guests swam and socialized outside, and someone manned a public address system, urging everyone to "give more than $50 because anything less will not help very much."[191] Such formal events were far less frequent than the informal. Nearly every summer Sunday when he was home, Nathan loaded coolers full of ice and drinks and, as Mary put it, "invited everybody in the world to come swim."[192]

It was a good place to raise a family. Nathan joined the PTA at nearby Pyle Middle School.[193] Nearly everyone in the neighborhood was Jewish and liberal, so there were carpools to take the children to religious school at Temple Sinai.[194] As always, Nathan tried, although often unsuccessfully, to keep weekends open for family. He made it to son Richard's bar mitzvah, although he had to pack right after the ceremony and head to Costa Rica, but he missed a lot of birthdays and felt bad about it.[195] The family vacations at the old spots continued: Key West, Kitty Hawk, and a new one, Massachusetts, so that Nathan could teach brief summer sessions at Brandeis with such other notables as Alfred

Kazin and Ashley Montagu.[196]   There was also the obligatory sixties family vacation to the Grand Canyon—in a station wagon, of course. The trip was all the more memorable because it was then that his cigar became too much for his usually compliant family, and Nathan gave up smoking entirely.[197]

There is no indication that Nathan had trouble giving up tobacco. Even though he was in his fifties, his self-control and concentration were razor sharp and he liked to show them off. Nathan Associates now had its holiday parties at Bannockburn and Nathan's house was not huge so they were crowded affairs. But even if Nathan was across the room, "you had a feeling of being very close to him" recalled Harriet Kriesberg.[198]   Inevitably, Nathan would then indulge in one of his characteristic feats: taking someone's new spouse or casual date by the arm he introduced the newcomer to every person in a house of 100-plus people. Joe Gunn understood that "it was designed to impress everybody." And it did.[199]

Nathan should have been good at knowing people, of course, because his contacts paid the bills. "It didn't seem to him that it was necessary to focus on marketing," recalled John Beyer. "Things just came to the firm."[200]   Like any influential businessman he cultivated his contacts through directorships. During the 1960s he was a director for Television Industries Incorporated, an early and unsuccessful Matty Fox pay-per-view venture, and Trans-Caribbean Airways, although he quit that post out of concern about conflicts when Roy Chalk bought a Central American airline.[201]   He also accepted financial directorships: Foundation Life Insurance and the D.C. National Bank, and of course there were also the Jewish connections—Nathan was on the board of the kosher food empire, Manischewitz, and he was on the board for a time at Reynolds Construction, a joint U.S.-Israeli contractor, and at Brager & Co., which sold Israeli bonds.[202]

As Nathan's list of directorships lengthened, he also worried about his own company. "I sometimes think that we are growing too rapidly and are getting too big," he wrote.[203]   In 1966 the firm had 88 full-time staff, about a quarter of them overseas.[204]   By the late 1960s the firm had outgrown the old doctor's office at 16th street, had expanded into the adjoining Jefferson Hotel and rented space at nearby 1220 16th Street.[205]   Up to 1966 Nathan had been the sole owner of the company. Then, deeming his company "definitely on the road to steady but moderate and healthy growth," Nathan decided to widen ownership.[206]   In March 1966, Nathan's 50 original shares were converted to 100,000, valued at $1 each, and made available in limited amounts to directors Atkin, Hollander, Jacobson, Lerner, and Wolf.[207]   Nathan Associates retained right of first refusal to ensure that the stock remained within the company.[208]

Nathan tried to take care of his team. He established a retirement plan in 1962, but he was also sensitive to his employees' social needs.[209]   While visiting abroad he gathered reports from his overseas staffers that he could relay to their families in a phone call back in the states. "They appreciate first-hand and up-to-date reports," he wrote.[210] Nathan's communications skills were substantial. No matter who it might be, said Atkin, he was comfortable "talking at their level and vocabulary."[211] When in 1967 Nathan decided to hire Joe Gunn, he called his house and Gunn's two-and-a-half-year-old daughter answered, whereupon the two began a conversation. Mrs. Gunn finally came in the room to find that her daughter had been talking with the famous economist for five minutes.[212]

Still, Nathan had his frailties. One, which likely stemmed from the same sense of insecurity and impulse to prove himself that he displayed at holiday parties, was the desire to dominate someone. "He always needed somebody around that he could beat up on," recalled Gunn. Maury Atkin most often came in for Nathan's verbal buffetings, perhaps because he was not an economist, perhaps just because he was so unquestionably loyal.[213]

Nathan had professional reasons to feel insecure as well. Sometime during the 1960s he began to understand that the economic assumptions that underpinned his ideal of New Deal liberalism were never really going to be tested. As his advice to Kennedy wound its way through the CEA, Nathan stewed. In late 1962 he filed one last formal statement of his old ideals in the academic journal *Industrial Relations*. Even a full year into the Kennedy Administration, he wrote, there was "little prospect that the United States is on the threshold of achieving, let alone maintaining, relatively full employment." In his article "The Road to Full Employment" he combined his old commitment to aggregate demand with his more recently acquired dedication to public investment. "For far too long," he concluded, "the word 'planning' has been a nasty word."[214]

Even in early 1964 when the advice given to one president was implemented by another as the "Kennedy-Johnson Tax Cut," Nathan was disappointed, convinced that cuts should be accompanied by ambitious social expenditures. It dismayed Nathan to realize that even at the zenith of their influence the best the Keynesians could do was to cut taxes.[215]

It was equally disturbing for Nathan to see his counterparts renounce the field of public policy entirely. By the 1960s, the "neoclassical synthesis"—a revived variant of classical economic theory and highly mathematical econometrics—had begun to take over the curriculum in most U.S. graduate programs. Keynesianism had been largely sidelined for special occasions. What one scholar has called the "mathematization of economics" was well under way.[216]

Nathan was suspicious of econometrics. It was not that he was afraid of numbers; long ago his father had encouraged him to do calculations in his head and Nathan still enjoyed the challenge. He was always a bit disappointed when, as one associate recalled, "the figures got a little beyond reach and he would reach into his drawer and pull out his slide rule."[217] Nathan believed that economists no longer employed calculations as levers to move the world—he was convinced that they were hiding behind their advanced mathematics instead. One of his criticisms of South Korea's first five-year plan was that it "relies too much on mathematical formulas and models."[218]

In a 1964 presentation to the American Economic Association, Nathan aired his concerns and pleaded for engagement. "In these days of automated economics," Nathan admitted to having only "limited mathematical training."[219] Nevertheless he insisted that economists had a duty to engage in public policy. He observed that the achievements of his own less methodologically distinguished generation were evident in the economic stability of the postwar decades. He implied that the future looked doubtful when, "whatever interest that has been manifested among economists has lagged behind public concern rather than led and stimulated debate."[220] Perhaps it was difficult for Nathan to see a new generation renounce policymaking when he hoped for one last opportunity for himself.

Two Steps into the Quagmire

In the fall of 1963, the King of Afghanistan visited Washington and received the requisite presidential reception. As Robert and Mary went through the line, President Kennedy grasped Nathan's hand and warmly asked, "when are you going to start advising us?" Nathan understood that the comment was really intended for the ears of the King standing next to the president, and was eternally grateful. In fact, Nathan was advising the U.S. government, although his role was sharply limited. When it really counted in 1960, after all, Nathan had stayed in the enemy camp. Nathan appreciated that Kennedy had been cordial, but admitted "I do think that I was sort of frozen out."[221]

Nathan had served on an economic task force, one of the many created to formulate policy during Kennedy's transition. In May 1961, he was named to the Food for Peace Council directed by former Congressman George McGovern. Since most of the Council's members were celebrities without much administrative experience, Nathan was invaluable to McGovern.[222] There was the task force that created USAID of course, and another "blue ribbon committee" on unemployment, but the former was temporary and the latter mostly for show.[223] A position that Nathan would truly have loved to fill did come up in the summer of 1961—an opening on the Federal Reserve System's Federal Open Market Committee. The CEA typically advised the president about appointments and Nathan's name was on Walter Heller's list. But the nominee, Heller understood, would have to be someone of whom "sound money" bankers approved. Nathan, Heller wrote, "fulfills every requirement except that of invulnerability to the charge—though not, we would gather, the fact—of unsoundness."[224]

In early 1964 the new president was seeking to mend fences with the intellectuals who had never liked him but whose support he now needed. Heller assured Johnson that Nathan was "the most reasonable, effective, and friendly ally we have in the liberal camp. He can make the difference between opposition and support among very influential liberals."[225] That summer Nathan came close to being appointed to a task force on foreign economic policy—but missed the opportunity.[226] All the while, Nathan ached to return to a position of influence in the government. "We should do more entertaining," he told Mary. In Washington, that was a phrase with special meaning.[227] But finally Nathan did get deeply involved—in a matter that tore the country apart and drove the Democrats from the White House.

At the Cai San Resettlement area in South Vietnam, Nathan and fellow economist Clifton Wharton are greeted by village elders.

By the end of 1965, Vietnam was crowding out Lyndon Johnson's Great Society program of domestic reform and consuming the president himself. Escalation was underway, and although U.S. troops had made military gains, it had also become clear that North Vietnamese forces had been able to filter into the South at twice the rate U.S. forces were entering.[228] Legislators and the public were beginning to be concerned.

In late December, hoping to manufacture some better Vietnam-related news, Johnson asked Secretary Orville Freeman to plan a mission that would "focus attention on agriculture and all the Department of Agriculture was doing" there. The "blue-ribbon ten-man presidential mission" was called up suddenly on the weekend of February 5, 1966.[229] "I am a little bit concerned lest it might have been set up for PR or propaganda purposes," Nathan wrote in his travel journal. He surely suspected the truth, but this was not the kind of assignment he believed that he could turn down.[230] After a briefing in Washington the group flew secretly to Honolulu, arriving a day after President Johnson, who had arranged secret meetings with South Vietnamese leadership. The next day the economists were waiting in the hallway outside Johnson's suite in the Royal Hawaiian Hotel when Averell Harriman encountered Nathan and asked what he was doing there. Nathan explained. "I've been trying to see the President for the past two days," the Ambassador complained. "Get in line," Nathan urged. He did.[231]

The "Honolulu Conference" marked the point at which the Vietnam War began to pivot from crusade to quagmire. Defense Secretary Robert McNamara, who had waged war confidently since the Kennedy Administration, appeared for the first time tired and circumspect. He admitted to reporters that "no amount of bombing can end the war."[232] Nathan and colleague Clifton Wharton also recognized some bad signs. They were the only economists on the mission with any experience in Southeast Asia, the rest being influential deans of agricultural schools at big American universities.[233] They could be counted on not to understand what they were seeing during their time in Vietnam, but to gain ample press coverage afterwards.

After meeting with Johnson, the economists continued to Vietnam. There they broke into smaller groups. Together, Nathan and Wharton—always with military escort—visited government agencies, toured markets, and visited the "strategic hamlets" created as part of the counterinsurgency program. At Cai San they encountered 55,000 forcibly uprooted North Vietnamese trying to get crops started on parched and long-abandoned rice fields. Local dignitaries and interested farmers turned out in front of the "land reform" office to honor the American economists, where Nathan and Wharton gladly shook hands with them.[234]

It was all over quickly. By February 12 the mission was back at the White House for photographs. Nathan expected little more than a "thank you" from the president.[235]

Instead, Johnson talked with the economists for 80 minutes. Nathan called it "one of the best presidential sessions I have ever been in. This guy was sensational, really pressing for views and judgment," he gushed to the *Dayton Daily News*. Nathan told the Dayton newspaper that it would likely take five years for development to work under "military shield."[236]

Lyndon Johnson must have seen the stars in Nathan's eyes, for within just a few days he decided that he wanted an "economic czar in Saigon" and wanted it to be Nathan. His was to be an ostensibly powerful position, reporting only to South Vietnamese Ambassador Henry Cabot Lodge.[237] Nathan turned down the offer. He wanted to work in government, but not at the expense of "extended separation from Mary and the children."[238] Few men could withstand the combination of flattery and abuse known as "the Johnson treatment." "Goddamn it," Nathan remembered the ADA's old adversary telling him. "You fought to kill me in 1956. I want you now." Nathan agreed to consult, but mostly from Washington.[239] Through the spring and summer of 1966, Nathan met regularly with Robert Komer, the special advisor whose job it was to win the "hearts and minds" of the South Vietnamese. Those were important months, during which Komer developed his Civil Operations and Revolutionary Development Support program, essentially an economic development effort under a military umbrella.[240]

By early August 1966, inflation fueled by the troop buildup had reached a crisis point.[241] Komer and Nathan discussed it with Johnson, who persuaded the latter to make another, more extended trip to Vietnam to look at inflation, study the general economic situation, and come up with development proposals.[242] On August 12, newspapers announced the beginning of the "Nathan Mission" to Vietnam.[243] Nathan steeled himself to "be skeptical and then try to get a meaningful feel of what is going on."[244]

Another round of embassy visits, conferences with Vietnamese officials, and tours of the countryside followed. There were unforgettable sights and experiences: seeing soldiers waterskiing in the Saigon river, flying in helicopters—fast and just above tree level for safety—and getting used to far-off explosions and routinely rattling windows. Nathan recognized that although currency devaluation had solved the inflation problem for a time, the huge and growing U.S. presence only guaranteed that it would return. It also guaranteed that—to use terms Nathan favored in the 1960s—with Americans doing so much of the heavy lifting, South Vietnam was unlikely to ever build up the economic "muscle" required to stand on its own.[245]

Nathan clearly felt an obligation to the administration. He urged a visiting *Washington Post* reporter to draw attention to "the more positive side of development." Nathan was assured that readers were only interested in battles, body counts, and defoliation. By then he was thinking hard about what Lyndon Johnson might be interested in, determined to draw up a report that was "constructively critical." Following the pattern of his work on development projects, Nathan concluded the trip with some high level visits. On August 22, Nathan met with U.S. Ambassador Lodge and South Vietnamese Prime Minster Ky. He then gave an hour-long "background briefing" to reporters. The next day, shorn of VIP status, Nathan left South Vietnam, stopping in the Trust Territories on the way home.[246]

With Robert Komer and Lyndon Johnson, July 1966.

On September 13, Nathan returned to the White House but met only with Harriman and Humphrey. "I cross-examined Bob Nathan rather carefully," the vice president reported to Johnson. "The single most important point he had to make was that we are not organized, not mobilized, not staffed in Vietnam to do the job that must be done."[247] Johnson was willing to send in staff. During the year the number of soldiers in Vietnam had increased by 144 percent. The number of casualties had increased twelvefold since Nathan first took Orville Freeman's call.[248] And so the gulf between the pragmatic liberal Nathan and his ideologically unalloyed ADA associates opened wider. "Almost all of my liberal friends are highly critical of the Vietnam situation and of anyone taking part in it," he acknowledged at the time.[249]

The most influential of them was John Kenneth Galbraith. The Harvard professor, bestselling author, and former ambassador to India had been a founding member of the ADA, but he was too much the celebrity to be so constrained, and had long ago drifted away from the ADA. In early 1965, Nathan wrote Galbraith that his recent articles and speeches on foreign policy "have generated much interest and enthusiasm," and invited him to speak at the ADA Convention.[250] A month later, Ed Hollander upped the ante, asking him to accept the chairmanship. Galbraith refused because he was writing a book and "would be moving into an organization of which I know too little." Hollander considered the refusal a rain check for two years hence, when *The New Industrial State* would be finished.[251] In 1966, Nathan invited Galbraith to an ADA conference. "I will do almost anything for liberalism but attend conferences, retreats or séances," Galbraith countered.[252] He was willing, however, to destroy the ADA to get America out of Vietnam.

By late 1966, Galbraith, Arthur Schlesinger, Jr., and former presidential speechwriter Richard Goodwin were all convinced that fighting the administration's Vietnam policy had to be top priority for liberals. "Almost immediately for me a platform presented itself," Galbraith wrote later, "the chairmanship of Americans for Democratic Action."[253] He accepted the post in a speech at the May 1967 convention that was typically clever and sarcastic. Galbraith proclaimed that he would work to bring students into the ADA and seek to correct former "mistakes of liberalism," most notably its intolerance of communism of any kind. He delighted in taking a slap at labor liberals who, on foreign policy were "well to the rear of Gerald Ford."[254]

The delegates debated a resolution on Vietnam. ADA veteran James Wechsler backed a strong stand. Nathan led the proponents of a softer stand, which assigned some fault for the mess to the North Vietnamese. The strong stand won 129 to 74.[255] Another notable development at the convention was the Galbraith-backed election to the vice chairmanship of Allard Lowenstein, a dynamic attorney and civil rights activist who had decided to launch a "dump Johnson" movement after meeting with an inexplicably arrogant Walt Rostow.[256]

A few weeks later, at a lightly attended meeting, the ADA board resolved that Vietnam was "the only issue." Nathan had missed the meeting, but assured labor liberal Gus Tyler that "it seems to me rather irresponsible to propose political decisions that are geared only to one's position on Vietnam."[257] Tyler, conferring fervidly with Nathan and other old-line liberals during the summer, warned, "it is when we become a one-issue outfit that we are finished."[258] But Joe Rauh, certain that if the "Vietnam war is just one among many issues," the ADA would lose support of "independent liberals and the young," decided to cast his lot with Galbraith and Schlesinger.[259] Still, as the summer of 1967 wound down, Rauh and Nathan were working together, attempting to craft a position that enabled the ADA to "avoid a bloody fight."[260]

Lowenstein, meanwhile, went looking for a candidate to challenge Johnson for the Democratic nomination. He asked Robert Kennedy, who refused but suggested

Minnesota Congressman Eugene McCarthy as the sacrificial lamb for the Democratic left. On November 30, McCarthy announced his candidacy on a "peace in Vietnam" platform consonant with the ADA's. That was about all McCarthy and ADA had in common—McCarthy's voting record had earned him an ADA score of 62 percent.[261] "Nobody cared that McCarthy was awful on domestic affairs," confessed Rauh. "He was right on the war, and the war was everything."[262]

Now that there was a candidate, the once-theoretical divisions in the ADA became material. In December, founder James Loeb, distressed to be on opposite sides of a big issue for the first time, wrote Rauh a desperate letter that concluded "I am, finally, pleading for ADA's survival."[263] In contrast, correspondence between Galbraith and Schlesinger in early 1968 sounds positively conspiratorial as they tried to figure out how to keep ADA from flying apart as they turned it into an anti-Vietnam phalanx. To Schlesinger's reports on the labor situation Galbraith replied, "continue to take soundings, and I will be prepared."[264] On February 10, 1968, the professors won their battle in a contentious and portentous ADA board vote.

Rauh softened up the lines with an unequivocal resolution for McCarthy. Galbraith put the assault across with a softer measure allowing members to vote as they pleased while endorsing McCarthy nonetheless. After eight hours of debate the measure passed 67 to 45.[265] Three labor leaders resigned from the ADA. So did Leon Keyserling. Nathan told a reporter that he would not leave, but that he was considering resigning his vice chairmanship.[266] He and his fellow stalwarts then penned an open letter calling the McCarthy campaign a "futile gesture" and stating, "we believe that a working coalition of all liberal political forces has been and continues to be essential."[267]

Nathan was appalled as the liberal group so dear to him rushed down the slope from deliberate action to passionate deed, but he had missed something. He knew that the achievements of the Great Society—the Civil Rights Act, Medicare, and a myriad of other laws and programs—were monumental. And he believed that Johnson, and even more Hubert Humphrey, should get the credit for them despite the grave mistake of Vietnam. But Nathan was a practical man and a statistician at heart. He counted the pluses and minuses and drew his conclusions. He did not understand that Vietnam, like slavery 100 years before, had achieved the power to crystallize and subsume every other issue in the American polity.

1968: "A Terrible Year"

On March 15, 1968, Nathan interrupted preparations for a trip to Israel to go downtown for a press conference. Speaking as a delegate to the 1968 Democratic

Convention, Nathan announced unequivocal support for the ticket of Lyndon Johnson and Hubert Humphrey. He was convinced—and the polls seemed to confirm—that McCarthy had no real chance of becoming president. "Vietnam is, of course, a major issue but does not lend itself to simple solutions," the *Washington Post* quoted him as saying. Johnson, Nathan insisted, was the candidate most likely to bring about a negotiated end.[268] The next day, when that story hit the newsstands, Robert Kennedy announced his own candidacy, upsetting all of Nathan's calculations. On the airplane to Israel on March 17, Nathan started a new travel journal. His journals usually began with reflections on recent domestic activities, but this one began with a prediction: "It looks as though the Democrats are in for a terrible year with all kinds of political maneuvering and manipulation which could conceivably result in the election of Nixon."[269]

Closer to home, Nathan had other things to worry about. His older sister Lillian had been battling cancer for about a year, and Larry had just come down with severe and undiagnosed pains in his jaw and neck.[270] When Nathan arrived in Israel he learned from Mary that sons David and Richard had been criticized for their father's "stand on Johnson and Humphrey" by students and even teachers in the liberal Montgomery County public schools.[271]

But Nathan's most immediate concern was Israel. His labors on behalf of the nation had subsided recently; he only gave two speeches a year for Israeli bonds.[272] That changed in March 1967, when the Israeli government asked him to help plan a major economic conference on Israel's four-year plan.[273] The assignments were familiar: to compile documentation and help formulate basic economic policy, but Nathan was uncharacteristically incapable of focusing.[274] Every day he scanned the *Jerusalem Post* and Paris edition of the *Herald Tribune* for news of the primaries, anxious "to get back and get into the swing of the campaign."[275]

By the time the conference convened on March 31, Nathan was exhausted. The corridors were full of people he knew, but he hoped to be left alone. At 6:30 the next morning came a telephone call. A newspaper reporter told him that Lyndon Johnson had stopped the bombing in Vietnam and had withdrawn from the race. Now no one else at the conference could concentrate either—most were worried about the implications for Israel. At midnight on April 1, Nathan telephoned Ed Hollander who reported, "no one has any idea what was going to happen, including plans for Humphrey." Nathan hung up and returned to his journal. "If Hubert Humphrey is going to run, he is going to have my all-out support," he wrote.[276]

On April 5, the conference over, Nathan was rushing through the gates at the Jerusalem Airport when he passed a delegate from Memphis who said that Martin Luther King had been shot. Nathan could not quite absorb it—he kept going. Transferring flights in Rome and then Paris he saw the headlines and began to assimilate the news. But Nathan was not prepared to see "perhaps a dozen fires burning" below as his last flight banked into Washington from the south.[277]

In the three weeks between the time that plane landed and Nathan boarded another for Malaysia on April 26, the vice president's supporters launched "United Democrats for Humphrey." At its head were Senators Fred Harris of Oklahoma and Walter Mondale of Minnesota; next tier down were Robert Nathan and Orville Freeman. In Malaysia, Nathan met Bob Johnson and Franz Wolf, who were wrapping up a preliminary transportation survey there.[278] Politics again dominated all the discussions and Nathan swore that he had not met a soul who was for Robert Kennedy, but then, he acknowledged, "we are all too old and don't know the young people or the militant minorities."[279]

Nathan was on the official campaign, but Humphrey had two other organizations going as well. "Citizens for Humphrey" was a vehicle for some of Humphrey's other oldest friends, including David Ginsburg. There was also the vice presidential staff, which included political advisors Larry O'Brien and Bill Welsh.[280] On May 9, a campaign staffer called Nathan's office. Hollander took the request to "help organize preparation of some position papers on different issues."[281] Nathan, it had been decided, would spearhead Humphrey's "task force." In 1968 everyone had a task force—a group of big names to come up with big ideas, but perhaps just as important, to impart intellectual sheen to a campaign. The economists were at the top of the heap—Nixon had monetarist Milton Friedman and McCarthy had Galbraith.[282]

Even before Nathan left for Malaysia, colleagues were forwarding issue papers for him to pass on to Humphrey. "I am close enough to get ideas up fairly high," Nathan assured one of them.[283] Hollander did some of this work while his boss was abroad, and when Nathan returned he moved almost immediately from 16th Street to new headquarters at 17th and L streets. Nathan took personal assistant Pauline "Polly" Wagner along with him and put her on the Humphrey payroll.[284] Nathan settled in for seven months as the campaign's unpaid Director of Research and Policy.[285]

Nathan was a good choice to lead the Humphrey effort. He had done the work before, having participated in the foreign economic problems task force of the Kennedy transition team along with Galbraith, Rostow, and other luminaries.[286] More important, Nathan knew how to prepare position papers, knew everyone—or someone who knew everyone—and was fully capable of dealing with self-important people. Some of the younger people on the campaign, alluding either to the age of the economist or to his outdated economics, dubbed Nathan "the Theda Bara of the intellectual set."[287] But then the Humphrey campaign was not expecting much support from the youth movement.

By July 1, scores had been invited to join the task force—those who did not want to be associated with the administration's Vietnam policy were not identified to the press.[288] Dozens of task force meetings had been scheduled and a few had convened. Some took place at the Brookings Institution, others at the University Club or the Cosmos Club, but at least half were conducted at the offices of Robert R. Nathan Associates.[289] Nathan carefully shepherded his task force members. Polly Wagner made travel arrangements, and Nathan ensured that expenses were paid—in some cases even for those reluctant to submit vouchers.[290] Once the effort was going full bore, Nathan had five paid staff and three volunteers overseeing the production of 33 separate task force reports, on subjects ranging from crime to taxation, and from agriculture to energy.[291] Marshall Loeb of *Time* magazine helped to edit them.[292]

Nathan was not office-bound for the entire campaign. He made trips to Los Angeles and Detroit to moderate meetings between the candidate and local academics, and went to the Bay Area on his own to meet with professors there.[293] "Gatherings of this sort can help immensely in winning back the confidence of the intellectual community," political scientist Nelson Polsby assured him.[294]

But most of the time Nathan edited furiously and, as he put it, "poured in lots of ammunition for campaign speeches." Some of the task force papers were excerpted in press releases. When Nathan tried to clear one with Humphrey, the vice president replied, "I trust you completely. Go ahead."[295] When it came time to make a statement on the Middle East, Humphrey waited to do so until he was sure that it had been approved by Nathan.[296] Through the summer Humphrey was in close touch with Nathan, sending brief memos with new ideas or requesting clarifications, sometimes more than once a day.[297] The vice president was pleased with Nathan's effort. "Our task forces are producing excellent material," he wrote in early August.[298] But inevitably some task force positions foundered on political shoals. In early September, Nathan told the press that Humphrey would not press for an immediate tax cut. Social programs are needed, Nathan maintained, because the country "is so torn up." The resulting headline was "Aide says HHH would Ban Tax Cut." One of Humphrey's political advisors made clear that Nathan had only summarized a task force report and that Humphrey would have more to say about taxes later.[299]

One issue, of course, loomed much larger than taxes. "I have engaged in more verbal battles on this subject than any other single one," Nathan confided to a friend in the midst of the campaign. "Vietnam seems to have precipitated a failure of mind and memory for many people who otherwise still seem to be quite normal and sane."[300] But if voters would not give up their obsession with Vietnam, neither would Humphrey detach himself from Johnson's commitment to fighting the war. It was easy to identify the administration's most inhumane act, the bombing along the Ho Chi Minh Trail in which B-52s were dropping more explosives than had been released during all of World War II in a futile attempt to stop infiltration of arms and fighters from the north. The foreign policy task forces led by Harvard's Samuel P. Huntington and Columbia's Doak Barnett all agreed that Humphrey should, at minimum, pledge to halt the bombing.[301] But Johnson believed that the bombing would force the North Vietnamese to the negotiating table, and Humphrey could not bring himself to be disloyal to the president he served. Anytime he even appeared to be modulating the president's tones, Johnson brutally put him down. As Nathan faithfully conveyed it to a mutual friend, "a new unequivocal position on the Vietnam War would be utterly impossible for the Vice President of the United States, whether he is a candidate or not." [302] Especially if the president was Lyndon Johnson.

For a while, everyone looked hopefully to Paris, where Averell Harriman and Cyrus Vance were negotiating with the North Vietnamese. But the polls kept dropping along with the bombs and there was no progress in Paris. David Ginsburg, who advised on foreign policy while Nathan handled domestic affairs, began carrying around a speech pledging a halt to the bombing to be deployed when the time came. By June, Humphrey was ready to make the move, but he still worried that a new stand might short-circuit the peace talks. Nathan had relayed information between Humphrey and Harriman by letter and telephone before, but this was a question to be posed in person.[303] Nathan asked Chester Cooper, a Harriman assistant leaving for Paris to get Harriman's approval. Harriman refused.[304]

Harriman had another idea, however. It was one that more than a few had considered. On August 21, Carl Kaysen, who had been on Kennedy's National Security Council and was then in Paris, wrote Nathan about it. Kaysen suggested that Humphrey pen a speech emphasizing his duty to run as an independent man and announcing his resignation from the vice presidency, submit it to the press, and then tell Johnson only after it could not be retracted.[305] Nathan showed the letter to Bill Welsh.[306] As the convention approached, that seemed like the most dramatic place to make the stand. There, Nathan recalled, it was hoped that Humphrey would accept the nomination and then resign, insisting, "I can do no less." In retrospect it would appear to have been a good move. But it was, Nathan emphasized later, "a very confused time, with great risk involved." Larry O' Brien took the idea to Humphrey who dismissed it out of hand. "I still cannot forgive myself for not personally pressing this plan all the way," Nathan said twelve years later.[307]

The 1968 Democratic Convention came later in the year than ever before. Lyndon Johnson had wanted to have it coincide with his birthday. It was in Chicago because that was where Johnson's hero Franklin Roosevelt had been nominated for his second term. So Nathan and Ginsburg went to a city that no one wanted to be in, to hammer out a platform that no one believed in, far too late to save the campaign—all because someone not even running wanted it that way. Nathan checked into room 2416 at the Conrad Hilton Hotel and on August 20 the platform committee began its work.[308]

As Nathan and Walter Heller worked over the economic planks, Ginsburg tried one more time to make Humphrey budge on Vietnam.[309] Ginsburg gave him a draft with a moderate position on bombing. Dean Rusk approved it and Johnson suggested that he might do so as well. Then, as Humphrey recalled, there was "a change of signals from the ranch."[310] Wait for a breakthrough in Paris, Johnson instructed Humphrey. The dutiful son did.[311]

The ADA made things no easier for Humphrey. Rauh and Galbraith had circulated a letter to the members asserting that Humphrey was "a candidate of the past—of a past and a policy that the people have rejected."[312] Furious, Nathan drafted a rebuttal of the "unwarranted and unjust charge," for the ADA board.[313] He sent an advance copy to Rauh, reminding him that the ADA was supposed to "keep the door open" for Humphrey. "Maybe the jugular instinct is essential in politics," Nathan wrote his old friend. "If so, perhaps I'd better retire from the field completely."[314]

Nathan well knew there was never any chance for McCarthy to win. At the Democratic convention the party regulars all pulled faithfully behind Humphrey because to do anything else would have meant the end of party politics as they knew it.[315] But things were to get worse. Along with the delegates to Chicago came protesters ranging from the earnest SDS to the absurd Yippies, all determined to assure that the party convention was a referendum on the war. Hemming them in at every corner were Chicago policemen, as apt to be uncompromising as Mayor Richard Daley. The trouble started early and by the time Humphrey was nominated on the August 28 it had reached alarming levels. In some respects the street violence was most troubling to television viewers who saw Democratic Party pomp and police brutality juxtaposed on their screens. In the early morning of August 29, Nathan scrawled his congratulations on Conrad Hilton stationery and asked to be included in the framing of the acceptance speech.[316] Shortly thereafter Nathan received a frantic telegram from MIT social scientist Ithiel Pool warning that "Michigan Avenue violence has overwhelmed convention for TV viewers."[317]

In the bleak days of September, Nathan returned to the task force work, trying to forget "the earthquake that hit us at Chicago."[318] He completed seven new reports in the first week of September, while keeping the lines open to Harriman. "If substantial progress were made in the Paris talks it certainly would be helpful," he wrote on September 7.[319]

In mid-September Nathan wrote to Freeman what everyone already knew. "Next to vacil-lating on issues, the whole image problem suffers most, in my judgment, from the feeling that the Vice President is not an independent power."[320] By then the polls put Humphrey in fifth place behind Nixon, Edward Kennedy, George Wallace, and Nelson Rockefeller.[321]

Finally, in Salt Lake City on September 30, Humphrey declared himself willing to stop the bombing in Vietnam. From that moment, the polls began to improve. On October 5, the ADA Executive Board was generous enough to endorse the Democratic candidate—although it was, Rauh emphasized, "an endorsement with reservations." Hollander complained bitterly about having to listen to the Galbraith, Schlesinger, and Rauh contingent "inveigh against the vice president, dissect his character, impose the test of their perfectionism, and examine his every imperfection under the magnificence of their self-righteousness."[322] Nathan only told reporters that they could have gotten a flat endorsement but the vote would have been closer—he had thin margins on his mind as November approached.[323]

Late in the campaign, when all the task forces had met, Nathan Associates had one more opportunity to help the Humphrey campaign. In a last-ditch effort, in the absence of a willing publisher, the company served as a vehicle for underwriting the publication and distribution of Polsby's *The Citizens Choice: Humphrey or Nixon*. The books were mailed out with a personal letter from Nathan.[324] Near the end there was little to do but agonize about the candidate's every move. When the pols aired some slick films intended to sell Humphrey like soap, Nathan wrote to Larry O'Brien "PLEASE, PLEASE, PLEASE get him on some kind of face-to-face, people-to-people discussion group rather than these films." Nathan told Humphrey the same thing—to air personal appearances, with him talking with people rather than to a camera. It may have been good advice but it was also irrelevant. As the Humphrey campaign wound down it also ran into the red—there was little money left for further television spots.[325]

Humphrey made an impressive comeback. Voters wanted peace in Vietnam and they wanted a viable candidate to provide it. On the eve of the election, at least one poll put Humphrey ahead in the three-way race with Nixon and Wallace, but it was not enough. Humphrey gave up only seven-tenths of a percent of the popular vote, but he lost by 110 electoral votes. On November 27, Humphrey wrote wistfully to Nathan that there were, "yes, some heartaches, which is inevitable under the circumstances, but no rancor. Only just sorry I didn't do better."[326] Nathan was at the time absorbed in putting Nathan Associates back in shape; his seven-month disappearance had taken a toll on the firm.[327]

Nathan had enjoyed political maneuvering since the days of the Goon Squad, and he believed that he was good at it, but there was truth in his angry letter to Rauh at the convention. He did not understand the jugular, passionate component of electoral politics. That is why he been asked to handle position papers and not political positions. In an election in which both Republican and Independent candidates exploited the hopes and preyed upon the fears of voters, the Democratic candidate—and to an even greater degree his director of research and policy—clung to a liberal belief in the rational voter. As Nathan informed a "law and order" task force member, "we can fan hatred and bitterness without solution and that is what Nixon and Wallace are doing. Or we can undertake meaningful, positive and effective programs which will truly serve to reduce crime and unite people. The latter is what Humphrey will do."[328]

To Nathan, politics was not, as columnist Frank Kent famously called it, "The Great Game." For him the pursuit had been about ideals and in earnest: "Hubert was a man of peace. Goddamn it, Hubert was not for war," he declared years later.[329] Above all he had been devastated to see the ADA put into play. When Nathan Associates employee David Chewning asked about joining, Nathan said he could, "but I don't advise it." After 1968 he wished he had never taken it up.[330] Galbraith was too sophisticated to be so earnest. In early 1969 he sent out a fundraising piece claiming that if the Democrats had nominated McCarthy they would have won. Nathan shot back that he well understood the role of puffery in fundraising flyers, but that the McCarthy claim was "sheer fantasy." What did it matter? Nathan asked, "Humphrey has lost and, unfortunately Nixon will be President in a few days." He told Galbraith not to write him back as he was leaving the country.[331] Galbraith wrote back anyway, eager to continue the game. "You may of course be right," he admitted. "Let us now fix things up."[332]

The ADA had received a quick membership boost during the McCarthy campaign, but the bubble as quickly collapsed. Marvin Rosenberg, who had been there to meet Kennedy in February 1961 commiserated to Joe Rauh. "We must try to get the Humphrey people back," he wrote. "I am talking about the Ed Hollanders." "Someone has to shake up the ADA," he continued, "Bob Nathan isn't going to bother anymore and I seem to be the only one left."[333] Nathan did not remain angry with Rauh—the two had years yet in which to banter and badger one another—but Nathan was done with ADA. He went back to work. Polly Wagner, the only Nathan Associate who had seen much of him during 1968, once remarked that her boss was "the only man I know who works 24 hours a day." She marveled that despite the pace he seldom dropped his straightforward, friendly and informal manner. "Maybe it's because he has a clear conscience," she concluded.[334]

5

THE VOICE OF EXPERIENCE

On September 23, 1980, the House Committee on Banking, Finance, and Urban Affairs held a hearing on "World War II and the Problems of the 1980s." It was the idea of chairman Henry Reuss, once a lawyer with the Office of Price Administration. To testify he brought in old colleague David Ginsburg, their former boss, John Kenneth Galbraith, and Robert Nathan. Nathan prepared their written report and he led off succinctly, "I believe that we are rather adrift in the eighties." Despite better technology, longer experience, and greater productive capacity, he said, "we seem lacking in confidence and the competence needed to manage the problems of the 1980s."[1] Nathan then settled into a comfortable recounting of the bold and effective steps that the nation had taken 40 years earlier.

It was a fine panel: Galbraith's sardonic wit still sparkled, and Ginsburg played the wise and low-key foil. Nathan's voice still boomed with enthusiasm, although with slighter force and a hint of the querulous. He was an old hand on the witness stand; between 1968 and his last appearance in 1986, Nathan testified before Congress no less than 45 times.[2] Some of these appearances were for clients in the telecommunications, music, retail, or energy industries. Others were on behalf of advocacy groups: through the end of his life Nathan remained a ready joiner and reliable fundraiser. But the testimony Nathan enjoyed the most came on occasions like this, where he served as the voice of experience. Nathan was usually well-prepared for his testimony, but he improvised at times, and on those occasions he often returned to the economic achievements of World War II.[3] Galbraith closed the session with praise for two giants of the era, former boss Leon Henderson and fellow panelist Robert Nathan. "He is not a notably modest man, but he was unduly modest this morning," Galbraith remarked. "All of us who were in Washington in those days owed more to the Nathan vision of what the American economy could produce than to the work of any other man."[4]

In the last decades of his life, Nathan's accomplishments were impressive by any standard. He was a resource to Congress, worked on the fringes of national politics, and pushed the postwar liberal agenda about as far as it would ever go, all the while building up his own company and ensuring its transition from a small personal firm to a sizeable independent company. But all was not in order. The economic problems of the 1970s baffled every economist, Nathan included. Unmoored by inflation, rising unemployment, double-digit interest rates, its first hostage crisis, and its second energy crunch, the nation was indeed adrift in the fall of 1980—some believed that it had already hit the rocks. Robert Nathan's voice of experience provided few answers to the troubling questions of these years, but it provided solace for a time and a livelihood to the end.

EVERYBODY'S EXPERT

As the 1960s turned into the 1970s and Nathan went from his fifties to his sixties he began to leave overseas assignments to others and settled into a new mentally challenging but less physically taxing role—the expert witness in litigation and regulatory matters. Most efforts were behind the scenes, but there were still headlines to be made, particularly in the case of a baseball player named Curt Flood.

Thanks to a 1920s exemption from antitrust laws, baseball had more authority over its employees than nearly any other industry—its "reserve clause" allowed players to be traded at the whim of the clubs, leaving them no control over their own careers. In 1969, after Curt Flood had played twelve years in the majors, the St. Louis Cardinals abruptly traded him to the Philadelphia Phillies. He refused to go and the player's union backed him up. Flood was African-American, and the language that he used in his letter to commissioner Bowie Kuhn set the tone for the legal proceedings to follow. "I do not feel I am a piece of property to be bought and sold irrespective of my wishes," he wrote. It was the liberal's dream: antitrust, civil rights, and "America's game." Stepping up to take the case was Arthur Goldberg, former United Steelworkers Union counsel, Supreme Court Justice, and United Nations Ambassador.[5]

Goldberg knew that since this was an antitrust case, economic analysis was indispensable. Robert R. Nathan Associates had an established record in sports economics; two years after the 1966 Milwaukee Braves case, the firm did an analysis of the regional economic impact of the Green Bay Packers.[6] Even if the lawyer and economist had not been friends there would have been ample cause for Goldberg to pick Nathan.

On May 22, 1970, Nathan appeared in Federal Court before Judge Irving Ben Cooper in the Southern District of New York in the matter of *Flood v. Kuhn*. On direct examination, he testified that the reserve clause brought about "total and complete imbalance between employer and employee," and that it "tends to depress wage levels because there is no opportunity to negotiate with alternative users of services." On cross-examination the league's attorney maintained that without the reserve clause wealthier clubs would monopolize talent. "There is not a tendency in the free enterprise system for all top talent to gravitate into one entity," Nathan countered. "Diversity tends to result, not concentration."[7]

Nathan did not persuade Judge Cooper, and Flood appealed all the way to the Supreme Court. Although Cooper's decision was upheld there, the salvo fired by Goldberg and Nathan had an effect. In 1970 the league allowed players with sufficient seniority to veto a trade. Nathan had been wrong about concentration, and so unwittingly did his part to spur the creation of the New York Yankees juggernaut.

In 1971 Nathan took another high-profile sports case. For years there had been two basketball leagues, but in the 1960s, while the National Basketball Association bounced along profitably, the American Basketball Association had deflated.[8] Deciding that two leagues were one too many, the ABA and the NBA decided to merge. The merger committees of the separate leagues hired a single economist, Nathan, to prepare a brief supporting the move.[9] This was no court case, but because the move required an antitrust exemption the merger had to be approved by Congress, so in September 1971, Nathan found himself facing the Senate Antitrust and Monopoly Subcommittee and Senator Sam Ervin of North Carolina.

Nathan and the North Carolina Senator had once been on the same side. Ervin had served on the Senate Select Committee to Investigate Campaign Practices that had helped bring down Joseph McCarthy. But he was tough, legally astute, personally opposed to the merger, and tough on basketball's witnesses. At issue was the question of whether having a single league would create undue market power in the sport and particularly over the players. Nathan's economic analysis indicated that there was no problem with the merger—or basketball's "option clause"—provided it was flexible enough.[10] Pointing to Nathan's steadfast opposition to any reserve clause in baseball, Ervin suggested that there was some inconsistency on Nathan's part.[11] Nathan did not get anywhere with the Senator—it was five years before the basketball leagues were allowed to merge—but he perhaps helped in a small way to keep Ervin in shape for his biggest quarry—President Richard Nixon, whom he brought down in the Watergate hearings of 1974.

Although he supported labor in baseball and ownership in basketball, Nathan was most often an expert witness for industry during these years. Some were regulated utilities such as Panhandle Eastern, a natural gas firm that had to beg for rate relief as inflation escalated. In his written brief, Nathan imaginatively found the 1946 Employment Act to be justification for a rate increase. It was necessary to enable Panhandle Eastern to ensure "maximum employment, production and purchasing power" required by the act.[12] In his testimony for an all-American trans-Alaska natural gas pipeline in 1975, Nathan took an equally expansive view, pointing to the payments benefits to be gained by cutting Canada out of the pipeline.[13]

Nathan also served, in one reporter's words, as the "key witness" when American Electric Power wished to merge with the Columbus and Southern Ohio Electric Company, insisting that even if the merger appeared contrary to antitrust laws, it "may not be contrary to the public interest in the electric utility industry and may even benefit the public." The industry journal *Electrical World* admiringly called this "the pro-merger or pro-consolidation argument, thoughtfully—even eloquently—expressed."[14]

Encountering Nathan as industry advocate came as a surprise to those who knew him only by reputation. Bernard Norwood joined in 1975 and quickly became one of the firm's top economists. "I'd have expected that he'd have been on the other side, the consumer side," Norwood admitted, but he soon realized that for the firm, free trade usually won out over other interests—even labor.[15] At the outset of its ultimately successful drive to take over a large share of the American market, for example, Nathan was the principal economic witness for the Japanese Automobile Manufacturers Association before the U.S. Tariff Commission.[16] The company also did a study on an obscure tax clause on behalf of manufacturers working on both sides of the U.S.-Mexico border. While Nathan's briefs were good, Norwood recalled, it was the "spark" that "often occurred in oral testimony" that Nathan's clients found most valuable.[17] In his testimony before the House Ways and Means Committee, Nathan extolled "Section 807" for bringing out the best in both economies, allowing unskilled Mexican labor to assemble parts made by skilled workers north of border.[18] Not surprisingly, organized labor was very unhappy about both of these appearances.

Ultimately, Nathan's testimony, like his economics, was influenced by enthusiasm. At one point an opportunity arose for Nathan to testify in favor of the Jones Act, venerable protective legislation intended to keep the domestic maritime fleet alive. John Beyer questioned whether the company should defend protectionism, but when meeting with the potential client, Beyer recalled, Nathan began to "wax eloquent and his arms would move around. You knew when he did that that we would take the assignment."[19] Nathan also represented the American Maritime Association, whose members were not subsidized, and protested that the protected lines should not benefit from special rates on military and government shipments and thus enjoy a "double subsidy."[20]

Meanwhile, work continued for one of the firm's highest profile corporate customers, which prompted one journalist to dub Nathan "Ma Bell's Boy." As he had in the mid-1960s, Nathan continued to argue that AT&T was a natural monopoly, appropriately regulated, but that it should nevertheless be awarded substantial rate increases so as to be able to ensure growth and full employment.[21]   In the 1970s things got stickier as the economy deteriorated and the Federal Communication Commission began to consider taking the Bell System apart. AT&T kept up a steady counteroffensive with Nathan as an eloquent front-rank witness. In March 1972, labor-friendly journalist John Herling deemed Nathan's position newsworthy. "In liberal circles over which Bob Nathan has customarily presided with charm, dignity and gusto, strong men and women suddenly fell silent as they contemplate the new role for their erstwhile leader," Herling wrote in the *Washington Daily News*. AT&T, he wrote, "bought itself a degree of credibility and an appearance of virtue by hiring Mr. Nathan."[22]   Leon Keyserling rushed to his fellow New Dealer's defense, insisting in a letter to the editor, "the very essence of liberalism includes that independence of mind and action which prompts an individual on an ad hoc basis to defend the cause he believes right."[23]   Keyserling's perspective was improved no doubt, by the fact that he had done work similar to Nathan's for the natural gas industry.[24]

Despite AT&T's efforts, pressure mounted and Nathan waxed ever more philosophic. In 1974, Clay T. Whitehead, the director of the White House office of telecommunications policy, intent on opening up the industry, drew attention to the Bell System's least defensible practice—that of forbidding its customers to use any equipment not manufactured by its Western Electric subsidiary.[25]   In July, before a Senate Subcommittee on Antitrust and Monopoly, Nathan defended his client in glowing terms, dismissing the Western Electric question as having to do merely with "compatibility," and calling AT&T "remarkably possessed of vision."[26]

But even as Nathan remained the face of the firm at the highest level, he was steadily building up an increasingly autonomous staff. Having long since outgrown the old doctor's office on 16th Street, in 1971 the company moved into new quarters, occupying a floor of a large commercial structure called the "Ring Building" at 1200 18th Street Northwest.[27] More and more the old triumvirate—Nathan, Hollander, and Wolf—increasingly passed down the work. Early in her career with the firm, Harriet Kriesberg sat in a meeting with Nathan and Hollander, trying hard to keep up with their discussion. She was relieved when the meeting ended only to realize that it was assumed that she would be writing the report. "I think it was really their philosophy," said Kriesberg—"swim or sink."[28]

By the early 1970s Robert R. Nathan Associates was being remade by a younger generation, some with roots in the Peace Corps. Nathan understood the importance of the new recruits but did not go out of his way to welcome them. In the spring of 1974 one such young economist, Roger Manring, came in for an interview. Nathan remained behind his desk, never stood, and hardly looked up. Instead, recalled Manring, "he went through the resumé in great detail so that he understood the chronology of everything. He was a detail-oriented guy and wanted it all to fit together neatly, and to know the facts." Manring passed this unusual interview, and a short time later he was given a few books and a sample proposal, and asked to write a technical proposal for a Nicaraguan transport system. Assuming that his job was on the line, Manring was toiling away on a Sunday night when Nathan came into the office. "What in the hell are you doing here?" Nathan asked. Enlightened, Nathan shook his head and grumbled, "good God, that isn't an appropriate task for you"—but left him to do it anyway. "It was not a place where you learned anything in a formal way," said Manring.[29]

Nathan continued to make hires in the 1970s, however, that followed the old model of bringing in a government veteran with established expertise. After retiring as assistant director of the Office of Management and Budget, Samuel M. Cohn joined the firm as a senior associate in August 1973.[30] Bernard Norwood was another ready-made "greybeard" for the firm. He had worked in the Foreign Service, the Office of the Special Trade Representative, and the Federal Reserve before joining the firm in 1975. Nathan had plans for each of them: Cohn was to handle statistical and economic surveys related to government policy; Norwood, matters related to foreign trade. But those plans changed when the project mix changed unexpectedly, much like the economy of the 1970s.

INFLATION ECONOMICS

In late October 1973, Nathan noticed that people were leaving the office without turning out the lights. He shot off two memos: one to his staff and one to the management of the building—other offices were leaving the lights on too. The building manager, recalled Nathan, "was a little shocked that anybody would be concerned."[31] But these were the days of the Arab oil embargo. The nation was in economic crisis and Nathan was deeply concerned—for good reason as it turned out. During the next seven years the economic earthquake of the 1970s would destroy for good the postwar liberal consensus that Nathan had taken for granted. His was among the loudest voices during the upheaval, even though he knew no better than anyone else what to do.

Inflation rose moderately in the early 1960s, then more than doubled as public spending for the Vietnam War and domestic programs overheated the economy. By 1970 the cost of living was steadily going up an alarming 4.2 percent per year and it was up to Richard Nixon to do something about it. During World War II Nixon was a low-level lawyer in the Office of Price Administration; although he worked in rationing, he liked to say that he had developed an aversion to price controls then.[32] Nevertheless, by the summer of 1971, public and professional opinion was overwhelmingly in favor of controlling both wages and prices in order to beat inflation. In August, Nixon imposed a 90-day freeze called "Phase I." The Council of Economic Advisors, led after 1972 by Herbert Stein, was in charge of making it work. No one knew then what "Phase II" would look like.

Testifying before the Joint Economic Committee of Congress on President Nixon's economic program, September 3, 1971. (© The Associated Press)

As the long prosperity of the 1960s came to an end, Americans became uncommonly concerned with economics, and the popular press was happy to oblige them with all the speculative analysis it could offer. *Newsweek* convened the most stellar panel, featuring Keynesian Paul Samuelson, monetarist Milton Friedman, and Yale anti-inflationist Henry Wallich.[33] *Time* countered with its own "Board of Economists," which included Walter Heller and Arthur Okun—both former chairs of the Council of Economic Advisors— Joseph Pechman of the Brookings Institution, and Beryl Sprinkel, a Chicago banker and follower of Freidman. The *Time* board also included two consultants: Otto Eckstein and Robert Nathan.[34] For a decade beginning in 1969, *Time* gave Nathan and his colleagues a platform for a plethora of predictions and pronouncements. They were lucky to be right half the time, but that was enough for *Time* magazine, confirming as Stein remarked later, that economics, like show business, was "a combination of information and entertainment."[35]

The earnest Nathan had a great deal in common with the puckish Herb Stein. They both had a working-class upbringing in a second-rank city (Stein was from Schenectady), but Stein was far more the academic—he studied for his Ph.D. under Jacob Viner, who inspired the neoclassical Chicago School developed more fully under Milton Friedman.[36] Stein was less dogmatic than the pure monetarists, but far more suspicious of deficit spending than the Keynesians. Putting Stein in charge of price controls, Nathan intoned in the October 11, 1971, issue of *Time*, was "like putting Polly Adler in charge of a convent."[37] Younger people might have scratched their heads, but contemporaries knew Adler as a notorious madame of the 1920s and 30s—score one for Nathan as *Time* talking head. Stein topped Nathan though, countering that it was more like putting a nun in charge of a brothel.[38]

Stein had a point. The economy had gone through a mild recession after 1969 and never fully recovered, making Nathan far more concerned about the "severe waste of resources" caused by unemployment than about the dangers of inflation—he wanted the Phase I freeze followed by an "expansionist fiscal policy."[39] When Phase II did go in— which allowed application for exemption—Nathan predicted "one of the most divisive, loud, screaming, scratching, gouging periods in a long time."[40] Regardless, the controls seemed effective. They "could have been tougher and administered a little more effectively," Nathan said, but they worked.[41]

But the key to beating inflation was curbing the self-fulfilling expectations of consumers and businesses that prices would continue to rise. If there ever had been a chance for them to work, the Nixon controls were on too briefly to succeed—people waited them out. And Nathan was right; they were half-hearted. When Phase II gave way to a much looser Phase III in 1972, the cost of living took off faster than before, heading toward 7 percent overall. The timing was terrible—bad weather was even then resulting in global crop failures and causing U.S. food prices to escalate steadily. It was "probably the worst economic mistake that has been made in decades," Nathan opined in the October 15 edition of *Washington Watch*.[42]

The next day things got much worse. On October 16, the Arab oil producing nations announced a 70 percent hike in oil prices in retaliation for U.S. support of Israel in the Yom Kippur War. Energy costs began to drive the overall cost of living ever higher. To cope, working people, especially unionized ones, began pushing for cost-of-living adjustments. Employers raised prices to keep up and the "inflationary spiral" began. Expectations were no longer of 4 percent inflation but of 8 percent inflation. Then in late 1973, the economy, undermined by precipitously rising costs and steadily falling productivity, plunged into full-blown recession. America was mired in "stagflation," a combination of unemployment and inflation that the Keynesians had generally assumed could not occur—one was supposed to automatically curb the other.

In this new climate it became a measure of preference, or perhaps ideology, as to whether an economist chose to target inflation or unemployment. Nathan's chief concern was clear. In November 1974, Nathan cautioned that labor was getting militant. "There is talk of violence and rioting in the street," he warned. At the very least, he predicted, workers would expect to reopen contracts ahead of their expiration for pay hikes.[43]

By then Nixon was gone, price controls had been completely discredited, and the genial Gerald Ford wondered what to do next. He planned a big economic summit for December, but scheduled a more select "pre-summit" in advance of that. Twenty-eight economists and eight legislators gathered in the East Room for the pre-summit. Ford started the proceedings and then turned them over to his new CEA chairman, Alan Greenspan. Most of those in attendance worried about inflation, but they still believed that recession—if allowed to continue—would eventually bring it under control.

When Nathan's turn came he told Greenspan that he was "considerably depressed and unhappy about the discussion up to now." Six percent unemployment, he stated, would not curb inflation. In what would turn out to be one of his most accurate predictions ever, he surmised that 8 or 10 percent unemployment, over two or more years might, but added, "I am not sure who it is that is willing to pay that kind of price."[44] Nathan was not. Even though the economy was sodden with steadily depreciating money, Nathan wanted the government to spend its way to full employment. "Let me add," he told the group, "that though it is battered and beaten we still have the Employment Act of 1946 on the books."[45]

Nathan did not dwell on the fact that while more spending might curb unemployment it would certainly—and ultimately did—fuel inflation. Instead, Nathan's prescriptions sometimes changed over time and according to venue. In October 1974, he told an advertising group, "I wouldn't be afraid to accept a 6 percent unemployment rate for a year or more if it could beat inflation."[46] Later he scolded Greenspan for suggesting that 4.9 percent unemployment would be acceptable.[47]

In general during the mid-1970s, Nathan's solution to economic trouble was a combination of the recent and the very old. The right mix, he suggested in the journal *Challenge*, would include a bit of coaxing ("moral suasion" and "price guideposts" in terminology then fashionable), some selective wage and price controls (but only if absolutely necessary), a heavy hand against the old bogey of "administered prices" through trade reform, and antitrust measures informed by a "new TNEC"—the late Depression effort to restart competition that had shaped Nathan's own career.[48] But mostly Nathan wanted growth regardless. "The important thing is to get that money out, to stimulate the economy and productivity, and that will generate tax revenues and reduce the deficit," he told a Congressional hearing in 1975.[49]

In the end it is doubtful whether even Nathan believed that the Keynesian solution that made so much sense during the Great Depression made sense in the 1970s. He must have included himself when, as *Washington Post* reporter James Rowe, Jr. heard him say in an unguarded moment at the 1978 annual meeting of the American Economic Association, "the profession has been devoid of any new ideas in recent years."[50]

In the midst of it all, Nathan still found an opportunity for mischief. Shortly after the pre-summit, Ford fixed on an unusual economic strategy—a public relations campaign that exhorted the public to buckle down, "whip inflation now," and wear a "WIN button" like the one on his own lapel.[51] Nathan ordered some buttons of his own that said BATH, for "Back Again to Hoover," and gave them out at every opportunity. He sent one to his friend, cartoonist Herb Block, explaining his dismay at the majority opinion expressed at the pre-summit. "These views given to the president were reminders of the 'wait for prosperity to come around the corner' philosophy of Herbert Hoover," he wrote Block. "That is why I ordered the buttons and have had to reorder."[52] And so, at least for economics enthusiasts, the Christmas season was lightened by Robert Nathan's BATH button. It was written up in the December 8 *Washington Post* and pictured in the December 23 issue of *Time*.[53]

In its reference to Hoover, of course, Nathan's button harkened back to a national economic crisis not comparable in cause or remedy to 1974. An editorial in the December 8 Sunday supplement of the same *Washington Post* entitled "The Good Old Days" did not refer to the button but made this point explicitly. Nathan, Keyserling, and Galbraith comprised an economic establishment "whose heritage and communal nightmare would be the Great Depression," it said. "This may explain why inflation appears to have baffled them so—they weren't trained or ready for it."[54]

LAST CHANCE AT PLANNING

Even as the old Keynesian fiscal tools failed to solve the nation's manifest problems, another solution equally treasured by the old establishment gained brief currency. One of the first indications came from an unlikely source: when Herb Stein mentioned at an American Economic Association meeting that "maybe we need an economic planning agency."[55] Stein was not serious, but other economists were.

Nathan was more than a long-time advocate of planning—it was his livelihood. He had been discouraged when the nation moved from comprehensive economic planning back towards free market solutions after the war, but had welcomed the chance to assist planning ministries abroad during the postwar years. Nathan never believed that free market mechanisms alone could ensure an equitable society at home or abroad, nor did he believe that economic failure should be accepted. As he told one interviewer in 1976, "I say, don't walk away from it. We have to analyze, evaluate, and appraise more carefully. We have to be more humane, more patient, more dedicated, more persistent." He concluded in Rooseveltian terms: "to me, it is worthwhile trying, experimenting, innovating."[56]

It was another economist, however, who got things going. In a March 1974 *New York Times* article, Wassily Leontief made the case for a "well-staffed, well-informed and intelligently guided planning board." He appealed unabashedly to the past, asking "isn't it time to revive President Franklin Roosevelt's National Resources Planning Board?"[57] Leontief was influential, having just won a Nobel prize, and he began gathering a group of economists, labor leaders, and even businessmen, all in agreement that "no reliable mechanism in the modern economy relates needs to available manpower, plant and materials." Among them were John Kenneth Galbraith, Robert Nathan, UAW President Leonard Woodcock, and Ford chairman Henry Ford II. In October the group was formally organized under a name suggested by Galbraith, the "Initiative Committee for National Economic Planning." As the title indicated, the committee members clearly expected to start something—they began drafting legislation to create an Office of Economic Planning in the White House and a Joint Congressional Planning Committee on Capitol Hill.[58]

For a time, the tide seemed to favor economic planning. By early 1975, some seventy economists had signed on, convincing one academic that this "does not look like the membership list of some small and clandestine group. They are people of experience and sophistication."[59] By February, the legislation was drafted and the effort had moved to Capitol Hill under the sponsorship of Senator Hubert Humphrey and the liberal Republican Senator Jacob Javits, both members of the Joint Economic Committee. "I know of no other single lesson which we can draw more clearly from this recession-depression than the need for some sort of economic planning mechanism in this country," Javits declared in a February 28 session.[60]

These words were glorious music to Robert Nathan, emanating from one of his favorite concert halls. The Joint Economic Committee was created by the Employment Act of 1946 to consult and coordinate action regarding the yearly economic report provided by the president's Council of Economic Advisors. It did not report legislation—it collected information, offered advice, and generally beat the drum for economic growth. Its members included such Nathan friends as Congressmen Richard Bolling of AVC days and Henry Reuss of wartime Washington. Nathan friends on the Senate side included Wisconsin's William Proxmire, New York's Jacob Javits, and of course Minnesota's Hubert Humphrey. Identified by Proxmire as "an old friend of the committee," Nathan was welcomed to expound on a variety of subjects throughout the 1970s.[61]

Nathan was in on the planning discussion at the outset. At the February 28 session the opening remarks of Javits were followed by a colloquy between Humphrey and Nathan on one of their favorite subjects. "I have deep concern, Mr. Chairman and members of the committee," Nathan stated, "that in essence that Employment Act is being breached in relation and truly ignored and, if anything, being violated." He then urged the legislators not to be daunted by critics of bureaucracy. When Proxmire noted that Council of Wage Stabilization Administrator Al Rees already had 40 people on his staff, Nathan countered, "well I think he needs 400."[62]

As winter turned to summer the momentum seemed to grow. The Initiative Committee had its manifesto featured in the March 16 *New York Times*.[63] In May, Humphrey and Javits introduced their bill, the "Balanced National Growth and Economic Planning Act of 1975." It called for an Office of Balanced Growth and Economic Policy in the Executive Office of the President. This was to be a super-agency like the War Production Board, its 16 members including cabinet members and agency heads. Just as the Employment Act of 1946 obliged the president to submit an economic plan, this legislation required submission to Congress of a "balanced economic growth plan" every two years.[64] The members of the Initiative Committee went out to champion their legislation only to learn that, tough economic times or not, Americans were as suspicious of planning as ever. Galbraith was sorry to have included the unwelcomed word "planning" in the group's title. As Michael Sharpe, the editor of the liberal periodical *Challenge* who helped coordinate the effort recalled, "We got it hot and heavy from the press and in retrospect the name was a mistake."[65]

As that effort bogged down, Nathan became deeply involved in less ambitious planning initiatives. He had already helped to found a short-lived group called The Council on National Priorities and Resources, which was "committed to promoting government action to meet human needs." Part of the idea was to give members, which included labor unions and religious organizations, the kind of long-range planning capacity that the executive and legislative branches had. But the Council could not help rating members of Congress just as the ADA had done. The chairman of the group at the outset was former Ohio Governor and short-lived liberal champion John Gilligan. Dovish diplomat Paul Warnke was the Council's Defense Chair and Nathan its Economic Chair.[66] By February 1976, when the Joint Economic Committee called upon Nathan to testify on behalf of the Council, he had moved up to Chairman.[67]

For a time it looked as if the energy crisis would provide the opportunity for planning that Nathan had been seeking for decades. When Senator Henry Jackson introduced legislation to create a National Energy Production Board, Nathan appeared before his committee to recount the War Production Board days and to dispel apprehensions about planning. "It doesn't mean government ownership. It doesn't mean government operation," Nathan insisted. "The problem is one of coordination, of planning, of programming and focusing."[68] While that idea stalled, Nathan participated in a non-governmental effort as Chairman of the Executive Committee of the Americans for Energy Independence.[69] At the end of the decade, Nathan was among those still pushing for a "high-level organization above the cabinet level and with direct access to the president," to deal with the energy crisis.[70] When President Carter finally proposed an Energy Mobilization Board in 1980, he had neither the skill nor support to push through what one centrist political scientist disparaged as "an expensive, inflationary, and growth oriented" plan.[71] Meanwhile, Nathan hung on as the Humphrey-Javits planning bill underwent a strange transformation.

The 1971 book, *The Future of the US Government*, grew out of the prestigious Commission on the Year 2000 convened by the American Academy of Arts and Sciences. For that volume Nathan contributed a chapter on relations between the public and private sectors at the century's end. Part of his millennial vision was that the decade of the 1970s would give rise to an "Opportunities Act," that would "make the federal government responsible for minimum social and welfare standards."[72]

The prediction was half right. The legislation came, but failed to make anyone responsible for anything. When the Humphrey-Javits planning bill stalled, California Congressman Augustus Hawkins seized the opportunity to revive a full employment measure that he had been keeping on life support for years. Humphrey, always eager to "put full employment back in the employment act," agreed to graft his bill to the Hawkins bill.[73]

Nathan and Humphrey had drawn close together during the liberal imbroglio of the 1960s, and they remained that way into the 1970s. "Both you and I have seen the issues pretty much alike," Humphrey wrote Nathan in late 1972, "and there are few, if any, whose judgment I respect more than yours."[74] In February 1976, Humphrey asked Nathan to work with Joint Economic Committee chief of staff Jerry Jasinowski "to go over in detail the revised Humphrey-Hawkins Full Employment Bill."[75] Whatever Nathan's contribution, the final bill owed much to another of the old liberals who had also been on the outs in the 1960s. In helping frame Humphrey-Hawkins, Leon Keyserling got a last chance to create the law that he had hoped for in drafting his 1946 "Full Employment" bill.[76]

The "Full Employment and Balanced Growth Act," unveiled in March 1976, did away with most of the planning and focused on employment—it directed the government to guarantee full employment within a specified time and keep unemployment to 3 percent in the interim.[77] The bill was unfortunately short on specifics as to how the federal government would create full employment without fueling inflation. Democrats liked the bill because it gave them a "job creation" hammer with which to beat Republicans during the election year. But few expected much more from "Humphrey-Hawkins" and little effort was made to resolve the contradictions; instead successive revisions weakened the bill even further.[78]

Nathan and Humphrey at the National Economists Club, February 1971.

By 1977, as the *Washington Post* put it, Humphrey-Hawkins was a "shadow of its former self." So was its author. Stricken with cancer, thin and frail, Humphrey kept tabs on his bill's progress by phone from Minnesota.[79] Humphrey died on January 13, 1978. When the bill cleared the House of Representatives two months later, Muriel Humphrey appeared on the floor to congratulate Hawkins on passing what was widely considered a symbolic memorial to her husband.[80] Jimmy Carter signed it in the same spirit.

Nathan had settled for symbolism all along, acknowledging that the Executive Branch could not be expected to enforce either the Employment Act of 1946 or Humphrey-Hawkins. Still, he insisted, "the fact that Congress will have access to both the Council of Economic Advisors and the National Economic Planning Board will at least afford opportunities to focus national attention on critical issues and constructive programs."[81] He expected, as he had written in his 1971 prognostication piece about the "Opportunity Act," that "the mere statement of goals and objectives served to clarify responsibility and guide the policies of government, labor, business, farmers and consumers as they related to the essential needs and wants of the people and the productive capabilities of the economy."[82]

Nathan had failed to anticipate one important development. The planning bill had been framed when at least a few lawmakers could still believe that the old Keynesian ideas of growing the economy out of recession would work during inflationary times. By the time Humphrey-Hawkins passed almost no one did. The cost of living was now rising at about 8 percent per year, faster than at any time in U.S. history. A stamp that cost eight cents in 1974 cost 20 cents in 1981.[83] Some economists liked to assert that consumers got back in wage gains what they lost in price hikes, but with the exception of a few unionized sectors, that had not been the case in the 1970s. As non-union workers paid for the gains of unionized ones, new fault lines appeared in the old Democratic coalition.

In taking issue with classical economists who insisted that market mechanisms would bring about recovery from economic crises "in the long run," Keynes famously countered, "in the long run we are all dead."[84] But as Herb Stein later wrote, "by 1979, forty-three years after the publication of Keynes' *General Theory*, we woke up to discover that we were living in the long run and were suffering for our failure to look after it."[85] In that year, Federal Reserve Chairman Paul Volcker, a Carter appointee, began to tighten the money supply and drive the country into recession. It took four painful years—two of them with unemployment around the 8 to 10 percent level that Nathan had deemed necessary—but inflation was tamed for more than a generation.[86]

RETIRING FROM THE FIELD

On May 24, 1972, Nathan received a most prestigious award—"Nishan-i-Astour," the Order of the Star—granted by Mohammed Zahir Shah, the King of Afghanistan. Although he was assured that "few could possibly ever hope to get such an award," Nathan was not terribly pleased. The emblem on its face was impressive, but its large and awkwardly-constructed pin ruined his suit.[87] Afghanistan had been a landmark: the firm's longest running contract and a large proportion of its international receipts.[88] But like the Order of the Star, Afghanistan only looked good from one side.

Afghan authorities had always been slow to implement economic development plans, but by 1969 forward movement had largely stopped, and for good reason: Nathan was recommending deficit spending at a time when inflation was already a problem. But beyond fiscal policy there were plenty of other Nathan recommendations that the Afghanis refused to implement—anything that would upset the status quo.[89] Corruption remained rampant, export-import restrictions were routinely violated by bureaucrats, and the government was reluctant to tax anyone. By the time Nathan arrived to check up on his Afghanistan team in early 1971, USAID had decided to cut off funding—the firm was on its last two-year contract.[90] On that trip Nathan made his usual rounds of parties, employee meetings, and visits to the ministries, but when it came time for his customary audience with the King, Nathan was unusually frank. There was "not enough decisiveness," Nathan complained. There was no lack of planning or direction, he insisted, "the problem was one of getting things done."[91]

When Nathan returned to Afghanistan that summer, things were worse. Domestic investment was down and foreign debt was up. But the biggest problem was agriculture. Two years of bad harvests had created what Nathan called an "emergency situation" in Kabul.[92] He would have known, since the firm had recently picked up a small Asia Development Bank contract to advise the government on agricultural policy. That task seemed to be ticking along well, but the main project advising the ministries had largely broken down and mission chief Glen Parker, disillusioned and demoralized, was soon replaced.[93]

In the summer of 1972 Nathan returned—his eighteenth trip in less than eleven years—to close out the contract.[94] By then the food shortage was dire. People were starving in Afghanistan's central province and there were regular demonstrations in Kabul.[95] As in Burma years before, Nathan made the best of it and worked hopefully. "Our most important task is to get out a good final report," he wrote in his travel journal. There were the usual rounds of meetings—now halfhearted—and at their culmination the receipt of the award and a last meeting with the King. "Nobody is ever held accountable and performance just isn't demanded," Nathan reported he had told the King. "There is never any penalty for failure to perform and never any reward for good performance." Nathan suggested that the King pick five incompetents in the ministries and fire them, and select five tax offenders and jail them.[96]

The King was not offended, but neither did he take Nathan's suggestions seriously. Like the rest of his government, he had too much at stake in the status quo. Nathan understood this. In its final report, produced in 1972, the Nathan team emphasized that at its core Afghanistan remained a traditional society in which "tribes, clans, families, economic classes, and possibly other groupings" were all in delicate balance. Within the government, therefore, "advice which brings with it the possibility of upsetting the equilibria is regarded as irrelevant." Since economic change always upsets balances this was a damning admission of failure. As the contract closed, the Afghan papers commented—most likely for overseas consumption—"in the opinion of Robert Nathan, Afghanistan is near the take-off point in economic development."[97] Nearer perhaps, but nowhere close. Within a year the King was gone, deposed in a bloodless coup. Instability ensued, resulting in a Marxist revolution in 1978, civil war, and in 1979, a Soviet invasion. For decades afterwards Afghanistan would pay a terrible price for maintaining the old "equilibria" in a modern world.

And what of Nathan's well-made plans? More than a decade later, development engineer Louis Berger, working in Pakistan, talked with some of the men responsible for economic development in Soviet-occupied Afghanistan. They told Berger that the best plans and policies left behind by the Afghan ministers were the Nathan reports. "It bothered the hell out of me that those bastards might have benefitted from my work," Nathan admitted.[98]

Afghanistan was the last international project in which Nathan was personally invested. For one thing, Nathan was now in his sixties; the kind of travel schedule that he had maintained in the 1960s was no longer possible. Increasingly during the 1970s, his travel journals make reference to fatigue and he longed for evenings alone in his hotel room more than he had before—even if they were still hard to achieve.[99] The project mix also began to change. In late 1968, for example, the firm completed a transportation survey of Malaysia done not for USAID, but for the United Nations Development Program and the World Bank. The company began working on an inception report afterward for a regional development program for Penang, and although Nathan helped sell the project on a trip to Penang in the summer of 1969, he left the work to Bob Johnson and Jim Leonard.[100]

Much of Nathan's traveling during the early 1970s was aimed at picking up business. John Beyer, who had left the Nathan firm in 1968 to work overseas with the Ford

Foundation, still made a few connections for Nathan Associates. Upon hearing that the Ford Foundation would be leaving Nepal, Beyer set up some meetings between Nepalese development officials and his old boss. Nathan duly appeared, and wrote of Beyer in his travel journal, "we are still hoping that he will return to our firm one of these days."[101]

Nathan also hoped to build on the record in Burma and establish a firm foothold in Southeast Asia with an office in Bangkok, Thailand.[102] Again, the goal was to diversify beyond USAID to get more World Bank, UN, and Asian Development Bank work.[103] Among the promising projects that came out of it was an opportunity to conduct a survey for a 50-mile canal through Thailand between the Indian Ocean and South China Sea.[104] The Bangkok office was short-lived, however. Instead, its former director, Hank Winter, went on a part-time basis and traveled around the region meeting with officials, identifying opportunities, and reporting back to Nathan.[105]

These sales efforts were necessary for several reasons. First, early in his administration Nixon had put a premium on channeling U.S. funding through these "multilateral" financial institutions. Nathan did not think much of USAID's orientation in these years, writing in the liberal *Saturday Review* that the U.S. foreign aid policy "measures progress mostly in qualitative physical terms, as if the human spirit were a numerical factor in the gross national product."[106] Later, Congress wrested control over USAID from the Executive Branch and shifted its focus to small farmer agricultural development in the "New Directions" program. Regardless, Nathan believed that his firm had once again been "sabotaged and blacklisted" during the Nixon years. Nathan recalled later that "eventually my friends remaining in the government told me not to bother bidding for contracts."[107]

As USAID was developing its new direction during the mid-1970s, Nathan Associates was also developing new leadership in its international operations. When Nathan arrived in Kabul in January 1972, he found a letter waiting for him; John Beyer wanted to return to the firm. "I am very pleased," Nathan wrote in his travel journal, "because John is exceptionally good."[108] It was Beyer rather than Nathan who supervised the firm's largest international project at mid-decade, one in Indonesia that involved four resident economists, including veteran Rufus Hughes and a number of short-term consultants. Beyer well understood, however, that even if Nathan the project supervisor could be effectively replaced, Nathan the name remained an invaluable asset. When he believed that the Indonesia project was not getting sufficient attention, Beyer encouraged Nathan to visit "and try to get more interest in the project." Nathan obliged. On the same mid-1975 trip Nathan visited another of the firm's largest overseas missions in Western Samoa. This one was staffed by some old-timers as well, including mission chief Glenn Craig and agricultural specialist Richard Wheeler. Among the younger staff were manpower specialist Elwood Shomo and Roger Manring. In Western Samoa, Nathan dutifully met with the prime minister before departing, but the extent of his rapidly acquired expertise was nowhere near the mastery he commanded in the projects where his supervision had been more sustained.[109]

As Nathan curtailed his involvement, the vacuum was filled by two men: John Beyer and Jim Leonard, who had worked in Malaysia and Indonesia. The two were a study in contrasts. Beyer was perhaps as much academic as entrepreneur, but he was mostly dedicated to development—his Ford Foundation background meshed well with the Peace Corps tutelage of many of the firm's younger hires. Leonard, on the other hand, had a hard-charging personality, oriented more toward business than benevolence. Beyer recalled that Leonard "clearly wanted to get rich fast."[110]   Still, Nathan liked to have Leonard around, perhaps because he provided a bracing dose of realism. Leonard was particularly exasperated by some of the younger staff's ideas about litigation work. "All you guys talk about justice. It's about settling a dispute," he once told Roger Manring.[111]

While Nathan took a small step back, his company continued to evolve in tandem with the national and international organizations that directed and funded economic development in the Third World. In the mid-1970s, the firm won USAID's first indefi-nite quantity contract. An IQC provided a master agreement under which a firm could conduct specific tasks with relatively little red tape. "If a mission somewhere wanted something done they would send a telegram or just ask you," explained Beyer.[112]

Whatever the benefits of the IQC, working for USAID, the Asia Development Bank, and the UN put ever greater demands on the firm's back office, never a robust operation in the first place. Nathan set his firm on a better track when he brought in James Penkusky, an accountant and comptroller with extensive experience in the defense industry. Penkusky figured out how far to push Nathan in continuing the evolution of the firm. Like many entrepreneurial types, Nathan was usually willing to cut rates in order to gain business. From the outset Penkusky insisted that the firm set a profitable rate structure and stick to it. It took some time for Nathan to adjust, but he went along.[113]   During the mid-1970s the need to conform to government standards also led to the abandonment of a curious relic of the past—the seven-hour day, 35-hour work week that Nathan had adopted in his idealistic younger days.[114]

The international economic development industry was growing up as well. The oldest firms were built around dynamic individuals. Along with Nathan was Vincent Checchi, who had built his small Washington, D.C., practice into a top USAID contractor by the 1970s, and Louis Berger, a Penn State engineer who started out building roads in Burma in the late 1950s.[115]   But new firms joining the ranks during the 1970s, including

Development Alternatives Incorporated and Chemonics, got their start in the USAID fold and were quick to adopt the more corporate approach to economic development work.[116]

Although by the 1970s Nathan had begun to retire from the field, he was still deeply disappointed that between Vietnam, stagflation, and Watergate, "U.S. leadership of the post-World War II era is gone." His expectations may have been lowered, but typically, Nathan's enthusiasm remained high.[117] After having lunch with him in the spring of 1977, John Gilligan, now USAID administrator, thanked Nathan. "As usual," he wrote, "I was left breathless from listening to you spin off ideas and concepts with a youth and vigor which has sadly almost disappeared from Washington."[118]

"CONTINUITY IS ASSURED"

There were systemic changes on the other side of the business as well during the 1970s. At one time Nathan had stood almost alone in the field of economic consulting. After modest growth in the 1950s and 1960s economic consulting boomed in the 1970s. Nathan himself attributed this to the fact that "as the economy became more complex and less predictable and more regulated and more litigious, the need for experts increased."[119] Michael Evans, who started with Chase Econometric Associates in New York and then opened an office in Washington, put a finer point on it. "The watershed came when Nixon put on the wage and price controls." "It was good for business."[120] By August 1974, according to the *Wall Street Journal*, businesses seeking economic guidance were "flocking to consulting firms as never before." The largest of these firms were companies that produced and sold economic forecasting models and data sets, including former CEA member Otto Eckstein's Data Resources Incorporated (DRI), Charles River Associates, Chase Econometric Associates, which was founded in 1971, and the venerable Lionel D. Edie and Company, which had been purchased by Merrill Lynch.[121]

By the 1970s, however, more economic consulting firms, mostly in Washington, were following the Nathan model of producing specialized studies rather than financial forecasting or reports. Another former government official, Norman Turé, set up a firm that favored neoclassical rather than Keynesian economic approaches. Former Commerce and Federal Reserve Board official Andrew Brimmer returned from Harvard Business School in 1976 to set up a shop that attracted big corporate customers. "You should think of us as something like lawyers, with economist's portfolios," said Brimmer in 1977. New York-based National Economic Research Associates, Inc. had opened a satellite office in Washington by the 1970s and was heavily involved in the kind of litigation, regulatory, and antitrust work that Nathan did.[122] But there was no disputing that Robert R. Nathan was, as Herb Stein said, "one of the outstanding figures in five decades of Washington economics," and one of the largest, with about 50 professional economists employed by 1977.[123]   When, in 1978, junior economist Richard Blankfeld was looking for work in Washington, he interviewed at Charles River Associates and at DRI. "I liked applied economics and Nathan was really known for that," he recalled. "I knew that I would be doing a whole range of different types of things, and that really appealed to me."[124]

By the 1970s the range had narrowed somewhat. The regional development business that had begun with Michigan's Upper Peninsula expanded briefly in the late 1960s on the strength of funding by the Great Society Economic Development Administration and the Office of Economic Opportunity.[125]   That funding dried up in the early 1970s at about the same time that Nathan Associates ventured into far more specialized development much farther north.

Through the 1960s, no one was much concerned about the hundreds of land claims held by native tribes throughout Alaska. Then, in 1968, Atlantic-Richfield found oil in Prudhoe Bay and began planning a pipeline to the south. It suddenly became very important to figure out what belonged to whom. Arthur Goldberg again made the crucial connection for Nathan. He represented the Alaska Federation of Natives, who were seeking an Act of Settlement from Congress, and decided that a plan showing how the proceeds of the settlement would be used would help speed passage. Not until 1971 was the Alaska Federation of Natives Charitable Trust created to fund the effort. That March, Nathan sent community development specialist Lee Gorsuch to Alaska to begin the study. By then the legislation was close to passage and a dozen regional and 200 community native corporations had been established. Nathan himself traveled to Kodiak in April 1972 to conduct a seminar for the directors of the corporations.[126]   After helping them organize, Gorsuch traveled the state looking for the best way for natives to get economic leverage, be it through control of coal, oil, or timber. In the summer of 1974, Nathan Associates undertook a second project, determining whether programs established earlier should be continued or not.[127]

The firm's longest running contract also had its origins in the Goldberg connection. Even though Curt Flood had not prevailed, the Paul, Weiss, Rifkind, Wharton & Garrison law firm had been impressed by Nathan's work.[128]   In 1974, the law firm recommended Nathan to another of its clients seeking to cut through a knotty economic problem. The American Society of Composers Authors and Performers (ASCAP) had been protecting the property rights of musicians for 60 years. The chief function of the group was to collect licensing fees from users of music and to distribute them to its members. The problem, of course, was that with music so ubiquitous in American culture it was impossible to determine precisely who was owed what; instead statistical sampling of one sort or another was always employed. In the aftermath of a lawsuit in the early 1960s, ASCAP agreed to let a third-party economist do the sampling. By 1974 the original third parties—two academic economists—had reached an advanced age and ASCAP turned to Nathan.[129] Although *Billboard* magazine would on occasion call Robert Nathan an "ASCAP economist," the actual assignment fell to Sam Cohn, who spent most of the rest of his career with Nathan Associates producing musical, rather than governmental, statistics.[130]

Nathan Associates had built up such a large catalogue of domestic work by the 1970s that Robert Nathan could be involved in only a small part of it. Work for organized labor had become rare by then, but when it did materialize, as when a coalition of Massachusetts unions wanted economic justification for a 12 percent across-the-board wage hike, Nathan, despite his commitment to guideposts and other anti-inflationary exhortations, was happy to personally facilitate what he called, "a moderate and reasonable effort to overcome only a part of the severe erosion."[131] Maury Atkin continued to go his own way, serving exporters and Israelis, but Nathan joined in when, during the 1970s, the company did two national inventories of ferrous scrap for Atkin's long-time client, the Institute of Scrap Iron and Steel.[132] He also participated in a Nathan Associates-run symposium on "economic concepts of short supply" conducted for the Institute in early 1980.[133]

Although domestic business remained strong, the clientele changed. Well into the 1970s the firm had done a great deal of work for federal agencies and foundations—clients included the National Science Foundation and the Department of Health, Education, and Welfare.[134] Indeed, as late as 1974 Nathan could claim that his economists were "keeping their hand on the pulse of the medical job market."[135] But during the Nixon Administration, the government agencies that had once hired generalists like Nathan began using specialized contractors and internal personnel.[136] By the 1980s, as specialists multiplied and competition among more generalized domestic government contractors intensified, the boom of the 1970s began to reverse and many smaller consulting firms were sold or shuttered.[137] At the same time, macroeconomic analysis like the modeling done by DRI fell out of favor. For one thing, such statistics were increasingly available in trade and popular publications. For another, businesses had begun to realize that the economists were more often wrong than right.[138]

Taking the place of the government work and specialized studies was a steadily growing litigation portfolio. Although John Beyer began to establish his credentials in litigation, during the mid-1970s, Nathan remained the firm's top expert witness.[139] Indeed, Nathan's withdrawal from overseas projects only deepened his involvement in such work.

One big case at mid-decade involved agricultural chemicals. Typically, Nathan had his associates, in this case Sam Cohn and Harriet Kriesberg, develop a body of information. He began to immerse himself in the details a month before he was due to testify, and was, in Kriesberg's recollection, "brilliant."[140]

One of Nathan's favorite assignments pertained to antitrust and milk, a case that also involved Joe Fries of Arent Fox, Nathan Associates' own law firm. At issue was a complex dispute in which the militant National Farmers' Organization sought to demonstrate that the major milk co-operatives were trying to force it out of business.[141] Nathan capped the three-year project in May 1978 with two weeks' testimony about the proper nature and extent of damages in Federal District Court in Kansas City, Missouri.[142] Afterwards, Nathan and Fries inevitably rehashed "the good old days in milk" at every opportunity.[143]

Nathan was an excellent expert witness because of an innate ability to become engrossed in the minutiae of any subject, be it industrial policy, insecticides, or milk. He pushed his assistants hard to provide him with the details and the basic analysis, insisting over and over, "you've got to tell me everything. You can't be doing some analysis and hand me the result and say, 'this is the result.' I've got to know how you did it."[144] But the big insights usually came from Nathan himself, and few of his subordinates would be so bold as to ask him how he "did it." Stephen Schneider joined the firm in 1984, largely to take over the ASCAP work from Sam Cohn, who was eager to retire.[145] On one occasion Schneider and Nathan were working on a project for the directors, actors, and writers guilds, trying to determine the effect of income on pension payments. Nathan found a sheet of paper, scrutinized it, and announced, "It's 10 percent." "Oh, I have to write that up" Schneider said knowingly. He and an assistant spent the next three days figuring out what Nathan had done. "He would just see things," Schneider recalled, and "he expected you to have it too."[146] In 1978 there was one sheet of paper that Nathan enjoyed scrutinizing above all others—the one that determined how the management transition in his company would go.

Just a few years earlier, the corporate governance of Robert R. Nathan Associates was still as it had been for most of a decade, with Nathan Chairman, Maury Atkin Secretary-Treasurer, and Ed Hollander and Franz Wolf sitting on the board. Sam Cohn had joined the board in early 1976, as did Bob Johnson.[147] By then the question of who would succeed Nathan was in the air. Jerry Jacobson, having figured out that it would not be him, had recently left the company. Bob Johnson may also have harbored some hopes, but was never a real contender. Why Nathan was considering transition at this point is not clear. He was interested in writing his biography and had certainly slowed down a bit, but slow for Nathan was fast for another man—he presumably had many more good years ahead. In any case, by the mid-1970s, Nathan, as James Penkusky recalled, was "testing the waters with people"—he asked Penkusky for his opinion about John Beyer's business acumen a few times.[148] By the summer of 1977, Nathan was pretty sure of his decision— he put Beyer on the board.[149]

Nathan in his office during the 1970s.

The problem for Robert R. Nathan Associates, as it was for many closely-held private businesses, was how the original shareholders were going to get their equity back out of the firm. Wolf, Hollander, and Atkin all held stock in the company, but at mid-decade the largest shareholder by far, with more than 71 percent of the company, was Nathan, who ran the company accordingly.[150] "He decided who would get promoted. He decided who would be recruited," said Beyer, and board meetings usually took up what was legally necessary and little else.[151] The most common solution for an aging owner in that situation was to sell out to a larger entity, something that Nathan clearly did not want to do.

In the late summer of 1977, Nathan dispatched Hollander to talk with John Beyer and Jim Leonard. "Bob has an offer from an engineering firm that he's seriously looking at," Hollander informed them. "If you guys want to do anything about it, now is your time." The two talked things through. It was understood that Beyer would be president—that Leonard did not have the disposition that would win Nathan's approval. They consulted counsel, put together a plan, and presented it to Nathan and Hollander. "I want to think about it," Nathan said, and that was the last word for weeks.[152]

In October, Nathan and Beyer were driving to the Hartford airport after the funeral of former staffer Richard Wheeler. Maybe it was the occasion or maybe it was just time, but Nathan was ready to talk. "It won't work," he told Beyer. "You will never get the money. But I want you to be president. Let me think about it."[153] Nathan turned the problem over to Joe Fries at Arent Fox. The solution was a stock buyback program in which the financial growth of the company would fund the transfer of stock from one generation to the next. Who would be included in that new generation and to what extent was now a subject for endless diversion on Nathan's part. He drew up a list—by hand— of who would be involved in the buyback program and how many shares they should receive. Nathan constantly revised it—crossing out numbers and putting in new ones. He admitted to Beyer that he was having fun.[154]

Too much fun, Beyer and the other directors finally decided. They gently suggested that the transition be completed. On June 8, 1978, Nathan turned the presidency of the company over to Beyer. He became chairman of the board, got the traditional "corner office," and as much secretarial help as required.[155] A month later the company was recapitalized, with most of the equity of the firm repurchased by the company—which took on debt to do so. All of the senior shareholders received assurance that the company would steadily buy back their shares.[156] Nathan ended up with a 20 percent nonvoting share of his company, and appeared to be happy with his decision. "Twenty years ago the firm would have folded if I left," he said. "Now I think the continuity is assured."[157]

Last Activism

Nathan had turned his company over to the new generation with an ease all the more surprising because he was a self-professed "workaholic." But he did not need his company as much as a man solely dedicated to business would have—there was too much to be done elsewhere in Washington for a man who also called himself a "liberal with a capital "L." If he was not at the office prepping a litigation case or meeting with friends at his favorite restaurant, Washington institution Duke Ziebert's, he could be found testifying on the Hill or tending to the business of one of the nearly dozen activist groups that continued to occupy his time.[158]

The AVC was still around, now more an old-timer's club than a collection of earnest young men.[159] Nathan had remained active in the group and was a member of the AVC National Advisory Committee since its establishment in the late 1950s. He could be counted on to raise money for AVC programs, including assistance for veterans with less-than-honorable discharges in the post-Vietnam years.[160] At the summer 1976 convention, Nathan received the group's highest honor, the Bessie Levine Memorial

Award, given to the member "who has done most to represent the ideals and objectives of AVC." Perhaps more enjoyable was a smaller affair held at Bolling Air Force Base in May 1984, a dinner and reception held in honor of Nathan's 75th birthday. Old ADA ally Gus Tyler presided as master of ceremonies, the dinner committee comprised a "who's who" of liberal Washington, and speakers included Joe Rauh, Walter Salant, and Louis Walinsky.[161]

With John Beyer around the time of the June 18, 1978, management transition.

Another venerable organization with strong New Deal ties was the National Consumers League, a group established in the early 20ᵗʰ century and headed up by such notables as Mary Dublin Keyserling and Esther Peterson. In 1967 Nathan became Chairman of the Board of the NCL; he served for 11 years, fundraising the entire time.[162] When he retired, Nathan received the NCL "Trumpeter Award" for guiding the group "through one of its most difficult periods," and for "innovative economic thinking" that put consumers and workers first.[163] Nathan also served on the board of the Washington-based Public Welfare Foundation, which he described as supporting "New Deal kinds of concepts," until late in life.[164]

There were also shorter involvements, including a stint in the early 1970s as head of the National Policy Panel of the United Nations Association of the United States, a mid-1970s term as Chairman of the non-profit Population Reference Bureau, and chairmanship of the development committee of the National Academy of Public Administration.[165] Nathan continued to serve on the Committee on Economic Development, joined the Council on Foreign Relations in 1962, and was a member of the board of overseers of the Wharton School of Business during the 1970s.[166] Nathan remained loyal to another alma mater as well, spearheading a drive for a new Georgetown Law Center along with Washington attorney and Redskins owner Edward Bennett Williams during the early 1970s, and receiving an honorary doctor of laws degree in June 1972.[167]

It was probably during his service as president of the American Freedom from Hunger Foundation that Nathan witnessed most closely the generational shift that remade the face of American culture and politics in the 1960s and 1970s. From 1968 through the early 1970s Nathan helped raise millions of dollars for the group by coordinating annual walks to fight world hunger. He was particularly fond of the cause because it promised to nurture a sense of world citizenship—and development mindedness—among America's youth. "They are convinced that the U.S. system can be made to work, not merely for Americans but for all people of the world," he wrote in a 1971 *Saturday Review* article. "I have come to admire not only their idealism and their ability to ask the right questions but their organizational skills as well," Nathan concluded.[168]

Nathan's closest involvement with America's youth, of course, was through his own family. When his oldest son Richard graduated from the University of Southern California with a theater degree and a professed desire to be a filmmaker, Nathan was remarkably open-minded for someone who had spent his own youth in more hard-headed pursuits. "I'll give you a year to get yourself a job in what you want to be," he told his son. After a year, however, Nathan informed Richard that he would have to go back and get a law degree. He did.[169]

When it came to national electoral politics in the 1970s, Nathan was definitely stuck on the wrong side of the generational divide, running as a Humphrey delegate in the 1972 Democratic primary. Like every other moderate in liberal Montgomery County, Nathan was buried in the McGovern landslide.[170] Nevertheless, as one of the stalwarts of the old Democratic Party, Nathan had a voice, however muted, in the 1972 cycle. It was largely an extension of his role in 1968.

Early in the decade Nathan had served on the party's policy advisory committee.[171] In 1972, Humphrey, still nominally in the running through the convention, tapped Nathan to serve as his representative in the drafting of the Democratic platform. The work was done in Washington in late June, where Nathan, as a member of the 15-member drafting subcommittee, put together the document that the Convention endorsed with few changes.[172] After the first few days of effort, when the subcommittee drafted the planks on domestic policy that guaranteed jobs for all Americans along with federal payments to ensure an income above poverty level, Nathan told a reporter that these were "liberal, forward-looking principles which I think Senator Humphrey could live with."[173] One plank that had Nathan's name on it was the party pledge of "improved access to the markets of industrial nations" for less-developed countries.[174] In mid-July, Humphrey thanked Nathan for "forging a progressive, yet responsible, document."[175]

In October, when Nathan spoke at a news conference for the Democratic candidate, the *Washington Post* called him a "McGovern economic advisor." If he was, however, it was short term. Even though Nathan and McGovern had been fairly close in the 1960s, any formal contribution to the 1972 effort appears to have been limited to membership in "economists for McGovern/Shriver."[176] The reason was not difficult to understand. In the year when procedural reforms—drawn up earlier by McGovern himself—first opened up the selection process to youth, women, and identity-based interest groups of all kinds, there was not much demand for what the charitable *Dayton Daily News* called an "elder Democratic statesman."[177]

There was still work to be done behind the scenes. In 1974, Nathan and Walter Heller headed up an economic study group organized under the Democratic National Committee. They decided that even though wage and price controls were in ill repute, the party should support their reintroduction, along with other measures—if necessary.[178] Nathan believed the 1976 election to be a critical one, coming in the wake of Vietnam and Watergate, a time of great disillusion at home and abroad. In one interview, Nathan warned, "if we get weak leadership, then I think we will be in real trouble."[179]

In May 1976, Nathan offered to help out in the Carter campaign. Carter promised to get back to him and wrote, "I will do my best never to disappoint you."[180] Nathan was optimistic after the election, believing that the Georgian was "bright and dedicated to making himself a great president."[181] But despite the president's assurances, Nathan's disappointment came early, not only at Carter's conservative economic policies but with his inept handling of the executive office.[182] Nathan had but slight opportunity to influence the administration, serving on the president's Pay Advisory Committee from 1979 to 1981.[183] Nevertheless, for a time Nathan was hopeful. Carter's program to fight inflation looked much like the one he had been advocating—a little of everything. He was disturbed when nearly everyone else in Washington wrote it off as insufficient.[184]

One of Nathan's sharpest critics was Carter's former treasury secretary, Michael Blumenthal, who put his finger on the dilemma that the new president and the old pro-growth liberals all faced: "there has been an effort to fight inflation, but not too hard. It was 'tighten the belt,' but 'don't cut out any important programs.'"[185] In the end, of course, Carter and the majority of the American public decided that repairing the economic machine required not a bigger kit, but the bold use of one brutally effective tool. He stood by as Paul Volcker's Federal Reserve contracted the money supply. "Overkill, overkill, overkill," snarled Nathan in one of the last *Time* economist sessions in 1979.[186] "The man doesn't have a learning curve," Nathan said of Carter in late 1980.[187]

Although he was deeply disappointed in President Jimmy Carter, Nathan seemed happy enough to meet him at the White House in October 1979.

Nathan was sure that tightening up the money supply and inducing a deep recession would never work. When it did, he credited not Volcker's monetary policy, but better harvests and bigger oil supplies.[188] There was little for Nathan to like in the conservative administration of Ronald Reagan, the man Nathan had once believed too radical for a position on the AVC National Planning Committee. "I abhor all these mergers and acquisitions; we've got to get back to price competition," he was quoted as saying in an early 1982 newspaper article. That fall Nathan was one of 34 economists who convened to produce a sharp critique of the administration: they called for national wage-price and industrial policies.[189] Behind the scenes, Nathan supported Walter Mondale—Hubert Humphrey's lineal political descendent—with money and economic advice, but his voice was surprisingly subdued during the Reagan years.[190] It could have been because he no longer seemed quotable in the mainstream press, but it could also be because the fires of liberal fury had finally been banked. Even his wife was a bit surprised. "He did not show the frustration the way I would have thought he would," recalled Mary years later.[191]

As is common with many aging warriors, Nathan began to channel at least a little of the old righteous indignation into the more pleasant pursuits of reunions and reminiscences. One of the first was a get-together, in March 1971, of what the Washington *Evening Star* called, "the small band who opposed McCarthy," organized around the National Committee for an Effective Congress.[192] Less than two years later, Nathan attended the memorial service at Washington's National Cathedral for Harry Truman. By then Nathan had achieved a greater appreciation of the president whom he had once believed not to be sufficiently liberal.[193]

For Nathan, as for every liberal of his generation, the presidency of Franklin Roosevelt was a golden moment in history that shone ever brighter as it receded in time. In 1977, Nathan and former Justice Department lawyer Joseph Borkin organized a reunion for New Dealers at Washington's Mayflower Hotel. Jimmy Carter, certainly no New Dealer, was invited but did not attend. Hubert Humphrey, who had come to Washington in the Truman years, was there, thin and frail with cancer. But the night belonged to the real New Dealers like Rexford Tugwell, Tommy Corcoran, and Leon Keyserling. Ben Cohen, who had spent a few evenings among the Goons at Nathan's apartment, paraphrased Wordsworth in a voice quavering with emotion: "We were the lucky ones. For us it was a time when to be alive was joy and to be young was very heaven. Indeed if we were not young we would not be here tonight."[194] When, in the summer of 1981 there was an advance screening of "A New Deal for Artists," produced by local public television station WETA, a reporter spied Nathan and Mary Dublin Keyserling in attendance. "Both had tears in their eyes."[195]

Nathan may have been sentimental about his part in the New Deal, but he was proudest of his role in mobilization for World War II. He considered the development of the Victory Program the greatest achievement of his life, and his favorite reminiscence was standing up to General Somervell, on paper, near the height of the feasibility dispute. "That non sequitur sentence," recalled Joe Gunn, who heard the story plenty of times, "boy he really liked that."[196] When Leon Henderson, the man who had stood up to Somervell in person, died in 1986, John Kenneth Galbraith memorialized him in an op-ed piece in the *Washington Post* and also gave credit to Nathan. Almost alone, Galbraith recalled, they understood "how great was the latent capacity of the depressed American economy for war production.[197] A year later, when Leon Keyserling died, it was Nathan's turn to write to the *Washington Post* to call attention to the neglected triumphs of an old New Dealer.[198]

But if in his elder days Nathan was as given to reminiscence as anyone, he was far more driven towards participation than most. And if some of his involvements, like chairmanship of the Harry Hopkins Public Service Institution, had a New Deal connotation, the group to which he probably dedicated the largest part of his autumn years grew out of his postwar involvement in Palestine.[199] Nathan had been involved with the Anti-Defamation League (ADL) of the B'nai B'rith, the Jewish "civil rights" organization founded early in the century, since at least the 1950s. By 1969 he had served as Chairman of the Washington, D.C.-Maryland regional board of the ADL and spent nine years as a member of the National Commission.

In the mid-1970s Nathan stepped up his involvement, becoming National Chairman of the ADL Society of Fellows.[200] It was in many respects a continuation of his older involvements in the cause of Israel, which involved incessant travel and fundraising.[201] When he took over the post, the ADL was in financial trouble, but Nathan presided over a dozen years of ever more successful "ADL Appeal" campaigns.[202] With all of the fundraising, of course, came plenty of speaking. One of his stock speeches during the stagflation years played on the theme, "troubled times lead to tendencies to place blame via stereotyped thinking and scare propaganda."[203] But in his earnest advocacy of Israel, some of Nathan's own pleas during these years could easily have been mistaken for scare propaganda.

Nathan could almost always come up with a good reason for taking on a contract.[204] "If it was money for the firm," Beyer recalled, "he didn't care." But there was one instance that called for a bit of uncharacteristic soul-searching. In the late 1970s, the company got an opportunity to do some work for the government of Saudi Arabia. The firm had done work for Muslim nations elsewhere in the world, but Saudi Arabia, so close and so opposed to Israel, was a different matter.[205] The senior leaders of the company, Atkin,

Wolf and Hollander, were all Jews and all opposed to taking it on. Nathan was against it as well, but the work was worth $200,000 and it was a sub rather than a prime contract. In the end Nathan decided to take on the job.[206]

In 1978 came another opportunity that Nathan could not turn down. The American Jewish Committee commissioned a study of Arab financial investment in the United States. To help with the project, Nathan brought Louis Walinsky back into the fold. Together they produced a document that calculated that Arabs had invested $50 billion in the United States. This investment, they noted, could be readily liquidated or even repudiated, posing a "potentially serious threat to the stability of the American economy."[207] Publications like the *Pittsburgh Jewish Chronicle* ran sensational headlines such as "Giant Arab Investments Threat to U.S.?" No one else paid much attention.[208]

Joe Rauh challenged Nathan on another controversial position stemming from involvement with Jewish causes. In 1985 the ADL scheduled a surprise event honoring Nathan. Larry Nathan invited Rauh. "Your brother Bob is not only one of my closest and dearest friends, but there are few people I admire and respect as much," Rauh replied, although declining the invitation due to the ADL's long-standing opposition to affirmative action programs.[209] The dinner over, Nathan wrote back to Rauh himself. He admitted that the group had some problems with affirmative action but asserted, "had it not been for ADL we would not be as far along in the fight against discrimination as we are."[210] "You are nuttier than a fruitcake about the ADL," Rauh shot back.[211] Nathan remained active in the John F. Kennedy Lodge of the B'nai B'rith until late in his life.[212]

VIEW FROM THE CORNER OFFICE

Although he stepped down as president, Nathan never truly "retired" from his firm until very late in life. Through the late 1990s, when he was not in Key West fishing or traveling on other business, Nathan was at his desk nearly every day. In 1995, a reporter visited Nathan there at the Colonial Place office complex in Arlington, Virginia. It was easy to see why Nathan might have liked to come in. Through his window one could see "every monument and major building" in Washington.[213] It was, to the reporter, a magnificent view. To Nathan it would have been the best reminder of the accomplishments of a lifetime. The Commerce Department building where Nathan first came to work still loomed in Federal Triangle. The temporaries on the Mall were gone, but the once-new Social Security Building immediately taken over by the War Production Board was still there. Despite the perfect view of the landmarks of his life, no one ever caught Nathan in reverie. He was still far too interested in what was going on inside, rather than outside, his office.

During the year following after the leadership transition things looked very good. For the fiscal year ending May 1979 the company's revenues exceeded $5 million for the first time.[214] At first Beyer managed the company as Nathan had, loosely. The veteran staffers were responsible for keeping the projects under their purview going and let overall performance take care of itself. Even before the transition Beyer had begun to take a more holistic look at the company by establishing budgets, to which no one paid much attention except Penkusky.[215] The problem was that budgets were not much good unless someone was obliged to meet them. Employees of the Nathan firm had long appreciated the variety that went along with the job—they might work on litigation one day and economic development the next. "In the olden days, everybody was doing everything. It was really nice," said Joe Gunn. "The problem was," he admitted, "nobody was responsible for anything."[216]

Nathan certainly had his own pet projects well into the 1980s. One was giving the Internal Revenue Service lots of economic reasons not to require that "direct sellers" like Avon and Amway pay withholding on their salespeople's income. No doubt one reason Nathan liked the subject was that he could identify with it—he himself had once sold Real Silk Hosiery door-to-door.[217] Withholding taxes, he maintained on good evidence, would kill the business that "provides the opportunity for individual initiative and innovation."[218] For Nathan, business was booming. In 1980, he wrote David Ginsburg that he faced "overwhelming pressures on a number of assignments."[219]

The company was feeling a different kind of pressure. In the fall of 1979, Beyer was out of town testifying in a 10-week trial when Ed Hollander called. "If you want this firm to exist when you come back, you better come back now," he said.[220] The problem was mostly on the international side of the business, which was slumping as USAID began to cut back its contracts.[221] When Ronald Reagan took office he assumed greater control over foreign aid spending and redirected it away from basic development and back toward national security.[222] The firm's international operations, which had been calibrated to the USAID priorities of the 1960s and 1970s, were suddenly adrift. "Government contracting just dried up," recalled Beyer. In the spring of 1982 the company began to run losses.[223]

For the second time in the firm's history, a drop in government business came just after an expensive move. This one was from the overcrowded Ring Building quarters to a brand new office building in the newly redeveloped "Penn Quarter" section of Washington.[224] Holding a set of books bleeding red ink, Penkusky informed Beyer that there was no choice: "we either trim back or you go out of business."[225] Ten senior people who worked mostly on international projects were let go.[226]

Nathan testifies before a House Ways and Means subcommittee on the tax status of independent contractors for the Direct Selling Association, July 1979. To his left are DSA counsel Arthur Rothkopf, President Neil Offen, and Chairman James Preston.

The crisis provided a compelling opportunity for Beyer to create coherent business divisions and distinct lines of accountability. Jim Fay, who had been brought into the company by Jerry Jacobson, took over the international business. Joe Gunn took on litigation. Beyer assigned Jim Leonard responsibility for the rest of the domestic work—a tough task since government studies and regulatory work had largely dried up as well. Leonard left and the division went to John Glennie, who had previously worked largely on litigation matters.[227] From that time on the main division in the company would be between the international work—which had thin margins even though the clients paid on schedule—and the litigation work, which was highly profitable, but involved long waits for payment since legal clients usually did not pay Nathan until they were paid.[228] The result was a healthy rivalry. As Roger Manring, who took over the International Division in 1989 put it, "they thought that they made much more money; we thought that we provided the cash flow."[229]

John Beyer had been worried when he took over that the founder would be "looking over my shoulder and calling the shots."[230] Although, by some reports, Beyer did spend a great deal of time in Nathan's office during the 1980s, he felt undue pressure on only a few occasions.[231] The first came when Beyer advocated taking on the Saudi Arabian subcontract. The second came when Beyer made an earnest effort to position the firm to recapture some of its lost international business.

The problem was that the scale of World Bank and USAID contracts had increased greatly. To win these contracts the firm needed to make sizeable investments up front. But Nathan himself had made that difficult—the transition agreement put a tight limit on the amount of additional debt the company could assume.[232] When Beyer raised the issue, Nathan countered, "put some more equity in it." The problem was that economic development professionals tended not to have a great deal of investment capital readily at hand. In the end, both Beyer and Fay greatly enlarged their stakes and ended up as the two largest shareholders.[233]

Nathan also differed with Beyer about the decision to get out of the kind of government economic consulting that had once comprised "Ed's shop." "We could do this as well as anybody," he insisted, but Beyer countered that the economic work available was all specialized and being won by firms that stuck closely to health, energy, or environmental work.[234] In addition, most of those competitors used a smaller percentage of career professionals than Nathan, pricing the firm out of the market.[235]

By far the biggest source of contention between Nathan and Beyer was over the attempt to establish a management consulting capability. The venture had its origins in John Glennie's efforts to build up his part of the business. William Kent was a "private sector" consulting firm with a respectable overseas record, particularly in the Middle East and Far East.[236] Its namesake, as could be expected for someone who makes a living working with businessmen, dressed well and held conservative views. His employees were MBAs rather than Peace Corps people. "There was definitely a cultural difference," recalled Manring.[237]

In 1986, Glennie proposed that William Kent become a subsidiary of Nathan Associates to take advantage of its global presence and extend its offerings from the economics of development to the economics of business management. Kent, who needed an infusion of capital, welcomed the deal and John Beyer stood behind it. Nathan, however, was deeply unhappy from the start. "He kept telling me that John was doing things that he didn't approve of," said Mary, referring to the episode. That Beyer was making the firm "something different from what Bob started out as."[238] In early 1988, Nathan reminded the board that "the biggest growth areas this past year were not the new areas of the firm's practice, but in our traditional activities."[239] If the enterprise had paid off, Nathan would likely have found much to appreciate, but it never did. Glennie, who had never established a very good relationship with Nathan to begin with, was soon out the door.[240] Roger Manring stepped in and made Kent more accountable, but there was still no retrieving the investment and in 1990, the firm unloaded William Kent.[241]

If Nathan worried about a new cultural identity for the company, he did not appear to have any concerns about its name. For years the firm had used the initials "RRNA," for Robert R. Nathan Associates, in its marketing materials. In 1989 management determined through market research that the initials RRNA were "not a widely recognized symbol for the firm." In September 1989, Robert R. Nathan Associates became legally and simply "Nathan Associates Inc."[242] Nathan was 80 years old by then, and his list of direct clients was finally growing shorter, but he still went to the office every day, as he confided to a friend, "to work with many staff members."[243]

That was not all that he did. Nathan's company continued to serve as a vehicle for the founder's many other interests. In the archives of political and nonprofit groups nationwide there are letters on a host of unrelated subjects written on company stationery. "I don't know how he kept his time sheet," marveled Joe Gunn.[244] Nathan might define his job-related pursuits broadly, but when it came to everyone else in the firm, he was always an indefatigable opponent of overhead. If anything, that aversion only increased in his later years. He closely scrutinized photocopy and long-distance telephone logs, and studied other people's timesheets carefully. When he determined that someone was billing too much of their time to overhead they heard about it. From behind his desk in the corner office of the Ring Building Nathan had a good look at the hallway. When a junior economist unlucky enough to be caught in an unproductive moment stepped from his office Nathan would bellow, "what the hell are you doing?"[245]

Nathan was hardly the compassionate boss idealized by some management manuals. He did not mind talking with younger employees, but he mostly wanted to know what they were charging their time to.[246] At Penn Quarter there was a line of small offices for the younger professionals soon dubbed "Kiddie Row." One Monday morning one of its denizens encountered Nathan, who asked "how's it going?" The junior economist began to recount a pleasant weekend's activities until Nathan clarified his question: "not you, stupid, your work!"[247] This crushed economist might have taken heart; as Stephen Schneider explained, "if he was nasty to you it meant he liked you. If he didn't like you, he would just ignore you."[248]

Although he was more sparing in its display, Nathan did have a softer side. At Christmas, the man who had once driven his red convertible around town with bags of gifts for his friends could still be counted on to fill his bag—with gifts for everyone in the office.[249] Edythe Crump, who joined the firm in 1990, recalled being "absolutely terrorized" by Nathan for a while—until he came to appreciate her work. After that, she said, "his voice would be a little softer when he spoke with me." Along with other women in the office Crump regularly received flowers—azaleas in the spring and dahlias in the fall—picked from the garden at Crail Drive.[250]

As the founder's involvement began to lessen, however, management fostered a set of principles that comprised a Nathan "value system." Unlike many consulting firms, the company did not set billing targets that ambitious professionals had to work overtime to meet. Instead, the company was generous in providing avenues for advancement for even the junior staff. Younger professionals in litigation were encouraged to take on the toughest tasks, including expert witness duties, as early as possible.[251] Even if it meant leaning hard on the staff at the development agencies, the company moved its best people into mission chief duties as early as possible.[252]

As in every consulting firm, however, there was great advantage in having a well-known name in reserve. Nathan's name was so valuable, in fact, that on one occasion in the late 1980s the board of directors considered the advisability of bringing another "senior economist" into the firm's orbit. Minutes show that "the name of Herb Stein was mentioned in passing."[253] Despite the ideological divide between them, Stein and Nathan were good friends. As Stein put it, both Republican and Democratic economists "seem to realize that although they are on different teams, they are in the same game and that they need each other."[254] Still, there is no record of Nathan's response and the issue did not come up again.

As Nathan aged, overseas trips, remarkably routine during the 1960s, once again became landmarks. In the summer of 1969, on one of his last trips around the world, Nathan took Mary along. They stopped in Israel—Nathan nearly always stopped in Israel—reviewed the project in Afghanistan, saw the Taj Mahal, flew to Thailand, and took a train to Penang to check up on work there.[255] One of the highlights of the trip came when their driver took them to the Sungai Kluang snake temple. "One had to be rather careful," Nathan wrote in his journal in his wooden style. "Mary held a couple of them in her hand while I took pictures and then I had two in my hand and one on my shoulder while she took some pictures. Their tongues were coming out but apparently I was not bitten and am OK but these pit vipers are deadly poisonous." The driver had assured them that the snakes were defanged. Nevertheless, recalled Mary, "I don't know why we did such stupid things."[256]

By the early 1970s, Nathan was confiding to these journals that he felt tired more and more often. He made his last extended trip—through Korea, Indonesia, the Philippines, and Samoa—in 1975, but there were still a few opportunities to play the tourist.[257] In 1974, Nathan joined the board of advisors of the Volvo Car Corporation, which meant a vacation in Sweden every year for the Nathans up through 1985.[258]

Nathan went on another, far more unusual, sightseeing trip in the fall of 1976. Among the numerous good causes to which Nathan contributed was the U.S.-China "People's Friendship Association." Mary was unable to go, so Nathan signed up alone for one of the first tour groups to visit the newly reopened China. It was an august assembly of doctors, college deans, at least one millionaire, and an ambassador. Nathan was the only economist, which was something of a disappointment because he had hoped to talk in depth with "economists, planners and policymakers" in China, rather than just be a member of a tour group. Still, it was an unusual place and a special time. While Nathan was there the Gang of Four was arrested, bringing China's Cultural Revolution to a close, and he saw the celebratory demonstrations in the streets of Wuhan.[259]

Nathan was also in the middle of historic events in early 1984 when, during the Lebanese civil war, he went to Beirut, where Nathan Associates was teamed with the Louis Berger Group in the Lebanon Reconstruction and Development program.[260] Nathan spent a week with American University of Beirut President Malcolm Kerr just before he was assassinated on January 18.[261]

There were shorter trips to Latin America for project reviews in the mid-1980s and in 1990 Nathan made his last important trip for the firm.[262] After 18 years, Nathan Associates was again working for Afghanistan, partnered with Louis Berger in a hopeless program to find agricultural substitutes for opium poppies. USAID requested Nathan's presence so he went—to Pakistan. Conditions were too hazardous in Afghanistan so this was, of necessity, a "cross border analysis." Nathan never again made it to Kabul.[263]

FADE

It was the time of life in which one learns to say goodbye. Nathan marveled at the statistical anomaly of a family, his, where all of the sisters died before the brothers.[264] The youngest sister Lillian died first, of cancer, in late 1968.[265] In a strange occurrence, the man who made that year most unpleasant by far also extended a last goodbye of sorts. Just a few months before his death in January 1973, Lyndon Johnson invited Nathan to stop in Texas, "so we can have a chance to reminisce quietly at the ranch over some of the satisfying moments we have shared."[266] Simon Kuznets died in the summer of 1985, 14 years after winning the Nobel Prize for the first "national accounts," the economic measurements that laid the basis for the modern GDP. It would be hard to say whether that invention changed Kuznets' life more than it did that of his disciple.

Larry Nathan had not been as fortunate in his health as his twin brother. After getting sick in 1968 he had been obliged to sell his Bruce Hunt stores to the Van Heusen chain, after which he spent a few years serving as a consultant to the Small Business

Administration, helping minority small businessmen better manage their firms.[267]   Larry loved Florida and fishing almost as much as his brother, and by the 1970s he and wife Dee were spending every winter in the Florida Keys near Marathon and every summer at Port Angeles on Washington's Olympic Peninsula.[268]   One thing Nathan loved about the Crail Drive property was that it was on a wooded lot, with azaleas and dogwoods that flowered in the spring.[269]   It was summer though, when Larry died, on July 30, 1989. His twin brother spent much of his time outdoors, trying to absorb the loss. "He used to go out and chop trees. He'd chop and chop and chop," remembered Mary.[270]

His closest friend in the company and in the ADA had retired for good while Nathan was still ambushing junior economists in the hallways. The Hollanders lived in a wooded lot on the east bank of the Potomac near Chain Bridge. Ed Hollander had a canoeing accident in the Potomac one day from which he never quite recovered.[271]   He died of cancer in November 1991.[272]   Although Joe Rauh had once insisted that he and Nathan were "in this together," it was Rauh who earned the reputation as "Mr. ADA" and the last great liberal with a capital "L." That is how the nation remembered him after he died of a heart attack in September 1993. Nathan Associates contributed to the Joseph Rauh Memorial Fund.[273]

Joe Rauh and Bob Nathan, late in life.

Illness—acromegaly and back trouble—had figured so heavily in his young life that perhaps Nathan had earned a reprieve later on. There were small problems, but nothing debilitating until the end. The back trouble recurred yet again in late 1969—so much so that Nathan was hospitalized for it, and when he went abroad that spring he carried along the old steel, leather, and canvas brace hoping it would hold together just a bit longer.[274] There were the kidney stones that stopped him temporarily a handful of times during his adult life, but more disturbing was an episode in October 1971, when Mary sent Nathan on an errand and he forgot why. He called her from a parking lot and subsequently spent four days in the hospital. Doctors insisted it was not a stroke.[275] He called it transient amnesia, and it never recurred.[276] Despite hip replacement surgery in 1987, Nathan continued to think more about what he could still accomplish than what he could not.[277] "I find that slowing down some is desirable on my part," he wrote Muriel Humphrey in 1988, "but somehow I have not been too successful in that respect."[278]

Nathan missed his first board of directors meeting due to illness in May 1992; Sam Cohn chaired in his absence.[279] Events like that heightened awareness of the founder's mortality, and provided focus for both him and his company. Accordingly, during the mid-1990s it became a corporate goal to "publish Nathan's book."[280] Nathan went through two writers, generated a great deal of text, but seemed to get stuck in an unsurprising place: no remaining notes take the story past World War II.[281] Nathan did not finish his own book, but he did his part for others, providing interviews for biographers of Simon Kuznets, Ed Prichard, and Hubert Humphrey.[282]

Although Nathan had begun to keep his own counsel—at least more than previously—about national affairs, he was deeply disappointed by the late 20th century rise of "anti-Washington" politics. In the late 1980s, young people still came to Nathan for professional advice and he inevitably suggested that they spend some time in government. "Most of them now say 'nothing doing,'" he grumbled.[283] When Bill Clinton was elected president in 1992, Nathan told the *Miami Herald* that "I'm more optimistic than I have been in a long time." "He's creative and flexible if he doesn't get chewed up in the political process."[284]

Although he had been luckier in his health than some, the kind of schedule Nathan was used to keeping could not help but "chew up" an aging man. In 1979, Richard Blankfeld was briefing his boss for congressional testimony on export controls of scrap metal. It was late in the day and Nathan seemed to nod off. Terrified, Blankfeld decided that the best thing to do was to keep on talking—when he made a mistake Nathan perked up and pointed it out.[285]

During most of the 1980s, Nathan's voice of experience rumbled—with perhaps a bit less concentrated force—through one congressional hearing after another. His last testimony, given in 1987 before the Senate Subcommittee on Energy Research and Development, was on behalf of a new client, the Solar Energy Industries Association. Near the end of his testimony in favor of tax incentives he returned to his favorite subject: "I happened to be Chairman of the Planning Committee of the War Production Board in World War II, and I assure you that at that time, if we had had an energy shortage we never would have undertaken successfully the mobilization we did." Ever the optimist, he closed by concluding that "I think the American people would rather pay a little more taxes and have energy security than to maintain the cuts that have been made and take tremendous risks in our society. Thank you."[286]

Into the early 1990s Nathan remained sharp, but as the middle of the decade approached he began to slow down noticeably.[287] Fewer employees had the chance to work with, or be reprimanded by, the founder, although it was exciting when famous old New Dealers showed up at the office from time to time.[288] By then Nathan worked almost entirely on litigation matters: there were a few cases in which Nathan lost his train of thought during testimony so Beyer and Gunn were careful in "managing his assignments." Finally, when prepping for a tax depreciation case, it became clear that Nathan could not testify—the case settled before Beyer had to.[289]

It was appropriate perhaps that Nathan's last testimony—as a fact witness rather than as an expert witness—returned him to World War II. During the conflict, the War Production Board had placed explicit production demands on the American Viscose plant in Front Royal, Virginia, that produced rayon for aircraft tires. By the 1990s the site was a toxic waste dump and the ultimate buyer, in *FMC Corporation v. United States Department of Commerce*, insisted that the government shared responsibility for the cleanup costs. In what Beyer recalled being "carefully crafted testimony," Nathan impressed one court after another—the case went through appeal—as to the gravity of the emergency and the powers resident in the War Production Board.[290]

The courts all found that the federal government was indeed a responsible party and therefore obliged to share in the costs of cleanup. The case had enormous implications, both legal and monetary. As one scholar wrote, it "sent a shock wave through both corporate America and the United States Department of Justice."[291] Stephen Schneider worked on some later environmental cases on behalf of Nathan Associates and had discussed the FMC case with Nathan. "The government was less apt to sue and more apt to settle to begin with. I remember Bob being very happy about that."[292]

Nothing had made Nathan happier during his life than being in Key West, but it carried much sadness as well, and at the end of Nathan's life there was more of both. By the 1970s the children were grown and establishing careers, Richard as a contractual lawyer for NBC, Ann as a television engineer for the same network, and David as an emergency room physician in the Philadelphia suburbs.[293] With less to hold him in Washington, Nathan was determined to spend more of every year in Key West, perhaps partly as a retreat into the past. As late as the 1980s Nathan was convinced that Key West "still has 80 percent of the old character." In 1976 the Nathans bought a house there that was anything but a thing of the past—a modern stucco, two-story structure with floor-to-ceiling windows secluded in a tree-covered lane off of Simonton Street in the heart of Key West. The living room was sunny, with brightly colored primitive paintings by local artist Mario Sanchez.[294] Nathan was determined to spend every January and February there, which was difficult for the first decade or so, but became easier.[295]

Not that being in the tropics altered Nathan's nature. He inevitably brought some Washington obligations with him, having told too many people, "come see us in Key West." They did, which left Mary to discharge the duties of host, cooking for guests in a cramped kitchen.[296] In the absence of other venues, Nathan could also be found speaking to the Key West Women's Club on subjects such as the economy and Afghanistan.[297] He even advised the Monroe County Commission on budgetary matters for a time, free of charge.[298] But his top priority was fishing, and he went out nearly every day.[299] Nathan entered a tournament in 1980 and caught a not terribly impressive bonefish.[300]

In 1996 things were different. The 20-year-old storm shutters had broken, leaving the living room dark. But Nathan, who could always be counted on to make things work, or at least to do a study on why they did not, simply sat in the dark. "He just did not seem to have the interest in getting things going," said Mary. Nathan ended up with a fever and swelling in his leg and Mary checked him into the hospital where he remained for at least two weeks. After that, said Mary, he was "never really quite the same." Back in Bethesda in March, Nathan had to learn to walk again—he shuffled up and down the driveway holding on to an assistant.[301]

The next winter Nathan did not want to return to Key West. They sold the house. Nathan was again able to walk, but now in his late 80s, he had begun to lose focus. "His brain was not very quick by that time," said Mary.[302] Nathan was quick enough, however, to go downtown in May 1997 to dedicate a plaque at the Willard Hotel where Jean Monnet had once run his British Purchasing Mission. "We must develop more leaders like Monnet," Nathan stated, "to ensure not only production to meet human requirements, but also to ensure peace and progress for all nations and all people."[303]

Through the late 1990s, Nathan insisted on coming in to the office. Nathan Associates would routinely send a car to pick him up and return him at the end of the day. By then, said Beyer, "his memory was just shot."[304] Although Nathan never kept a clean desk, he had always been master of the amiable clutter around him. But the papers started to mount higher on the windowsill next to the Venetian blinds in his office, until one day the pile stopped growing.[305] Nathan could no longer leave home.[306]

All the time spent fishing in the Florida sun also took its toll and Nathan had to undergo facial surgery for skin cancer.[307] Macular degeneration destroyed one eye and left him only partial vision in another.[308] Nathan made it out one more time, in December 1999, to the Commerce Department where he was honored by Secretary William M. Daley for his role as a "young economist" in helping Kuznets develop the national accounts. Nathan could not go to the rostrum so Daley came to him and urged everyone to stand "and recognize true greatness."[309]

Around that time Richard Blankfeld frequently stopped by Crail Drive to see the boss, whom he usually found resting in the back bedroom. Blankfeld sometimes talked about what he was billing his time to, but mostly Nathan just told the old stories. "They were always interesting the second time around," Blankfeld recalled.[310] It seemed for a while that it was Alzheimer's disease, but the signs were not right. A specialist finally explained it to Mary. Nathan was experiencing a sudden deterioration followed by seeming recovery and then a sudden deterioration again, stair-step fashion. He was having, as his father had before him, a series of small strokes. Louis Nathan had lost the use of his limbs; Robert Nathan was losing his memory.[311]

By March 2000, Nathan's memory was "very selective" as Mary put it to Clifton Wharton, the economist who had accompanied Nathan to Vietnam and wanted help with his memoirs. There was not much left: a dinner at the Kennedy White House, meetings with Eleanor Roosevelt, the days at the War Production Board.[312] Not surprisingly, politics were among the few things that filtered in from without. On Christmas Day, 2000, just after the contentious Bush-Gore "butterfly ballot" election, the company held a birthday party at Crail Drive. Someone said they couldn't believe how old Nathan was. Nathan replied that he could not believe it either, and that he was "going to get a recount in Florida."[313]

By the next spring Nathan could no longer stay at home. Mary checked him in to Auxiliary House, a special care facility for people with memory loss near Bethesda's Suburban Hospital.[314] Joe Gunn and his wife visited twice in a special sitting room. The second time Nathan was wheeled in, he thanked them for coming and said "now if you'll excuse me, I think I'll go back to my room."[315] He died Tuesday, September 4, 2001.

The memorial service was the next Friday morning. The man who never went to temple, even on high holidays—"that's for other people," he used to say—was buried in a Jewish cemetery, King David Memorial Garden in Falls Church, Virginia. There was a brief ceremony back at Crail Drive. That was the end of it. The voice of experience fell silent at the close of the American epoch that had begun with Pearl Harbor. September 11, 2001, was less than four days away.[316]

CONCLUSION

In the spring of 1958 the nation was in recession—the worst since the Great Depression—and as head of the Joint Economic Committee Subcommittee on Fiscal Policy Senator Paul Douglas hoped to put through a tax cut to get the economy going. Douglas was himself an economist, but he ran out of patience as the panel of specialists equivocated. So at the end of the hearings he tried one last time to pin the economists down. "The bell is ringing; the clerk is calling the roll," Douglas told them. "He is calling your name. You have to say yes or no; you can't say maybe." When Douglas himself called the roll the economists remained on the fence—with one exception. As Senate aide Howard Shurman recalled it, "the only one who answered directly was Bob Nathan."[1]

Robert R. Nathan was a confident man, sure of his capabilities and sure of his objectives. He discovered at a young age the exhilaration of participating in the market-place and from then on he was certain that the free market was the best economic arrangement for human affairs. The Great Depression did nothing to shake that certainty; instead it convinced him that it only required political democracy to make capitalism good. Along the way he found an equally exhilarating pursuit: the fight for liberal reform. Thereafter, Nathan reveled in the American political process and carried his commitment abroad to launch the profession of development economics. He boldly undertook complex social, cultural, and political challenges in Burma, Korea, and Afghanistan. With a bit less confidence he even waded into Vietnam, all the while strikingly sure that a free market, tempered by a benevolent government, would eventually lift the impoverished to plenitude.

Liberal reform and economic development were always his chief pursuits, but with the same enthusiasm with which he once hawked newspapers, orangeade, and Real Silk hosiery, Nathan loved to promote his economic expertise in the marketplace. That led him to work enthusiastically for labor unions, regulated industries, law firms, developing nations, and corporations in matters that were sometimes more ethically ambiguous than Nathan's profession of principles. Nathan was less likely to tout this entrepreneurial opportunism than he was to promote his liberal principles, but both complemented the delight he took in earnest participation in the most urgent of human affairs, whether making a living or ordering a society.

Nathan transmitted this sense of personal commitment to his firm, but to endure, Nathan Associates had to find a way beyond the founder. For most of his time as president, in fact, Nathan Associates remained more a loose band of economic entrepreneurs than a tightly integrated corporation. The first trait that Nathan Associates inherited from its founder was a commitment, as the company put it during its fiftieth year, to "Free Enterprise in the Public Interest." A close second was its emphasis on personal professional expertise, but along with that came a suspicion of size.[2] Ironically, Nathan, who believed in growth as a universal objective, was deeply concerned lest his firm expand beyond the point at which he could personally vouch for its work.

John Beyer shared this concern.[3] "The essence of our product," he once wrote, "is the people that we are in a position to provide for our project work."[4] As a result, intent on safeguarding its reputation for economic and technical expertise, Nathan Associates hired carefully and grew slowly through the 1990s and 2000s, even as competitors reformulated their identities as project managers and multiservice USAID consultants to grow rapidly.[5]

Nathan Associates did pursue growth, but more modestly, by acquiring existing practices or incorporating established professionals. Not all were successful: the company came very close to buying one small development consultancy before hitting a cash crunch in the early 2000s. An attempt to set up a litigation shop around a Houston-based economist ended after a year of steep losses. But there were more successes: opening a litigation office in Orange County, California, acquisition of a London-based specialist in emerging market economics, and establishment of an economic consulting firm in India. By 2012 there were more than a dozen professionals at work at each of these locations.[6]

As Nathan's successors pushed the firm's footprint beyond Washington, D.C., they also moved the company figuratively beyond the shadow of its founder. Concentration of ownership had always presented a challenge. When Nathan died, John Beyer held more than half of the firm's shares.[7] He instituted an "equity task force" that devised programs to spread ownership more widely and then took on the additional responsibility of creating a more sophisticated corporate governance structure.[8] Nathan had been content to guide his business personally, but Beyer believed that more dispassionate supervision, by a board with a majority of outside directors, could provide insight and discipline not available in company ranks.[9] By the time that goal was realized in 2011, Beyer had stepped down as president.[10] Lakhbir Singh, an economist who came up in the firm, had been among the most effective in helping move the company ahead on a variety of governance, ownership, and management fronts. In 2002, Singh became executive vice president. Six years later he became president and in 2013 he succeeded Beyer as CEO.

As the company moved beyond the shadow of the founder, it created the Robert R. Nathan Memorial Foundation. Work began shortly after Nathan's death on a "broad-based directed campaign to friends of Bob Nathan and other firms."[11] The non-profit was established in 2002, its directors including Beyer, Joe Gunn, Maurice Atkin, economist Andrew Brimmer, Maryland liberal Michael Barnes, and Richard Nathan. By the mid-2000s, the foundation was sponsoring a fellowship in applied economics for graduate students at Wharton.[12] By 2013, the Nathan Fellowship had been reoriented to enable two economics graduates from Burma to study in the United States.[13]

It had been fifty-five years since the Nathan team was ignominiously ejected from the country. Despite Nathan's plans and the hard work of his associates, Burma had entered half a century of political and economic deep freeze. Such tough realities can turn a youthful do-gooder into a seasoned skeptic, but that was not the case with Robert Nathan. Although his temperament was well-suited for the sometimes quixotic pursuits of economic development abroad and liberal reform at home, Nathan was never a starry-eyed idealist. He realized that outside help could only go so far, that "in the final analysis, the area will develop only as you develop."[14] He understood that there were limits to reform, but hoped that economic growth would usually suppress what he called "revolutionary and disruptive tendencies."[15] Nathan nearly always remained confident that expert economic advice coupled with enlightened political leadership could create abundance for the masses. And even if it might be necessary to wait for the benefits, it was never too soon to begin the work.

Aware that causes and consequences can be staggeringly complex, economists are usually a cautious lot. President Truman shared the frustrations of Senator Douglas and supposedly called for a one-armed economist who could not resort to "on the other hand" equivocation. Robert Nathan was that one-armed economist. He was willing to take a stand and defend it, seldom retreating to the safer ground of assuming the most efficient outcome to be the best. Long-time employee Robert Damuth observed that Nathan usually acted on the conviction that "an efficient outcome might not be an equitable outcome, and equitable outcomes matter most."[16] This ensured that Nathan would always be something of a heretic in the economics brotherhood.

"I couldn't help but be a liberal," Nathan admitted. "I had respect for conservative economists. But they were dealing with abstract theories and so often ignoring the hardships of individuals. The depression was something I could never overcome."[17] Indeed, the Great Depression gave Nathan two important things: the desire to become an economist, and the conviction that economics should be a problem-solving tool as much as an academic discipline. As Roger Manring said, "He believed in evidence, facts, application of facts, and the tools of economics to solve real world problems, to make the world a better place."[18]

It was this faith in the facts, and, when stubborn facts did not provide clarity, commitment to the equitable outcome, that gave Nathan the certainty that most contemporaries lacked. He was always willing to grab the levers of the economic machine and pull. Economists and politicians before the 1930s were reluctant to intervene in the supposedly self-regulating market economy. Economists after the 1970s worried greatly about unintended consequences—negative effects stemming from policies framed with the best of intentions. In either case the result was the same: deference to the status quo and a tendency toward drift. Robert Nathan came into his profession at a time in which it was possible to believe that well-intentioned experts could remake societies as—or at least approximately as—they desired. His experience during World War II convinced him that experts had not merely the option, but the obligation, to intervene economically and politically for the greater good. If there was scarcity and deprivation anywhere in the world, the bell was ringing and Nathan was ready to go on record.

The New Deal economist shared this confidence with a New Deal congressman who also wished to pursue the promise of "bold, persistent experimentation" made by Franklin Roosevelt to its end. Lyndon Johnson shared Nathan's belief in the democratic free market, opposition to communism, trust in expertise, and after winning national office freed him from his Deep-South constituency, a commitment to liberal reform. Johnson tried in the 1960s to remake America and the world quickly and thoroughly and in so doing destroyed postwar liberalism. One by one voters and interest groups fell away as the free market undermined industries and devastated cities, the civil rights movement unleashed a divisive rights revolution, and the anti-communist crusade plunged America into Vietnam. All along the way, well-intentioned liberals brought about unintended consequences, and social progressives and cultural conservatives pulled steadily apart.

Although he never expected his plans to succeed entirely, the prospect of unintended consequences did not worry Nathan—where problems remained, a new plan could be provided. Nathan seemed always to be in a hurry, but his belief in a steady, incremental push toward progress and his innate respect for human ability kept him moving cheerfully, even if slowly, ahead. In great measure he possessed faith in technical expertise, belief in activist government, and trust that abundance could reconcile all the conflicts that might undermine the New Deal order. He never faced up to their limitations in maintaining that order. By the 1990s, when *The Economist* noted that "one of the rudest things you can call an American politician nowadays is a liberal," Nathan was well out of the fray.[19]

"I guess I'm inherently an optimist or I wouldn't have worked all these years in the less developed countries," Nathan acknowledged in 1976. "It's been very frustrating. Nor would I have spent as much time as I have in do-good organizations and in volunteering my time and energy to so many causes, if I didn't have an inherent optimism about our country and about the world."[20]   For those less the optimist than Nathan, success and failure depend on perspective. In 2013, the conservative counterrevolution that displaced postwar liberalism appears to be in retreat. Reform—safely dubbed "progressive" rather than liberal—seems cautiously resurgent. Although Afghanistan remains in the shadows, the Nathan Foundation can today hope, in a small way, to help lead Burma out of its political and economic dark age. South Korea was once a benighted nation as well, but as it turns out, Robert Nathan did his part to change that.

Shortly after Nathan's death, Illinois Senator Paul Simon wrote to Mary to tell her about a visit he had made to South Korea during the 1970s and a discussion with Park Chung-Hee. By then, South Korea had become Asia's economic miracle, and then-Congressman Simon asked the Korean leader what had made the difference. Park forgot the name, but knew the man. Advice, he said, "from the American economist with the big hands."[21]

Notes

Introduction

1. For a recent exposition of Nathan's pro-consumption faith (although one laden with postmodern academic apparatus), see *Against Thrift: Why Consumer Culture Is Good for the Economy, the Environment, and Your Soul* (New York: Basic Books, 2011).

2. Arthur M. Schlesinger, *The Vital Center: The Politics of Freedom* (Boston: Houghton Mifflin, 1949).

3. William Leuchtenberg, *Franklin Roosevelt and the New Deal, 1932-1940* (New York: Harper & Row, 1963), 5.

4. Bernard Norwood, telephone interview by Kenneth Durr, February 10, 2012, 11.

5. For this insight I am indebted to Robert Damuth. See "Nathan Associates Inc. Strategic Plan," Winter 1995, in Nathan Associates Corporate Records.

6. The exception is Jim Lacey, *Keep From All Thoughtful Men: How U.S. Economists Won World War II* (Annapolis, MD: Naval Institute Press, 2011). The standard history of the ADA makes little reference to Nathan, even though he dominated the organization during most of the 1950s. Steven M. Gillon, *Politics and Vision: The ADA and American Liberalism, 1947-1985* (New York: Oxford University Press, 1987).

7. 118 Cong. Rec. 20,792–94 (1972).

Chapter 1

1. Robert R. Nathan, interview by Niel M. Johnson, June 22, 1989, 7, Harry S. Truman Library (hereafter Nathan Oral History, HSTL).

2. Nathan Oral History, 7, HSTL.

3. See "NATHAN-#70421-v1-RRNHistory," undated document obtained from Nathan Associates (hereafter Wharton MS), 29-30.

4. http://www.jewishgalicia.net/website/modules/database/Item.aspx?type=9&id=20&pid=407.

5. Philip Taylor, *The Distant Magnet: European Emigration to the U.S.A.* (New York: Harper & Row, 1971), 51-57.

6. See Piotr Wrobel, "The Jews of Galicia under Austrian-Polish Rule, 1867-1918," accessed at http://www.jewishgen.org/galicia/html/jews_of_galicia.pdf.

7. Taylor, *Distant Magnet*, 65.

8. The FBI identified Nathan's father and mother as being born in 1873 and 1874, respectively, in Rohaytn, Austria. See reference slips dated March 9, 1966, in the Federal Bureau of Investigation files obtained under the Freedom of Information Act (hereafter Nathan FBI File). While traveling in Poland, Nathan noted in his diary that his parents were actually from nearby Burshtyn. See May 1947 Sweden-Poland Journal, 28, Box 1, Robert R. Nathan Papers, Division of Rare and Manuscript Collections, Cornell University Library (hereafter Cornell MS).

9. *Dayton Daily News*, March 24, 1970.

10. *Dayton Daily News*, June, n.d., 1984.

11. "Bob Nathan: A Truly Remarkable Life," in *Washington Jewish Week*, n.d., circa 1995, Robert R. Nathan Scrapbooks, Nathan Associates (hereafter Nathan Scrapbooks); Fifteenth Population Census of the United States, 1930. The various censuses give differing accounts; this one squares with Nathan's recollections and appears to be more accurate in other respects as well.

12. 1903 *Dayton City Directory*.

13. 1908 *Dayton City Directory*.

14. The *Dayton City Directory* for 1908 lists the family as Nathan. The directories for 1909 and 1910 identify the family as Nathanson. The 1910 U.S. federal census also lists the family as Nathanson. The *Dayton City Directory* for 1911 lists the family as Nathan again. See Thirteenth Population Census of the United States, 1910.

15. Nathan Oral History, 2, HSTL.

16. Nathan's birth record lists his name as Robert Nathanson. See Cincinnati Field Office report dated July 17, 1940, Nathan FBI File. The family had a number of issues with names. Brother Larry was named Philip at his birth and identified as "Lorenz" in the 1910 federal census. Older brother Louis was identified as "Israel Nathanson" in the 1910 federal census.

17. Thirteenth Population Census of the United States, 1910.

18. *Dayton Daily News*, June [n.d.], 1984, Nathan Scrapbooks; on the markets that were all-important in the Nathan's lives, see http://www.urbanohio.com/forum2/index. php?topic=13169.0.

19. *Washington Jewish Week*, Nathan Scrapbooks.

20. Wharton MS, 117.

21. Wharton MS, 117.

22. Thirteenth Population Census of the United States, 1910.

23. Wharton MS, 117.

24. *Dayton Daily News*, June [n.d.], 1984 in Nathan Scrapbooks; *Washington Jewish Week*, Nathan Scrapbooks.

25. *Dayton Daily News*, February [n.d.], 1942, Nathan Scrapbooks; *National Jewish Monthly*, October 1948; *Dayton Daily News*, February 18, 1961.

26. *Dayton Daily News*, February [n.d.], 1942, Nathan Scrapbooks; *Dayton Daily News*, December 22, 1923.

27. *Dayton Daily News*, October 25, 1966.

28. *Dayton Daily News*, December 22, 1923.

29. http://www.daytonhistorybooks.com/083095_2.html.

30. http://www.daytonhistorybooks.com/page/page/3531803.htm.

31. http://www.daytonhistorybooks.com/083095_2.html.

32. *Dayton Daily News*, February [n.d.], 1942, in Nathan Scrapbooks; *Dayton Daily News*, May 4, 1931.

33. *Stivers News*, February 26, 1942.

34. *Stivers News*, March 3, 1927.

35. *Dayton Daily News Record,* October 25, 1966.

36. Wharton MS, 1.

37. Nathan Oral History, 3, HSTL.

38. Wharton MS, 1.

39. Biographical summary dated October 12, 1945, and attached to J. Edgar Hoover to Harry Vaughan, October 12, 1945, in Nathan FBI File; Fifteenth Population Census of the United States, 1930.

40. Wharton MS, 2.

41. Washington, D.C., Field Office Case File, July 12, 1940, 3-4, Nathan FBI File.

42. *Washington Jewish Week,* Nathan Scrapbooks; Wharton MS, 4.

43. See "Room and Board—Descriptive List Published by Nathan–Miller Tutoring Service," n.d., in Nathan Scrapbooks.

44. Wharton MS, 33.

45. Joseph J. Thorndike Jr., "Bob Nathan: Donald Nelson's Young Braintruster Sticks Pins in Bureaucrats," *Life,* April 13, 1942, 47-50. See p. 49.

46. Wharton MS, 4; *Dayton Daily News,* February [n.d.], 1942, in Nathan Scrapbooks; Cleveland Field Office Report, August 7, 1940, 1–2, Nathan FBI File.

47. *Washington Jewish Week,* Nathan Scrapbooks.

48. Cincinnati Field Office Case File, August 9, 1940, 2, Nathan FBI File.

49. *Washington Jewish Week,* Nathan Scrapbooks.

50. Philadelphia Field Office Case File, March 16, 1966, 1, Nathan FBI File.

51. See program in Nathan Scrapbooks.

52. *National Jewish Monthly,* October 1948.

53. Biographical summary dated October 12, 1945, and attached to J. Edgar Hoover to Harry Vaughan, October 12, 1945, in Nathan FBI File.

54. Wharton MS, 9.

55. Wharton MS, 6-7.

56. Wharton MS, 15.

57. See Alan H. Gleason, "Foster and Catchings: A Reappraisal," *Journal of Political Economy* (April 1959): 156–72.

58. Gleason, "Foster and Catchings: A Reappraisal," 156-72.

59. One very important acolyte was Marriner Eccles, future chairman of the Federal Reserve under FDR.

60. Wharton MS, 21.

61. Robert Nathan, interview by Robert W. Fogel, Washington, D.C., December 26, 1990, 2, Box 3, Nathan Accession 22614, Library of Congress Manuscript Division (hereafter Fogel Nathan Interview).

62. Wharton MS, 23-29.

63. Nathan Oral History, 6, HSTL.

64. J. Frederic Dewhurst and Robert R. Nathan, *Social and Economic Character of Unemployment in Philadelphia, April, 1930* (Washington, D.C.: GPO, 1932), 1-6.

65. Nathan Oral History, 7, HSTL.

66. Bonnie R. Fox, "Unemployment Relief in Philadelphia, 1930-1932: A Study of the Depression's Impact on Volunteerism," *Pennsylvania Magazine of History and Biography* (January 1969): 87, 90.

67. Dewhurst and Nathan, *Social and Economic Character of Unemployment in Philadelphia,* 1.

68. *Dayton Daily News Record,* October 25, 1966.

69. Fogel Nathan Interview, 4.

70. "50 Years of Free Enterprise in the Public Interest," n.d., unattributed manuscript in files of Nathan Associates.

71. Wharton MS, 30.

72. Wharton MS, 36.

73. Philadelphia Field Office Case File, March 16, 1966, 1, Nathan FBI File.

74. Undated newspaper clippings in Nathan Scrapbooks.

75. *Miami Herald,* February 22, 1974; *Dayton Daily News*, May 4, 1931; *Ad-Clubber*, April 18, 1950, in Nathan Scrapbooks.

76. "50 Years of Free Enterprise in the Public Interest"; Harold U. Ribalow, "Robert R. Nathan: Brain-Truster," April 24, 1942, press release, Nathan FBI File.

77. Wharton MS, 40.

78. Robert W. Fogel, "Simon S. Kuznets: April 30, 1901–July 9, 1985," *NBER Working Paper Series* (July 2000): 5.

79. Vibha Kapuria-Foreman and Mark Perlman, "An Economic Historian's Economist: Remembering Simon Kuznets," *Economic Journal* (November 1995): 1525–30.

80. Wharton MS, 41.

81. Wharton MS, 42.

82. Fogel Nathan Interview, 4.

83. Robert R. Nathan, "GNP and Military Mobilization," *Journal of Evolutionary Economics* 4 (1994): 1-16. See p. 1.

84. Robert R. Nathan, "Operating Results of Manufacturing Plants in Minnesota, 1926–1930, by George Filipetti, William Dachtler and Judson Burnett," *Annals of the American Academy of Political and Social Science* (May 1933): 236; Robert R. Nathan, "A New Plan for Unemployment Reserves by Alvin H. Hansen, Merrill G. Murray," *Annals of the American Academy of Political and Social Science* (July 1933): 247.

85. Fogel Nathan Interview, 4, 5; Wharton MS, 50.

86. Wharton MS, 52–58.

87. Adolph Berle and Gardiner Means, *The Modern Corporation and Private Property* (New York: Macmillan, 1932); Richard Pells, *Radical Visions and American Dreams: Culture and Social Thought in the Depression Years* (New York: Harper & Row, 1973), 69.

88. Nathan Oral History, 7, HSTL.

89. Wharton MS, 61–62.

90. Kuznets noted in 1940 that Nathan had "not shown much originality in dealing with theoretical statistical problems." See Albany Field Office Case File, August 10, 1940, Nathan FBI File.

91. Wharton MS, 44.

92. Nathan, "GNP and Military Mobilization," 1; Fogel Nathan Interview, 5.

93. Fogel Nathan Interview, 9.

94. Philadelphia Field Office Case File, March 16, 1966, 1, Nathan FBI File; Washington Field Office Case File, July 12, 1940, 4, Nathan FBI File.

95. Wharton MS, 62.

96. Nathan Oral History, 8, HSTL.

97. Nathan, "GNP and Military Mobilization," 1–2.

98. Wharton MS, 71.

99. Carol S. Carson, "The History of the United States National Income and Product Accounts: The Development of an Analytical Tool," *Income and Wealth* (June 1975): 155–56.

100. Mark Perlman, "Political Purpose and the National Accounts," *The Politics of Numbers* (1987): 138.

101. John Kenneth Galbraith, "The National Accounts: Arrival and Impact," *Reflections of America: Commemorating the Statistical Abstract Centennial* (Washington, D.C.: GPO, 1980), 75.

102. Jim Lacey, *Keep From All Thoughtful Men: How U.S. Economists Won World War II* (Annapolis, MD: Naval Institute Press, 2011), 39–40.

103. Carson, "History of the United States National Income and Product Accounts," 157.

104. Perlman, "Political Purpose and the National Accounts," 136.

105. See Robert W. Fogel, "Academic Economics and the Triumph of the Welfare State," Paper Presented at the Association of American Universities Centennial Meeting, Washington, D.C., April 17, 2000.

106. Kapuria-Foreman and Perlman, "An Economic Historian's Economist," 1525–30.

107. Kapuria-Foreman and Perlman, "An Economic Historian's Economist," 1531.

108. Wharton MS, 72; Nathan, "GNP and Military Mobilization," 3.

109. *Washington Jewish Week*, Nathan Scrapbooks.

110. Wharton MS, 81.

111. Carson, "History of the United States National Income and Product Accounts," 158.

112. *Washington Jewish Week*, Nathan Scrapbooks.

113. Fogel Nathan Interview, 9.

114. Nathan Oral History, 8, HSTL.

115. Wharton MS, 83.

116. *Washington Jewish Week*, Nathan Scrapbooks.

117. Wharton MS, 103; Nathan Oral History, 9, HSTL.

118. Biographical summary dated October 12, 1945, and attached to J. Edgar Hoover to Harry Vaughan, October 12, 1945, in Nathan FBI File; Fogel Nathan Interview, 10.

119. Wharton MS, 104.

120. Wharton MS, 108.

121. *Washington Jewish Week*, Nathan Scrapbooks.

122. Nathan, "GNP and Military Mobilization," 4.

123. See queries from Nathan dated September 15, September 29, and October 4, Box 14, PI 183 Entry 4, Committee on Economic Security Staff Correspondence, RG 47, Records of the Social Security Administration, National Archives and Records Administration (NARA).

124. Wharton MS, 110; Nathan to Edwin F. Witte, n.d., Box 14, PI 183 Entry 4, Committee on Economic Security Staff Correspondence, RG 47, Records of the Social Security Administration, NARA.

125. Wharton MS, 111; Howard Egbert to Nathan, August 22, 1935, Nathan Scrapbooks.

126. Washington Field Office Case File, July 12, 1940, 4, Nathan FBI File.

127. Wharton MS, 113.

128. *Washington Jewish Week*, Nathan Scrapbooks.

129. Robert R. Nathan, "National Income Increased Five Billion Dollars in 1934," *Survey of Current Business*, August 1935, 16–18.

130. 1935 *Washington, D.C., City Directory*.

131. Wharton MS, 115.

132. Wharton MS, 114–15.

133. 1934 *Dayton City Directory*.

134. *Dayton Daily News*, February [n.d.], 1942, in Nathan Scrapbooks.

135. Wharton MS, 118.

136. Wharton MS, 118.

137. Clipping from *Dayton Daily News*, n.d., in Nathan Scrapbooks.

138. Wharton MS, 104.

139. Washington Field Office Case File, March 17, 1966, Nathan FBI File.

140. Wharton MS, 128.

141. Wharton MS, 128.

142. Clipping from the *Miami Herald,* n.d., 1993, Nathan Scrapbooks.

143. Wharton MS, 129.

144. Clipping from the *Miami Herald,* n.d., 1993, Nathan Scrapbooks.

145. Robert R. Nathan, "Key West," in Bureau of Foreign and Domestic Commerce *Fortnightly*, April 1, 1938, 5–7, Nathan Scrapbooks.

146. August 1946 Paris Journal, 39, Box 1, Nathan Papers, Cornell MS. One of Nathan's closest friends during these years testified that he drank only about "ten times a year." See Cleveland Field Office Case File, August 7, 1940, Nathan FBI File.

147. Wharton MS, 130.

148. Wharton MS, 131–32.

149. Wharton MS, 110.

150. See Robert R. Nathan, "Estimates of Unemployment in the United States, 1929-1935," *International Labour Review* 49 (1936): 49–73; "An 'Accepted' Estimate of Unemployment," *Economic Notes*, April 1936, 7, Nathan Scrapbooks.

151. Arnold J. Katz, "A Tribute to Robert Nathan," February 2002, accessed at http://www.bea. gov/scb/pdf/2002/02%20February/0202Tribute.pdf.

152. Perlman, "Political Purpose and the National Accounts," 139.

153. Nathan, "GNP and Military Mobilization," 4–5.

154. Wharton MS, 122–23.

155. Jordan A. Schwarz, *The New Dealers: Power Politics in the Age of Roosevelt* (New York: Knopf, 1993), 144–45; Joseph P. Lash, *Dealers and Dreamers: A New Look at the New Deal* (New York: Doubleday, 1988), 388.

156. *Washington Jewish Week*, Nathan Scrapbooks.

157. Marion Fourcade, *Economists and Societies: Discipline and Profession in the United States, Britain, and France, 1890s to 1990s* (Princeton: Princeton University Press, 2009), 102.

158. Lash, *Dealers and Dreamers*, 318.

159. *Washington Jewish Week*, Nathan Scrapbooks.

160. Nathan Oral History, 10, HSTL.

161. Harold U. Ribalow, "Robert R. Nathan: Brain-Truster," April 24, 1942, press release, Nathan FBI File.

162. Kate Louchheim, *The Making of the New Deal* (Cambridge: Harvard University Press, 1983), 280.

163. Wharton MS, 123.

164. *Washington Post,* January 21, 1982; *Life,* April 13, 1942, 49.

165. Wharton MS, 125–26.

166. Convocation Program, October 12, 1938, Nathan Scrapbooks; biographical summary dated October 12, 1945, and attached to J. Edgar Hoover to Harry Vaughan, October 12, 1945, Nathan FBI File; Washington Field Office Case File, March 17, 1966, Nathan FBI File.

167. Wharton MS, 125–26.

168. *New York Post,* January 8, 1945.

169. 1937 *Washington, D.C., City Directory*.

170. *Dayton Daily News*, February, n.d., 1942, Nathan Scrapbooks.

171. Washington, D.C., Case File, July 12, 1940, 10, Nathan FBI File; 1938 *Washington D.C. City Directory*.

172. Sixteenth Population Census of the United States, 1940.

173. *Washington Post,* June 13, 2001.

174. Wharton MS, 127.

175. *New York Post,* January 8, 1945; Harold U. Ribalow, "Robert R. Nathan: Brain-Truster," April 24, 1942, press release, Nathan FBI File; *Life,* April 13, 1942, 50.

176. *Life,* April 13, 1942, 50; Washington, D.C., Case File, July 12, 1940, 11, Nathan FBI File.

177. *Life,* April 13, 1942, 50.

178. Lash, *Dealers and Dreamers*, 332.

179. Wharton MS, 139.

180. "For Release Tuesday A.M.," December 19, 1939, Nathan Scrapbooks.

181. Alan Barth, "Washington," December 16, 1939, Nathan Scrapbooks.

182. *Washington Jewish Week*, Nathan Scrapbooks.

183. *Survey of Current Business*, July 1937.

184. Isador Lubin to Nathan, April 1, 1959, Box 69, Isador Lubin Papers, Franklin Delano Roosevelt Library (hereafter FDR Library).

185. Wharton MS, 137.

186. Schwarz, *The New Dealers*, 185.

187. Carson, "History of the United States National Income and Product Accounts," 166; Herbert Stein, *The Fiscal Revolution in America* (Washington: AEI Press, 1990), 168; Wharton MS, 143.

188. Lash, *Dealers and Dreamers*, 319; Stein, *Fiscal Revolution in America*, 107, 115.

189. Wharton MS, 142.

190. Galbraith, "The National Accounts," 76.

191. Galbraith, "The National Accounts," 76.

192. *Banking*, October 1938, 21.

193. Wharton MS, 148.

194. Wharton MS, 151; Nathan Oral History, 12, HSTL.

195. William E. Leuchtenberg, *Franklin Roosevelt and the New Deal, 1932-1940* (New York: Harper & Row, 1963), 298.

196. Ernest Draper to Nathan, March 22, 1940, and Sheridan Downey to Nathan, April 1, 1940, Nathan Scrapbooks; Wharton MS, 116.

197. James Fesler et al., *Industrial Mobilization for War: History of the War Production Board and Predecessor Agencies, 1940-1945* (Washington, D.C.: GPO, 1947), 19.

198. Lash, *Dealers and Dreamers*, 457.

199. Robert R. Nathan, "An Unsung Hero of World War II," in *Jean Monnet: The Path to European Unity*, ed. Douglas Brinkley and Clifford Hackett (London: St. Martin's Press, 1992), 69.

200. Fogel Nathan Interview, 25.

201. Perlman, "Political Purpose and the National Accounts," 142; Lacey, *Keep From All Thoughtful Men*, 46–47.

202. Washington, D.C., Office Case File, July 12, 1940, 4, Nathan FBI File.

203. "WFO Airtel," attached to SAC, WFO to Director, FBI, March 24, 1966, Nathan FBI File; "The Modern Forum," November 20, 1938, Nathan Scrapbooks.

204. *New York Times*, October 26, 1939.

205. *Life*, April 13, 1942, 49.

206. Paul Mallon column in unidentified newspaper, November 6, 1939, Nathan Scrapbooks.

207. See "NATHAN-#250782-v1-RRN_govt_service_and_the_victory_program," undated document from Nathan Associates (hereafter Victory MS), 7; J. Edgar Hoover to Matthew McGuire, September 4, 1941, and Washington D.C. Report, August 7, 1940, 5, Nathan FBI File.

208. "Activities of the Bureau of Research and Statistics," August 15, 1940, Box 7, Entry 1, Policy Documentation File, RG 179, War Production Board (hereafter WPB Policy Doc File), NARA.

209. Robert R. Nathan, *An Appraisal of the War Production Board: Industrial College of the Armed Forces Publication Number L50-144* (Washington, D.C.: GPO, 1950), 6–7.

210. John E. Brigante, *The Feasibility Dispute: Determination of War Production Objectives for 1942 and 1943* (Washington: Committee on Public Administration, 1950), 17.

211. Nathan, "GNP and Military Mobilization," 6.

212. Nathan, "GNP and Military Mobilization," 7.

213. Nathan, "An Unsung Hero of World War II," 70.

214. Nathan, "An Unsung Hero of World War II," 69.

215. Harold U. Ribalow, "Robert R. Nathan: Brain-Truster," April 24, 1942, press release, Nathan FBI File.

216. *Newsweek,* March 1942.

217. Nathan, *An Appraisal of the War Production Board,* 3.

218. Victory MS, 8.

219. Nathan, *An Appraisal of the War Production Board,* 3.

220. Brigante, *Feasibility Dispute,* 18.

221. Robert Nathan, interview by François Duchêne, May 15, 1987, 9, Jean Monnet Collection, Historical Archives of the EU, European University Institute (hereafter Duchêne Nathan Interview).

222. *Washington Jewish Week*, Nathan Scrapbooks.

223. Brigante, *Feasibility Dispute,* 19.

224. Nathan, *An Appraisal of the War Production Board,* 8.

225. Victory MS, 21.

226. Nathan, "An Unsung Hero of World War II," 76; Victory MS, 17–18.

227. Duchêne Nathan Interview, 11.

228. Robert R. Nathan, "Problems of Statistical Control—Economic Aspects," *Journal of the American Statistical Association* (March 1941): 18–26.

229. *Future: The Magazine for Young Men*, January 1941, 8.

230. American Statistical Association Bulletin, December 8, 1939, Nathan Scrapbooks.

231. E. J. Coil to Nathan, April 28, 1941, Nathan Scrapbooks.

232. *Life*, April 13, 1942, 50.

233. *Evening Star,* December 30, 1934; Maurice Atkin, interview by Kenneth Durr, Bethesda, MD, January 4, 2012, 12.

234. See programs in Nathan Scrapbooks.

235. See programs in Nathan Scrapbooks. Quote from October 4, 1942, program.

236. *Boston Globe,* May 31, 1942.

237. *Poughkeepsie New Yorker,* July 25, 1942.

238. *Washington Jewish Week*, Nathan Scrapbooks.

239. Duchêne Nathan Interview, 8.

240. Eliot Janeway, *Struggle for Survival: The Memorable Account of Roosevelt's Economic Mobilization for World War II* (New York: Weybright and Talley, 1968), 190; Fesler et al., *Industrial Mobilization for War,* 137.

241. Fesler et al., *Industrial Mobilization for War,* 137.

242. Nathan, *An Appraisal of the War Production Board,* 12.

243. Fesler et al., *Industrial Mobilization for War,* 134–35. The 1940 U.S. national income was

just over $100 billion. See *U.S. Statistical Abstract of the United States, 1955* (Washington, 1955), 287.

244. *Dayton Journal-Herald,* February 28, 1941.

245. "The Defense Program: Magnitude and Tempo," Box 11, Richard Gilbert Papers, FDR Library.

246. Brigante, *Feasibility Dispute*, 22.

247. Brigante, *Feasibility Dispute*, 21–24.

248. Fesler et al., *Industrial Mobilization for* War, 138.

249. Steven Fraser, *Labor Will Rule: Sidney Hillman and the Rise of American Labor* (New York: Free Press, 1991), 483.

250. Katherine Graham, *Personal History* (New York: Knopf, 1998), 134–35.

251. Fraser, *Labor Will Rule*, 482–83.

252. Alan Brinkley, *The End of Reform: New Deal Liberalism in Recession and War* (New York: Knopf, 1995), 181.

253. Nathan, *An Appraisal of the War Production Board*, 9; Nathan Oral History, 19, HSTL.

254. Nathan, "An Unsung Hero of World War II," 80.

255. "Feasibility of the Victory Program," December 1, 1941, 4, attached to Stacy May to Donald M. Nelson, December 4, 1941, Box 550, WPB Policy Doc File, NARA.

256. Brigante, *Feasibility Dispute*, 27.

257. "Feasibility of the Victory Program," December 1, 1941, 9, attached to Stacy May to Donald M. Nelson, December 4, 1941, Box 550, WPB Policy Doc File, NARA.

258. *Dayton Daily News*, February, n.d., 1942, Nathan Scrapbooks; *Boston Globe,* May 31, 1942; *Ad Clubber*, April 18, 1950, Nathan Scrapbooks.

259. There is no good record of when these meetings started. Different dates are suggested, but the last half of 1941 is the most plausible since Prichard was a pacifist until then and Nathan appears to have met Rauh and Graham in August.

260. Duchêne Nathan Interview, 13–15.

261. Brinkley, *End of Reform*, 180.

262. Duchêne Nathan Interview, 13–15.

263. Graham, *Personal History*, 136.

264. Nathan Oral History, 31, HSTL.

265. Federal Bureau of Investigation files on William Walter Remington, File Number 101-1185, Section 2, Part 2, obtained at http://vault.fbi.gov/william-remington (hereafter Remington FBI File), 227.

266. Fogel Nathan Interview, 35; Duchêne Nathan Interview, 18; Remington FBI File, 232.

267. Remington FBI File, 227.

268. Tracy Campbell, *Short of the Glory: The Fall and Redemption of Edward F. Prichard Jr.* (Lexington: University Press of Kentucky, 1998), 74.

269. Graham, *Personal History*, 136.

270. Fraser, *Labor Will Rule*, 483.

271. Brigante, *Feasibility Dispute*, 29–30.

272. Brigante, *Feasibility Dispute*, 30.

273. Nathan Oral History, 19, HSTL; Lash, *Dealers and Dreamers*, 457.

274. Calvin L. Christman, "Donald Nelson and the Army: Personality as a Factor in Civil-Military Relations during World War II," *Military Affairs* (October 1973): 81–83.

275. Brinkley, *End of Reform*, 182.

276. Janeway, *Struggle for Survival*, 226.

277. "For Immediate Release," February 19, 1942, Box 548, WPB Policy Doc File, NARA.

278. *Stivers News,* February 26, 1942.

279. *Boston Globe,* May 21, 1942.

280. *Dayton Daily News*, February, n.d., 1942, Nathan Scrapbooks.

281. *Life*, April 13, 1942, 47.

282. *Dayton Daily News*, February, n.d., 1942, Nathan Scrapbooks.

283. Remington FBI File, 286.

284. *New York Times,* April 2, 1942.

285. Duchêne Nathan Interview, 19.

286. *Life*, April 13, 1942, 50.

287. Brinkley, *End of Reform*, 190.

288. Gardner Jackson to Nathan, April 6, 1942, Box 52, Gardner Jackson Papers, FDR Library.

289. *PM*, April 26, 1942.

290. *Washington Post,* April 15, 1942; Nathan to Donald M. Nelson, March 16, 1942, 1, attached to Donald M. Nelson "to Division Heads," March 21, 1942, Box 551, WPB Policy Doc File, NARA.

291. Nathan to Donald M. Nelson, January 12, 1943, Box 550, WPB Policy Doc File, NARA.

292. Nathan to Fred Searles, Jr., March 10, 1942, Box 551, WPB Policy Doc File, NARA.

293. Simon Kuznets to Nathan, June 25, 1942, Box 552, WPB Policy Doc File, NARA.

294. Nathan Oral History, 20, HSTL.

295. Nathan, "GNP and Military Mobilization," 11.

296. Brinkley, *End of Reform*, 187.

297. Robert D. Cuff, "Organizational Capabilities and U.S. War Production: The Controlled Materials Plan," *Business and Economic History* 19 (1990): 103–12; Brigante, *Feasibility Dispute*, 35.

298. Brigante, *Feasibility Dispute*, 34.

299. Nathan to "Planning Committee," December 17, 1942, Box 554, WPB Policy Doc File, NARA; Nathan to Donald M. Nelson, January 12, 1943, Box 550, WPB Policy Doc File, NARA.

300. Brigante, *Feasibility Dispute*, 52.

301. Brigante, *Feasibility Dispute*, 59.

302. Brinkley, *End of Reform*, 187.

303. Nathan Oral History, 21, HSTL.

304. Fesler et al., *Industrial Mobilization for War*, 284.

305. Brigante, *Feasibility Dispute*, 66.

306. Brigante, *Feasibility Dispute*, 66.

307. Nathan to Donald M. Nelson, January 12, 1943, Box 550, WPB Policy Doc File, NARA.

308. As early as mid-April, Kuznets had suggested to Nathan that "what is needed is a continuously operating Resources and Requirements Planning Committee."; see Simon Kuznets to Nathan, April 13, 1942, 10, Box 551, WPB Policy Doc File, NARA.

309. Brigante, *Feasibility Dispute*, 69; Fesler et al., *Industrial Mobilization for War*, 285.

310. Nathan, *An Appraisal of the War Production Board*, 18.

311. Janeway, *Struggle for Survival*, 240.

312. Fesler et al., *Industrial Mobilization for War*, 284.

313. Brigante, *Feasibility Dispute*, 76.

314. Christman, "Donald Nelson and the Army," 82.

315. Lacey, *Keep From All Thoughtful Men*, 80.

316. Brinkley, *End of Reform*, 188.

317. Remington FBI File, 227.

318. Brigante, *Feasibility Dispute*, 86.

319. Brigante, *Feasibility Dispute*, 81.

320. Brehon Somervell, "Memorandum for Mr. Nathan," September 12, 1942, Box 552, WPB Policy Doc File, NARA.

321. Brigante, *Feasibility Dispute*, 80.

322. Brehon Somervell, "Memorandum for Mr. Nathan," September 12, 1942, Box 552, WPB Policy Doc File, NARA.

323. Brigante, *Feasibility Dispute*, 84.

324. Nathan, "GNP and Military Mobilization," 13.

325. Nathan to "Lieut. General Somervell," September 17, 1942, Box 553, WPB Policy Doc File, NARA.

326. *Washington Jewish Week*, Nathan Scrapbooks.

327. Brigante, *Feasibility Dispute*, 86, 90.

328. Brigante, *Feasibility Dispute*, 90, 89.

329. Brigante, *Feasibility Dispute*, 91–93.

330. Nathan to Donald M. Nelson, January 12, 1943, Box 550, WPB Policy Doc File, NARA.

331. Brigante, *Feasibility Dispute*, 94–95.

332. *Life*, September 14, 1942, 106.

333. Brigante gives this as $90 billion, which it could not have been—the upper limit number that the Army was upset with was $80 billion.

334. Brigante, *Feasibility Dispute*, 94–95.

335. Brigante, *Feasibility Dispute*, 98–100.

336. Nathan to "Planning Committee," December 17, 1942, Box 554, WPB Policy Doc File, NARA.

337. Janeway, *Struggle for Survival*, 240, 245.

338. Brinkley, *End of Reform*, 195.

339. *Washington Post,* October 11, 1942.

340. Brigante, *Feasibility Dispute*, 106.

341. Campbell, *Short of the* Glory, 88.

342. *Washington Post,* April 30, 1943.

343. Janeway, *Struggle for Survival*, 244–45. Nathan never told this story but did admit that he tried to support Nelson "in the press and with the Pearson stories." See Nathan Oral History, 34, HSTL. Nathan also admitted "Prich knew, there's no question." See Robert Nathan, interview by Tracy Campbell, Arlington, VA, June 9, 1995, 23, Louie B. Nunn Center for Oral History, University of Kentucky Libraries.

344. Nathan Oral History, 32, HSTL.

345. Duchêne Nathan Interview, 25.

346. *Washington Post*, March 16, 1943.

347. *Washington Post*, October 11, 1942.

348. *Newsweek*, December 6, 1943.

349. Wharton MS, 116.

350. *National Jewish Monthly*, October 1948; *Wall Street Journal*, February 5, 1943.

351. *Washington Post*, March 21, 1943.

352. Nathan Oral History, 34, HSTL; Nathan to Donald M. Nelson, April 3, 1943, Box 550, WPB Policy Doc File, NARA.

353. *Washington Post*, April 30 and May 1, 1943.

354. Nathan to Donald M. Nelson, Charles E. Wilson, Ralph J. Cordiner, and J. A. Krug, May 5, 1943, Box 554, WPB Policy Doc File, NARA.

355. Nathan Oral History, 34, HSTL; *Pittsburgh Press,* May 5, 1943.

356. Galbraith, "The National Accounts," 77.

Chapter 2

1. Maurice D. Atkin, *Life's Voyage: Dedicated to Making a Difference* (Marco Island, FL: Keller Publishing, 2005), 47.

2. *Boston Globe*, July 1, 1949.

3. "Smaller War Plants Corporation: Meeting of Regional Directors, Deputy Regional Directors and Regional Loan Agents," April 30, 1945, 4, Robert R. Nathan Scrapbooks, Nathan Associates (hereafter Nathan Scrapbooks).

4. David Ginsburg notes for Nathan Tribute Dinner, April 27, 1999, Box 121, David Ginsburg Papers, Library of Congress.

5. Mary Nathan, interview by Kenneth Durr, Bethesda, MD, February 15, 2012, 3 (hereafter Mary Nathan Oral History); Toby Shafter, "Success Story in Washington," *National Jewish Monthly* (October 1948): 77–78.

6. Nathan to "Lube, Lauch, Ben and Pritch," May 30, 1943, Box 69, Isador Lubin Papers (hereafter Lubin Papers), Franklin D. Roosevelt Library (hereafter FDR Library).

7. *Dayton Daily News*, n.d., 1961, Nathan Scrapbooks.

8. *Washington Post,* July 17, 1943.

9. Nathan to "Lube, Lauch, Ben and Pritch," May 30, 1943, Box 69, Lubin Papers, FDR Library; *Newsweek*, December 6, 1943.

10. *Newsweek*, December 6, 1943.

11. Mary Nathan to author, February 16, 2012; Robert Nathan, interview by Robert W. Fogel, Washington, D.C., December 26, 1990, 48, Box 3, Nathan Accession 22614, Library of Congress Manuscript Division (LCMS) (hereafter Fogel Nathan Interview).

12. *Washington Post,* July 17, 1943.

13. "Bob Nathan: A Truly Remarkable Life," in *Washington Jewish Week*, n.d., circa 1995 (hereafter *Washington Jewish Week*), Nathan Scrapbooks.

14. Mary Nathan Oral History, 2.

15. Mary Nathan to author, February 16, 2012.

16. *Newsweek*, December 6, 1943; Grace G. Tully to Nathan, November 13, 1943, Folder 8575, Franklin D. Roosevelt Personal File, FDR Library.

17. Robert R. Nathan, interview by Niel M. Johnson, June 22, 1989, 35, Harry S. Truman Library (hereafter Nathan Oral History, HSTL).

18. *Newsweek,* December 6, 1943.

19. Robert R. Nathan, *Mobilizing for Abundance* (New York: Whittlesey, 1944), vii-xiii.

20. *New York Times,* April 14, 1943.

21. Toby Shafter, "Success Story in Washington," *National Jewish Monthly* (October 1948): 77–78.

22. Alan Wolfe, *America's Impasse: The Rise and Fall of the Politics of Growth* (New York: Pantheon, 1981), 13.

23. David R. Henderson, "The U.S. Postwar Miracle," *Working Paper* (November 2010): 3–4.

24. Nathan, *Mobilizing for Abundance,* 213.

25. Nathan, *Mobilizing for Abundance*, vii-xiii.

26. Nathan Oral History, 35, HSTL; Robert Nathan, interview by Tracy Campbell, Arlington, VA, June 9, 1995, 26, Louie B. Nunn Center for Oral History, University of Kentucky Libraries.

27. Nathan to Franklin D. Roosevelt, November 6, 1943, Folder 8575, Franklin D. Roosevelt Personal File, FDR Library.

28. *Newsweek*, December 6, 1943.

29. Robert A. Brady, "The C.E.D.—What Is It and Why?" *Antioch Review* (Spring 1949): 21–46.

30. Robert M. Collins, "Positive Business Responses to the New Deal: The Roots of the Committee for Economic Development, 1933-1942," *Business History Review* (Autumn 1978): 369–91.

31. *Dayton Daily News,* December 19, 1943.

32. Eddie Cantor to Nathan Blumberg, February 22, 1944, Nathan Personal Correspondence, Nathan Associates.

33. Isador Lubin to Nathan, February 4, 1944, Box 69, Lubin Papers, FDR Library. Nathan got his old friend from Wharton, Emmet Welch, to assist him in the study *Manpower Demobilization and Reemployment*, but as of October 1945 it was still in preparation; see list of CED publications accessed February 2, 2013, from FRASER, http://fraser.stlouisfed.org/docs/historical/eccles/043_15_0005.pdf.

34. *Newsweek,* December 6, 1943.

35. *Washington Post*, March 8, 1944; Franklin D. Roosevelt to Nathan, March 21, 1944, Folder 8575, Franklin D. Roosevelt Personal File, FDR Library.

36. A. Morgner, "Mobilizing for Abundance by Robert R. Nathan," *Accounting Review* (April 1945): 251–52.

37. G. Haberler, "Mobilizing for Abundance by Robert R. Nathan," *American Economic Review* (September 1944): 604–6.

38. Morgner, "Mobilizing for Abundance by Robert R. Nathan," 251–52.

39. *New York Times*, March 11, 1944.

40. "Needed: 20,000,000 Postwar Jobs," University of Chicago Round Table Radio Transcript, August 13, 1944, 5.

41. *UP,* August 13, 1944.

42. Robert R. Nathan, "Nations Stake in American Reconversion," *Free World* (October 1944): 335–38, see p. 338.

43. R. C. Tress, "Mobilising for Abundance by Robert R. Nathan," *Economic Journal* (March 1946): 115–19.

44. Mary Nathan Oral History, 11.

45. *Washington Jewish Week*, May 18, 1995, Nathan Scrapbooks.

46. Peter Grose, *Israel in the Mind of America* (New York: Knopf, 1983), 177.

47. *Washington Jewish Week*, n.d., Nathan Scrapbooks.

48. *Washington Jewish Week,* May 11, 1989, Nathan Scrapbooks.

49. *Washington Jewish Week*, n.d., Nathan Scrapbooks.

50. Isador Lubin to Nathan, February 4, 1944, Box 69, Lubin Papers, FDR Library.

51. S. Ilan Troen, "American Experts in the Design of Zionist Society: The Reports of Elwood Mead and Robert Nathan," in *Envisioning Israel: The Changing Ideals and Images of North American Jews* (Detroit: Wayne State University Press, 1996), 205; Eli Ginzberg, *My Brother's Keeper* (New Brunswick: Transaction Publishers, 2008), 8.

52. *Washington Jewish Week*, n.d., Nathan Scrapbooks.

53. "An Economist Looks at Palestine," reprint of a January 9, 1947, San Francisco speech, 3, Nathan Scrapbooks.

54. *Washington Jewish Week*, n.d., Nathan Scrapbooks.

55. *New York Times,* April 24, 1944.

56. Nathan to Isador Lubin, February 17, 1944, Box 69, Lubin Papers, FDR Library.

57. December 1944 Palestine Journal, 67, Box 1, Robert R. Nathan Papers (hereafter Nathan Papers), Division of Rare and Manuscript Collections, Cornell University Library (hereafter Cornell MS).

58. *Jewish Telegraphic Agency*, August 4, 1944; *Jewish Telegraphic Agency*, June 27, 1944.

59. "An Economist Looks at Palestine," 5.

60. Fogel Nathan Interview, 39.

61. Oscar Gass to Isador Lubin, November 13, 1944, Box 69, Lubin Papers, FDR Library.

62. "An Economist Looks at Palestine," 4.

63. December 1944 Palestine Journal, 6, 22, Nathan Papers, Cornell MS.

64. December 1944 Palestine Journal, 30, Nathan Papers, Cornell MS; *Washington Jewish Week*, n.d., Nathan Scrapbooks.

65. December 1944 Palestine Journal, 47, Nathan Papers, Cornell MS.

66. *Jerusalem Post*, March 3, 1968.

67. December 1944 Palestine Journal, 53–65, Nathan Papers, Cornell MS; "Translation from the Hebrew Daily Paper *Haboker*," January 26, 1945, Nathan Scrapbooks.

68. Maurice Atkin, interview by Kenneth Durr, Bethesda, MD, January 4, 2012, 19 (hereafter Atkin Oral History I).

69. *Washington Jewish Week*, n.d., Nathan Scrapbooks.

70. *Washington Jewish Week*, n.d., Nathan Scrapbooks.

71. December 1944 Palestine Journal, 80, Nathan Papers, Cornell MS.

72. December 1944 Palestine Journal, 116–125, 135, Nathan Papers, Cornell MS.

73. Robert R. Nathan, Oscar Gass, and Daniel Creamer, *Palestine: Problem and Promise* (Washington: Public Affairs Press, 1946), vii; *Washington Jewish Week,* May 11, 1989, Nathan Scrapbooks.

74. Unidentified newspaper clipping, January 9, 1946, Nathan Scrapbooks.

75. *Jewish Telegraphic Agency*, January 7, 1946.

76. December 1944 Palestine Journal, 125, Nathan Papers, Cornell MS.

77. Troen, "American Experts in the Design of Zionist Society," 206; Nachum T. Gross, "Israeli Economic Policies, 1948–1951: Problems of Evaluation," *Journal of Economic History* (March 1990): 70.

78. Nathan, Gass and Creamer, *Palestine: Problem and Promise*, 4.

79. *Washington Post,* October 4, 1943.

80. December 1944 Palestine Journal, 66, 71, Nathan Papers, Cornell MS.

81. Tracy Campbell, *Short of the Glory: The Fall and Redemption of Edward F. Prichard Jr.* (Lexington: University Press of Kentucky, 1998), 90.

82. Herman Miles Somers, *Presidential Agency: The Office of War Mobilization and Reconversion* (Cambridge: Harvard University Press, 1950), 84.

83. Nathan Oral History, 19, HSTL; Somers, *Presidential Agency*, 85.

84. Nathan Oral History, 19, HSTL.

85. Isador Lubin to Nathan, June 3, 1943, Box 69, Lubin Papers, FDR Library.

86. *Washington Jewish Week*, n.d., Nathan Scrapbooks.

87. *Washington Jewish Week*, n.d., Nathan Scrapbooks; Nathan Oral History, 41, HSTL.

88. Alonzo L. Hamby, "The Liberals, Truman, and FDR as Symbol and Myth," *Journal of American History* (March 1970): 859–67.

89. Mary Nathan Oral History, 9–11.

90. Sixteenth Population Census of the United States, 1940.

91. *Newsweek,* December 6, 1943.

92. *New York Post,* August 14, 1944.

93. *Washington Star,* August 24, 1944.

94. *Time,* April 30, 1945.

95. Barton J. Bernstein, "The Removal of War Production Board Controls on Business, 1944-1946," *Business History Review* (Summer 1965): 248.

96. Somers, *Presidential Agency,* 86.

97. *Newsweek,* December 6, 1943.

98. Nathan to "Judge Vinson," June 15, 1945, Box 234, A1 Entry 38, RG 250, Records of the Office of War Mobilization and Reconversion (hereafter RG 250), NARA.

99. Lincoln Fairley to Nathan, June 4, 1945, Box 230, A1 Entry 38, RG 250, NARA.

100. Nathan Oral History, 42, HSTL.

101. *Newsweek,* December 6, 1943.

102. *Washington Post,* July 27, 1945.

103. Nathan Oral History, 43–44, HSTL; Fogel Nathan Interview, 40.

104. Nathan to D. A. Fitzgerald, August 23, 1945, Box 390, Entry 125, RG 250, NARA.

105. John W. Snyder, *From War to Peace: A Challenge* (Washington, D.C.: GPO, 1945), 1, 5; see Everett E. Hagen, "The Reconversion Period: Reflections of a Forecaster," *Review of Economics and Statistics* (May 1947): 95–101.

106. John W. Snyder, interview by Jerry N. Hess, February 7, 1968, 277, Harry S. Truman Library.

107. John H. Tolan, interview by James R. Fuchs, March 5, 10, and 17, 1970, and February 8, 1974, 181, Harry S. Truman Library; Somers, *Presidential Agency,* 89.

108. Nathan Oral History, 53, HSTL; Fogel Nathan Interview, 41.

109. Arthur F. McClure, *The Truman Administration and the Problems of Postwar Labor, 1945-1948* (Rutherford, NJ: Fairleigh Dickinson University Press, 1969), 186–87.

110 "Economic Projections Prepared within the Technical Staff," September 8, 1945, 21, Box 389, Entry 125, RG 250, NARA.

111. *Christian Science Monitor,* October 31, 1945.

112. See http://www.trumanlibrary.org/publicpapers/index.php?pid=190&st=&st1=.

113. *Christian Science Monitor,* October 31, 1945.

114. John W. Snyder, interview by Jerry N. Hess, February 21, 1968, 353, Harry S. Truman Library.

115. Broadus Mitchell to Nathan, November 20, 1945, Box 232, Entry 38, RG 250, NARA.

116. *Washington Post,* October 22, 1945; Somers, *Presidential Agency,* 89.

117. *Business Week,* November 17, 1945 .

118. "OWMR Press Release," December 4, 1945, Nathan Scrapbooks.

119. *Washington Post,* January 3, 1946. This is documented by Drew Pearson, who seemed to be getting his copy directly from Nathan, as well as a December 21 entry in Truman's schedule of an "off the record" meeting alone with Nathan. See the daily appointment book at the Truman library on-line at: http://www.trumanlibrary.org/calendar/main. php?currYear=1945&currMonth=12&currDay=21.

120. *Wall Street Journal,* December 17, 1945.

121. See, for example, Harry S. Truman to "My dear Bob" Nathan, May 28, 1946, Nathan Scrapbooks.

122. Robert L. Tyler, "The American Veterans Committee: Out of the Hot War and into the Cold," *American Quarterly* (Fall 1966): 419–36. See p. 420.

123. *Christian Science Monitor*, May 11, 1946.

124. "Veterans Elect Bob Nathan," AVC Press Release, March 25, 1946, Nathan Scrapbooks.

125. Toby Shafter, "Success Story in Washington," *National Jewish Monthly* (October 1948): 77–78.

126. *Capital Veteran,* June 1946.

127. *Cincinnati Enquirer,* March 8, 1948.

128. "Save OPA Day," event program, May 11, 1946, Nathan Scrapbooks.

129. A *Washington Post* columnist offered pointers on public speaking; he cautioned that "we're not all as adept as Bob Nathan, the economist, whose mind churns up ideas faster than his machine gun delivery can give them expression." See *Washington Post*, November 8, 1950.

130. "Should OPA Be Modified Along the Lines of Congressional Action," The American Forum of the Air Radio Transcript, June 18, 1946, 5, Nathan Scrapbooks.

131. Joseph Goulden, *The Best Years, 1945-1950* (New York: Atheneum, 1976), 103–4.

132. *Washington Post,* July 10, 1946.

133. *Washington Post*, June 9, 1946.

134. *Washington Post,* June 18, 1946.

135. *Washington Evening Star*, June 14, 1946; see "Proceedings of the First Constitutional Convention of American Veterans Committee," June 14–16, 1946, in Box 97, AVC Papers, George Washington University Archives.

136. *Times-Herald,* January 7, 1947.

137. *New York Times*, January 7, 1973.

138. *Christian Science Monitor*, May 11, 1946.

139. Tyler, "The American Veterans Committee," 423.

140. *New York Times*, August 10, 1948.

141. *Christian Science Monitor*, May 11, 1946.

142. Notes from Carl Solberg interview with Robert R. Nathan, November 18, 1980, 4, Box 147.E.11.3B, Papers of Carl Solberg, Minnesota Historical Society.

143. "American Veterans Committee, Inc. National Planning Committee," November 10, 1946, Box 101, AVC Papers, George Washington University Archives.

144. Tyler, "The American Veterans Committee," 429; *AVC Bulletin*, July 1947. The tickets are in the Joseph Lash Papers; see Box 1, Joseph Lash Papers, FDR Library.

145. *New York Times*, January 7, 1973.

146. Washington Office Report, January 29, 1951, 2, Federal Bureau of Investigation files obtained under the Freedom of Information Act (hereafter Nathan FBI File).

147. August 1946 Paris Journal, 41, Box 1, Nathan Papers, Cornell MS.

148. Mary Nathan Oral History, 2–3.

149. *Chicago Sun Times,* July 18, 1947.

150. Mary Nathan Oral History, 5.

151. *Daily Times,* July 19, 1947; Mary Nathan Oral History, 23.

152. *New Republic,* April 5, 1948.

153. *Waterbury Republican,* March 15, 1948.

154. "American Veterans Committee, Inc. National Planning Committee," July 19, 1947, Box 102, AVC Papers, George Washington University Archives.

155. *New York Times,* August 10, 1948.

156. Tyler, "The American Veterans Committee," 431–33.

157. "American Veterans Committee, Inc. National Planning Committee," September 18, 1948, Box 102, AVC Papers, George Washington University Archives.

158. "American Veterans Committee, Inc. National Planning Committee," September 18, 1948, Box 102, AVC Papers, George Washington University Archives.

159. Tyler, "The American Veterans Committee," 432–33; *New York Times,* November 28, 1948.

160. *AVC Bulletin,* December 1948.

161. *AVC Bulletin,* April 1949.

162. Nathan to Marriner S. Eccles, May 11, 1949, from The Marriner S. Eccles Document Collection, accessed February 2, 2013, from FRASER, http://fraser.stlouisfed.org/eccles/record.php?id=16581.

163. Nathan Oral History, 38, HSTL.

164. *Washington Post,* February 18, 1946.

165. *Dayton Daily News,* February 5, 1946.

166. Nathan Oral History, 63, HSTL.

167. *Washington Post,* May 9, 1946.

168. Donald M. Nelson to T. V. Soong, February 13, 1945, Nathan Accession 22614, LCMS.

169. Nathan to Isador Lubin, December 4, 1947, Box 69, Lubin Papers, FDR Library.

170. *Washington Post,* October 22, 1945.

171. Gerlof D. Homan, "American Business Interests in the Indonesian Republic, 1946–1949," *Indonesia* (April 1983): 125–32; see p. 129.

172. Typescript by Nathan entitled "Draft 1/28, Second Cassette," 49, in Nathan Corporate Records (hereafter Nathan Draft 1/28).

173. R. Burr Smith, interview by James R. Fuchs, April 10, 1974, 7, Harry S. Truman Library.

174. Nathan Draft 1/28, 49.

175. "Robert R. Nathan Associates, Inc., Minutes of Meeting of Incorporators," January 14, 1946, Nathan Associates Corporate Records.

176. "Robert R. Nathan Associates, Inc., Minutes of First Meeting of Board of Directors," January 15, 1946, Nathan Associates Corporate Records.

177. *Dayton Daily News,* March 10, 1946.

178. Mary Nathan Oral History, 37.

179. Atkin Oral History I, 13.

180. *Washington Star,* March 30, 1946.

181. "Robert R. Nathan Associates, Inc.," Press Release, April 2, 1946, Nathan Scrapbooks.

182. Nathan Draft 1/28, 57.

183. Undated document entitled "Nathan Transcript (Source Unknown)," 2–3, Nathan Associates Corporate Records.

184. "An Internationally Famous Economist…Robert Nathan Discusses a New Trend in Consumer Purchasing," n.d., circa 1946, Nathan Scrapbooks.

185. "Robert Nathan Forms Public Relations Firm," in Pittsburgh Field Office Report, February 11, 1947, Nathan FBI File.

186. *New York Times,* December 24, 1946.

187. *Fashion Trades,* July 23, 1947.

188. *Times-Herald,* July 1, 1949.

189. *New York Times,* July 26, 1946.

190. *Tide,* November 22, 1946.

191. *Tide,* July 12, 1946.

192. August 1946 Paris Journal, 5, 11, Box 1, Nathan Papers, Cornell MS.

193. *Washington Times-Herald,* August 25, 1944.

194. Edgar Beigel, "France Moves Toward National Planning," *Political Science Quarterly* (September 1947): 387.

195. Shafter, "Success Story in Washington," 77–78.

196. August 1946 Paris Journal, 12, 55, 65, Box 1, Nathan Papers, Cornell MS.

197. Nathan, Gass, and Creamer, *Palestine: Problem and Promise,* 4.

198. *Washington Jewish Week,* n.d., Nathan Scrapbooks.

199. Troen, "American Experts in the Design of Zionist Society," 208–9.

200. Nathan to Isador Lubin, October 1, 1946, Box 69, Lubin Papers, FDR Library.

201. August 1946 Paris Journal, 40, Box 1, Nathan Papers, Cornell MS; Joseph Francis Rishel, *Pittsburgh Remembers World War II* (Charleston: History Press, 2001), 29; Nathan Oral History, 48, HSTL.

202. Nathan Oral History, 50, HSTL.

203. *Newsweek,* December 23, 1946.

204. "Extemporaneous Remarks of Vice President Wallace," speech given before the American Business Conference, March 17, 1944, Nathan Scrapbooks; *Tide,* December 20, 1946.

205. *St. Louis Star Times,* December 12, 1946.

206. Nelson Lichtenstein, *The Most Dangerous Man in Detroit: Walter Reuther and the Fate of American Labor* (New York: Basic Books, 1995), 235–46.

207. *Key West Citizen,* January 17, 1946.

208. U.S. Department of Commerce, *Historical Statistics of the United States, Colonial Times to 1957* (Washington: GPO, 1961), 99.

209. McClure, *The Truman Administration and the Problems of Postwar Labor*, 74, 70.

210. Nathan to Averell Harriman, December 4, 1946, Box 249, Averell Harriman Papers, Library of Congress Manuscript Division (hereafter LCMS).

211. *New York Times*, December 15, 1946; *Washington Post*, December 12, 1946.

212. *Washington Post*, December 12, 1946.

213. *New Republic*, December 23, 1946.

214. Robert Roy Nathan and Oscar Gass, *A National Wage Policy for 1947* (Washington, D.C: Robert R. Nathan Associates, Inc., 1946), 1–2.

215. "For Release 2 P.M., Wednesday," Press Release, December 11, 1946, Box 249, Averell Harriman Papers, LCMS.

216. *Washington Post*, December 19, 1946.

217. *New Republic*, December 23, 1946.

218. "Statement by the Honorable W. Averell Harriman," attached to cover sheet "Draft—Not to be Used in Any Way," December 12, 1946, Box 249, Averell Harriman Papers, LCMS.

219. *New York Times*, December 13, 1946.

220. *Washington Post*, January 4, 1947.

221. *Washington Post*, December 12, 1946.

222. *Business Week*, December 21, 1946.

223. *Time*, December 23, 1946.

224. *Tide*, December 20, 1946.

225. *Business Week*, December 21, 1946.

226. For good exposition, see "The Nathan Report and Its Critics," *American Economic Review* (June 1947): 386–91.

227. *Cleveland News*, January 17, 1950.

228. *Washington Star*, January 3, 1947.

229. *Pittsburgh Post-Gazette*, December 16, 1946.

230. See Director of Economic Research to General Fleming, December 18, 1946, Box 249, Averell Harriman Papers, LCMS. "Take to cabinet" is written on the document.

231. "Can We Have a 25 Percent Wage Boost Without Raising Prices?" *Town Meeting*, January 23, 1947, 7.

232. *Washington Post*, December 12, 1946.

233. *New York Times*, December 13, 1946; *New York Times*, April 6, 1947; *U.S. News & World Report*, July 22, 1944.

234. *New York Times*, December 4, 1947.

235. *U.S. News & World Report*, July 22, 1944.

236. Robert R. Nathan Associates, Inc., *A National Economic Policy for 1949*, July 1949, 3, Box 69, Lubin Papers, FDR Library.

237. *New York Times*, July 12, 1949.

238. Nathan Associates, *A National Economic Policy for 1949*, 2.

239. *Washington Post*, July 12, 1949.

240. *New York Times*, July 13, July 8, and July 16, 1949.

241. *Boston Globe*, July 17, 1949; *New York Times,* July 30, 1949.

242. "Should the Steel Wage Recommendation Be Accepted?" University of Chicago Round Table Transcript, September 11, 1949, 1, Nathan Scrapbooks.

243. *Washington Post,* September 30, 1949.

244. Nathan Oral History, 51, HSTL.

245. December 1944 Palestine Journal, 71, Nathan Papers, Cornell MS.

246. *Dayton Daily News,* March 10, 1946.

247. *Jewish Telegraphic Agency*, January 15, 1947.

248. Address by Robert Nathan before the National Conference for Palestine of the United Palestine Appeal, October 12, 1947, Box 69, Lubin Papers, FDR Library.

249. Peter Grose, "Story Behind Truman Recognition of Israel," undated newspaper article, Nathan Scrapbooks.

250. Isador Lubin to Nathan, June 3, 1943, Box 69, Lubin Papers, FDR Library; Nathan Oral History, 73, HSTL.

251. *Washington Jewish Week*, May 11, 1989.

252. Nathan Oral History, 76, HSTL. "I really even got involved with some of the politicking with countries about votes and the partition," said Nathan.

253. Fraser Wilkins, interview by Richard D. McKinzie, June 20, 1975, no page number, Harry S. Truman Library.

254. Edwin M. Wright, interview by Richard D. McKinzie, July 26, 1974, 111–14, Harry S. Truman Library.

255. Grose, *Israel in the Mind of America*, 252.

256. Walter Millis, ed., *The Forrestal Diaries* (New York: Viking, 1951), 346.

257. Isador Lubin to Nathan, December 2, 1947, Box 69, Lubin Papers, FDR Library.

258. Grose, "Story Behind Truman Recognition of Israel."

259. *Baltimore Sun*, March 22, 1948.

260. Grose, *Israel in the Mind of America*, 280.

261. Leonard Slater, *The Pledge* (New York: Simon and Schuster, 1970), 76.

262. Grose, *Israel in the Mind of America*, 280.

263. Grose, "Story Behind Truman Recognition of Israel."

264. Grose, "Story Behind Truman Recognition of Israel."

265. Unidentified newspaper clipping, March 20, 1948, Nathan Scrapbooks.

266. Grose, "Story Behind Truman Recognition of Israel."

267. Nathan to Robert A. Lovett, March 24, 1948, Truman Papers on-line at http://www.trumanlibrary.org/whistlestop/study_collections/israel/large/documents/newPDF/3-22.pdf#zoom=100.

268. Grose, "Story Behind Truman Recognition of Israel."

269. *Washington Post,* May 15, 1948.

270. *Southern Jewish Weekly,* February 23, 1951.

271. *Philadelphia Inquirer,* April 8, 1949; *Philadelphia Inquirer,* April 11, 1949; *New York Times,* June 23, 1949.

272. "How the Import of Private Capital Is Being Encouraged," translation of article published in *Haaretz,* September 29, 1949, Nathan Scrapbooks.

273. *Jewish Telegraphic Agency,* June 22, 1949.

274. Troen, "American Experts in the Design of Zionist Society," 215.

275. Nathan to Harry S. Truman, January 31, 1949, Nathan Personal Correspondence.

276. Troen, "American Experts in the Design of Zionist Society," 209.

277. Nathan to Louis Harris, January 14, 1948, attached to Nathan to Isador Lubin, January 19, 1948, Box 69, Lubin Papers, FDR Library.

278. Nathan to Rensis Likert, February 16, 1948, Box 69, Lubin Papers, FDR Library.

279. Troen, "American Experts in the Design of Zionist Society," 212–13; *Washington Jewish Week,* n.d., Nathan Scrapbooks.

280. Troen, "American Experts in the Design of Zionist Society," 210.

281. *Jerusalem Post,* September 6, 1950.

282. Troen, "American Experts in the Design of Zionist Society," 214–15.

283. *Brandeis Report,* July 1951.

284. See various newspaper clippings in the Nathan Scrapbooks.

285. *Kansas City Times,* June 13, 1951.

286. Troen, "American Experts in the Design of Zionist Society," 216.

287. *New York Times,* May 4, 1947.

288. *P.M.,* January 24, 1947; *New York Times,* February 8, 1947.

289. *World Report,* February 11, 1947; *Hampton Roads Daily Press*, September 13, 2006.

290. *P.M.,* January 24, 1947; Ronald C. Newton, "The Neutralization of Fritz Mandl: Notes of Wartime Journalism, the Arms Trade, and Anglo-American Rivalry in Argentina During World War II," *Hispanic American Historical Review* (August 1986): 574.

291. *Jewish Times,* February 28, 1947.

292. August 1946 Paris Journal, 59, Box 1, Nathan Papers, Cornell MS.

293. "Robert R. Nathan Associates, Inc. Certificate of Secretary," September 20, 1949, Nathan Associates Corporate Records; Nathan Draft 1/28, 50.

294. *New York Times,* February 23, 1947.

295. *New Yorker,* April 25, 1959, 37.

296. *New York Times,* February 14, 1947.

297. *New York Times,* November 21, 1948.

298. *New York Times,* March 22 and June 28, 1948.

299. *Washington Post,* April 26, 1947.

300. *Look,* November 20, 1951.

301. May 1947 Sweden-Poland Journal, 36, Nathan Papers, Cornell MS.

302. June 1948 Far East Journal, 1, Nathan Papers, Cornell MS.

303. Homan, "American Business Interests in the Indonesian Republic," 125–32. See pp. 129–30.

304. June 1948 Far East Journal, *passim.*

305. June 1948 Far East Journal, 19, Nathan Papers, Cornell MS.

306. Maurice Atkin, interview by Kenneth Durr, Bethesda, MD, January 10, 2012, 50 (hereafter Atkin Oral History II).

307. June 1948 Far East Journal, 48, Nathan Papers, Cornell MS.

308. Washington Office Report, April 22, 1942, 11, Nathan FBI File.

309. Philip Murray to Nathan, November 22, 1949, Box 165, Philip Murray Papers, American Catholic History Research Center and University Archives (ACUA).

310. Gerald Pomper, "The Public Relations of Organized Labor," *Public Opinion Quarterly* (Winter 1959–1960): 485; *New York Times,* December 29, 1949. On brief notes for commentary, see Charles F. Zimmerman to Marriner Eccles, from The Marriner S. Eccles Document Collection, accessed February 2, 2013, from FRASER, http://fraser.stlouisfed.org/eccles/record.php?id=15569.

311. "Liberal Tax Spokesman Makes Impression on Chairman Doughton," Labor Press Association Release, March 2, 1950, Nathan Scrapbooks; *CIO News*, February 9, 1953.

312. Nathan Draft 1/28, 60.

313. Nathan to Murray, November 7, 1950, and Nathan to Murray, November 28, 1950, Box 165, Philip Murray Papers, ACUA.

314. Nathan to Murray, March 12, 1951, Box 165, Philip Murray Papers, ACUA. Potential subscribers included the largest CIO unions, however—the UAW, USW, IUE, ILGWU, and ACW. See Nathan to Alfred Baker Lewis, December 27, 1957, Box 10, Robert R. Nathan Associates Papers, Library of Congress.

315. December 1944 Palestine Journal, 61–66, Nathan Papers, Cornell MS; June 1948 Far East Journal, 93, Nathan Papers, Cornell MS. Nathan read George Orwell and Hilaire Belloc while flying across the Pacific Ocean in 1948.

316. "Miami Breaks Precedent, Negroes, Whites Dine Together," Federated Press Release, March 4, 1947, Nathan Scrapbooks.

317. Michael Barone, *Our Country: The Shaping of America from Roosevelt to Reagan* (New York: Free Press, 1990), 197.

318. Robert R. Nathan, "American Business Today and Tomorrow," in *Twentieth Century Unlimited: The Vantage Point of the First Fifty Years*, ed. Bruce Bliven (Philadelphia: Lippincott, 1950), 167.

319. See Robert Lekachman, *The Age of Keynes* (New York: Viking, 1966), 164–65.

320. Hagen, "The Reconversion Period: Reflections of a Forecaster," 101.

321. Herbert Stein, "The Washington Economics Industry," *AEA Papers* (May 1986): 1–9.

322. December 1944 Palestine Journal, 17, Nathan Papers, Cornell MS.

CHAPTER 3

1. *Niagara Falls Gazette*, May 18, 1948.

2. Edward Hollander to "All Members of the ADA Executive Committee," August 2, 1954, Box 15, Joseph Rauh Papers, Library of Congress Manuscript Collections (hereafter Rauh Papers, LCMS).

3. Robert R. Nathan, interview by John F. Stewart, June 9, 1967, 26, John F. Kennedy Library (hereafter Nathan Oral History, JFKL).

4. Washington Field Office Case File, March 17, 1966, 32, in Federal Bureau of Investigation files obtained under the Freedom of Information Act (hereafter Nathan FBI File); *Dayton Daily News,* July 27, 1951.

5. Nathan Oral History, 26, JFKL.

6. Samuel Hale Butterfield, *U.S. Development Aid—An Historic First: Achievements and Failures in the Twentieth Century* (Westport: Praeger, 2004), 2-3.

7. Butterfield, *U.S. Development Aid,* 1.

8. Robert R. Nathan, interview by Niel M. Johnson, June 22, 1989, 85, Harry S. Truman Library (hereafter Nathan Oral History, HSTL).

9. See Harry S. Truman to Nelson Rockefeller, January 13, 1951, Truman Papers on-line at http://www.trumanlibrary.org/whistlestop/study_collections/pointfourprogram/documents/pdfs/1-7.pdf#zoom=300.

10. "Partners in Progress, A Report to the President," March 1951, Truman Papers on-line at http://www.trumanlibrary.org/whistlestop/study_collections/pointfourprogram/documents/pdfs/3-2.pdf#zoom=300.

11. Robert A. Packenham, *Liberal America and the Third World: Political Development Ideas in Foreign Aid and Social Science* (Princeton: Princeton University Press, 1973), 35.

12. Butterfield, *U.S. Development Aid,* 8.

13. "Program: National Conference on International Economic and Social Development," April 7, 8, 9, 1952, in Robert R. Nathan Scrapbooks, Nathan Associates (hereafter Nathan Scrapbooks).

14. Although the country is now named Myanmar, it was Burma for Nathan and will be referred to as such here.

15. David I. Steinberg, "Economic Growth with Equity? The Burmese Experience," *Contemporary Southeast Asia* (September 1982): 124–28.

16. Stan Sesser, "A Rich Country Gone Wrong," *New Yorker,* January 9, 1989, 55–96. See p. 63.

17. Steinberg, "Economic Growth with Equity?" 127.

18. Sesser, "Rich Country Gone Wrong," 63.

19. Steinberg, "Economic Growth with Equity?" 133.

20. Nathan Oral History, 98, HSTL.

21. August 1951 Burma-Israel Journal, 2, Box 1, Robert R. Nathan Papers, Division of Rare and Manuscript Collections, Cornell University Library (hereafter Cornell MS).

22. Typescript by Nathan entitled "Draft 1/28, Second Cassette," 6, in Nathan Corporate Records (hereafter "Draft 1/28). Strangely, Nathan also took along a friend, Washington contractor Donald Brown, who was merely sightseeing.

23. August 1951 Burma-Israel Journal, 18–29, Box 1, Nathan Papers, Cornell MS.

24. Draft 1/28, 7–8.

25. August 1951 Burma-Israel Journal, 29, Box 1, Nathan Papers, Cornell MS.

26. Nathan later recalled his first trip to Burma as being something of a sales venture, but in truth the deal was done before Nathan arrived—his team was right behind him. Nathan Oral History, 99, HSTL.

27. *Chicago News,* August 16, 1951.

28. August 1951 Burma-Israel Journal, 23, Box 1, Nathan Papers, Cornell MS.

29. Draft 1/28, 9.

30. Everett E. Hagen, "My Life Philosophy," *American Economist* (Spring 1991): 10–18.

31. Nathan Oral History, 99, HSTL.

32. Maurice Atkin, interview by Kenneth Durr, Bethesda, MD, January 10, 2012, 18 (hereafter Atkin Oral History II); Maurice D. Atkin, *Life's Voyage: Dedicated to Making a Difference* (Marco Island, FL: Keller Publishing, 2005), 51.

33. Draft 1/28, 107.

34. January 1952 Burma Journal, 30, Box 1, Nathan Papers, Cornell MS.

35. August 1951 Burma-Israel Journal, 30–34, Box 1, Nathan Papers, Cornell MS.

36. April 1953 Korea-Burma Journal, 42, Box 33, Robert R. Nathan Associates Records, 1951-1961 (hereafter Nathan Associates Records), LCMS.

37. January 1952 Burma Journal, 15, Box 1, Nathan Papers, Cornell MS.

38. January 1952 Burma Journal, 24, 15, Box 1, Nathan Papers, Cornell MS.

39. Nathan Oral History, 78, HSTL.

40. Steinberg, "Economic Growth with Equity?" 134.

41. Laurence D. Stifel, "Economic Development in Burma: Book Review," *American Economic Review* (September 1963): 780.

42. Louis J. Walinsky, *Economic Development in Burma, 1951-1960 (*New York: Twentieth Century Fund, 1962), 547.

43. Walinsky, *Economic Development in Burma,* 135, 305.

44. Janet Welsh, "Burma's Development Problems," *Far Eastern Survey* (August 1956): 115.

45. January 1952 Burma Journal, 28, Box 1, Nathan Papers, Cornell MS.

46. *New York Times,* March 2, 1952.

47. Draft 1/28, 12.

48. See Nathan to Isador Lubin, October 22, 1951, and "An Economic Survey and Program for Korea," May 6, 1952, in Box 69, Isador Lubin Papers, Franklin D. Roosevelt Library (hereafter Lubin Papers, FDRL).

49. *New York Times,* October 22, 1952.

50. Robert R. Nathan, "Panel 2. The Period of Reconstruction and Rapid Growth (1953–Present): Korea," 2, typescript in Nathan Associates Corporate Records; Robert Nathan, interview by Robert W. Fogel, Washington, D.C., December 26, 1990, 56, Box 3, Nathan Accession 22614, LCMS (hereafter Fogel Nathan Interview); October 1952 Korea-Burma Journal, 1, Box 1, Nathan Papers, Cornell MS.

51. October 1952 Korea-Burma Journal, 9–14, Box 1, Nathan Papers, Cornell MS.

52. Draft 1/28, 12.

53. Nathan Oral History, 79–82, HSTL.

54. Nathan Oral History, 79–82, HSTL; *Pathfinder,* February 4, 1953.

55. April 1953 Korea-Burma Journal, 31, Box 33, Nathan Associates Records, LCMS.

56. For example, see column by Walter Trohan in *Chicago Tribune*, October 23, 1952.

57. October 1952 Korea-Burma Journal, 54, Box 1, Nathan Papers, Cornell MS.

58. October 1952 Korea-Burma Journal, 60, Box 1, Nathan Papers, Cornell MS.

59. *New York Times,* February 7, 1953.

60. *Washington Post,* February 8, 1953.

61. *New York Times,* February 7, 1953.

62. Nathan to "Reg and Staff," May 7, 1953, Reel 44, Americans for Democratic Action Papers on Microfilm (hereafter ADA Microfilm).

63. Nathan to Louis Walinsky, October 8, 1953, Box 3, Louis Walinsky Papers, Cornell MS (hereafter Walinsky Papers); David Ekbladh, *The Great American Mission: Modernization and the Construction of an American World Order* (Princeton: Princeton University Press, 2010), 138.

64. Robert R. Nathan Associates, Inc., *An Economic Programme for Korean Reconstruction* (Washington, D.C.: Robert R. Nathan Associates, Inc., 1954), xii–xiv.

65. *Washington Post,* June 14, 1954.

66. Gregg Andrew Brazinsky, "From Pupil to Model: South Korea and American Development Policy During the Early Park Chung Hee Era," *Diplomatic History* (January 2005): 85.

67. Nathan Associates, *An Economic Programme for Korean Reconstruction,* iii.

68. Ekbladh, *The Great American Mission,* 139.

69. Nathan to Louis Walinsky, December 4, 1953, Box 3, Walinsky Papers, Cornell MS.

70. Nathan to Louis Walinsky, June 24, 1954, Box 3, Walinsky Papers, Cornell MS.

71. Draft 1/28, 13.

72. Nathan to J. Russell Andrus, January 28, 1958, Box 17, Nathan Associates Records, LCMS.

73. Brazinsky, "From Pupil to Model," 83.

74. Clifton Brock and Max Lerner, *Americans for Democratic Action: Its Role in National Politics* (Washington, D.C.: Public Affairs Press, 1962), 49.

75. James Loeb, Jr., to Nathan, December 10, 1946, Reel 60, ADA Microfilm.

76. Nathan Oral History, 69, HSTL. There is some question on this. In some instances he claimed not to have been there, nor does he show up on membership lists. But he does show up on invitation lists, and in one instance he claimed to have remembered Eleanor Roosevelt's remarks at the event. His recollection that he was there but not a member makes the most sense.

77. See "Program: Fifteenth Annual Roosevelt Day Dinner," January 31, 1963, Nathan Scrapbooks.

78. "For Immediate Release," January 4, 1947, Box 5, Gardner Jackson Papers, FDR Library.

79. Joseph Rauh, interview by Niel M. Johnson, June 21, 1989, 52, HSTL.

80. See ADA "Report of the Committee on Economic Stability," Box 12, John Kenneth Galbraith Papers, JFKL. The committee was chaired by former OPA administrator Chester Bowles and included such notables as Lauchlin Currie, John Kenneth Galbraith, David Ginsburg, Richard V. Gilbert, Leon Henderson, and Joseph Rauh.

81. William Benton to Nathan, October 23, 1957, Box 3, Maurice Rosenblatt Papers, LCMS (hereafter Rosenblatt Papers).

82. Brock and Lerner, *Americans for Democratic Action,* 98.

83. Nathan Oral History, 69, HSTL.

84. *ADA World,* June 1952; Nathan to "All Executive Committee Members," August 8, 1952,

Box 16, Rauh Papers, LCMS.

85. Minutes of the ADA Executive Committee meeting, April 5, 1955, Box 14, Rauh Papers, LCMS.

86. *Jewish Criterion*, August 15, 1952.

87. Nathan to Isador Lubin, October 23, 1953, Box 16, Lubin Papers, FDRL.

88. Nathan to "Reg and Staff," May 7, 1953, Box 44, ADA Microfilm.

89. Nathan to Leon Shull, August 15, 1952, Box 44, ADA Microfilm.

90. Nathan to Louis Walinsky, July 21, 1954, Box 3, Walinsky Papers, Cornell MS.

91. See "Nathan Visit Cheers Los Angeles ADA," July 1954 press clipping, Nathan Scrapbooks.

92. *Washington Post,* November 11, 1953.

93. "For Immediate Release," January 4, 1947, Box 5, Gardner Jackson Papers, FDR Library.

94. Washington Field Office Case File, March 17, 1966, 6, Nathan FBI File.

95. See Allen Weinstein and Alexander Vassiliev, *The Haunted Wood: Soviet Espionage in America: The Stalin Era* (New York: Random House, 2000).

96. See Robert Griffith, *The Politics of Fear: Joseph McCarthy and the Senate* (Lexington: University Press of Kentucky, 1970), 212–16.

97. See University of Pennsylvania Nathan obituary at http://www.upenn.edu/ gazette/0102/0102obits.html.

98. See ADA to Joseph McCarthy, July 15, 1953, Box 15, Rauh Papers, LCMS.

99. *ADA World,* April 1953.

100. *Washington Post,* April 7, 1953.

101. ADA to Joseph McCarthy, July 15, 1953, Box 15, Rauh Papers, LCMS.

102. Reinhold Niebuhr to "Dear Friend," April 14, 1953, Box 16, Lubin Papers, Cornell MS.

103. *ADA World*, April 1953.

104. October 1952 Korea-Burma Journal, 3, Box 1, Nathan Papers, Cornell MS.

105. Maurice Rosenblatt to Nathan, March 4, 1953, Box 3, Rosenblatt Papers, LCMS.

106. Maurice Rosenblatt "Nathan Memo," March 4, 1953, Box 21, Rosenblatt Papers, LCMS.

107. Maurice Rosenblatt to Nathan, June 10, 1952, Box 3, Rosenblatt Papers, LCMS.

108. Maurice Rosenblatt to Nathan, September 12, 1952, Box 3, Rosenblatt Papers, LCMS.

109. Maurice Rosenblatt to Ruth Aull, October 2, 1952, Box 3, Rosenblatt Papers, LCMS.

110. Maurice Rosenblatt "Nathan Memo," March 4, 1953, Box 21, Rosenblatt Papers, LCMS.

111. Maurice Rosenblatt to Nathan, March 4, 1953, Box 3, Rosenblatt Papers, LCMS.

112. Maurice Rosenblatt to John W. Oliver, May 1, 1953, Box 1, Rosenblatt Papers, LCMS.

113. "The Clearing House," n.d., Box 21, Rosenblatt Papers, LCMS.

114. *Evening Star,* March 24, 1971.

115. Maurice Rosenblatt "Nathan Memo," March 4, 1953, Box 21, Rosenblatt Papers, LCMS.

116. Griffith, *The Politics of Fear*, 229–35.

117. *ADA World*, April 1954.

118. Griffith, *The Politics of Fear*, 252.

119. Nathan to Frieda Fromm-Reichman, April 12, 1954, Reel 44, ADA Microfilm.

120. Edward D. Hollander to Nathan, June 11, 1954, Reel 46, ADA Microfilm.

121. James T. Patterson, *Grand Expectations: The United States, 1945-1974* (New York: Oxford University Press, 1996), 269.

122. Press Clipping, "Nathan Visit Cheers Los Angeles ADA," July 1954, Nathan Scrapbooks. See also Nathan to Louis Walinsky, May 5, 1954, Box 3, Walinsky Papers, Cornell MS.

123. "Notes on Operation Anti-McCommunism," n.d., Box 21, Rosenblatt Papers, LCMS.

124. Maurice Rosenblatt to Oscar Pattis, June 26, 1954, and Rosenblatt to Joseph Shane, June 30, 1954, Box 21, Rosenblatt Papers, LCMS.

125. L. B. Nichols to Clyde Tolson, July 28, 1954, Nathan FBI File.

126. *Chicago Daily Tribune,* August 17, 1954.

127. Maurice Rosenblatt to George Backer, May 20, 1953, Box 21, Rosenblatt Papers, LCMS.

128. Griffith, *The Politics of Fear,* 282–90.

129. Nathan to Maurice Rosenblatt, July 17, 1962, Box 3, Rosenblatt Papers, LCMS.

130. Robert Nathan, interview by Tracy Campbell, Arlington, VA, June 9, 1995, 40, Louie B. Nunn Center for Oral History, University of Kentucky Libraries.

131. Maurice Atkin, interview by Kenneth Durr, Bethesda, MD, January 4, 2012, 9–10 (hereafter Atkin Oral History I).

132. Mary Nathan, interview by Kenneth Durr, Bethesda, MD, February 15, 2012, 29, 18 (hereafter Mary Nathan Oral History).

133. *Labor's Daily,* May 24, 1955.

134. September 1949 Israel Journal, 6, Box 1, Nathan Papers, Cornell MS.

135. January 1952 Burma Journal, 19, Box 1, Nathan Papers, Cornell MS.

136. November 1959 Iran Journal, 26, Box 1, Nathan Papers, Cornell MS.

137. October 1952 Korea-Burma Journal, 29, Box 1, Nathan Papers, Cornell MS.

138. See "NATHAN-#70421-v1-RRNHistory," undated document obtained from Nathan Associates, 132.

139. Atkin Oral History I, 34.

140. Nathan to Louis Walinsky, November 8, 1956, Box 3, Walinsky Papers, Cornell MS.

141. Mary Nathan Oral History, 26.

142. Nathan to Louis Hexter, September 29, 1955, Box 14, Rauh Papers, LCMS.

143. September 1949 Israel Journal, 14, Box 1, Nathan Papers, Cornell MS.

144. Mary Nathan Oral History, 7; Washington Field Office Case File, March 17, 1966, 16, Nathan FBI File.

145. Nathan to National Advisory Committee of the Anti-Defamation League, May 20, 1959, Box 12, Rauh Papers, LCMS.

146. Mary Nathan Oral History, 6.

147. February 1954 Burma-Israel Journal, 15, Box 1, Nathan Papers, Cornell MS.

148. Nathan to Herbert Block, April 4, 1958, Herbert Block Papers, LCMS.

149. Mary Nathan Oral History, 5.

150. Mary Nathan Oral History, 30.

151. Nathan to Louis Walinsky, July 5, 1955, Box 3, Walinsky Papers, Cornell MS.

152. October 1952 Korea-Burma Journal, 39, Box 1, Nathan Papers, Cornell MS.

153. July 1956 Burma Journal, 61–62, Box 1, Nathan Papers, Cornell MS.

154. October 1952 Korea-Burma Journal, 41, Box 1, Nathan Papers, Cornell MS.

155. Mary Nathan Oral History, 8.

156. January 1952 Burma Journal, 16, Box 1, Nathan Papers, Cornell MS; February 1957 Burma Journal, 4, Box 1, Nathan Papers, Cornell MS.

157. October 1952 Korea-Burma Journal, 26, Box 1, Nathan Papers, Cornell MS.

158. In the interim between TCA and ICA, the agency was called the Foreign Operations Administration.

159. Draft 1/28, 66.

160. Washington Field Office Case File, March 17, 1966, 5-6, Nathan FBI File.

161. Cincinnati Field Office Case File, March 22, 1966, 2, Nathan FBI File.

162. *Washington Post,* February 28, 1950; *Washington News,* November 1954; *CIO News,* February 2, 1953.

163. Nathan to Louis Walinsky, April 2, 1954, Box 3, Walinsky Papers, Cornell MS.

164. Draft 1/28, 73.

165. Nathan to Louis Walinsky, December 4, 1953, Box 3, Walinsky Papers, Cornell MS.

166. *New York Times,* February 14, 1955.

167. Nathan to David McDonald, December 16, 1957, Box 10, Nathan Associates Records, LCMS; Joseph L. Rauh to Edward Hollander, September 28, 1953, Box 15, Rauh Papers, LCMS.

168. Nathan to Louis Walinsky, November 8, 1956, Box 3, Walinsky Papers, Cornell MS; July 1956 Burma Journal, 14, Box 1, Nathan Papers, Cornell MS.

169. Teletype of UPI Press Release "Add 8 Steel," October 13, 1959, Nathan Scrapbooks.

170. *New York Times,* September 26, 1958.

171. Nathan Oral History, 6, JFKL; Draft 1/28, 75.

172. Draft 1/28, 38, 40; Nathan Oral History, HSTL, 102.

173. *Washington Post,* July 9, 1958; *Washington Post,* June 10, 1959; Nathan to Louis Walinsky, October 15, 1958, Box 3, Walinsky Papers, Cornell MS. Nathan was up against Adolf Berle who represented Gray Lines.

174. Nathan to Louis Walinsky, November 8, 1956, Box 3, Walinsky Papers, Cornell MS.

175. Atkin Oral History I, 17–18.

176. August 1951 Burma-Israel Journal, 1, Box 1, Nathan Papers, Cornell MS.

177. Atkin Oral History I, 16.

178. Atkin Oral History I, 23.

179. Draft 1/28, 60.

180. Atkin Oral History I, 27.

181. *New York Times,* January 31, 1956.

182. Draft 1/28, 87.

183. *Sarasota Herald Tribune,* March 17, 1954.

184. *New York Times,* June 8, 1953.

185. Nathan to Louis Walinsky, October 8, 1953, Box 3, Walinsky Papers, Cornell MS.

186. Atkin, *Life's Voyage*, 51.

187. Nathan to Louis Walinsky April 2, 1954, Box 3, Walinsky Papers, Cornell MS.

188. *Journal of Commerce,* August 26, 1952; Nathan to Louis Walinsky, March 25, 1958, Box 3, Walinsky Papers, Cornell MS.

189. Congressional Information Bureau Press Release, September 22, 1959, Nathan Scrapbooks.

190. Nathan to Doyle Willis, December 18, 1957, Box 10, Nathan Associates Records, LCMS.

191. "The Experience of Robert R. Nathan Associates, Inc. in Economic Analysis of Sports Enterprises," n.d., Nathan Scrapbooks.

192. Nathan to Richardson Dilworth, November 5, 1957, Box 10, Nathan Associates Records, LCMS.

193. July 1956 Burma Journal, 86, Box 1, Nathan Papers, Cornell MS.

194. Draft 1/28, 99.

195. Atkin Oral History II, 11.

196. Louis Walinsky to Nathan, May 15, 1954, Box 3, Walinsky Papers, Cornell MS.

197. Nathan to Louis Walinsky, December 4, 1953, Box 3, Walinsky Papers, Cornell MS.

198. Mary Nathan Oral History, 16.

199. Louis Walinsky to Nathan July 25, 1957, Box 11, Walinsky Papers, Cornell MS.

200. Atkin Oral History II, 15–16.

201. Atkin Oral History I, 27; see invitation, Nathan to Gardner Jackson, December 6, 1954, in Box 52, Gardner Jackson Papers, FDR Library.

202. Robert R. Nathan Associates, Inc., Minutes of the Annual Meeting of Stockholders, February 11, 1959, Nathan Associates Corporate Records.

203. Atkin Oral History II, 21; Atkin Oral History I, 26, 19.

204. Atkin Oral History II, 24.

205. Nathan to Arthur Schlesinger, Jr., April 1, 1955, Box P-20, Arthur Schlesinger, Jr., Papers, JFKL.

206. Brock and Lerner, *Americans for Democratic Action*, 166; Joseph Rauh to Walter Reuther, April 14, 1955, Box 15, Rauh Papers, LCMS.

207. Joseph Rauh to Eugene McCarthy, February 8, 1957, Box 13, Rauh Papers, LCMS.

208. Atkin Oral History I, 4.

209. *Washington Post,* April 1, 1957.

210. Robert Nathan, "The Other Side of Prosperity," reprinted from *ADA Voting Guide 1956,* in Nathan Scrapbooks.

211. Hubert Humphrey to Edward Hollander, April 13, 1957, Reel 44, ADA Microfilm.

212. For example, see A. J. Creshkoff to Nathan, April 24, 1959, Box 16, Nathan Associates Records, LCMS.

213. Edward Hollander to "Dear Member," n.d., circa February 1, 1947, Box 43, Rauh Papers, LCMS.

214. Stanley Gewirtz to Joseph Rauh, March 7, 1953, Box 15, Rauh Papers, LCMS.

215. Edward Hollander to Nathan, April 1, 1955, Reel 44, ADA Microfilm; Edward D. Hollander to Nathan, August 5, 1958, Reel 45, ADA Microfilm.

216. Edward D. Hollander to ADA National Board, June 3, 1955, Reel 46, ADA Microfilm.

217. Brock and Lerner, *Americans for Democratic Action*, 18.

218. Eleanor Roosevelt to Nathan and attached Eleanor Roosevelt to Joseph L. Rauh July 18, 1957, Box 12, Rauh Papers, LCMS.

219. Edward Hollander to Nathan, December 4, 1958, Box 12, Rauh Papers, LCMS.

220. Steven M. Gillon, *Politics and Vision: The ADA and American Liberalism, 1947-1985* (New York: Oxford University Press, 1987), 124; Edward Hollander to Reinhold Niebuhr, August 16, 1957, Box 12, Rauh Papers, LCMS.

221. Gillon, *Politics and Vision*, 125.

222. Minutes of the ADA Executive Committee Meeting, December 1, 1953, and July 13, 1954, Box 15, Rauh Papers, LCMS.

223. Nathan to Ben D. Zevin, July 21, 1955, Box 14, Rauh Papers, LCMS.

224. Nathan to Louis Walinsky, June 17, 1954, Box 3, Walinsky Papers, Cornell MS.

225. Nathan to James G. Patton, October 4, 1955, Box 14, Rauh Papers, LCMS.

226. Joseph Rauh to Nathan, October 27, 1955, Box 14, Rauh Papers, LCMS.

227. Marvin Rosenberg to Joseph Rauh, March 29, 1955, Box 15, Rauh Papers, LCMS.

228. Robert R. Nathan to Joseph L. Rauh, August 11, 1954, Box 15, Rauh Papers, LCMS.

229. Arthur Schlesinger, Jr., to Joseph Rauh, December 15, 1954, Box 15, Rauh Papers, LCMS.

230. Nathan to Arthur M. Schlesinger, Jr., December 8, 1954, Box P-20, Arthur Schlesinger, Jr., Papers, JFKL.

231. Nathan to Edward Hollander, August 7, 1956, Reel 44, ADA Microfilm.

232. Nathan to Irving Rosenbloom, November 26, 1957, Box 10, Nathan Associates Records, LCMS.

233. Nathan to Mrs. David M. Levy, December 12,1958, Reel 45, ADA Microfilm; Nathan to Mrs. Albert Lasker, May 2, 1956, Reel 44, ADA Microfilm.

234. Marvin Rosenberg to Nathan, December 13, 1957, Reel 44, ADA Microfilm.

235. Edward Hollander to Nathan, December 4, 1958, Box 12, Rauh Papers, LCMS.

236. James Wechsler to Elmer Davis, March 11, 1955, Box 15, Rauh Papers, LCMS.

237. *Economic Intelligence,* February 1955; *Boston Globe,* January 5, 1954.

238. *ADA World,* June 1959.

239. "Chairman's Report," May 9, 1959, Box 1, Samuel Beer Papers, JFKL.

240. Nathan to Walter Reuther, July 24, 1957, Box 12, Rauh Papers, LCMS.

241. "Report of National Chairman Robert R. Nathan, 11th ADA Convention," May 16, 1958, Box 1, Beer Papers, JFKL.

242. "For Release," September 24, 1957, Box 2, Beer Papers, JFKL.

243. Edward Hollander to Joseph Rauh and Susanna H. Davis, November 18, 1955, Box 14, Rauh Papers, LCMS.

244. *Cleveland News,* February 25, 1953; *New York Times,* January 20, 1953.

245. *New York Times,* January 11, 1953.

246. Gillon, *Politics and Vision*, 122–23, 116.

247. Edward D. Hollander to ADA National Board, June 3, 1955, Reel 46, ADA Microfilm.

248. January 1952 Burma Journal, 39, Box 1, Nathan Papers, Cornell MS.

249. Nathan to Mrs. Albert Lasker, May 2, 1956, Reel 44, ADA Microfilm; Gillon, *Politics and Vision*, 118.

250. Herbert Stein, *The Fiscal Revolution in America* (Washington: AEI Press, 1990), 319–20.

251. *New York Times,* January 3, 1958.

252. Stein, *Fiscal Revolution in America*, 324.

253. "Draft of Speech before I.U.D—AFL-CIO," April 22, 1958, Reel 44, ADA Microfilm.

254. "Report of National Chairman Robert R. Nathan, 11th ADA Convention," May 16, 1958, Box 1, Beer Papers, JFKL.

255. "Draft of Speech before I.U.D—AFL-CIO," April 22, 1958, Reel 44, ADA Microfilm.

256. "Report of National Chairman Robert R. Nathan, 11th ADA Convention," May 16, 1958, Box 1, Beer Papers, JFKL.

257. "Report of the National Chairman, Robert R. Nathan," May 8–10, 1959, Reel 46, ADA Microfilm.

258. Joseph Rauh to Isador Lubin, March 20, 1959, and Nathan to Isador Lubin, May 22, 1959, Box 69, Lubin Papers, Cornell MS.

259. Joseph Rauh to Herbert H. Lehman, April 30, 1959, Box 12, Rauh Papers, LCMS.

260. James Loeb, Jr., to Nathan, n.d., circa 1959, Nathan Personal Correspondence, Nathan Associates Corporate Records.

261. Samuel H. Beer to Nathan, April 4, 1959, Nathan Personal Papers, Nathan Associates.

262. Joseph Rauh to Nathan, April 24, 1959, Box 12, Rauh Papers, LCMS.

263. July 1954 Burma Journal, 1, Box 1, Nathan Papers, Cornell MS.

264. Draft 1/28, 9–10.

265. Everett E. Hagen, "My Life Philosophy," *American Economist* (Spring 1991): 10–18. See p. 16.

266. Walinsky, *Economic Development in Burma,* 455.

267. October 1952 Korea-Burma Journal, 33, Box 1, Nathan Papers, Cornell MS.

268. Walinsky, *Economic Development in Burma,* 408.

269. Nathan Oral History, 101, HSTL.

270. January 1959 Burma Journal, 143, Box 1, Nathan Papers, Cornell MS.

271. Nathan Oral History, 100–101, HSTL.

272. January 1952 Burma Journal, 14, Box 1, Nathan Papers, Cornell MS.

273. Walinsky, *Economic Development in Burma,* 556; Louis Walinsky to Nathan, January 10, 1954, Box 3, Walinsky Papers, Cornell MS.

274. *New York Times*, March 1, 2002.

275. Eugene M. Feinblatt to Nathan, August 10, 1953, Box 15, Rauh Papers, LCMS; ADA Press Release, July 5, 1951, Box 16, Rauh Papers, LCMS.

276. Louis Walinsky to Nathan, October 5, 1953, Box 3, Walinsky Papers, Cornell MS.

277. Louis Walinsky to Nathan, April 30, 1954, Box 3, Walinsky Papers, Cornell MS.

278. April 1953 Korea-Burma Journal, 73, Box 33, Nathan Associates Records, LCMS.

279. Louis Walinsky to Nathan, July 23, 1955, Box 3, Walinsky Papers, Cornell MS.

280. *New Times of Burma*, February 16, 1954; Louis Walinsky to Nathan, June 2, 1954, Box 3, Walinsky Papers, Cornell MS.

281. April 1953 Korea-Burma Journal, 72, Box 33, Nathan Associates Records, LCMS.

282. July 1954 Burma Journal, 1, Box 1, Nathan Papers, Cornell MS.

283. July 1954 Burma Journal, 8, 12, Box 1, Nathan Papers, Cornell MS.

284. February 1954 Burma-Israel Journal, 15, Box 1, Nathan Papers, Cornell MS.

285. July 1954 Burma Journal, 25, Box 1, Nathan Papers, Cornell MS; *Burma Star*, August 20, 1954.

286. July 1954 Burma Journal, 30, 36, Box 1, Nathan Papers, Cornell MS.

287. Louis Walinsky to Nathan, June 8, 1955, Box 3, Walinsky Papers, Cornell MS.

288. *Washington Post,* July 3, 1955.

289. *Burmese Review and Monday New Times*, May 23, 1955, in Box 20, Nathan Associates Records, LCMS.

290. Steinberg, "Economic Growth with Equity?" 135.

291. February 1955 Burma-Israel Journal, 46–53, Box 1, Nathan Papers, Cornell MS.

292. February 1954 Burma-Israel Journal, 43, 35, Box 1, Nathan Papers, Cornell MS; January 1959 Burma Journal, 105, Box 1, Nathan Papers, Cornell MS.

293. Nathan to Louis Walinsky, December 23, 1954, Box 3, Walinsky Papers, Cornell MS.

294. Steinberg, "Economic Growth with Equity?" 135.

295. January 1959 Burma Journal, 20, Box 1, Nathan Papers, Cornell MS; July 1956 Burma Journal, 79, Box 1, Nathan Papers, Cornell MS.

296. Walinsky, *Economic Development in Burma,* 561.

297. See Nathan to Louis Walinsky, December 23, 1954, Nathan to Walinsky, July 8, 1955, and Nathan to Walinsky, February 8, 1956, in Box 3, Walinsky Papers, Cornell MS; Louis Walinsky to Nathan, July 25, 1957, Box 11, Walinsky Papers, Cornell MS.

298. Nathan to Louis Walinsky, May 31, 1957, Box 5, Walinsky Papers, Cornell MS.

299. February 1957 Burma Journal, 39, Box 1, Nathan Papers, Cornell MS.

300. Louis Walinsky to Nathan, December 3, 1957, Box 3, Walinsky Papers, Cornell MS; David Chewning, *A Life Worth Living* (McLean, VA: Lulu Enterprises, 2009), 201–3.

301. February 1954 Burma-Israel Journal, 14, Box 1, Nathan Papers, Cornell MS.

302. David Chewning, interview by Kenneth Durr, McLean, Virginia, January 26, 2012 (hereafter Chewning Oral History), 11.

303. January 1959 Burma Journal, 3, Box 1, Nathan Papers, Cornell MS.

304. July 1954 Burma Journal, 39, Box 1, Nathan Papers, Cornell MS.

305. *Rangoon Nation*, August 26, 1954.

306. Sesser, "Rich Country Gone Wrong," 63.

307. January 1959 Burma Journal, 2, Box 1, Nathan Papers, Cornell MS.

308. Welsh, "Burma's Development Problems," 122.

309. Walinsky, *Economic Development in Burma*, 520–21, 527.

310. Tawfik Ismail and Oai Kee Beng, *Malaya's First Year at the United Nations: As Reflected in Dr. Ismail's Reports Home to Tunku Abdul Rahman* (Singapore: Institute of Southeast Asian Studies, 2009), 5.

311. Ismail and Beng, *Malaya's First Year at the United Nations*, 5.

312. Hugh Tinker, "Economic Development in Burma, 1951-1960: Book Review," *Pacific Affairs* (Autumn 1963): 327.

313. Louis Walinsky to Nathan, April 29, 1955, Box 3, Walinsky Papers, Cornell MS.

314. Louis Walinsky "Daily Records," Entry for December 1, 1958, Box 12, Walinsky Papers, Cornell MS.

315. The termination memo dated December 2, 1958, is in Box 8, Nathan Associates Records, LCMS.

316. Nathan to Louis Walinsky, December 3, 1958, Box 3, Walinsky Papers, Cornell MS.

317. January 1959 Burma Journal, 12, Box 1, Nathan Papers, Cornell MS.

318. Robert R. Nathan Associates, Inc., "Summary of Policy Recommendations, 1953-1959," February 1959, Mimeographed Manuscript at the Library of Congress.

319. January 1959 Burma Journal, 7, 47–52, Box 1, Nathan Papers, Cornell MS.

320. Walinsky, *Economic Development in Burma,* 595–96.

321. The critic was Dr. Alexander Shakow. See "Economic Development in Burma, 1951-1960: Book Review," 327.

322. February 1957 Burma Journal, 16-20, Box 1, Nathan Papers, Cornell MS.

323. Nathan to Dore Schary, January 1, 1959, Reel 45, ADA Microfilm.

324. January 1959 Burma Journal, 142, Box 1, Nathan Papers, Cornell MS.

325. Robert R. Nathan Associates, Inc., *Three Steps From the Ivory Tower* (Washington, D.C.: Robert R. Nathan Associates, Inc., 1960), in Nathan Scrapbooks; Nathan to Isador Lubin, March 22, 1956, Box 69, Lubin Papers, Cornell MS.

326. Nathan to Louis Walinsky, October 20, 1954, Box 3, Walinsky Papers, Cornell MS.

327. Louis Walinsky to Nathan, December 3, 1958, Box 12, Walinsky Papers, Cornell MS.

328. "A Very Brief History of Nathan Associates Inc.," 2, Nathan Associates Corporate Records; Draft 1/28, 52.

329. Nathan to Louis Walinsky, June 12, 1957, Box 3, Walinsky Papers, Cornell MS; Nathan to Doyle Willis, December 18, 1957, Box 10, Nathan Associates Records, LCMS.

330. Mary Nathan Oral History, 37.

331. October 1958 Colombia Journal, 10, Box 1, Nathan Papers, Cornell MS.

332. Nathan to Louis Walinsky, December 12, 1958, Box 3, Walinsky Papers, Cornell MS.

333. Washington Field Office Case File, March 17, 1966, 6, Nathan FBI File.

334. January 1952 Burma Journal, 30, Box 1, Nathan Papers, Cornell MS.

335. Nathan to Louis Walinsky, December 12, 1958, Box 3, Walinsky Papers, Cornell MS.

336. November 1959 Iran Journal, 3, Box 1, Nathan Papers, Cornell MS; Nathan to Walter Reuther, November 17, 1959, Box 12, Rauh Papers, LCMS.

337. November 1959 Iran Journal, 41–42, Nathan Papers, Cornell MS.

338. April 1953 Korea-Burma Journal, 7, Box 33, Nathan Associates Records, LCMS.

339. Nathan to Louis Walinsky, September 29, 1958, Walinsky Papers, Box 3.

340. October 1958 Columbia Journal, 12, 8–9, Box 1, Nathan Papers, Cornell MS.

341. Draft 1/28, 13.

342. Nathan to Mrs. David M. Levy, January 27, 1959, Reel 45, ADA Microfilm; October 1958 Colombia Journal, 6, Box 1, Nathan Papers, Cornell MS.

343. Samuel Beer to Nathan, October 9, 1956, Box 2, Beer Papers, JFKL.

344. Nathan to Dorothy Kenyon, March 6, 1956, Box 14, Rauh Papers, LCMS.

345. Patterson, *Grand Expectations*, 254.

346. Patterson, *Grand Expectations*, 244.

347. *Washington Post*, August 8, 1956.

348. Robert R. Nathan, "Some Observations and Highlights on the Democratic National Convention in Chicago," August 16, 1956, pp. 13 and 9, Reel 44, ADA Microfilm.

349. Nathan to J. M. Kaplan, January 18, 1957, Reel 44, ADA Microfilm.

350. Robert R. Nathan, *An Appraisal of the War Production Board: Industrial College of the Armed Forces Publication Number L50-144* (Washington, D.C.: GPO, 1950), 1–27.

351. *Forbes*, March 15, 1951.

352. Nathan to Louis Walinsky, June 4, 1958, Box 3, Walinsky Papers, Cornell MS.

353. Calvin L. Christman, "Donald Nelson and the Army: Personality as a Factor in Civil-Military Relations during World War II," *Military Affairs* (October 1973): 418.

354. *Money and Credit: Their Influence on Jobs, Prices, and Growth: The Summary of the Report of the Commission on Money and Credit*, Supplement to the June 25, 1961, *New York Times*, 2–3; Nathan to John W. Hight, November 2, 1959, Reel 45, ADA Microfilm.

355. Arthur Smithies, "The Commission on Money and Credit," *Quarterly Journal of Economics* (November 1961): 546, 553.

356. Smithies, "The Commission on Money and Credit," 546, 553; *Money and Credit*, 4.

357. *Money and Credit*, 4.

358. Smithies, "Commission on Money and Credit," 545.

359. *Washington Post*, July 6, 1958; *Washington Post*, July 5, 1959; *Washington Post*, September 27, 1959.

360. *Washington Post*, November 6, 1959; Nathan Oral History, 8, JFKL.

361. Brock and Lerner, *Americans for Democratic Action*, 177.

362. Hubert H. Humphrey to Mary Nathan, March 10, 1960, Box 150.D.5.8F, Hubert Humphrey Senate Political Files, Minnesota Historical Society.

363. Hubert H. Humphrey to Nathan, March 29, 1960, Box 150.D.5.7B, Hubert Humphrey Senate Political Files, Minnesota Historical Society.

364. *Washington Post*, April 29, 1960.

365. Michael E. Parrish, *Citizen Rauh: An American Liberal's Life in Law and Politics* (Ann Arbor: University of Michigan Press, 2011), 138.

366. Patterson, *Grand Expectations*, 435.

367. Nathan Oral History, 1–4, JFKL.

368. Brock and Lerner, *Americans for Democratic Action*, 15.

369. *Washington Post,* December 30, 1954.

370. Richard L. Neuberger to Nathan, March 27, 1956, Box 13, Rauh Papers, LCMS.

371. Nathan Oral History, 10–15, JFKL.

372. Parrish, *Citizen Rauh,* 143. Nathan denied this as he did regarding other instances in which his alleged maneuvering seemed less than upright. But coupled with Rauh's request for assurance, it is the most plausible account.

373. Patterson, *Grand Expectations,* 439.

374. Nathan Oral History, 28, JFKL. On Freeman, see notes from Carl Solberg interview with Robert R. Nathan, November 18, 1980, 4, Box 147.E.11.3B, Papers of Carl Solberg, Minnesota Historical Society; Robert Caro, *Passage to Power: The Years of Lyndon Johnson* (New York: Knopf, 2012), 140.

375. Nathan Oral History, 17, JFKL.

376. Brock and Lerner, *Americans for Democratic Action*, 193.

377. Nathan Oral History, 19, JFKL.

378. *Dayton Daily News*, February 18, 1961.

CHAPTER 4

1. May 1961 Afghanistan Journal, 1–2, Box 1, Robert R. Nathan Papers (hereafter Nathan Papers), Division of Rare and Manuscript Collections, Cornell University Library (hereafter Cornell MS).

2. See W. W. Rostow, *The Stages of Economic Growth: A Non-Communist Manifesto* (London: Cambridge University Press, 1960), 4–16.

3. Robert R. Nathan Associates marketing brochure, n.d., circa 1967, in Robert R. Nathan Scrapbooks, Nathan Associates (hereafter Nathan Scrapbooks).

4. Gregg Andrew Brazinsky, "From Pupil to Model: South Korea and American Development Policy During the Early Park Chung Hee Era," *Diplomatic History* (January 2005): 85.

5. Arthur M. Schlesinger, Jr., *A Thousand Days: John F. Kennedy in the White House* (Boston: Houghton Mifflin, 1965), 588.

6. Robert R. Nathan, interview by John F. Stewart, June 9, 1967, 25, John F. Kennedy Library (hereafter Nathan Oral History, JFKL).

7. Nathan Oral History, 25, JFKL.

8. Samuel Hale Butterfield, *U.S. Development Aid—An Historic First: Achievements and Failures in the Twentieth Century* (Westport: Praeger, 2004), 62–63.

9. December 1962 Korea Journal, 1, Box 1, Nathan Papers, Cornell MS.

10. "Robert Nathan on Afghanistan," 7, transcript of an unidentified, undated cassette tape in Nathan Associates Corporate Records.

11. Nathan's travel journal does not even mention the cemetery, although it does detail the trip to the area with Hai Aziz. In later years, Nathan loved to tell the cemetery story, however.

12. "Robert Nathan on Afghanistan," 3, transcript of an unidentified, undated cassette tape in Nathan Associates Corporate Records.

13. "Amendment No. 3 to Contract Between the Royal Government of Afghanistan and Robert R. Nathan Associates, Inc.," April 29, 1964, at http://www.fara.gov/docs/352-Exhibit-AB-19641123-21.pdf .

14. October 1961 Afghanistan Journal, 1, Box 1, Nathan Papers, Cornell MS.

15. Typescript by Nathan entitled "Draft 1/28, Second Cassette," 21–22, in Nathan Associates Corporate Records (hereafter Draft 1/28); Robert R. Nathan Associates, Inc., "Economic Advisory Services Provided to the Ministry of Planning, Royal Government of Afghanistan, September 1961 to June 1972, Final Report" (hereafter Afghanistan Final Report), July 1972, at http://pdf.usaid.gov/pdf_docs/PDABU535.pdf, xiv, xv.

16. May 1961 Afghanistan Journal, 59–64, Box 1, Nathan Papers, Cornell MS.

17. Afghanistan Final Report, viii, 198.

18. April 1963 Afghanistan Journal, 1, 33, Box 1, Nathan Papers, Cornell MS.

19. August 1964 Korea Journal, 16, Box 1, Nathan Papers, Cornell MS.

20. David Chewning, interview by Kenneth Durr, McLean, VA, January 26, 2012, 13 (hereafter Chewning Oral History).

21. March 1964 Afghanistan Journal, 6–7, Box 1, Nathan Papers, Cornell MS; November 1966 Afghanistan Journal, 36, Box 2, Nathan Papers, Cornell MS.

22. April 1966 Afghanistan Journal, 1, Box 2, Nathan Papers, Cornell MS.

23. Joe Gunn, interview by Kenneth Durr, Arlington, VA, February 9, 2012, 6 (hereafter Gunn Oral History).

24. Afghanistan Final Report, 10–11; January 1968 Afghanistan Journal, 12, Box 2, Nathan Papers, Cornell MS.

25. Walter LaFeber, *Inevitable Revolutions: The United States in Central America* (New York: Norton, 1983), 148–49.

26. Robert R. Nathan Associates, Inc., *Investment and Industrial Development in El Salvador* (Washington, D.C.: Robert R. Nathan Associates, Inc., 1961), i.

27. February 1963 El Salvador Journal, 5, Box 1, Nathan Papers, Cornell MS.

28. LaFeber, *Inevitable Revolutions*, 172.

29. May 1961 Afghanistan Journal, 14, Box 1, Nathan Papers, Cornell MS.

30. August 1963 El Salvador Journal, 3, Box 1, Nathan Papers, Cornell MS.

31. February 1963 El Salvador Journal, 5, Box 1, Nathan Papers, Cornell MS.

32. August 1963 El Salvador Journal, 59–62, Box 1, Nathan Papers, Cornell MS.

33. April 1963 Afghanistan Journal, 47, Box 1, Nathan Papers, Cornell MS.

34. August 1963 El Salvador Journal, 59–62, Box 1, Nathan Papers, Cornell MS.

35. Robert R. Nathan Associates marketing brochure, n.d., circa 1967, Nathan Scrapbooks.

36. January 1965 Costa Rica Journal, 67, Box 1, Nathan Papers, Cornell MS.

37. April 1964 El Salvador Journal, 15, Box 1, Nathan Papers, Cornell MS.

38. February 1963 El Salvador, 12–20, Box 1, Nathan Papers, Cornell MS.

39. LaFeber, *Inevitable Revolutions*, 173–74.

40. LaFeber, *Inevitable Revolutions*, 184.

41. January 1965 Costa Rica Journal, 1, Box 1, Nathan Papers, Cornell MS.

42. April 1964 El Salvador Journal, 36, Box 1, Nathan Papers, Cornell MS.

43. January 1965 Costa Rica Journal, 2, 7, 16, Box 1, Nathan Papers, Cornell MS.

44. E. D. Hollander, "Observations on the Political Economy of Manpower in Ghana," *Economic Bulletin of Ghana* 4, no. 6 (June 1960): 9–18.

45. David Chewning, *A Life Worth Living* (McLean, VA: Lulu Enterprises, 2009), 298–302.

46. February 1964 Nigeria Journal, *passim*, Box 1, Nathan Papers, Cornell MS.

47. John Beyer, interview by Kenneth Durr, Arlington, VA, 10, January 18, 2012 (hereafter Beyer Oral History).

48. Robert R. Nathan Associates, Inc., *Economic Review of the Turkey-Iran Railway Link* (Washington, D.C.: Robert R. Nathan Associates, Inc., 1963).

49. May 1961 Afghanistan Journal, 109, Box 1, Nathan Papers, Cornell MS; May 1967 Israel Journal, 1, Box 2, Nathan Papers, Cornell MS.

50. December 1962 Korea Journal, 16–17, Box 1, Nathan Papers, Cornell MS.

51. Program for "Joe Rauh Testimonial," January 16, 1971, Nathan Scrapbooks.

52. *ADA World*, February 1961.

53. Alan P. Grimes, "Contemporary American Liberalism," *Annals of the American Academy* (November 1962): 27.

54. Samuel H. Beer to Kenneth O'Donnell, January 27, 1961, Box 1, Samuel Beer Papers, John F. Kennedy Presidential Library (JFKL).

55. *New York Times Magazine*, February 19, 1961.

56. Joseph L. Rauh, Jr., interview by Robert S. Peck, "Mississippi Freedom Tape," 149, at http://www.dcchs.org/JosephLRauh/rauh_transcript_8.pdf.

57. Schlesinger, *Thousand Days*, 628.

58. Nathan Oral History, 22, JFKL.

59. Schlesinger, *Thousand Days*, 629.

60. Marion Fourcade, *Economists and Societies: Discipline and Profession in the United States, Britain, and France, 1890s to 1990s* (Princeton: Princeton University Press, 2009), 107.

61. Walter Heller, Kermit Gordon, James Tobin, Gardner Ackley, and Paul Samuelson, interview by Joseph Pechman, August 1, 1964, 289, 294, JFKL (hereafter CEA OH).

62. Steven M. Gillon, *Politics and Vision: The ADA and American Liberalism, 1947-1985* (New York: Oxford University Press, 1987), 147.

63. Joseph L. Rauh, Jr., interview by Robert S. Peck, "Mississippi Freedom Tape," 149, at http://www.dcchs.org/JosephLRauh/rauh_transcript_8.pdf.

64. *ADA World*, February 1961.

65. Grimes, "Contemporary American Liberalism," 32.

66. *ADA World*, April 1961.

67. *U.S. News & World Report*, May 11, 1963.

68. *New York Times*, November 22, 1962.

69. *Washington Post*, July 31, 1960.

70. Gillon, *Politics and Vision*, 149, 153.

71. *Washington Post*, November 17, 1964.

72. Robert R. Nathan and Joseph L. Rauh, Jr., to Walter P. Reuther, August 9, 1963, Box 12, Joseph Rauh Papers, Library of Congress Manuscript Collections (hereafter Rauh Papers, LCMS).

73. Rauh to unidentified correspondent, June 5, 1963, Box 12, Rauh Papers, LCMS.

74. Robert R. Nathan and Joseph L. Rauh, Jr., to Walter P. Reuther, August 9, 1963, Box 12, Rauh Papers, LCMS.

75. See Alan Draper, *A Rope of Sand: The AFL-CIO Committee on Political Education, 1955–1967* (New York: Praeger, 1988).

76. Grimes, "Contemporary American Liberalism," 32.

77. May 1961 Afghanistan Journal, 49, Box 1, Nathan Papers, Cornell MS.

78. Andrew Kopkind, "Humphrey's Old Pals: An Account of the ADA Convention," *New Republic*, May 7, 1966, 21.

79. August 1964 Korea Journal, 153, Box 1, Nathan Papers, Cornell MS.

80. *St. Petersburg Times,* September 16, 1964.

81. Gillon, *Politics and Vision*, 169.

82. Hubert Humphrey to Nathan, April 17, 1962, Nathan Personal Correspondence, Nathan Associates Corporate Records (hereafter Nathan Personal Correspondence).

83. Kopkind, "Humphrey's Old Pals," 19–22.

84. *ADA World,* July 1966.

85. *Washington Post,* March 31, 1967.

86. *Washington Post*, March 20, 1966.

87. *New York Times*, December 31, 1966.

88. *Washington Post*, March 20, 1966, and July 3, 1951.

89. *Washington Post*, March 20, 1966.

90. *Washington Post*, July 30, 1966.

91. *Washington Post*, June 11, 1962.

92. *Washington Post,* March 20, 1966, and March 21, 1966.

93. Nathan to Isador Lubin, April 21, 1967, Box 69, Isador Lubin Papers, Franklin D. Roosevelt Library (FDR Library).

94. "Minutes of the Annual Meeting of the Board of Directors of Robert R. Nathan Associates, Inc.," February 9, 1962, Nathan Associates Corporate Records.

95. Samuel Beer to Edward Hollander, February 20, 1962, Box 2, Samuel Beer Papers, JFKL.

96. Beyer Oral History, 19–20.

97. Harriet Kriesberg, interview by Kenneth Durr, Bethesda, MD, March 2, 2012, 4 (hereafter Kriesberg Oral History).

98. "Minutes of the Annual Meeting of the Board of Directors of Robert R. Nathan Associates, Inc.," February 4, 1963, Nathan Associates Corporate Records.

99. Maurice Atkin, interview by Kenneth Durr, Bethesda, MD, January 4, 2012, 20 (hereafter Atkin Oral History I); Maurice Atkin, interview by Kenneth Durr, Bethesda, MD, January 10, 2012, 8–9 (hereafter Atkin Oral History II).

100. *Washington Post*, July 2 and July 8, 1964.

101. *Labor,* February 11, 1967.

102. Robert R. Nathan Associates marketing brochure, n.d., circa 1967, Nathan Scrapbooks; *Chemical & Engineering News,* December 6, 1965.

103. Edward D. Hollander, *The Future of Small Business* (New York: F. A. Praeger, 1967).

104. *Business Week,* July 31, 1965.

105. Draft 1/28, 42; *Escanaba Daily Press,* January 14, 1963.

106. Unidentified news clipping dated February 11, 1964, in Nathan Scrapbooks.

107. Draft 1/28, 69.

108. *Escanaba Daily Press,* February 9, 1963.

109. *Mining Journal,* June 12, 1963, in Nathan Scrapbooks.

110. Unidentified news clipping dated February 11, 1964 in Nathan Scrapbooks.

111. Robert R. Nathan Associates marketing brochure, n.d., circa 1967, Nathan Scrapbooks.

112. *New York Times,* May 25, 1966, and January 17, 1967.

113. Robert R. Nathan Associates, Inc., *Protection and Development for Recreational Resources* (Boston: New England Regional Commission, 1968) and *Developing Marine Industries* (Boston: New England Regional Commission, 1968).

114. *New York Times,* November 13, 1962; "Office of Coal Research Contractor Sees Coal Export Opportunities," U.S. Department of Interior Press Release, September 16, 1963, in Nathan Scrapbooks.

115. Nathan to Samuel Lasky, September 6, 1963, front attachment to Robert R. Nathan Associates, Inc., *The Foreign Market Potential for United States Coal* (Washington, D.C.: GPO, 1963).

116. August 1963 El Salvador Journal, 23, Box 1, Nathan Papers, Cornell MS.

117. Nathan Associates, *Foreign Market Potential,* 1-6; *New York Times,* September 18, 1963.

118. 114 Cong. Rec. 13,717 (1968).

119. Robert R. Nathan Associates, Inc., *The Potential Market for Far Western Coal and Lignite* (Washington, D.C.: GPO, 1965); *New York Times,* September 18, 1963.

120. DOE Energy Information Administration, *Coal Production in the United States,* October 2006, 8, accessed at http://www.eia.gov/cneaf/coal/page/coal_production_review.pdf.

121. May 1961 Afghanistan Journal, 1, Box 1, Nathan Papers, Cornell MS.

122. May 1962 Afghanistan Journal, 2, Box 1, Nathan Papers, Cornell MS; December 1962 Korea Journal, 2, Box 1, Nathan Papers, Cornell MS.

123. April 1963 Afghanistan Journal, 4, Box 1, Nathan Papers, Cornell MS.

124. February 1964 Nigeria Journal, 1, Box 1, Nathan Papers, Cornell MS.

125. "Minutes of the Annual Meeting of the Board of Directors of Robert R. Nathan Associates, Inc.," May 28, 1963, Nathan Associates Corporate Records.

126. January 1965 Costa Rica Journal, 2, Box 1, Nathan Papers, Cornell MS.

127. March 1965 Afghanistan, India, Israel Journal, 80, Box 1, Nathan Papers, Cornell MS.

128. *Washington Post,* May 17, 2008; Beyer Oral History, 8; "Minutes of the Annual Meeting of the Board of Directors of Robert R. Nathan Associates, Inc.," June 21, 1965, Nathan Associates Corporate Records.

129. Brazinsky, "From Pupil to Model," 86–87; David Ekbladh, *The Great American Mission:*

Modernization and the Construction of an American World Order (Princeton: Princeton University Press, 2010), 197.

130. Brazinsky, "From Pupil to Model," 92.

131. December 1962 Korea Journal, 2, 4, Box 1, Nathan Papers, Cornell MS.

132. August 1964 Korea Journal, 3, Box 1, Nathan Papers, Cornell MS.

133. Ekbladh, *The Great American Mission*, 198.

134. December 1962 Korea Journal, 41, Box 1, Nathan Papers, Cornell MS.

135. Brazinsky, "From Pupil to Model," 90.

136. April 1965 Saipan-Korea Journal, 95–99, 138, 136, Box 1, Nathan Papers, Cornell MS.

137. Brazinsky, "From Pupil to Model," 101–3.

138. David C. Cole and Young Woo Nam, *The Pattern and Significance of Economic Planning in Korea* (Cambridge, MA: Development Advisory Service, 1968), 3.

139. June 1966 Korea Journal, 2, Box 2, Nathan Papers, Cornell MS.

140. June 1966 Korea Journal, 52, Box 2, Nathan Papers, Cornell MS.

141. Draft 1/28, 18.

142. April 1965 Saipan-Korea Journal, 77–79, 2, Box 1, Nathan Papers, Cornell MS.

143. *Washington Post*, February 26, 1991.

144. April 1965 Saipan-Korea Journal, 95–99, Box 1, Nathan Papers, Cornell MS.

145. "Press Translations: Korea," May 22, 1965, Nathan Scrapbooks.

146. Brazinsky, "From Pupil to Model," 114.

147. Dirk Anthony Ballendorf, "The New Freely-Associated States of Micronesia: Their Natural and Social Environmental Challenges," *GeoJournal*, March 1988, 139.

148. Chewning Oral History, 29.

149. See April 1965 Saipan-Korea Journal, Box 1, Nathan Papers, Cornell MS.

150. August 1966 Vietnam Journal, 71, Box 1, Robert R. Nathan Accession 22614, LCMS. The unsuccessful chief of mission was Ivan Bloch.

151. August 1966 Vietnam Journal, 84, Box 1, Robert R. Nathan Accession 22614, LCMS.

152. Chewning Oral History, 30.

153. April 1965 Saipan-Korea Journal, 37, Box 1, Nathan Papers, Cornell MS.

154. Robert R. Nathan Associates, Inc., *Economic Development Plan for Micronesia: Summary and Index* (Washington, D.C.: Robert R. Nathan Associates, Inc., 1967).

155. Hubert Humphrey to Nathan, April 17, 1962, Nathan Personal Correspondence; *San Juan Star,* November 30, 1965.

156. *San Juan Star,* December 5, 1965.

157. Robert R. Nathan Associates marketing brochure, n.d., circa 1967, Nathan Scrapbooks.

158. October 1961 Afghanistan Journal, 30, Box 1, Nathan Papers, Cornell MS; *Washington Post,* October 27, 1961; May 1962 Afghanistan Journal, 66, Box 1, Nathan Papers, Cornell MS.

159. *Steel Valley News,* October 19, 1964; Robert R. Nathan Associates marketing brochure, n.d., circa 1967, Nathan Scrapbooks.

160. Draft 1/28, 69.

161. April 1963 Afghanistan Journal, 2, Box 1, Nathan Papers, Cornell MS.

162. Gunn Oral History, 23.

163. Robert R. Nathan, "Antitrust and International Competition: Courting the 'Cartel Malignancy,'" *Antitrust Law and Economics Review* 79 (1985): 86.

164. Gunn Oral History, 22.

165. See decision in *Automatic Radio Mfg. Co. Inc., et al. v. Ford Motor Company*, at https://bulk.resource.org/courts.gov/c/F2/390/390.F2d.113.7021_1.html; Gunn Oral History, 21; Draft 1/28, 100.

166. *Sporting News*, March 19, 1966.

167. *Milwaukee Journal*, March 8, 1966.

168. "The Experience of Robert R. Nathan Associates, Inc. in Economic Analysis of Sports Enterprises," n.d., circa 1984, Nathan Scrapbooks; *Milwaukee Journal*, March 8, 1966.

169. *Milwaukee Journal*, March 8, 1966.

170. *Sporting News*, March 19, 1966.

171. Draft 1/28, 70.

172. Draft 1/28, 84.

173. Robert R. Nathan Associates marketing brochure, n.d., circa 1967, Nathan Scrapbooks; Draft 1/28, 74.

174. Beyer Oral History, 16.

175. *Business Week,* June 4, 1966.

176. *Washington Post,* June 8, 1966.

177. Unidentified summary of FCC rate hearings, August 1, 1966, in Nathan Scrapbooks.

178. *Business Week,* June 4, 1966.

179. *Washington Post,* June 8, 1966.

180. *Washington Post,* June 11, 1966.

181. Draft 1/28, 84.

182. "The legal profession learns from law school and repeatedly thereafter that all clients have the right to get the best possible legal advice," wrote Nathan, pointing out that the same did not go for economists. See Draft 1/28, 79.

183. *Washington Post,* June 8, 1966.

184. *Milwaukee Journal,* March 8, 1966.

185. *Dayton Journal Herald*, n.d., in Nathan Scrapbooks.

186. *Washington Post*, February 19, 1961.

187. Washington Field Office Case File, March 17, 1966, 20, in Federal Bureau of Investigation files obtained under the Freedom of Information Act (hereafter Nathan FBI File).

188. Mary Nathan, interview by Kenneth Durr, Bethesda, MD, February 15, 2012, 30–31 (hereafter Mary Nathan Oral History).

189. May 1961 Afghanistan Journal, 3, Box 1, Nathan Papers, Cornell MS.

190. Mary Nathan Oral History, 27.

191. Mary Nathan Oral History, 41–42; Washington Field Office Case File, March 17, 1966, 17, Nathan FBI File.

192. Mary Nathan Oral History, 30.

193. SAC, WFO to Director, FBI, March 25, 1966, Nathan FBI File.

194. Mary Nathan Oral History, 13.

195. May 1966 Costa Rica Journal, 7, Box 2, Nathan Papers, Cornell MS; October 1961 Afghanistan Journal, 2, Box 1, Nathan Papers, Cornell MS.

196. October 1961 Afghanistan Journal, 1, Box 1, Nathan Papers, Cornell MS.

197. Mary Nathan Oral History, 40.

198. Kriesberg Oral History, 23.

199. Gunn Oral History, 8.

200. Beyer Oral History, 32.

201. *New York Times*, December 19, 1959; New York Field Office Case File, March 16, 1966, 2, Nathan FBI File; February 1963 El Salvador Journal, 58, Box 1, Nathan Papers, Cornell MS.

202. Edward C. Mayberry, "The Two Mr. Nathans," in unidentified publication, circa 1965, Nathan Scrapbooks; *Washington Post,* November 19, 1963; *New York Times,* September 16, 1972; May 1961 Afghanistan Journal, 50, Box 1, Nathan Papers, Cornell MS; Baltimore Field Office Case File, March 14, 1966, Nathan FBI File; New York Field Office Case File, March 16, 1966, 5, Nathan FBI File; *Washington Star,* June 19, 1960.

203. October 1965 El Salvador Journal, 2, Box 1, Nathan Papers, Cornell MS.

204. *Washington Post,* March 20, 1966; *Washington Post,* March 21, 1966.

205. Kriesberg Oral History, 6; Draft 1/28, 52.

206. Draft 1/28, 51.

207. "Written Consent to Action by Stockholders of Robert R. Nathan Associates, Inc.," Nathan Associates Corporate Records.

208. Draft 1/28, 51.

209. "Minutes of the Annual Meeting of the Board of Directors of Robert R. Nathan Associates, Inc." April 9, 1962, Nathan Associates Corporate Records.

210. November 1966 Afghanistan Journal, 49, Box 2, Nathan Papers, Cornell MS.

211. Atkin Oral History II, 3.

212. Gunn Oral History, 11.

213. Gunn Oral History, 16.

214. Robert R. Nathan, "The Road to Full Employment," *Industrial Relations: A Journal of Economy and Society,* October 1962, 29–38.

215. *ADA World*, April 1963.

216. Fourcade, *Economists and Societies*, 90.

217. Gunn Oral History, 30; Bernard Norwood, telephone interview by Kenneth Durr, February 10, 2012, 10 (hereafter Norwood Oral History).

218. December 1962 Korea Journal, 17, Box 1, Nathan Papers, Cornell MS.

219. Robert R. Nathan, "Economic Analysis and Public Policy: The Growing Hiatus," *American Economic Association,* May 1964, 611.

220. Nathan, "Economic Analysis and Public Policy," 615.

221. Nathan Oral History, 27, 29, JFKL.

222. *Washington Post*, May 7, 1961.

223. CEA OH, 253.

224. Walter W. Heller, "Memoranda for the President," June 12, 1961, Papers of John F. Kennedy, Presidential Papers, Office Files, at http://www.jfklibrary.org/Asset-Viewer/Archives/ JFKPOF-073-005.aspx.

225. Gillon, *Politics and Vision*, 266, n. 26.

226. Washington Field Office Case File, March 17, 1966, 10, Nathan FBI File.

227. Mary Nathan Oral History, 20.

228. Stanley Karnow, *Vietnam: A History* (New York: Penguin, 1983), 479–80.

229. *International Agricultural Development*, monthly newsletter of the International Agricultural Development Service, U.S. Department of Agriculture, March 1966; Washington Field Office Case File, March 17, 1966, 13, Nathan FBI File.

230. February 1966 Vietnam Conference in Hawaii Journal, 4, Box 2, Nathan Papers, Cornell MS.

231. Manuscript by Clifton Wharton, February 23, 2000, 4, in Mary Nathan Personal Collection.

232. Karnow, *Vietnam*, 498.

233. February 1966 Vietnam Conference in Hawaii Journal, 22, Box 2, Nathan Papers, Cornell MS.

234. Manuscript by Clifton Wharton, February 23, 2000, in Mary Nathan Personal Collection, 6.

235. February 1966 Vietnam Conference in Hawaii Journal, 22, Box 2, Nathan Papers, Cornell MS.

236. *Dayton Daily News*, February 27, 1966.

237. *Foreign Relations of the United States, 1964-1968*, vol. 4, *Vietnam, 1966*, ed. David C. Humphrey (Washington, D.C.: GPO, 1998), 260–64. In March 1966, the White House initiated a security check "for a Presidential appointment, position not stated." See W. V. Cleveland to "Mr. Gale," March 7, 1966, Nathan FBI File.

238. August 1966 Vietnam Journal, 1, Box 1, Robert R. Nathan Accession 22614, LCMS.

239. Notes from Carl Solberg interview with Robert R. Nathan, November 18, 1980, 4, Box 147.E.11.3B, Papers of Carl Solberg, Minnesota Historical Society (MNHS) (hereafter Solberg interview notes).

240. Ekbladh, *Great American Mission*, 202–3.

241. *Washington Post*, August 12, 1966.

242. August 1966 Vietnam Journal, 1, Box 1, Robert R. Nathan Accession 22614, LCMS.

243. *Washington Post*, August 12, 1966.

244. August 1966 Vietnam Journal, 5, Box 1, Robert R. Nathan Accession 22614, LCMS.

245. August 1966 Vietnam Journal, 35, Box 1, Robert R. Nathan Accession 22614, LCMS; August 1966 Vietnam Journal, 18–33, Box 1, Robert R. Nathan Accession 22614, LCMS.

246. August 1966 Vietnam Journal, 42, 39, 60, Box 1, Robert R. Nathan Accession 22614, LCMS.

247. Hubert Humphrey to Lyndon Johnson, September 16, 1966, Box 150.E.13.6F, Hubert H. Humphrey Papers, 1968 Presidential Campaign Files, MNHS (hereafter Humphrey 1968 Files).

248. James T. Patterson, *Grand Expectations, The United States, 1945-1974* (New York: Oxford University Press, 1996), 595.

249. August 1966 Vietnam Journal, 1, Box 1, Robert R. Nathan Accession 22614, LCMS.

250. Nathan to John Kenneth Galbraith, February 10, 1965, Box 144, John Kenneth Galbraith Papers, JFKL (hereafter Galbraith Papers).

251. John Kenneth Galbraith to Edward Hollander, March 4, 1965, and Edward Hollander to John Kenneth Galbraith, March 5, 1965, Box 496, Galbraith Papers, JFKL.

252. John Kenneth Galbraith to Robert R. Nathan, March 28, 1966, Box 144, Galbraith Papers, JFKL.

253. John Kenneth Galbraith, *A Life in Our Times: Memoirs* (Boston: Houghton Mifflin, 1981), 484–85.

254. "Address by John Kenneth Galbraith on Accepting the National Chairmanship of Americans for Democratic Action in Washington, D.C., April 2, 1967," Box 188, Galbraith Papers, JFKL.

255. *ADA World,* May 1967.

256. Leon H. Keyserling, "What Has Happened to ADA?" January 29, 1968, 30, Box 188, Galbraith Papers, JFKL; Gillon, *Politics and Vision*, 191.

257. Nathan to Gus Tyler, June 5, 1967, Box 7, James Wechsler Papers, Wisconsin State Historical Society.

258. Samuel Beer to James A. Wechsler, July 7, 1967, Box 2, Samuel Beer Papers, JFKL.

259. Arthur Schlesinger, Jr., "Memorandum to Members of the ADA National Board," June 16, 1967, Box 11, Rauh Papers, LCMS.

260. Marvin Rosenberg to John Kenneth Galbraith, July 28, 1967, Box 11, Rauh Papers, LCMS.

261. Keyserling, "What Has Happened to ADA?" 5, Box 188, Galbraith Papers, JFKL.

262. Gillon, *Politics and Vision*, 208.

263. James Loeb, Jr., to John Kenneth Galbraith, Box 496, Galbraith Papers, JFKL.

264. Arthur Schlesinger, Jr., to John Kenneth Galbraith, January 10, 1968, and John Kenneth Galbraith to Arthur M. Schlesinger, Jr., January 23, 1968, Box 496, Galbraith Papers, JFKL.

265. Gillon, *Politics and Vision*, 211–12.

266. *Washington Post*, February 14, 1968.

267. *ADA World*, March–April 1968.

268. *Washington Post,* March 16, 1968.

269. March 1968 Israel Journal, 2, Box 2, Nathan Papers, Cornell MS.

270. February 1965 El Salvador Journal, 3, Box 1, Nathan Papers, Cornell MS.

271. March 1968 Israel Journal, 24, Box 2, Nathan Papers, Cornell MS.

272. May 1967 Israel Journal, 3, Box 2, Nathan Papers, Cornell MS.

273. June 1969 Jerusalem Journal, 1, Box 2, Robert R. Nathan Accession 22614, LCMS.

274. November 1967 Israel Journal, 1, Box 1, Robert R. Nathan Accession 22614, LCMS.

275. March 1968 Israel Journal, 13, Box 2, Nathan Papers, Cornell MS.

276. March 1968 Israel Journal, 44, 47–48, Box 2, Nathan Papers, Cornell MS.

277. March 1968 Israel Journal, 65–67, Box 2, Nathan Papers, Cornell MS.

278. April 1968 Malaysia Journal, 1–6, 46, Box 2, Nathan Papers, Cornell MS; *Straits Echo and Times of Malaya,* July 22, 1969.

279. April 1968 Malaysia Journal, 55, Box 2, Nathan Papers, Cornell MS.

280. Lewis Chester, Godfrey Hodgson, and Bruce Page, *American Melodrama: The Presidential Campaign of 1968* (New York: Viking, 1969), 151–52.

281. April 1968 Malaysia Journal, 60, Box 2, Nathan Papers, Cornell MS.

282. *Washington Post,* June 30, 1968.

283. Nathan to Hyman Minsky, April 17, 1968, Box 148.B.13.16F, Humphrey 1968 Files.

284. Nathan to Hyman Minsky, June 11, 1968, Box 148.B.13.16F, Humphrey 1968 Files; Solberg interview notes, 3.

285. Nathan to George L. P. Weaver, June 3, 1968, Box 148.B.13.15B, Humphrey 1968 Files.

286. See "Report to the Honorable John F. Kennedy by the Task Force on Foreign Economic Policy," December 31, 1960, Box 1073, Subcollection 5, Transition Files, 1960-1961, Series 17.5, Pre-Presidential Papers of John F. Kennedy, JFKL.

287. Theodore White, *The Making of the President, 1968* (New York: Atheneum, 1969), 316.

288. Solberg interview notes, 3.

289. Memorandum to Nathan, July 1, 1968, Box 95, David Ginsburg Papers, Library of Congress.

290. Gerald W. Bush to "Task Force Members and Consultants," July 19, 1968, Box 95, David Ginsburg Papers, Library of Congress; Nathan to Frank McDermott, September 9, 1968, attached to Nathan to Robert Short, October 4, 1968, Box 148.B.13.15B, Humphrey 1968 Files.

291. Nathan to Secretary Freeman, September 6, 1968, Box 148.B.13.16F, Humphrey 1968 Files.

292. Solberg interview notes, 3.

293. Transcript attached to Dee O'Brien to Bill Welsh, August 7, 1968, Box 148.B.14.1B, Humphrey 1968 Files.

294. Nelson Polsby to Nathan, July 28, Box 148.B.13.16F, Humphrey 1968 Files.

295. Solberg interview notes, 1, 3.

296. Humphrey to Bob Nathan et al., June 27, 1968, attached to Humphrey to Nathan, June 27, 1968, Box 148.B.15.8F, Humphrey 1968 Files.

297. See multiple correspondence, Humphrey to Nathan, July 6, 1968, Box 148.B.15.8F, Humphrey 1968 Files.

298. Humphrey to Nathan, August 3, 1968, Box 148.B.14.4F, Humphrey 1968 Files.

299. *Washington Post,* September 6, 1968.

300. Nathan to Stuart A. Rice, July 31, 1968, Box 148.B.13.16F, Humphrey 1968 Files.

301. Chester, Hodgson, and Page, *American Melodrama,* 422.

302. Nathan to Harry Kahn, June 17, 1968, Box 148.B.13.15B, Humphrey 1968 Files.

303. Nathan to W. Averell Harriman, July 16, 1968, Box 148.B.13.15B, Humphrey 1968 Files.

304. *Los Angeles Times,* February 5, 1978.

305. Carl Kaysen to Nathan, August 21, 1968, Box 147.E.11.3B, Carl Solberg Papers, MNHS.

306. Nathan to Carl Solberg, March 18, 1983, Box 147.E.11.3B, Carl Solberg Papers, MNHS.

307. Solberg interview notes, 1–2; Carl Solberg, *Hubert Humphrey, A Biography* (New York: Norton, 1984), 361.

308. William Benton to Nathan, August 16, 1968, Box 148.B.13.15B, Humphrey 1968 Files; Galbraith, *A Life in Our Times*, 501; Solberg interview notes, 1; Nathan to Humphrey, August 29, 1968, Box 148.B.15.8F, Humphrey 1968 Files.

309. "Memorandum for the Vice President and Robert R. Nathan," August 10, 1968, Box 92, David Ginsburg Papers, Library of Congress.

310. Humphrey to David Ginsburg, June 26, 1969, Box 95, David Ginsburg Papers, Library of Congress.

311. Solberg, *Hubert Humphrey*, 349.

312. Gillon, *Politics and Vision*, 219.

313. "RRN 8/3/67 Draft," Box 148.B.13.15B, Humphrey 1968 Files.

314. Nathan to Joseph L. Rauh Jr., August 22, 1968, Box 148.B.13.15B, Humphrey 1968 Files.

315. Chester, Hodgson, and Page, *American Melodrama*, 547.

316. Nathan to Humphrey, August 29, 1968, Box 148.B.15.8F, Humphrey 1968 Files. An early draft with Nathan's notations is in Box 148.B.13.16F, Humphrey 1968 Files.

317. Ithiel Pool to Nathan, August 29, 1968, Box 148.B.13.16F, Humphrey 1968 Files.

318. Nathan to Edward K. Smith, November 2, 1968, Box 148.B.13.15B, Humphrey 1968 Files.

319. Nathan to Secretary Freeman, September 7, 1968, Box 148.B.13.15B, Humphrey 1968 Files.

320. Nathan to Secretary Freeman, September 12, 1968, Box 148.B.13.16F, Humphrey 1968 Files.

321. Chester, Hodgson, and Page, *American Melodrama*, 645. Curiously, the Harris poll included Rockefeller and Kennedy even though they had long since been eliminated as potential candidates.

322. Edward Hollander to Joseph Duffey, October 14, 1968, Box 11, Rauh Papers, LCMS.

323. *Washington Post,* October 6, 1968.

324. Nathan to Robert Short, October 17, 1968, and Nathan to "Fellow Democrat," October 23, 1968, Box 148.B.13.16F, Humphrey 1968 Files.

325. Nathan to Humphrey, October 21, 1968, Box 148.B.13.16F, Humphrey 1968 Files.

326. Hubert Humphrey to Nathan, November 23, 1968, Nathan Personal Correspondence.

327. John Beyer, interview by Kenneth Durr, Arlington, VA, February 27, 2012, 9.

328. Nathan to John Stewart, October 9, 1968, Box 148.B.14.3B, Humphrey 1968 Files.

329. Robert R. Nathan, interview by Niel M. Johnson, June 22, 1989, 68, Harry S. Truman Library.

330. Chewning Oral History, 26.

331. Robert R. Nathan to John Kenneth Galbraith, January 9, 1969, Box 144, Galbraith Papers, JFKL.

332. John Kenneth Galbraith to Robert R. Nathan, January 21, 1969, Box 144, Galbraith Papers, JFKL.

333. Marvin Rosenberg to Joseph Rauh, July 24, 1969, Box 11, Rauh Papers, LCMS.

334. *Dayton Daily News,* October 25, 1966.

CHAPTER 5

1. *World War II and the Problems of the Eighties, Hearing Before the Committee on Banking, Finance and Urban Affairs, House of Representatives*, 96th Cong., 2d Sess., 5, 12 (September 23, 1980).

2. Robert R. Nathan resume, n.d., Nathan Associates Corporate Records.

3. *Federal Energy Administration Act (1973), Hearings Before the Committee on Government Operations, United States Senate*, 93rd Cong., 1st Sess., 137–39 (December 6 and 7, 1973).

4. *World War II and the Problems of the Eighties*, 39.

5. In an unusual turn of events, Lyndon Johnson had persuaded Goldberg to resign from the Supreme Court, ostensibly to take the United Nations job, but actually to make a place for Johnson (and Nathan) friend Abe Fortas. Why Goldberg agreed is speculated upon but unknown. See David L. Stebenne, *Arthur J. Goldberg: New Deal Liberal* (New York: Oxford University Press, 1996), 348.

6. *Professional Basketball, Hearing Before the Subcommittee on Antitrust and Monopoly of the Committee on the Judiciary, United States Senate*, 92nd Cong., 1st Sess. (September 21, 22, and 23, 1971).

7. *Stars and Stripes*, May 25, 1970.

8. *Washington Post*, November 16, 1971.

9. *Professional Basketball*, 179.

10. *New York Times*, September 22, 1971.

11. *Professional Basketball*, 162.

12. "Inflation and Regulation," uncited, undated interview with Nathan circa 1969, in Robert R. Nathan Scrapbooks, Nathan Associates (hereafter Nathan Scrapbooks).

13. "U.S. Will Save $10 Billion in Balance of Payments if El Paso Trans-Alaska Gas Project is Approved," El Paso Company Press Release, September 30, 1975, Nathan Scrapbooks.

14. *Electrical World*, January 19, 1970.

15. Bernard Norwood, telephone interview by Kenneth Durr, February 10, 2012, 13 (hereafter Norwood Oral History).

16. Typescript by Nathan entitled "Draft 1/28, Second Cassette," 76, in Nathan Corporate Records (hereafter Draft 1/28).

17. Norwood Oral History, 15.

18. *Tariff and Trade Proposals, Hearings Before the Committee on Ways and Means, House of Representatives*, 91st Cong., 2nd Sess., 3202 (May 11–June 25, 1970).

19. John Beyer, interview by Kenneth Durr, Arlington, VA, February 27, 2012, 27 (hereafter Beyer Oral History II).

20. *Journal of Commerce*, February 5, 1971; *Wall Street Journal*, March 2, 1971.

21. See *Tax Reform, 1969, Hearings Before the Committee on Ways and Means, House of Representatives*, 91st Cong., 1st Sess., 3655–3706 (February 18–April 24, 1969).

22. *Washington Daily News*, March 7, 1972. Herling had succeeded where Nathan failed, publishing *John Herling's Labor Letter* since 1947.

23. *Washington Daily Times*, March 7, 1972.

24. *Tax Reform, 1969*, 3706.

25. *Washington Star,* July 9, 1974.

26. *The Industrial Reorganization Act, Hearings Before the Subcommittee on Antitrust and Monopoly of the Committee on the Judiciary, United States Senate,* 93rd Cong., 2d Sess., 3957 (July 9, 30, and 31, 1974).

27. Draft 1/28, 52.

28. Harriet Kriesberg, interview by Kenneth Durr, Bethesda, MD, March 2, 2012, 6 (hereafter Kriesberg Oral History).

29. Roger Manring, telephone interview by Kenneth Durr, February 3, 2012, 7, 16 (hereafter Manring Oral History).

30. *Washington Post,* August 31, 1973.

31. Robert R. Nathan, "Advice to the Next President," *Challenge,* January/February 1976, 30.

32. Hobart Rowen, *Self-Inflicted Wounds: From LBJ's Guns and Butter to Reagan's Voodoo Economics* (New York: Times Books, 1994), 55.

33. *Washington Post,* November 16, 1969.

34. *Time,* June 14, 1971.

35. Herbert Stein, "The Washington Economics Industry," *AEA Papers and Proceedings,* May 1986, 1.

36. Herbert Stein, "The Principles Behind the Policies," *Challenge,* March–April 1973, 31–38.

37. *Time,* October 11, 1971.

38. Rowen, *Self-Inflicted Wounds,* 76.

39. *The President's New Economic Program, Hearings Before the Joint Economic Committee, Congress of the United States,* 92nd Cong., 1st Sess., pt. 2, 346, 352 (August 30–September 3, 1971).

40. *Time,* October 18, 1971.

41. *Washington Watch,* October 15, 1973.

42. *Washington Watch,* October 15, 1973.

43. *Time,* November 25, 1974.

44. "The White House: Remarks of the President at the Closing of the Conference on Inflation," September 5, 1974, Gerald R. Ford Library on-line at http://www.fordlibrarymuseum.gov/library/document/0248/whpr19740905-011.pdf.

45. *Washington Post,* September 22, 1974.

46. *New York Times,* October 29, 1974.

47. *Full Employment and Balanced Growth Act of 1978, Hearings Before the Committee on Banking, Housing, and Urban Affairs, United States Senate,* 95th Cong., 2d Sess., 151, 157 (May 8, 9, and 10, 1978).

48. Nathan, "Advice to the Next President," 23–33.

49. *The 1975 Economic Report of the President, Hearings Before the Joint Economic Committee, Congress of the United States,* 94th Cong., 1st Sess., 945 (February 19–28, 1975).

50. *Los Angeles Times,* February 5, 1978.

51. Rowen, *Self-Inflicted Wounds,* 107.

52. Nathan to Herbert Block, December 4, 1974, Box 55, Herbert Block Papers, Library of Congress Manuscript Collections (hereafter Block Papers, LCMS).

53. *Washington Post,* December 8, 1974; *Time,* December 23, 1974.

54. *Washington Post,* December 8, 1974.

55. *New York Times,* March 14, 1974.

56. Nathan, "Advice to the Next President," 28.

57. *New York Times,* March 14, 1974.

58. "For a National Economic Planning System," *Challenge,* March–April 1975, 51–53.

59. *New York Times,* February 28, 1975; Margaret Weir, *Politics and Jobs: The Boundaries of Employment Policy in the United States* (Princeton: Princeton University Press, 1992), 133.

60. *The 1975 Economic Report of the President,* 683.

61. *Price and Wage Control: An Evaluation of Current Policies, Hearings Before the Joint Economic Committee, Congress of the United States,* 96th Cong., 2d Sess., pt. 1, 73 (November 13, 14, and 15, 1972).

62. *The 1975 Economic Report of the President,* 897, 926.

63. *New York Times,* March 16, 1975.

64. Mike Sharpe, "The Planning Bill," *Challenge,* May–June 1975, 3–8.

65. Mike Sharpe, "Review: John Kenneth Galbraith: His Life, His Politics, His Economics," *Challenge,* May–June 2005, 125–29.

66. *New York Times,* March 4, 1975.

67. *Fiscal Year 1977 Budget and the Economy, Hearings Before the Committee on the Budget, House of Representatives,* 94th Cong., 2d Sess., 526 (January 26–March 17, 1976).

68. *National Energy Production Board, Hearings Before the Committee on Interior and Insular Affairs, United States Senate,* 94th Cong., 2d Sess., 115 (March 20, April 14, and April 15, 1975).

69. Bulletin, "Americans for Energy Independence," Spring 1986, Nathan Scrapbooks; *AFL-CIO News,* June 23, 1979.

70. *Evening Post,* June 30, 1980.

71. Alan Wolfe, *America's Impasse: The Rise and Fall of the Politics of Growth* (New York: Pantheon, 1981), 46.

72. Robert R. Nathan, "The Year 2000: Relations of the Public and Private Sectors," in *The Future of the United States Government: Toward the Year 2000,* ed. Harvey S. Perloff (New York: George Brazillier, 1971), 232–241. See p. 238.

73. Weir, *Politics and Jobs,* 135.

74. Hubert Humphrey to Nathan, December 18, 1972, Nathan Personal Correspondence, Nathan Associates Corporate Records (hereafter Nathan Personal Correspondence).

75. Hubert Humphrey to Nathan, February 23, 1976, Nathan Personal Correspondence.

76. Weir, *Politics and Jobs,* 137.

77. "The New Humphrey-Hawkins Bill," *Challenge,* May–June 1976, 21–29. See p. 21.

78. Weir, *Politics and Jobs,* 136.

79. *Washington Post,* November 24, 1977.

80. *Washington Post,* March 17, 1978.

81. *National Economic Planning, Balanced Growth, and Full Employment, Hearings Before the Joint Economic Committee, Congress of the United States*, 94th Cong., 1st Sess., 159, 165 (June 11 and 12, 1975).

82. Nathan, "The Year 2000," 238.

83. James T. Patterson, *Restless Giant: The United States from Watergate to Bush v. Gore* (New York: Oxford University Press, 2005), 65.

84. John Maynard Keynes, *A Tract on Monetary Reform* (London: Macmillan, 1923), 80.

85. Herbert Stein, *Presidential Economics: The Making of Economic Policy from Roosevelt to Reagan and Beyond* (New York: Simon and Schuster, 1984), 232.

86. Allan H. Meltzer, *A History of the Federal Reserve, Volume 2, Book 2, 1970-1986* (Chicago: University of Chicago Press, 2009), 1008–1131.

87. May 1972 Afghanistan Journal, 40, Box 2, Nathan Papers, Cornell MS.

88. *Business Abroad,* February 1969.

89. January 1969 Afghanistan Journal, 14, Box 2, Nathan Papers, Cornell MS.

90. December 1970 Afghanistan-Nepal Journal, 1, Box 2, Nathan Papers, Cornell MS; May 1972 Afghanistan Journal, 1, Box 2, Nathan Papers, Cornell MS.

91. December 1970 Afghanistan-Nepal Journal, 22, 20, Box 2, Nathan Papers, Cornell MS.

92. August 1971 Afghanistan-Tehran-Israel Journal, 36, 17, 9, Box 2, Nathan Papers, Cornell MS.

93. January 1972 Afghanistan Journal, 16, Box 2, Nathan Papers, Cornell MS.

94. Draft 1/28, 21.

95. *New York Times,* June 16, 1972; May 1972 Afghanistan Journal, 28, Box 2, Nathan Papers, Cornell MS.

96. May 1972 Afghanistan Journal, 3, 42–45, Box 2, Nathan Papers, Cornell MS.

97. "Afghanistan Nears the Take-Off Point," Depth News Release, July 22, 1972, Nathan Scrapbooks.

98. Robert R. Nathan, interview by Niel M. Johnson, June 22, 1989, 103, Harry S. Truman Library (hereafter Nathan Oral History, HSTL).

99. August 1971 Afghanistan-Tehran-Israel Journal, 31, Box 2, Nathan Papers, Cornell MS.

100. *Straits Echo and Times of Malaya,* July 22, 1969; *Straits Echo and Times of Malaya*, April 30, 1970, and *Straits Echo and Times of Malaya*, May 2, 1970.

101. December 1970 Afghanistan-Nepal Journal, 50, Box 2, Nathan Papers, Cornell MS.

102. *Bangkok Post*, October 30, 1971, in Nathan Scrapbooks.

103. *Washington Post,* September 10, 1971.

104. *U.S. News & World Report,* January 1, 1973.

105. Manring Oral History, 10; July 1975 Far East-Korea Journal, 58, Box 2, Nathan Papers, Cornell MS.

106. Robert R. Nathan, "Youth, Dollars, and Development," *Saturday Review,* May 1, 1971, 24–25, 64.

107. *Business Week,* March 7, 1977.

108. January 1972 Afghanistan Journal, 16, Box 2, Nathan Papers, Cornell MS.

109. July 1975 Far East-Korea Journal, 37, 83, Box 2, Nathan Papers, Cornell MS.

110. Beyer Oral History II, 1.

111. Manring Oral History, 24.

112. John Beyer, interview by Kenneth Durr, Arlington, VA, January 18, 2012, 32 (hereafter Beyer Oral History).

113. James Penkusky, interview by Kenneth Durr, Arlington, VA, January 25, 2012, 9 (hereafter Penkusky Oral History).

114. Penkusky Oral History, 25.

115. *Business Abroad*, February 1969; http://www.louisberger.com/Who-We-Are.

116. Manring Oral History, 56.

117. *National Security Policy and the Changing World Power Alignment, Hearing-Symposium Before the Subcommittee on National Security Policy and Scientific Developments of the Committee on Foreign Affairs*, 92nd Cong., 2d Sess., 200 (May 24–August 8, 1972).

118. John J. Gilligan to Nathan, April 29, 1977, Nathan Personal Correspondence.

119. *National Journal*, June 6, 1987.

120. *Washington Post*, January 2, 1984.

121. *Wall Street Journal*, August 21, 1974.

122. http://www.nera.com/7250.htm.

123. Stein, "The Washington Economics Industry," 4; *Business Week*, March, 7, 1977.

124. Richard Blankfeld, interview by Kenneth Durr, Rockville, MD, January 16, 2012, 3 (hereafter Blankfeld Oral History).

125. See Nathan Associates marketing brochure, *Counsel for Decision*, in Nathan Scrapbooks.

126. *Kodiak Mirror*, April 26, 1972.

127. See Lee Gorsuch oral history at http://www.litsite.org/index.cfm?section=history-and-culture&page=ancsa-at-30&cat=Lecture-Series&viewpost=2&ContentId=830&pg=64&crt=14; "Robert R. Nathan Associates Chosen to Conduct Alaska 2 (c) Studies," Department of Interior Press Release, June 28, 1974, Nathan Scrapbooks.

128. Stephen Schneider, telephone interview by Kenneth Durr, December 6, 2012, 7 (hereafter Schneider Oral History).

129. Schneider Oral History, 5.

130. *Billboard*, April 12, 1980.

131. *Boston Herald American,* September 24, 1976.

132. *American Metal Market,* August 24, 1977.

133. *National Journal,* February 2, 1980.

134. Beyer Oral History II, 13.

135. *Army Times,* January 30, 1974.

136. Beyer Oral History, 18.

137. *National Journal,* June 6, 1987.

138. *Industry Week*, April 20, 1992.

139. Beyer Oral History, 25.

140. Kriesberg Oral History, 15.

141. Manring Oral History, 26.

142. *RRN/A Newsletter*, Summer 1978, 3.

143. Beyer Oral History, 29.

144. Manring Oral History, 27.

145. "History of Nathan Associates Inc.," August 5, 2009, 2, Nathan Associates Corporate Records.

146. Schneider Oral History, 18–19.

147. "Minutes of Meeting of Shareholders of Robert R. Nathan Associates, Inc.," December 23, 1957, and January 23, 1976, Nathan Associates Corporate Records.

148. Penkusky Oral History, 14, 13.

149. "Minutes of Special Meeting of the Board of Directors of Robert R. Nathan Associates, Inc.," June 21, 1977, Nathan Associates Corporate Records.

150. "Robert R. Nathan Associates, Inc. Shareholders of Record," December 31, 1975, Nathan Associates Corporate Records. Nathan's children owned another 750 shares.

151. Beyer Oral History, 40.

152. Beyer Oral History, 33, 34; Beyer Oral History II, 3.

153. Beyer Oral History II, 4. Richard Wheeler died in early October 1977.

154. Beyer Oral History, 34; Beyer Oral History II, 4–5.

155. "Minutes of Special Meeting of the Board of Directors of Robert R. Nathan Associates, Inc.," June 8, 1978, Nathan Associates Corporate Records.

156. "A Very Brief History of Nathan Associates, Inc.," 8, Nathan Associates Corporate Records.

157. "Minutes of Special Meeting of the Board of Directors of Robert R. Nathan Associates, Inc.," June 8, 1978, Nathan Associates Corporate Records; *Washington Post,* September 5, 1978.

158. *Washington Times*, May 16, 1989.

159. The AVC's last director, elected in 1965, was June Willenz.

160. Nathan to Freeman, December 7, 1979, Box 151, AVC Papers, George Washington University Archives; Nathan to Petrey, June 6, 1974, Box 55, AVC Papers, George Washington University Archives.

161. See program in Box 176, AVC Papers, George Washington University Archives.

162. Robert R. Nathan resume, n.d., Nathan Associates Corporate Records.

163. Program: "National Consumers League Annual Trumpeter Award Dinner," April 3, 1979, Nathan Scrapbooks; "National Consumers League Honors Robert Nathan," National Consumers League Press Release, April 3, 1979, Nathan Scrapbooks.

164. *Washington Jewish Week*, May 18, 1995.

165. "UN's 'Antiquated' Communications System Requires Access to Satellites, Panel Says," United Nations Association Press Release, May 8, 1971, and "Wartime Technology to be Made Available for Peacekeeping Missions," CBS Laboratories Press Release, June 10, 1971, both in Nathan Scrapbooks; *Washington Post,* June 7, 1974.

166. Program: "Toward a Working Economy," 1977 National Conference of the National Alliance of Businessmen, September 12–14, 1977, Nathan Scrapbooks.

167. *Bethesda-Chevy Chase Tribune*, April 9, 1971; *Dayton Jewish Chronicle*, June 29, 1972.

168. *Wall Street Journal,* March 2, 1971.

169. Mary Nathan, interview by Kenneth Durr, Bethesda, MD, February 15, 2012, 34 (hereafter

Mary Nathan Oral History).

170. *Washington Post,* May 18, 1972.

171. *New York Post,* December 2, 1971.

172. Denis G. Sullivan, Jeffrey L. Pressman, Benjamin I. Page, and John J. Lyons, *The Politics of Representation: The Democratic Convention of 1972* (New York: St. Martin's Press, 1974), 91.

173. *Mobile Register,* June 26, 1972.

174. *Washington Post,* August 4, 1972.

175. Hubert Humphrey to Nathan, July 14, 1972, Nathan Personal Correspondence.

176. *New York Times,* October 21, 1972, and *New York Times,* November 5, 1972.

177. *Dayton Daily News,* September 17, 1972.

178. *New York Times,* November 17, 1974.

179. Nathan, "Advice to the Next President," 32.

180. Jimmy Carter to Nathan, May 15, 1976, Nathan Personal Correspondence.

181. *Indianapolis Star,* March 31, 1977.

182. *Washington Star,* September 13, 1977.

183. Robert R. Nathan resume, n.d., Nathan Associates Corporate Records.

184. Robert R. Nathan, "Imperfect Markets and Government Policy," *Society,* July–August 1979, 5, 14–15.

185. Rowen, *Self-Inflicted Wounds,* 201–2.

186. *Time,* October 22, 1979.

187. Notes from Carl Solberg interview with Robert R. Nathan, November 18, 1980, 4, Box 147.E.11.3B, Papers of Carl Solberg, Minnesota Historical Society (hereafter Solberg interview notes).

188. *Fellowship,* Fall 1981.

189. *Washington Post,* March 24 and September 6, 1982.

190. Walter F. Mondale to Nathan, December 21, 1981, and July 11, 1983, Nathan Personal Correspondence.

191. Mary Nathan Oral History, 21.

192. *Washington Evening Star,* March 24, 1971.

193. See program for memorial services for Harry S. Truman, January 5, 1973, in Nathan Scrapbooks.

194. *New York Times,* March 6, 1977.

195. *Washington Post,* June 30, 1981.

196. *Washington Times,* May 16, 1989; Joe Gunn, interview by Kenneth Durr, Arlington, VA, February 9, 2012, 28 (hereafter Gunn Oral History).

197. *Washington Post,* November 2, 1986.

198. *Washington Post,* August 19, 1987.

199. Jennings Randolph to John Heinz, April 9, 1987, in John Heinz Papers on-line at http://doi.library.cmu.edu/10.1184/pmc/heinz/box00111/fld00009/bdl0002/doc0001.

200. *Intermountain Jewish News,* April 5, 1974.

201. *San Jose Mercury,* October 15, 1974.

202. ADL *Fellowship* (Winter 1975) in Nathan Scrapbooks.

203. ADL *Fellowship* (Fall 1975) in Nathan Scrapbooks.

204. Beyer Oral History II, 22.

205. Beyer Oral History, 26, 20.

206. Beyer Oral History II, 33–34.

207. *New York Post*, October 27, 1978; *Jewish Times*, November 3, 1978.

208. *Jewish Chronicle*, November 2, 1979.

209. Joseph Rauh to Lawrence M. Nathan, April 10, 1985, Box 285, Rauh Papers, LCMS.

210. Nathan to Joseph Rauh, May 6, 1985, Box 285, Rauh Papers, LCMS.

211. Joseph Rauh to Nathan, May 7, 1985, Box 285, Rauh Papers, LCMS.

212. *Washington Jewish Week*, May 18, 1995.

213. *Washington Jewish Week*, May 18, 1995.

214. "Minutes of Annual Meeting of the Board of Directors of Robert R. Nathan Associates, Inc.," May 18, 1979, Nathan Associates Corporate Records.

215. Penkusky Oral History, 27.

216. Gunn Oral History, 36.

217. Draft 1/28, 90.

218. *Direct/Current*, June 1979.

219. Nathan to David Ginsburg, September 11, 1980, Box 121, David Ginsburg Papers, Library of Congress.

220. Beyer Oral History II, 10.

221. "Minutes of Annual Meeting of the Board of Directors of Robert R. Nathan Associates, Inc.," December 27, 1979, Nathan Associates Corporate Records.

222. Samuel Hale Butterfield, *U.S. Development Aid—An Historic First: Achievements and Failures in the Twentieth Century* (Westport: Praeger, 2004), 199.

223. Beyer Oral History II, 13.

224. Draft 1/28, 52.

225. Penkusky Oral History, 22.

226. Beyer Oral History, 35.

227. Beyer Oral History II, 14–15.

228. Penkusky Oral History, 21.

229. Manring Oral History, 39.

230. Beyer Oral History, 40.

231. Blankfeld Oral History, 39.

232. Beyer Oral History II, 7.

233. Beyer Oral History, 35–36.

234. Beyer Oral History, 19.

235. Draft 1/28, 62.

236. "Minutes of the Meeting of the Board of Directors, Robert R. Nathan Associates, Inc.," September 3, 1986, Nathan Associates Corporate Records.

237. Manring Oral History, 40.

238. Mary Nathan Oral History, 38.

239. "Minutes of the Meeting of the Board of Directors, Robert R. Nathan Associates, Inc.," February 22, 1988, Nathan Associates Corporate Records.

240. Schneider Oral History, 17.

241. Beyer Oral History II, 31; Mary Nathan Oral History, 38; "A Very Brief History of Nathan Associates Inc.," 13, Nathan Associates Corporate Records.

242. "Minutes of the Special Meeting of the Board of Directors, Robert R. Nathan Associates, Inc.," September 20, 1989, Nathan Associates Corporate Records.

243. Nathan to Muriel Humphrey Brown, March 21, 1988, Nathan Personal Correspondence.

244. Gunn Oral History, 35.

245. Penkusky Oral History, 10.

246. Gunn Oral History, 41.

247. Blankfeld Oral History, 12–13.

248. Schneider Oral History, 28–29.

249. Lakhbir Singh, interview by Kenneth Durr, Arlington, VA, February 2, 2012, 10.

250. Edythe Crump to author, March 14, 2013.

251. Beyer Oral History II, 19–20.

252. Manring Oral History, 18.

253. "Minutes of the Meeting of the Board of Directors, Robert R. Nathan Associates, Inc.," December 12, 1989, Nathan Associates Corporate Records.

254. Stein, "The Washington Economics Industry," 7.

255. June 1969 Jerusalem Journal, Box 1, Nathan Accession 22614, LCMS.

256. Mary Nathan Oral History, 20.

257. August 1971 Afghanistan-Tehran-Israel Journal, 31, Box 2, Nathan Papers, Cornell MS.

258. Robert R. Nathan resume, n.d., Nathan Associates Corporate Records.

259. See October 1976 China Journal, 1, Box 1, Nathan Accession 22614, LCMS; typescript, "Report on Trip to People's Republic of China," November 17, 1976, 1, 14–15, Mary Nathan Personal Collection.

260. Draft 1/28, 36.

261. *Dayton Daily News*, June 1984.

262. Draft 1/28, 32–33.

263. Manring Oral History, 57.

264. Nathan Oral History, 2, HSTL.

265. *Washington Post*, December 6, 1968.

266. Lyndon Johnson to Nathan, August 2, 1972, Nathan Personal Correspondence.

267. *Dayton Daily News*, March 31, 1970.

268. *Miami Herald*, February 22, 1974; Nathan to Edward Levin, November 5, 1985, Nathan Personal Correspondence.

269. April 1970 Switzerland Journal, 62, Box 2, Nathan Papers, Cornell MS.

270. Mary Nathan Oral History, 9.

271. Mary Nathan Oral History, 25.

272. *Washington Post*, November 28, 1991.

273. "Minutes of the Special Meeting of the Board of Directors, Nathan Associates, Inc.," January 28, 1994, Nathan Associates Corporate Records.

274. April 1970 Switzerland Journal, 1, Box 2, Nathan Papers, Cornell MS.

275. Mary Nathan to author, November 26, 2012.

276. Simon Kuznets to Nathan, October 20, 1971, Nathan Personal Correspondence.

277. Nathan to Mark Perlman, November 5, 1987, Nathan Personal Correspondence.

278. Nathan to Muriel Humphrey Brown, March 21, 1988, Nathan Personal Correspondence.

279. "Minutes of the Annual Meeting of the Board of Directors, Nathan Associates, Inc.," May 19, 1992, Nathan Associates Corporate Records.

280. See "Summary of the 1994 Corporate Plan," 2, in Nathan Associates Corporate Records.

281. Gunn Oral History, 44–45; "Minutes of the Special Meeting of the Board of Directors, Nathan Associates, Inc.," January 30, 1995, Nathan Associates Corporate Records.

282. Tracy Campbell, *Short of the Glory: The Fall and Redemption of Edward F. Prichard Jr.* (Lexington: University of Kentucky Press, 1998); Carl Solberg, *Hubert Humphrey, A Biography* (New York: Norton, 1984); Robert William Fogel, Enid M. Fogel, Mark Guglielmo, and Nathaniel Grotte, *Political Arithmetic: Simon Kuznets and the Empirical Tradition in Economics* (Chicago: University of Chicago Press, 2013).

283. *Washington Jewish Week*, May 25, 1989.

284. *Miami Herald*, n.d., circa 1992, in Nathan Scrapbooks.

285. Blankfeld Oral History, 14. Blankfeld recalled it as the 1980s, but the testimony was actually in 1979.

286. *Renewable Energy Technologies, Hearings Before the Subcommittee on Energy Research and Development of the Committee on Energy and Natural Resources, United States Senate*, 100th Cong., 1st Sess., 46 (March 24 and 26, 1987).

287. Manring Oral History, 48.

288. Norwood Oral History, 27.

289. Beyer Oral History II, 35, 37.

290. See Van S. Katzman, "The Waste of War: Government Cercla Liability at World War II Facilities," *Virginia Law Review*, August 1993, 1191–1233; *Washington Jewish Week*, May 18, 1995.

291. Katzman, "Waste of War."

292. Schneider Oral History, 24.

293. Mary Nathan Oral History, 13.

294. *Keys News*, February 13, 1983.

295. Mary Nathan Oral History, 16.

296. Mary Nathan Oral History, 17.

297. *Key West Citizen*, January 10, 1980.

298. *Keys News*, February 13, 1983.

299. Mary Nathan Oral History, 17.

300. "Metropolitan South Florida Fishing Tournament Official Entry Form," January 26, 1980, Nathan Scrapbooks.

301. Mary Nathan Oral History, 45, 44.

302. Mary Nathan to author, February 16, 2012.

303. Luanne Crayton, "Nathan Honors Father of European Union," *Exchange*, Summer 1997, 5.

304. Beyer Oral History II, 37.

305. Norwood Oral History, 26.

306. Mary Nathan Oral History, 48.

307. Mary Nathan Oral History, 17.

308. Mary Nathan to Clifton R. Wharton Jr., March 2, 2000, Mary Nathan Personal Collection.

309. A summary of the award ceremony is at http://www.nathaninc.com/news/nathan-honored-role-commerce-departments-achievement-century.

310. Blankfeld Oral History, 41.

311. Mary Nathan Oral History, 11.

312. Mary Nathan to Clifton R. Wharton Jr., March 2, 2000, Mary Nathan Personal Collection.

313. Mary Nathan Oral History, 48.

314. Mary Nathan Oral History, 49.

315. Gunn Oral History, 49.

316. Beyer Oral History II, 41.

CONCLUSION

1. Howard E. Shuman, interview by Donald A. Ritchie, September 17, 1987, United States Senate Historical Office, accessed at http://www.senate.gov/artandhistory/history/resources/pdf/Shuman_interview_6.pdf. Nathan was in favor of the tax cut.

2. *Exchange*, Autumn 1995, 1.

3. Lakhbir Singh, interview by Kenneth Durr, Arlington, VA, February 2, 2012, 13 (hereafter Singh Oral History).

4. "Minutes of Meeting of Shareholders of Nathan Associates, Inc.," August 5, 1999, Nathan Associates Corporate Records.

5. Roger Manring, telephone interview with Kenneth Durr, February 3, 2012, 46 (hereafter Manring Oral History).

6. Singh Oral History, 31.

7. "Minutes of the Meeting of the Board of Directors, Nathan Associates, Inc.," February 2, 2000, Nathan Associates Corporate Records.

8. "Minutes of the Meeting of the Board of Directors, Nathan Associates, Inc.," August 10, 1999, and November 3, 1999, Nathan Associates Corporate Records.

9. "Minutes of Meeting of Shareholders of Nathan Associates, Inc.," July 29, 2004, Nathan Associates Corporate Records.

10. John Beyer, interview by Kenneth Durr, Arlington, VA, February 27, 2012, 46.

11. "Minutes of the Meeting of the Board of Directors, Nathan Associates, Inc.," November 8,

2001, Nathan Associates Corporate Records.

12. "Minutes of Meeting of Shareholders of Nathan Associates, Inc.," August 14, 2002, Nathan Associates Corporate Records.

13. "Status Report for the Robert R. Nathan Memorial Foundation," February 14, 2013, in author's possession.

14. *Dayton Daily News*, September 17, 1972.

15. February 1963 El Salvador Journal, 66, Box 1, Nathan Papers, Cornell MS.

16. Nathan Associates Inc. Strategic Plan, Winter 1995, Nathan Associates Corporate Records.

17. *Washington Jewish Week,* May 18, 1995.

18. Manring Oral History, 15.

19. Otis L. Graham, Jr., "Liberalism After the Sixties: A Reconnaissance," in *The Achievement of American Liberalism: The New Deal and Its Legacies*, ed. William H. Chafe (New York: Columbia University Press, 2003), 293.

20. Robert R. Nathan, "Advice to the Next President," *Challenge*, January/February 1976, 32.

21. Paul Simon to Mary Nathan, September 19, 2001, Nathan Personal Correspondence, Nathan Associates Corporate Records.

BIBLIOGRAPHY

ORAL HISTORIES

Harry S. Truman Library

Robert R. Nathan, June 22, 1989, by Niel M. Johnson

Joseph L. Rauh, Jr., June 21, 1989, by Niel M. Johnson

R. Burr Smith, April 10, 1974, by James R. Fuchs

John W. Snyder, February 7 and 21, 1968, by Jerry N. Hess

John W. Snyder, February 21, 1968, by Jerry N. Hess

John H. Tolan, March 5, 10, and 17, 1970, and February 8, 1974, by James R. Fuchs

Fraser Wilkins, June 20, 1975, by Richard D. McKinzie

Edwin M. Wright, July 26, 1974, by Richard D. McKinzie

John F. Kennedy Library

Walter Heller, Kermit Gordon, James Tobin, Gardner Ackley, and Paul Samuelson, August 1, 1964, by Joseph Pechman

Robert R. Nathan, June 9, 1967, by John F. Stewart

Library of Congress Manuscript Division

Robert Nathan, December 26, 1990, by Robert W. Fogel, Nathan Accession 22614, Box 3

European University Institute, Historical Archives of the EU

Robert Nathan, May 15, 1987, by François Duchêne

Historical Society of the District of Columbia Circuit

Joseph L. Rauh, Jr., n.d., by Robert S. Peck

University of Kentucky Libraries, Louie B. Nunn Center for Oral History

Robert Nathan, June 9, 1995, by Tracy Campbell

By the Author

Maurice Atkin, January 4 and 10, 2012, Bethesda, Maryland

John Beyer, January 18 and February 27, 2012, Arlington, Virginia

Richard Blankfeld, January 16, 2012, Rockville, Maryland

David Chewning, January 26, 2012, McLean, Virginia

Joe Gunn, February 9, 2012, Arlington, Virginia

Harriet Kriesberg, March 2, 2012, Bethesda, Maryland

Roger Manring, February 3, 2012, by telephone

Mary Nathan, February 15, 2012, Bethesda, Maryland

Bernard Norwood, February 10, 2012, by telephone

James Penkusky, January 25, 2012, Arlington, Virginia

Stephen Schneider, December 6, 2012, by telephone

Lakhbir Singh, February 2, 2012, Arlington, Virginia

GOVERNMENT DOCUMENTS

U.S. Bureau of the Census. *Fifteenth Population Census of the United States.* 1930.

————. *Sixteenth Population Census of the United States.* 1940.

————. *Thirteenth Population Census of the United States.* 1910.

U.S. Federal Bureau of Investigation. Files on Robert Roy Nathan.

————. Files on William Walter Remington.

U.S. Congress. "National Economic Planning, Balanced Growth, and Full Employment." *Hearings Before the Joint Economic Committee.* 94th Cong., 1st Sess., June 11 and 12, 1975.

————. "National Security Policy and the Changing World Power Alignment." *Hearing-Symposium Before the Subcommittee on National Security Policy and Scientific Developments of the Committee on Foreign Affairs.* 92d Cong., 2d Sess., May 24–August 8, 1972.

————. "Price and Wage Control: An Evaluation of Current Policies." *Hearings Before the Joint Economic Committee.* 96th Cong., 2d Sess., pt. 1, November 13, 14, and 15, 1972.

————. "The 1975 Economic Report of the President." *Hearings Before the Joint Economic Committee.* 94th Cong., 1st Sess., February 19–28, 1975.

————. "The President's New Economic Program." *Hearings Before the Joint Economic Committee.* 92d Cong., 1st Sess., pt. 2, August 30–September 3, 1971.

U.S. Congress. House. "Fiscal Year 1977 Budget and the Economy." *Hearings Before the Committee on the Budget.* 94th Cong., 2d Sess., January 26–March 17, 1976.

————. "Tariff and Trade Proposals." *Hearings Before the Committee on Ways and Means.* 91st Cong., 2d Sess., May 11–June 25, 1970.

————. "Tax Reform, 1969." *Hearings Before the Committee on Ways and Means.* 91st Cong., 1st Sess., February 18–April 24, 1969.

————. "World War II and the Problems of the Eighties." *Hearings Before the Committee on Banking, Finance and Urban Affairs.* 96th Cong., 2d Sess., September 23, 1980.

U.S. Congress. Senate. "Federal Energy Administration Act (1973)." *Hearings Before the Committee on Government Operations.* 93rd Cong., 1st Sess., December 6 and 7, 1973.

————. "Full Employment and Balanced Growth Act of 1978." *Hearings Before the Committee on Banking, Housing, and Urban Affairs.* 95th Cong., 2d Sess., May 8, 9, and 10, 1978.

————. "National Energy Production Board." *Hearings Before the Committee on Interior and Insular Affairs.* 94th Cong., 2d Sess., March 20, April 14 and 15, 1975.

————. "Professional Basketball." *Hearings Before the Subcommittee on Antitrust and Monopoly of the Committee on the Judiciary.* 92d Cong., 1st Sess., September 21, 22, and 23, 1971.

————. "Renewable Energy Technologies." *Hearings Before the Subcommittee on Energy Research and Development of the Committee on Energy and Natural Resources.* 100th Cong., 1st Sess., March 24 and 26, 1987.

————. "The Industrial Reorganization Act." *Hearings Before the Subcommittee on Antitrust and Monopoly of the Committee on the Judiciary.* 93rd Cong., 2d Sess., July 9, 30, and 31, 1974.

Books

Atkin, Maurice D. *Life's Voyage: Dedicated to Making a Difference*. Marco Island, FL: Keller Publishing, 2005.

Barone, Michael. *Our Country: The Shaping of America from Roosevelt to Reagan*. New York: Free Press, 1990.

Berle, Adolph, and Gardiner Means. *The Modern Corporation and Private Property*. New York: Macmillan, 1933.

Brigante, John E. *The Feasibility Dispute: Determination of War Production Objectives for 1942 and 1943*. Washington, D.C.: Committee on Public Administration, 1950.

Brinkley, Alan. *The End of Reform: New Deal Liberalism in Recession and War*. New York: Knopf, 1995.

Brock, Clifton, and Max Lerner. *Americans for Democratic Action: Its Role in National Politics*. Washington, D.C.: Public Affairs Press, 1962.

Butterfield, Samuel Hale. *U.S. Development Aid—An Historic First: Achievements and Failures in the Twentieth Century*. Westport: Prager, 2004.

Campbell, Tracy. *Short of the Glory: The Fall and Redemption of Edward F. Prichard Jr*. Lexington: University Press of Kentucky, 1998.

Caro, Robert. *Passage to Power: The Years of Lyndon Johnson*. New York: Knopf, 2012.

Chester, Lewis, Godfrey Hodgson, and Bruce Page. *American Melodrama: The Presidential Campaign of 1968*. New York: Viking, 1969.

Chewning, David. *A Life Worth Living*. McLean, VA: Lulu Enterprises, 2009.

Cole, David C., and Young Woo Nam. *The Pattern and Significance of Economic Planning in Korea*. Cambridge, MA: Development Advisory Service, 1968.

Dewhurst, J. Frederic, and Robert R. Nathan. *Social and Economic Character of Unemployment in Philadelphia, April, 1930*. Washington, D.C.: GPO, 1932.

Draper, Alan. *A Rope of Sand: The AFL-CIO Committee on Political Education, 1955-1967*. New York: Praeger, 1988.

Ekbladh, David. *The Great American Mission: Modernization and the Construction of an American World Order*. Princeton: Princeton University Press, 2010.

Fesler, James, et al. *Industrial Mobilization for War: History of the War Production Board and Predecessor Agencies, 1940–1945*. Washington, D.C.: GPO, 1947.

Fogel, Robert William, Enid M. Fogel, Mark Guglielmo, and Nathaniel Grotte. *Political Arithmetic: Simon Kuznets and the Empirical Tradition in Economics*. Chicago: University of Chicago Press, 2013.

Fourcade, Marion. *Economists and Societies: Discipline and Profession in the United States, Britain, and France, 1890s to 1990s*. Princeton: Princeton University Press, 2009.

Fraser, Steven. *Labor Will Rule: Sidney Hillman and the Rise of American Labor*. New York: Free Press, 1991.

Galbraith, John Kenneth. *A Life in Our Times: Memoirs*. Boston: Houghton Mifflin, 1981.

Gillon, Steven M. *Politics and Vision: The ADA and American Liberalism, 1947–1985*. New York: Oxford University Press, 1987.

Ginzberg, Eli. *My Brother's Keeper*. New Brunswick: Transaction Publishers, 2008.

Goulden, Joseph. *The Best Years, 1945–1950*. New York: Atheneum, 1976.

Graham, Katherine. *Personal History*. New York: Knopf, 1998.

Griffith, Robert. *The Politics of Fear: Joseph McCarthy and the Senate*. Lexington: University Press of Kentucky, 1970.

Grose, Peter. *Israel in the Mind of America*. New York: Knopf, 1983.

Hollander, Edward D. *The Future of Small Business*. New York: Praeger, 1967.

Ismail, Tawfik, and Oai Kee Beng. *Malaya's First Year at the United Nations: As Reflected in Dr. Ismail's Reports Home to Tunku Abdul Rahman*. Singapore: Institute of Southeast Asian Studies, 2009.

Janeway, Eliot. *Struggle for Survival: The Memorable Account of Roosevelt's Economic Mobilization for World War II*. New York: Weybright and Talley, 1968.

Karnow, Stanley. *Vietnam: A History*. New York: Penguin, 1983.

Keynes, John Maynard. *A Tract on Monetary Reform*. London: Macmillan, 1923.

Lacey, Jim. *Keep From All Thoughtful Men: How U.S. Economists Won World War II*. Annapolis: Naval Institute Press, 2011.

LaFeber, Walter. *Inevitable Revolutions: The United States in Central America*. New York: Norton, 1983.

Lash, Joseph P. *Dealers and Dreamers: A New Look at the New Deal*. New York: Doubleday, 1988.

Lekachman, Robert. *The Age of Keynes*. New York: Random House, 1966.

Leuchtenberg, William E. *Franklin Roosevelt and the New Deal, 1932–1940*. New York: Harper & Row, 1963.

Lichtenstein, Nelson. *The Most Dangerous Man in Detroit: Walter Reuther and the Fate of American Labor*. New York: Basic Books, 1995.

Louchheim, Kate. *The Making of the New Deal*. Cambridge: Harvard University Press, 1983.

McClure, Arthur F. *The Truman Administration and the Problems of Postwar Labor, 1945–1948*. Rutherford: Fairleigh Dickinson University Press, 1969.

Meltzer, Allan H. *A History of the Federal Reserve, Volume 2, Book 2, 1970–1986*. Chicago: University of Chicago Press, 2009.

Millis, Walter, ed. *The Forrestal Diaries*. New York: Viking, 1951.

Nathan, Robert R. *An Appraisal of the War Production Board: Industrial College of the Armed Forces Publication Number L50-144*. Washington, D.C.: GPO, 1950.

Nathan, Robert R., Oscar Gass, and Daniel Creamer. *Palestine: Problem and Promise*. Washington, D.C.: Public Affairs Press, 1946.

Packenham, Robert A. *Liberal America and the Third World: Political Development Ideas in Foreign Aid and Social Science*. Princeton: Princeton University Press, 1973.

Parrish, Michael E. *Citizen Rauh: An American Liberal's Life in Law and Politics*. Ann Arbor: University of Michigan Press, 2011.

Patterson, James T. *Grand Expectations: The United States, 1945–1974*. New York: Oxford University Press, 1996.

———. *Restless Giant: The United States from Watergate to Bush v. Gore*. New York: Oxford University Press, 2005.

Pells, Richard. *Radical Visions and American Dreams: Culture and Social Thought in the Depression*

Years. New York: Harper & Row, 1973.

Rishel, Joseph Francis. *Pittsburgh Remembers World War II*. Charleston: History Press, 2001.

Rostow, W. W. *The Stages of Economic Growth: A Non-Communist Manifesto*. London: Cambridge University Press, 1960.

Rowen, Hobart. *Self-Inflicted Wounds: From LBJ's Guns and Butter to Reagan's Voodoo Economics*. New York: Times Books, 1994.

Schlesinger, Arthur M., Jr. *A Thousand Days: John F. Kennedy in the White House*. Boston: Houghton Mifflin, 1965.

———. *The Vital Center: The Politics of Freedom*. Boston: Houghton Mifflin, 1949.

Schwarz, Jordan A. *The New Dealers: Power Politics in the Age of Roosevelt*. New York: Knopf, 1993.

Slater, Leonard. *The Pledge*. New York: Simon and Schuster, 1970.

Snyder, John W. *From War to Peace: A Challenge*. Washington, D.C.: GPO, 1945.

Solberg, Carl. *Hubert Humphrey, A Biography*. New York: Norton, 1984.

Somers, Herman Miles. *Presidential Agency: The Office of War Mobilization and Reconversion*. Cambridge: Harvard University Press, 1950.

Stebenne, David L. *Arthur J. Goldberg: New Deal Liberal*. New York: Oxford University Press, 1996.

Stein, Herbert. *The Fiscal Revolution in America*. Washington, D.C.: AEI Press, 1990.

———. *Presidential Economics: The Making of Economic Policy from Roosevelt to Reagan and Beyond*. New York: Simon and Schuster, 1984.

Sullivan, Denis G., Jeffrey L. Pressman, Benjamin I. Page, and John J. Lyons. *The Politics of Representation: The Democratic Convention of 1972*. New York: St. Martin's Press, 1974.

Taylor, Philip. *The Distant Magnet: European Emigration to the U.S.A.* New York: Harper & Row, 1971.

Walinsky, Louis J. *Economic Development in Burma, 1951–1960*. New York: Twentieth Century Fund, 1962.

Weinstein, Allen, and Alexander Vassiliev. *The Haunted Wood: Soviet Espionage in America: The Stalin Era*. New York: Random House, 2000.

Weir, Margaret. *Politics and Jobs: The Boundaries of Employment Policy in the United States*. Princeton: Princeton University Press, 1992.

White, Theodore. *The Making of the President, 1968*. New York: Atheneum, 1969.

Wolfe, Alan. *America's Impasse: The Rise and Fall of the Politics of Growth*. New York: Pantheon, 1981.

ARTICLES

Ballendorf, Dirk Anthony. "The New Freely-Associated States of Micronesia: Their Natural and Social Environmental Challenges." *GeoJournal*, March 1988, 137–42.

Beigel, Edgar. "France Moves Toward National Planning." *Political Science Quarterly*, September 1947, 381–97.

Bernstein, Barton J. "The Removal of War Production Board Controls on Business, 1944–1946." *Business History Review*, Summer 1965, 243–60.

Brady, Robert A. "The C.E.D.—What Is It and Why?" *Antioch Review*, Spring 1949, 21–46.

Brazinsky, Gregg Andrew. "From Pupil to Model: South Korea and American Development Policy During the Early Park Chung Hee Era." *Diplomatic History,* January 2005, 83–115.

Carson, Carol S. "The History of the United States National Income and Product Accounts: The Development of an Analytical Tool." *Income and Wealth,* June 1975, 153–81.

Christman, Calvin L. "Donald Nelson and the Army: Personality as a Factor in Civil-Military Relations during World War II." *Military Affairs,* October 1973, 81–83.

Collins, Robert M. "Positive Business Responses to the New Deal: The Roots of the Committee for Economic Development, 1933–1942." *Business History Review,* Autumn 1978, 369–91.

Cuff, Robert D. "Organizational Capabilities and U.S. War Production: The Controlled Materials Plan." *Business and Economic History* 19 (1990): 103–12.

Fogel, Robert W. "Simon S. Kuznets: April 30, 1901–July 9, 1985." *NBER Working Paper Series,* July 2000, 1–28.

Fox, Bonnie R. "Unemployment Relief in Philadelphia, 1930–1932: A Study of the Depression's Impact on Volunteerism." *Pennsylvania Magazine of History and Biography,* January 1969, 86–108.

Galbraith, John Kenneth. "The National Accounts: Arrival and Impact." *Reflections of America: Commemorating the Statistical Abstract Centennial."* Washington, D.C.: GPO, 1980), 75–80.

Gleason, Alan H. "Foster and Catchings: A Reappraisal." *Journal of Political Economy,* April 1959, 156–72.

Grimes, Alan P. "Contemporary American Liberalism." *Annals of the American Academy,* November 1962, 25–34.

Gross, Nachum T. "Israeli Economic Policies, 1948–1951: Problems of Evaluation." *Journal of Economic History,* March 1990, 70.

Hagen, Everett E. "My Life Philosophy." *American Economist,* Spring 1991, 10–18.

Hamby, Alonzo L. "The Liberals, Truman, and FDR as Symbol and Myth." *Journal of American History,* March 1970, 859–67.

Hildebrand, George H. "The Nathan Report and Its Critics." *American Economic Review,* June 1947, 386–91.

Homan, Gerlof D. "American Business Interests in the Indonesian Republic, 1946-1949." *Indonesia,* April 1983, 125–32.

Kapuria-Foreman, Vibha, and Mark Perlman. "An Economic Historian's Economist: Remembering Simon Kuznets." *Economic Journal,* November 1995, 1525–47.

Katzman, Van S. "The Waste of War: Government Cercla Liability at World War II Facilities." *Virginia Law Review,* August 1993, 1191–1233.

Kopkind, Andrew. "Humphrey's Old Pals: An Account of the ADA Convention." *New Republic,* May 7, 1966, 19–22.

Nathan, Robert R. "Advice to the Next President." *Challenge,* January–February 1976, 23–33.

———. "American Business Today and Tomorrow." In *Twentieth Century Unlimited: The Vantage Point of the First Fifty Years,* edited by Bruce Bliven, 161–82. Philadelphia: Lippincott, 1950.

————. "Antitrust and International Competition: Courting the "Cartel Malignancy." *Antitrust Law and Economics Review* 79 (1985): 79–100.

————. "Economic Analysis and Public Policy: The Growing Hiatus." *American Economic Association*, May 1964, 610–22.

————. "Estimates of Unemployment in the United States, 1929–1935." *International Labour Review* 49 (1936): 49–73.

————. "GNP and Military Mobilization." *Journal of Evolutionary Economics*, Spring–Summer 1994, 1–16.

————. "Imperfect Markets and Government Policy." *Society*, July–August 1979, 5–15.

————. "National Income Increased Five Billion Dollars in 1934." *Survey of Current Business*, August 1935, 16–18.

————. "Nations' Stake in American Reconversion." *Free World*, October 1944, 335–38.

————. "The Planning Bill." *Challenge*, May—June 1975, 3–8.

————. "Problems of Statistical Control—Economic Aspects." *Journal of the American Statistical Association*, March 1941, 18–26.

————. "The Reconversion Period: Reflections of a Forecaster." *Review of Economics and Statistics*, May 1947, 95–101.

————. "The Road to Full Employment." *Industrial Relations: A Journal of Economy and Society*, October 1962, 29–38.

————. "An Unsung Hero of World War II." In *Jean Monnet: The Path to European Unity*, edited by Douglas Brinkley and Clifford Hackett, 67–85. New York: St. Martin's Press, 1991.

————. "The Washington Economics Industry." *AEA Papers and Proceedings*, May 1986, 1–9.

————. "The Year 2000: Relations of the Public and Private Sectors." In *The Future of the United States Government: Toward the Year* 2000, edited by Harvey S. Perloff, 232–41. New York: George Brazillier, 1971).

Newton, Ronald C. "The Neutralization of Fritz Mandl: Notes of Wartime Journalism, the Arms Trade, and Anglo-American Rivalry in Argentina During World War II." *Hispanic American Historical Review*, August 1986, 541–79.

Perlman, Mark. "Political Purpose and the National Accounts." In *The Politics of Numbers*, edited by William Alonso and Paul Starr, 133-51. New York: Russell Sage, 1987.

Pomper, Gerald. "The Public Relations of Organized Labor." *Public Opinion Quarterly*, Winter 1959–1960), 483–94.

Sesser, Stan. "A Rich Country Gone Wrong." *New Yorker*, January 9, 1989, 55–96.

Shafter, Toby. "Success Story in Washington." *National Jewish Monthly*, October 1948, 77–78.

Sharpe, Mike. "Review: John Kenneth Galbraith: His Life, His Politics, His Economics." *Challenge*, May–June 2005, 125–29.

Smithies, Arthur. "The Commission on Money and Credit." *Quarterly Journal of Economics*, November 1961, 544–68.

Stein, Herbert. "The Principles Behind the Policies." *Challenge*, March–April 1973, 32–38.

Steinberg, David I. "Economic Growth with Equity? The Burmese Experience." *Contemporary Southeast Asia*, September 1982, 124–52.

Thorndike, Joseph J. Jr. "Bob Nathan: Donald Nelson's Young Braintruster Sticks Pins in Bureaucrats." *Life*, April 13, 1942, 47–50.

Tinker, Hugh. "Economic Development in Burma, 1951–1960: Book Review." *Pacific Affairs*, Autumn 1963, 325–27.

Tress, R. C. "Mobilising for Abundance by Robert R. Nathan." *Economic Journal*, March 1946, 115–19.

Troen, S. Ilan. "American Experts in the Design of Zionist Society: The Reports of Elwood Mead and Robert Nathan." In *Envisioning Israel: The Changing Ideals and Images of North American Jews*, edited by Allon Gal, 193–218. Detroit: Wayne State University Press, 1996.

Tyler, Robert L. "The American Veterans Committee: Out of the Hot War and into the Cold." *American Quarterly*, Fall 1966, 419–36.

Welsh, Janet. "Burma's Development Problems." *Far Eastern Survey*, August 1956, 115.

Manuscripts

Division of Rare and Manuscript Collections, Cornell University

Robert R. Nathan Papers

Louis Walinsky Papers

Library of Congress Manuscripts Division

Herbert Block Papers

David Ginsburg Papers

Averell Harriman Papers

Robert R. Nathan Associates Papers, 1951–1961

Robert R. Nathan Papers, Accession 22614

Joseph Rauh Papers

Maurice Rosenblatt Papers

National Archives and Records Administration

RG 47, Records of the Social Security Administration

RG 179, Records of the War Production Board

RG 250, Records of the Office of War Mobilization and Reconversion

Franklin D. Roosevelt Library

Franklin D. Roosevelt Personal File

Richard Gilbert Papers

Gardner Jackson Papers

Joseph Lash Papers

Isador Lubin Papers

Special Collections Research Center, George Washington University

American Veterans Committee Papers

Minnesota Historical Society

Carl Solberg Papers

Hubert H. Humphrey Papers

American Catholic History Research Center, Catholic University

Philip Murray Papers

John F. Kennedy Library

Samuel Beer Papers

John Kenneth Galbraith Papers

John F. Kennedy Pre-Presidential Papers

Arthur Schlesinger Papers

Wisconsin State Historical Society

Americans for Democratic Action Papers

James Wechsler Papers

NATHAN STUDIES

Robert R. Nathan Associates, Inc. *Developing Marine Industries*. Washington, 1968.

———. *Economic Advisory Services Provided to the Ministry of Planning, Royal Government of Afghanistan, September 1961 to June 1972, Final Report*. Washington, 1972.

———. *Economic Development Plan for Micronesia: Summary and Index*. Washington, 1967.

———. *An Economic Programme for Korean Reconstruction*. Washington, 1954.

———. *Economic Review of the Turkey-Iran Railway Link*. Washington, 1963.

———. *The Foreign Market Potential for United States Coal*. Washington, 1963.

———. *A National Economic Policy for 1949*. Washington, 1949.

———. *A National Wage Policy for 1947*. Washington, 1946.

———. *The Potential Market for Far Western Coal and Lignite*. Washington, 1965.

———. *Protection and Development for Recreational Resources*. Washington, 1968.

INDEX

***Boldface** indicates illustrations.

A

B

C

D

E

F

H

I

J

K

L

M

Q

R

S

T

U

V

W